Vocabulary Their Way™

Word Study with Middle and Secondary Students

Shane Templeton
University of Nevada, Reno

Donald R. Bear
University of Nevada, Reno

Marcia Invernizzi
University of Virginia

Francine Johnston
University of North Carolina at Greensboro

PEARSON

Boston   New York   San Francisco
Mexico City   Montreal   Toronto   London   Madrid   Munich   Paris
Hong Kong   Singapore   Tokyo   Cape Town   Sydney

Executive Editor: *Aurora Martínez Ramos*
Development Editor: *Hope Madden*
Series Editorial Assistant: *Jacqueline Gillen*
Vice President, Marketing and Sales Strategies: *Emily Williams Knight*
Vice President, Director of Marketing: *Quinn Perkson*
Marketing Manager: *Danae April*
Production Editor: *Annette Joseph*
Editorial Production Service: *Omegatype Typography, Inc.*
Composition Buyer: *Linda Cox*
Manufacturing Manager: *Megan Cochran*
Electronic Composition: *Omegatype Typography, Inc.*
Cover Administrator: *Linda Knowles*

For Professional Development resources, visit www.allynbaconmerrill.com.

Between the time website information is gathered and then published, it is not unusual for some sites to have closed. Also, the transcription of URLs can result in typographical errors. The publisher would appreciate notification where these errors occur so that they may be corrected in subsequent editions.

Many of the designations used by manufacturers and sellers to distinguish their products are claimed as trademarks. Where those designations appear in this book, and Allyn and Bacon was aware of a trademark claim, the designations have been printed in initial or all caps.

Printed in the United States of America

10   9   8   7   6   5   B-R   13   12   11

www.pearsonhighered.com

ISBN-10:   0-13-155535-9
ISBN-13:   978-0-13-155535-8

Contents

Preface

"The most powerful source of vocabulary instruction is the well-focused mind, seeking actively to understand" (Henderson, 1980). Our students learn vocabulary *their* way when they are focused on a topic of keen interest, trying to figure out the what, why, and how of it all. The focus may be a videogame, a novel, a car engine, setting up a webpage—it doesn't matter, really, so long as they are focused. Students acquire the vocabulary of their focus with relative ease. Our challenge is to help them apply that natural tendency to areas in which they may not at first be as interested. You can help students become engaged with the *content* of what we are teaching and reveal aspects of words to them that they might not otherwise notice, and the effect on their academic performance will be noticeable.

Vocabulary knowledge—the understanding of words and the concepts they represent—is the single best indicator of students' reading ability, comprehension, and familiarity with academic discourse (Anglin, 1993; Baumann, Kame'enui, & Ash, 2003; McKeown & Curtis, 1987; Schleppegrell, 2004; Stahl & Nagy, 2006). Because of this, vocabulary is one of the best predictors of students' success in school. As a teacher, because you are in the position to affect your students' vocabulary development significantly, you will also open their worlds more expansively to them.

To teach vocabulary to our students effectively and engagingly is to teach vocabulary *their* way. In contrast to the traditional emphasis on learning a set number of specific words every week or every unit, this book is focused on helping you give students the tools to learn quite literally tens if not hundreds of thousands of words independently—and that is a more learner-friendly and effective approach.

You may teach Freshman English or Senior Honors English; you may teach biology, eighth grade history, or seventh grade math. Regardless of the ages, grades, and subjects you teach, however, you work with students whose brains are organized to detect *patterns:* patterns in the real world, patterns in topics and themes within and across specific content areas such as history/social studies and science, and patterns in *words.* Patterns in words exist on three levels: sound, spelling, and meaning.

Understanding the relationship between spelling and meaning at the middle and secondary grades will be a profoundly important insight for students. Understanding the *meaning* of a word is often a clue to its spelling, and understanding the spelling of a word may in turn be a key to understanding its meaning. You can provide the support students need by helping them detect these patterns in words. In so doing, you help them learn specific words and you help them learn *about* words.

In recent years, vocabulary researchers have emphasized the role of *word consciousness* in vocabulary learning: the knowledge and predisposition to learn, appreciate, and effectively use words (Graves, 2006; Graves & Watts-Taffe, 2002; Stahl & Nagy, 2006). Teachers play a pivotal role in developing this awareness in their students and in helping students grow their vocabularies effectively and engagingly—*their* way. Toward this end, teachers develop their own knowledge base about words and how they work, and as a consequence their vocabulary instruction is much more confident, enjoyable, and effective.

We hope this book will help you build a strong foundation in this knowledge base for English vocabulary, as well as the vocabulary of specific academic areas. There is much that teachers can learn right along with students. If you're open to the possibilities such learning offers, you will also find that your teaching and your students' learning will be much, much more effective and rewarding.

A GUIDE TO USING THIS BOOK

- Chapter 1 sets the stage for teaching vocabulary *their* way, briefly presenting what we know about how words are learned based on the significant research that has explored how to teach words and how to teach about words.
- Chapter 2 and Chapter 3 will provide the foundation in how words work in English and where words come from. You'll find answers to the questions students and teachers often ask about words, such as why a single word can have several different meanings or why we don't spell words the way they sound (and why there are different spellings for the same sound). This knowledge will be a strong support for your instruction, and equally important, will provide you with the confidence to explore words more deeply with your students. Although you are encouraged to page through the whole book, sampling here and there, looking for your own specific teaching interests and responsibilities, you are also encouraged to return for a careful reading of Chapters 2 and 3. If you do so, the payoff for your instruction should be significant, and you may further develop your own vocabulary and spelling!
- Chapter 4 addresses the essentials of vocabulary instruction—how to select which words to teach, how to select the meaningful features of words on which to focus (prefixes, suffixes, bases, and roots), and how to teach specific words as well as how to teach *about* words.
- Chapters 5 and 6 apply the essentials presented in Chapter 4 to instruction in specific subject matter areas. Chapter 5 addresses vocabulary in narratives and the instruction about words that most often is the responsibility of English/language arts teachers, while Chapter 6 addresses vocabulary in the different content areas. Building on the basic approach presented in Chapter 4, Chapters 5 and 6 emphasize how to teach about the important Greek and Latin roots and affixes that are reflected in the vocabulary of English, mathematics, social studies/history, and the sciences.
- While English learners are mentioned throughout the book, Chapter 7 directly addresses the challenges and opportunities for English learners' vocabulary instruction in the middle and secondary grades. Instruction in cognates is highlighted, supporting an approach that begins with obvious relationships among words across languages and moves to more subtle but important relationships that cognates reflect.
- Chapter 8 provides straightforward ways to assess students' vocabulary knowledge in your specific subject matter area. Many of these assessments reflect the types of instructional strategies and activities that have been presented throughout the book. Informed assessment is based on an understanding of the literacy and learning development of your students, and Chapter 8 elaborates on a developmental model that should help guide your instructional decisions.
- The Appendixes at the end of the book provide (1) lessons that may serve as templates for your instruction; (2) assessment materials; and (3) games for developing and reinforcing understanding of words and important structural or *morphological* features of words.

In closing, we wish to point out that we include quite a bit of *narrative* in this book—explanations about words in examples of teacher conversation and in student lessons. Our hope is that you may try on the language of these narratives as you become comfortable with them, adapting them to your own style, and using some or all of them as "templates" for your own narratives and conversations about words.

ACKNOWLEDGMENTS

We would like to thank the reviewers for their considerable time and effort; specifically, for the care and precision with which they read the manuscript at various stages of development and offered both insightful critiques as well as affirmation. With gratitude, we wish to acknowledge that this book may be of greater benefit to novice and experienced teachers alike because of their considerable efforts: Cathy Blanchfield, California State University, Fresno; Jackie Glasgow, Ohio University; Joseph W. Guenther, University of Wisconsin, Platteville; James Johnston, Central Connecticut State University; Margot Kinberg, National University; Timothy Shanahan, University of Illinois at Chicago; David L. Smith, University of Nevada, Reno; Nancy Williams, University of South Florida; and Roderick E. Winters, Winona State University.

We also wish to extend our heartfelt thanks and appreciation to Linda Bishop, whose support, guidance, and unfailing encouragement made this book, and so much else, possible; Hope Madden, developmental editor extraordinaire, without whose encouragement, support, and hard work this book would not have been possible; Heather Gauen, Mary Young, and Karla Walsh at Omegatype Typography for their impressively thorough copyediting and production in an apologetically short amount of time; and Joanne Carlisle, for her very timely feedback and suggestions.

We also thank Lori Helman, Kara Moloney, Dianna Townsend, Cindy Brock, Julie Pennington, Diane Barone, Sandra Madura, Shari Dunn, Tamara Baren, Carol Casserta-Henry, Regina Smith, Judy Otteson, Sally Kelley, Mandy Grotting, Brenda Sabey, and the many other colleagues and friends who have provided encouragement and constructive critiques. A special expression of gratitude to the Northern Nevada Writing Project Summer Invitational Institute—an exceptional and welcoming group of writing teachers who provided encouraging feedback (as well as a timely critique!) of Chapter 3.

We also acknowledge our families, unfailingly supportive and understanding; and once again, for so many reasons, Ed Henderson, who most definitely encouraged "word consciousness" in all of us; and Achsah Henderson, who may not realize how much she, too, encouraged and nourished all along the way.

And last, but most certainly not least, we thank our students—undergraduate and graduate, and the teachers they've become—from whom we have learned so very, very much.

1 CHAPTER

The Nature of Vocabulary Development and Instruction

Every teacher is a teacher of language. Regardless of the subject you teach—English, math, social studies/history, chemistry, or another subject—you teach the *language* of a subject. The most important part of that language is the *vocabulary*, because the important words in a subject area stand for the most important concepts and ideas in that subject. By providing this language—the vocabulary—you are giving your students the keys to accessing the important ideas and concepts of your subject. Teaching this vocabulary "is more than teaching words, it is teaching *about* words: how they are put together, how they are learned, and how they are used" (Nagy, 2007, p. 71).

WHY TEACH VOCABULARY *THEIR* WAY?

Our students are naturally set up to learn words and to be interested in words. They thrive on learning and using words that are a part of their world and their interests—the words of popular culture and of niche subcultures. These words are valuable to students, and are the coin of everyday language that helps define their worth in the eyes of their peers and their independence in the eyes of adults. As students move into middle school and beyond, they thrive on communicating in ways that defy adults' attempts to comprehend. Of course, it is this way with every generation, because this is, after all, human nature. How can we capitalize on our students' natural disposition to learn words and teach them the vocabulary we know is "good for them"—the vocabulary that will help them grow beyond the coin of their own language realms and open up the informational treasures of the worlds beyond? The vocabularies that represent the combined ideas, insights, and knowledge expressed through the subject areas we teach? The simple though challenging answer is that we make the exploration of the words and the concepts the words represent as engaging, compelling, and intriguing as we can. We hope that this book will be a valuable resource as you address that challenge.

To get a feel for this type of exploration, let's observe a slice of one teacher's vocabulary instruction as she places a transparency on the overhead projector with the following sentence:

> Hurricane Katrina decimated much of the Gulf Coast region of the southern United States.

Pointing to *decimated*, Ms. Baren asks, "Ladies and gentleman, what do you think this word means in this sentence? . . . Yes, Regina?"

"It's like destroying it or like making things really bad."

"That may make sense here, Regina. Let's see . . . any other ideas . . . yes, Cody?"

"Like flooding? Like it flooded a lot of places?"

"That would make sense, too. I'm wondering *why* Regina and Cody are thinking this word might have this type of meaning. . . yes, Caitlyn?"

"Well, it's like we know Katrina caused a lot of damage, and we know it was in that area."

"Okay, good! Good thinking here all around . . . Now let's look at the next two sentences."

Ms. Baren slides a covering page over the transparency:

Hundreds of people died, hundreds of square miles were flooded, and thousands of buildings were blown down. Rarely has the United States seen such widespread damage from a single natural event.

"Do these sentences help us with our thinking about this word? Cody?"

"Yeah! See? It says 'flooded.'"

Tyrone interjects, "But that's not all it says!"

"Interesting point, Tyrone. I wonder what you're thinking?"

"Well, it also talks about the people who died and about buildings being blown down."

Fadila adds, "And it also talks about 'widespread damage,' which could mean lots of different kinds of damage."

"Interesting observations, Tyrone and Fadila! You know, I'm not wondering any more about how Regina, Cody, Caitlyn, Tyrone, and Fadila are thinking about this word! They've shown us some pretty perceptive use of the *context*—the sentences and words around this particular word—to try to figure it out. Ahhhh . . . I see Álvero surreptitiously slipping his pocket dictionary out! Okay, Álvero, please tell us what you've found."

"It says 'to destroy or kill a large part of a group.'"

"Interesting! Would that meaning work in this passage? Yes, Brittany?"

"Kind of, but it only talks about 'killing,' and Katrina did more that that."

"Good point. Álvero, was that the only definition listed for *decimate*?"

"No, the next one says 'to inflict great destruction or damage on.' I think *that* fits better!"

"Ladies and gentleman, by a show of hands, how many of us concur with Álvero? . . . Well! Apparently most of us! Okay, let's read back over these three sentences and see how that definition fits."

The class concurs that it does. Ms. Baren continues: "Let's look just at the word *decimate* itself. Are there any clues in how the word *looks* that might suggest its meaning? Any prefixes, suffixes, word roots that leap out at us?"

After a few seconds, she continues: "I see a lot of squinched and puzzled faces! You know, nothing leapt out at me, either, when I first looked at this word. What if I reminded you about the Latin word root *dec* that all of us have learned about? Think of the words *decimal* and *decade*." She writes them on the transparency. "What meaning does the root *dec* have? Yes, Carey?"

"Ten!"

"Right you are! What do you think? . . . Might the *dec* in *decimate* also mean 'ten'? . . . Ah, I see more squinched and puzzled faces as you're thinking this one through.

"Let me share a story with you. Back during the Roman Empire, when those Roman legions were busy trying to conquer just about everybody else in the known world, from time to time some troops or soldiers would get unhappy about things. Maybe not enough good food, working conditions weren't all that good, they missed their families, whatever. Anyway, if things got bad enough for them they might start talking about a mutiny—about rising up and taking over from their general. Well, if the general somehow became aware of this kind of talk he had a very effective way of putting an end to it: He would select one-tenth of his troops by lot—he probably pulled names from a helmet in those days—and those selected would be killed . . . *And the other soldiers* would have to do the killing! So originally, when you talked about 'decimating the ranks' it literally meant 'killing a tenth.' Over time, as we have learned, the meanings of words usually grow and evolve, and this happened with *decimate*. It came to have the meanings that Álvero found in the dictionary: either killing not just a tenth but a large part of a group, or as it means in our Katrina example, inflicting great destruction or damage."

Let's reflect on what's happened in this lesson. Ms. Baren draws out the students' thinking about the word *decimate* and encourages more than one contribution. She acknowledges the quality of the students' ideas ("That would make sense, too"). She good-naturedly teases yet appreciates Álvero checking the dictionary. She asks if there is a consensus about the meaning but checks to make sure one last time. She also uses a few more "scholarly" words along the way—*perceptive, surreptitiously,* and *concur.* She then tells a story about the word, and in doing so reminds students what they know and are learning about Latin word roots, a critical aspect of vocabulary development. These "stories" about words are also, as we will see, a critical aspect of vocabulary development. This type of quality interaction with students, of course, doesn't happen out of the blue. Most students do not spontaneously volunteer information, for example, and check definitions in dictionaries. Most students do not talk about other information in a passage and how it can contribute to figuring out the meaning of an unfamiliar word. Many students would be put off by a teacher's spontaneous use of words such as *surreptitiously* and *concur,* as well as by her talking about Latin word parts.

We're talking about changing those student attitudes. What facilitates and sustains Ms. Baren's type of vocabulary instructional climate? Over the course of the year, she has modeled these ways of thinking and strategizing about words: using context clues and whatever information is in the passage to help determine the meaning of a word, and usually referring to the dictionary only as a last resort. She has taught and modeled how to look *within* words for clues to their meaning. She has also taught and modeled the use of more academic vocabulary and included just enough of it in her speech to reinforce the type of attitude toward words she has worked to establish in her classroom. And she has told interesting stories about words. (If students were not familiar with the meaning of *dec,* they will not now likely forget it.)

Can you tell what grade level or subject Ms. Baren teaches? Geography, science, history, English? It may be difficult to pin down, because this way of talking and thinking about words engages fourth-graders and high school seniors alike, and it works across all subject areas. The attention to word parts such as *dec* and the context in which they occur will help students be more aware of, and learn, many more new words through their reading.

One last example may illustrate this point. Assume a student who has never encountered and is not familiar with the word *decathlon* is reading the following sentence:

Gerry had trained for years before he attempted to compete in the decathlon.

The student will not only understand from the context of the sentence that a decathlon is a very demanding type of competition but will also know how to look at the structure of the word to home in on a more precise meaning. The letters *athl* recall *athlete* or *athletic* and remembering that *dec* is the Latin root meaning "ten" helps the student determine that a *decathlon* is an athletic competition with ten events. Further reading confirms by context that this is the appropriate meaning. The only reason now to look the word up in the dictionary is to seek additional information—for example, to find out which ten events are part of this competition.

Many of us were fortunate enough to have had teachers like Ms. Baren—teachers who made learning come alive for us by telling stories about words. Some stories may have been humorous, some astonishing or alarming—but these stories always gave us insight into where a word came from and how it grew into the meaning it has today. These teachers demonstrated and talked about how words work to give language its precision, appropriateness, and impact. Perhaps even more important, this way of talking and thinking—stories and conversations about words—intrigued us and hooked us on words more generally. And once we were curious about words, we were more motivated to attend to the meanings and nuances of new words we encountered, what researchers call *word consciousness,* the "interest in, awareness of, and appreciation of words" (Stahl & Nagy, 2006, p. 140; Lubliner & Scott, 2008). Our students need to develop this critical aspect of vocabulary improvement, and they also need to learn *strategies* for learning new words they encounter. For example, Ms. Baren shows her students how words "work"—how word parts such as prefixes and suffixes combine with other word parts and how to use this information in the context of what they are reading.

This book seeks to help you become this type of teacher. Throughout *Vocabulary Their Way,* we will be examining how you can organize and present your vocabulary instruction to best take advantage of students' predispositions to learn about word meaning and structure. As you help them become attracted to and excited about words—their meanings, associations, sounds, and histories—your instruction will reflect the following research-based findings:

- We do not learn words one at a time, like adding beads on a string. Words and the concepts they represent are interconnected in many different ways.
- For almost every word we learn, there are potentially many, many more words we could learn at the same time.
- The way words are spelled in English makes more sense than most of us think—and this knowledge can be a powerful tool for helping us learn the meaning of thousands of words.

WHAT ARE THE DIFFERENT TYPES OF VOCABULARY?

Over the years, researchers and educators have used a number of terms to describe different types of vocabulary, with a traditional perspective represented in Figure 1.1. Beginning in the center of the diagram, our *listening/speaking* vocabulary is primary in human development. Estimates vary, but children entering kindergarten average a listening/speaking vocabulary of approximately 5,000 words. As children develop their abilities to read and write, we refer to their *reading/writing* vocabularies, which over

FIGURE 1.1   Traditional Perspective on Types of Vocabulary

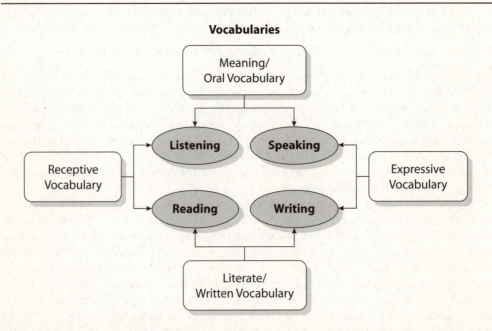

Source: Adapted from J. Pikulski and S. Templeton, 2004.

time grow to include most of the words in students' listening/speaking vocabularies. Significantly, from the upper elementary grades onward our reading/writing vocabularies come to include more words than our listening/speaking vocabularies. Written language contains many words that do not usually occur in most spoken language. Writers use words that they would not normally use in their speech. When readers encounter these new words, they need to decipher them. They are often able to figure out word meanings if they have been taught strategies for doing so.

As an example, suppose you encounter the word *eleemosynary* in an article about charitable organizations in the following sentence: "In contrast to the apparent miserliness of millionaires over 40 years of age, a greater number of younger millionaires seem to be developing eleemosynary tendencies." You may have never seen this word before, but given the *context* of this sentence—the word seems to be contrasted with *miserliness*—and the *topic* of the article—charitable organizations—you can make a pretty good guess that the word might have something to do with giving to charity or behaving in a charitable fashion. Because this is an interesting-looking word, you'll make a note to look it up in the dictionary when you finish reading the article. The dictionary confirms your guess, but you may still be a bit uncertain about how to pronounce a word that isn't really in your speaking vocabulary—and for good reason. How many social situations will you be in where this word would be appropriate and not make you sound like a know-it-all? On the other hand, if you were writing an essay for a required economics course, the word could fit quite appropriately.

Another way of regarding vocabulary refers to *receptive* vocabulary as the words we "receive" or take in and understand through listening and reading, whereas *expressive* vocabulary refers to words we are able to use in speaking or writing. The bottom line, however, is that the vocabulary most of us draw on when reading and writing is larger than the vocabulary we use in our own everyday speech.

Because most new words we encounter come from print or specific content areas, more recently some educators and researchers have fine-tuned the traditional perspective represented in Figure 1.1. Table 1.1 presents the labels that are now most commonly used to represent distinctions in types of vocabulary, subdivided into three broad classifications: conversational vocabulary, core academic vocabulary, and content-specific academic vocabulary.

Conversational vocabulary includes the most common and most frequently occurring words in the spoken language, such as *talk, have,* and *upon.* Beck, McKeown, and Kucan (2002, 2008) refer to these words as "tier 1" vocabulary because they are so easily picked up conversationally and rarely require instruction. The other two categories capture the types of vocabulary we encounter primarily in print.

Core academic vocabulary includes those words that may not occur a lot in everyday spoken language but which students may encounter frequently in their reading and, because of the high utility of the words, should be able to use in their writing. These words also occur in more formal oral discourse, such as a lecture format, and are equally likely to occur across all content areas. Students usually have the underlying conceptual understanding that these words represent, but they simply lack the label. Beck and colleagues target core academic vocabulary words such as *transmit, energetic,* and *paradox* for instruction because these "tier 2" words can more precisely express concepts that are already understood.

Content-specific academic vocabulary refers to words that occur in specific content or subject matter areas such as science, history and social science, mathematics, and the arts. In contrast to core academic vocabulary, much content-specific academic vocabulary represents significantly new concepts, and can therefore be more difficult to learn. For this reason, Beck and colleagues categorize content-specific words such as *rectilinear, potentate,* and *mercantilism* as "tier 3" vocabulary. Nevertheless, students are expected to learn content-specific vocabulary in their content classes, which are most often taught by subject area teachers.

TABLE 1.1   Contemporary Perspectives on Types of Vocabulary

Types of Vocabulary	Definitions and Examples
Conversational Vocabulary	
Tier 1 vocabulary (Beck, McKeown, & Kucan, 2002, 2008)	Words that students learn through everyday conversation with parents, other family members, and peers. Examples: *happy, walk, about*
Core Academic Vocabulary	
General purpose vocabulary (Diamond & Gutlohn, 2007) High-utility general vocabulary (Stahl & Nagy, 2006) Tier 2 vocabulary (Beck, McKeown, & Kucan, 2002, 2008) Responsibility for teaching: Elementary teachers, middle and secondary English/language arts teachers	Words that students may encounter frequently in their reading and should be able to use in their writing. They probably already have an underlying concept for the word. Examples: *encounter, significant, advantage*
Academic Language	
Responsibility for teaching: Elementary teachers, English/ language arts teachers	Words and phrases that indicate logical operations and tasks. Examples: *consequently, evaluate, distinguish between*
Content-Specific Academic Vocabulary	
Tier 3 vocabulary (Beck, McKeown, & Kucan, 2002, 2008) Responsibility for teaching: Elementary teachers, middle and secondary subject matter teachers	Words that refer to new concepts *in a particular content area* that are important for students to learn. Examples: *pollution, alliance, papacy, algebraic expression*

We have included *academic language* in our core academic vocabulary category rather than in our content-specific academic vocabulary category because this type of language occurs across all content areas. *Academic language* is the term that educators use to refer to words and phrases that signal relationships among ideas and information, such as *therefore, as a result, compare and contrast,* and *analyze.* Although the words and phrases of academic language must be learned and applied in the context of the tasks and tests with which students engage across all subject matter areas, it generally falls to the English, reading, or language arts teacher to make sure that students understand academic language.

On occasion there is some overlap between core academic and content-specific academic vocabularies. For example, when students are first introduced to the word *sanctuary* it may be a part of the content-specific academic vocabulary in science, referring to a reserved and protected area for animals or birds. As time goes on, however, students will learn that the word occurs in other content areas as well, such as English and history/ social sciences, so it becomes a core vocabulary word. However, despite this occasional overlap, when you think about the students, subjects, and grade levels you teach, it will still be useful to keep these distinctions among types of vocabulary in mind.

WHAT ARE THE DIFFERENT LEVELS OF KNOWING A WORD?

Consider the words *hand, teach, condensation, prehensile, surfeit,* and *apophasis.* For each word, think about the following questions:

- Do you know the word and feel confident about using it?
- Do you have knowledge of the word but lack sufficient familiarity to readily use it in appropriate situations?

- Do you have only a *general* sense of the word?
- Have you heard or seen the word but do not know what it means?
- Have you never heard nor seen the word before?

For most of us, these questions capture the range of our familiarity with any word we encounter. This is how vocabulary knowledge works; our brains do not have on/off switches for each word, such that we either know it or we don't. Rather, our knowledge falls along a continuum from feeling pretty confident to total unfamiliarity. Dale (1965) popularized this way of thinking about vocabulary knowledge and suggested that it is one of the best ways to assess our students' vocabulary knowledge.

Consider for a moment the types of knowledge underlying every word that you in some sense "know":

- The *range of meanings* of the word, both literal and figurative. For example, *effervescent* refers to a carbonated or fermenting liquid in which small bubbles of gas are emitted, but it may also refer to an individual's behavior or personality.
- The *situations and contexts* to which the word applies, including informal and formal speech and writing.
- How the *grammatical form* of a word affects its meaning—*effervesce*, a verb, is the action of bubbling up; *effervescence*, a noun, refers to the process of bubbling up; and *effervescent*, an adjective, attributes the nature and qualities of that process to something or someone.
- Knowing other words that are likely to occur with the word.
- Knowing the probability of encountering the word.

HOW DO WE DECIDE WHICH WORDS TO TEACH?

In Chapter 4 we will explore how you can teach your students the strategies for learning new words on their own, as they are reading independently. As we have just seen, however, much of your instruction will involve teaching words that fall within the *core academic* vocabulary and the *content-specific* academic vocabulary categories. In the intermediate grades and up, how do we determine which words within these categories should be directly taught?

Over the years, educators in different content areas—English/language arts, math, science, history and social science, and so forth—have identified the words that they believe represent the concepts that are most important to learn in their respective fields (Marzano, 2004). These words are characterized by their scope and sequence across the grades and are reflected in the curriculum materials that publishers develop for each grade level. The required textbooks you use for the subjects and grade levels that you teach include most of these important words. Your state and school district have also developed standards that reflect the content and concepts that are important to teach at different levels and usually designate the most important vocabulary for this material. Table 1.2 provides examples of concepts and the words that represent these concepts for several subject matter areas across the intermediate, middle, and high school levels.

WHAT DOES THE RESEARCH SAY ABOUT VOCABULARY LEARNING AND INSTRUCTION?

Research clearly supports the need for students to be actively involved in vocabulary learning, and an important effect of this involvement is the development of favorable attitudes toward words and word learning—that *word consciousness* mentioned earlier.

TABLE 1.2   Examples of Concepts and Words That May Be Taught at the Upper Elementary, Middle School, and High School Levels

	Upper Elementary (Grades 4–5)	Middle School (Grades 6–8)	High School (Grades 9–12)
English/Language Arts	affix genre paragraph prepositional phrase summarize voice	adverb clause dialect editorial metaphor predicate adjective simile	allegory alliteration consonance interrogative pronoun literary criticism omniscient point of view
Mathematics	associative property commutative property distributive property fraction measurement negative number	algebraic expression circumference constant ratio polygon perpendicular bisector rotation symmetry	correlation exponential function logarithm polynomial sinusoidal function vector
Science	astronomical object condensation density microscope pollution prehistoric organism	atom chemical element ecosystem gene metamorphic parasite	biological evolution chromosome DNA geochemical cycle mitochondria paradigmatic plate tectonics
General History	Allied Powers archaeology Cinco de Mayo diplomacy immigration Latin America	bourgeoisie industrialization sovereign state totalitarian regime women's suffrage	depression entrepreneurial spirit Federalist mercantilism reunification
The Arts	diction rhythm improvisation tempo legato scale quarter note	aesthetic criteria texture repertoire meter tonality design element hue	negative space oratorio archetype choreographic penultimate movement decrescendo

Teachers should attend to the following three broad aspects of vocabulary learning and instruction (bearing in mind that real-world instruction blurs the boundary lines among them):

- Immersion in *rich oral language* and wide reading
- Word or *lexical-specific* vocabulary instruction
- *Generative* vocabulary instruction

Immersion in Rich Oral Language and Wide Reading

Rich oral language includes your use of important words the students are learning and have yet to learn, as well as your comments on and observations about words during a period or throughout the day. Part of this rich oral language environment includes reading aloud to your students, from both narrative and informational materials. These read-alouds allow you many opportunities to make words interesting—yet again, raising students' word consciousness. Beyond the elementary grades, however, most teachers rarely read to their students. If you teach at the middle or secondary level, it is essential that you plan to read to your students at least once a week from an example of good writing in your subject area no matter what grade you teach.

The role of wide reading is critical. To illustrate, on average, fifth grade students who score at the 98th percentile on a standardized reading test read about an hour every day outside of school, whereas students who score at the 50th percentile read about 4½ minutes every day outside of school (Anderson, Wilson, & Fielding, 1988). Another way of thinking about the role of independent reading is expressed by Cunningham and Stanovich (1998) when they observed that "the entire year's out-of-school reading for the child at the 10th percentile amounts to just two days reading for the child at the 90th percentile!" (p. 4). From the intermediate grades on, many other things besides books are claiming our students' attention, so it is especially important that we find ways to keep them motivated and engaged to continue reading independently outside of school.

While wide reading is indeed necessary if not critical in increasing vocabulary, for most students it is not sufficient. They also need direct instruction in specific words and in how words work. This is where teachers play their most important role in students' vocabulary learning, as shown by the other two aspects of the previous list.

Word or Lexical-Specific Vocabulary Instruction

Researchers refer to instruction that targets individual words as *lexical-specific* instruction. Once you have selected the words to address directly, how you go about teaching them will depend on your purposes and on your students' background knowledge. Some words will be merely mentioned, whereas others will be explored deeply, involving many exposures to the words in meaningful contexts, both in and out of texts. This latter category of words represents essential *core academic* and *content-specific academic* vocabulary, and research emphasizes that these words should be experienced on the average of at least 12 to 15 times each. Such experiences include attending to the words before reading, during reading, and after reading, as well as in more than one context—in addition to being *read*, they must be *heard, spoken,* and *written.*

Generative Vocabulary Instruction

Researchers refer to instruction to help students understand the processes of word formation in English—how prefixes, suffixes, base words, and Greek and Latin word roots combine—as *generative* vocabulary instruction. Understanding these processes of word formation will *generate* student learning about thousands of words they will encounter in their instructional and independent reading (Templeton, 2004b). These processes are taught directly, because most students do not discover them on their own. In a classic study, Nagy and Anderson observed, "Knowledge of word-formation processes opens up vast amounts of vocabulary to the reader" (1984, p. 314). When students understand these word formation processes—how to put together and take apart these word elements—they have a powerful strategy for independent word learning (Kieffer & Lesaux, 2007). When they encounter an unfamiliar word in their reading they will be able to analyze its parts through a "take apart" strategy, thinking about the meaning that each word part contributes and how the combined meaning of the parts works in the context in which they encounter the word—as we did with the word *decathlon.*

There are many opportunities to teach vocabulary in a generative way. Take the word *courage,* for example. When examining this word more closely and extending students' understanding of it, teachers may also present other words that are related in structure and meaning:

courage
courage *ous*
courage *ously*
en courage
en courage *ment*
dis courage
dis courage *ment*
dis courag *ing*
dis courag *ingly*

When we point out this generative aspect of words, we help students understand another important, if not critical, understanding about words: "Words that are related in meaning are often related in spelling as well, despite changes in sound" (Templeton, 1979, 1983, 2004). We refer to this as the *spelling–meaning connection,* an awareness that powerfully supports students' spelling development as well as vocabulary development.

HOW DOES VOCABULARY DEVELOPMENT ENHANCE LITERACY LEARNING?

Exploring vocabulary development guides our efforts to facilitate students' literacy learning. Given the strong relationship between vocabulary knowledge and reading development, the wide variation in students' reading development has implications for students' vocabulary learning. In fact, students' reading achievement affects how easily they can read the words and then uncover the meanings of the new vocabulary words they encounter in their reading. Students who read well do not have to concentrate on the mechanics of reading and therefore have the time and energy to think and focus on the *meaning* of what they read.

Table 1.3 presents a developmental model that describes the relationships, or "synchrony," among reading, writing, and word knowledge across the three developmental stages of literacy we primarily see in the middle and secondary grades. By taking a developmental perspective to match these behaviors and look for the relationships, teachers find it easier to gauge their students' progress as readers and learners and to differentiate and plan for instruction more appropriately, as well as predict the relative ease students will have in learning new vocabulary. We will take a more in-depth look at the relationships among reading, writing, and word knowledge in Chapter 8, in which the role of assessment in guiding instruction is explored.

Most students in the middle and secondary grades are in the last two stages of reading, writing, and word knowledge development. *Intermediate* readers and writers read at least at a fourth-grade level. Vocabularies expand through the reading in which students engage, in both narrative literature and in specialized content area reading. Students in this stage of development are usually more advanced readers who learn the meanings of more complex prefixes, suffixes, and word roots. If they wish, teachers can use Figure 1.1 and examples of students' reading and writing at the beginning of the school year to explain literacy learning and development both to students and parents. They then may better understand what literacy behaviors go together and what they can look for to assess progress.

TABLE 1.3 *A Model of Reading and Writing Development*		
	Transitional	**Intermediate**	**Advanced**
Early	• Approaching phrasal fluency • Some expression in oral reading • Prefer silent reading by the end of this stage	• Prefer silent reading • Develop a variety of reading styles • Begin to skim and scan and vary rate and style for purpose • Practice study skills	• Read fluently, with expression • Develop a variety of reading styles • Vocabulary grows with experience reading
Later Development	• Approaching writing fluency • More organization • Several paragraphs	• Understanding of prefixes, suffixes, bases, and easy roots grows • Increasingly fluent writing builds expression and voice • Experiences different writing styles and genres • Writing shows personal problem solving and personal reflection • Editing and revising processes are refined	• Critical thinking and analysis is evident in writing • Various forms of professional writing styles are practiced
Reading Rates (in words per minute)	• 60–100 oral	• 80–100 oral • 100–180 silent	• 100–120 oral • 150–250 silent

LOOKING AHEAD

This chapter has sketched in broad strokes the vocabulary instructional terrain that will be explored throughout this book. The next two chapters lay the foundation for this exploration. Chapter 2 describes the nature of words and how they work, and Chapter 3 explores the nature of the historical journeys that words travel and how those journeys are a part of understanding and appreciating words and how they work. This foundational information should support quite powerfully the balance of the information provided in this book. In addition to providing appropriate and engaging activities and teaching students strategies for learning words independently, this foundation should develop your own confidence with respect to discussing words with your students and in telling the stories about words that will engage them and motivate them to become lifelong word learners.

2 CHAPTER

The Meaning and Structure of Words

If you have one "glunch" and I give you another "glunch," you now have two _____.

Today we are "glunching," and yesterday we _____.

If it is easy for us to "glunch" together, you might say we are _____.

Try to complete the sentences above (answers appear at the bottom of the page). Chances are you got at least two out of three, if not all of them. Why? You probably have not encountered these words before—but they are similar to words that you _do_ know, and without thinking too terribly much about it you plugged in rules that you carry around in your head telling you how to create plural nouns, past tense verbs, and words that modify and describe nouns and verbs. You might even have begun to picture what "glunching" looks like—it's hard to prevent associations from going off in our minds.

These examples help illustrate an important aspect of our language knowledge—that we somehow "just know" because we have grown up exposed to others who use the language and who have given us feedback as we learned the language. Almost effortlessly, we understood the rules about how words are formed and how they behave in speech. There comes a point, however, where what we need to know is not obvious in speech, and that's the point at which we will need a knowledgeable teacher.

HOW WORDS WORK: FEELINGS AND CONNECTIONS

Figurative Language

Denotation and Connotation. Words have _denotative_ meanings describing what the words literally mean or refer to. They also have _connotative_ meanings, which refer to what the words suggest to us, how they make us feel, and the associations we bring to them beyond their literal meanings. For example, it makes a difference if we refer to a person as _old_ or as _elderly_; elderly has a kinder, more respectful association than if we were to refer to someone simply as old. Both words literally denote an older person, but we select one over the other in most contexts because of its more effective and appropriate connotative meaning. The relationship between denotative and connotative meaning exists everywhere.

Let's say you're a history or social studies teacher, and you wish to teach about the origins of the Republican and the Democratic parties. As soon as you write these terms on the overhead, however, you discover you've ignited a debate. "Republicans are spoiled rich people." "Democrats just want to take our money and give it to people who

---

Answers: _glunches_, _glunched_, _glunchable_ (_glunching_ and _glunchers_ are also acceptable).

don't want to work." Yes, these are usually attitudes and understandings the students pick up at home, but they are nonetheless real for your students. You want to address the literal or denotative meaning of these terms, but your students are revealing their connotative meanings for these terms; associations very often with affective and emotional overlays that are suggested by the words. The word *republican* literally means or *denotes* "having to do with a republic"; depending on your experiences and attitudes, the term may *connote* "the party of spoiled rich people" or "the party that preserves important values of family, country, and religious faith."

It's not just hot lava terms like Republican and Democrat. The word *dog*, while having a literal meaning that most children could agree on, also has a connotative meaning—a meaning not shared in common by all of us. If your experiences with dogs have been pleasant, warm, and fuzzy, you have a very positive connotative meaning. In contrast, if your experiences include being attacked by a dog, your connotative meaning is negative. These connotative meanings are the filter through which you will examine *dog* and the concepts it represents.

Simile and Metaphor.   Simile and metaphor are much more common than we often realize in our language (Bartel, 1983; Nilsen & Nilsen, 2004). Students can learn the straightforward definitions. *Simile* expresses a comparison using the terms *like* or *as.* In *Timothy of the Cay* (1993), Theodore Taylor writes in the first person of how young Phillip was rescued from the cay on which he had been stranded: "I'd been brought aboard from the rescue boat, naked as a plucked pigeon" (p. 2). Taylor has used a simile, "naked as a plucked chicken," to describe Phillip's condition. In *Gulliver's Travels,* Jonathan Swift describes Gulliver's perception of a crowd of brightly clad women in Lilliput as "spread out like an embroidered petticoat."

Metaphor also expresses a comparison, but without the words *like* or *as.* In *On My Honor* (1986), Marion Dane Bauer offers the following description as young Joel finally staggers onto the riverbank after nearly drowning: "When the river bottom came up to meet his feet, he stood. The sky was an inverted china bowl above his head" (p. 33). Of course, the sky is not literally an inverted china bowl; through the use of metaphor, Bauer has helped us construct a vivid mental image. The starkness of this image—a white glare after he had been struggling underwater—also captures Joel's sense of being caught in a nightmare from which he cannot escape. He has just realized that his friend Tony, who has also been swimming in the river, has probably drowned.

Scott O'Dell, in *Black Star, Bright Dawn* (1988), describes Bright Dawn's realization that she is caught in a whiteout while on the grueling Alaskan Iditarod: "There was nothing to see except swirling curtains of white cotton. There was no sky above me, no ice beneath my feet" (p. 83). O'Dell does not have to say "The snow was like swirling curtains of white cotton." We know he is talking about the snow, and his description is more effective because he states it directly. In *The Brief Wondrous Life of Oscar Wao* (2007), Junot Díaz enfolds one metaphor after another as he describes, through the adolescent Lola's eyes, the first time she fell in love. From "a sweet morenito named Max Sánchez" came "the bruja feeling that comes singing out of my bones, that takes hold of me the way blood seizes cotton" (p. 72). In poetry, William Blake described the soldier's sigh that "runs in blood down palace walls," and in her poem "Bees Are Black, with Gilt Surcingles," Emily Dickinson refers to bees as "Buccaneers of Buzz" (Bartel, 1983).

We should let students know that our purpose for exploring simile and metaphor is to identify instances when words have been used to express something in a fresh, new, compelling way. We then help them apply this awareness in their writing and in their appreciation of what they read (see also Beck et al., 2008).

Writers who use words effectively usually have a deep sensitivity to the sounds, structures, and meanings of words. This is why they can select and link those words that work most effectively in a particular context. Similarly, readers who read most effectively have a solid awareness of sound, structure, and meaning. Our ultimate goal is of course to grow *wordsmiths*—students who know how words are put into play (for example, how writers use them to craft images, to engage feelings, and to prompt action). Chapter 5 explores how we may help students understand this process by identifying instances of effective word use and learning the terms that help us talk about this usage, such as denotation, connotation, simile, and metaphor.

Idioms and Idiomatic Expressions.   Phrases such as *flying off the handle, tongue-tied,* and *kick the bucket* may not be understood by putting together the literal meanings of the words. Rather, their meaning is purely figurative. *Idioms* and *idiomatic expressions* work like words, although their meanings are hidden in underlying concepts. Idiomatic expressions exist in conversational English but also occur within each academic domain or content area.

Etymology.   *Etymology* refers to the study of the origin or history of words. The classroom vignette in Chapter 1 of the history behind the word *decimate* is an example of etymology at work. Through sharing these historical narratives with students, we make words more interesting and provide students with a deeper sense of how words work. And the stories are everywhere. For example, according to some etymologists, Julius Caesar's surname—*Caesar*—came from a Latin word meaning "cut," and when we learn the procedure by which he was supposedly born we not only appreciate the power of the origin of a word or name but learn in a more compelling sense what the medical term *caesarian section* means. Chapter 3 explores etymology in greater depth, because an understanding of the history of the English language includes an understanding of the processes by which words are generated and come to mean what they mean today.

HOW WORDS WORK: MEANINGS

Linguists spend their lives studying language, and psychologists spend their lives studying the brain and the mind. Together, they provide us insights into how we learn and use language. Not surprisingly, one of the most intensively studied topics is words. Words help us convey with great varieties of precision and meaning what we want to express to others. They don't do the whole job, of course; if we're talking to someone we are also conveying meanings through body language, expressions, tone of voice, and so forth.

Nevertheless, words are critically important, the indispensable nuggets that allow us to communicate our conceptual understanding to others through speech or writing. Linguists and psychologists tell us that the relationship between spoken and written words and the concepts they represent is more complex than a lot of us assume. This chapter will explore this complexity, beginning with the ways that learners probably come to understand words and their meanings.

At first glance, it would seem that from a very early age we learn words by matching them up with objects and actions in the environment, using pretty much a one-to-one mapping. However, the actual process is somewhat more complex. Toddlers, for example, may use *bow wow* to refer not only to dogs but to cats and cows as well—but given time and experience, they manage to sort out the beings in their environment. Older students learn words in ways that are similar in many respects to those used by toddlers, but with some significant differences as well. They may learn that *simile* and *metaphor* are words for comparing, yet still identify *Her eyes were limpid pools of alabaster* as a simile and *Her eyes were like limpid pools of alabaster* as a metaphor—until they get a bit more feedback from the teacher to help them sort out the defining characteristics of a simile and a metaphor.

Similar confusion may accompany learning about and differentiating *viruses* from *bacteria* in biology, *abscissa* from *ordinate* in math, and *World War I* from *World War II* in world history. In contrast to younger children, however, older students must usually think more deliberately about new vocabulary—words and the concepts they represent—and also think about *how* they are thinking about the new vocabulary: They must be aware of their own efforts and strategies and how to get back on track when things get confusing.

Linguists and psychologists describe four types of knowledge that language users possess: phonological, semantic, syntactic, and morphological. *Phonological knowledge* refers to the sound system of the language. More specifically, it refers to our knowledge of how we speak using the sounds we make as well as stress or accent and intonation contours—the rising and falling of our speech. *Semantic knowledge* refers to establishing and growing an understanding of the relationship between words and their underlying meanings. *Syntactic knowledge* refers to our ability to arrange words into expressions. In many languages, particularly in English, this knowledge about the *order* of words in speech and writing also carries meaning. In English, syntactic knowledge often determines the meanings of words themselves—for example, *record* has a different meaning as well as pronunciation depending on whether it functions as a noun or a verb. *Morphological knowledge* refers to how meaningful word parts are put together—as, for example, the prefix *re-* attaches to the word *apply* to make another word, *reapply*. Morphological knowledge underlies students' generative knowledge about words: Once we move beyond the most frequent words used in the English language—words such as *the, talk, those*—we find that most words are created by combining prefixes, suffixes, bases, and roots: *unkind, replay, disconsolately*. Understanding and applying this type of knowledge can generate knowledge of literally tens of thousands of words.

Much of what we "know" about these types of knowledge is implicit or subconscious—we just seem to develop it in the course of growing up and learning how to speak our native language. Effective teachers help us bring some of this knowledge to the surface and apply it in our learning. By understanding the underlying nature of these types of knowledge, we'll be better able to help our students grow their understanding of words. Let's take a closer look at each of them.

Phonological Knowledge

When we hear the words *light* and *right*, how do we know they are different? Only by their beginning sounds or *phonemes:* /līt/, /rīt/. We can clearly hear the difference between these two sounds. Our knowledge of the phonemes in our language—the sounds that make a difference—is part of our *phonological knowledge*. When we are growing up and learning to speak the language, no one sits us down and tells us about these sounds. We acquire knowledge of them through listening and speaking in meaningful contexts. Individuals growing up in parts of Asia, however, do not hear the sounds /l/ and /r/ as different, because these phonemes do not signal meaningful differences in those languages. On the other hand, speakers growing up in English-speaking environments do not hear any difference between the beginning sounds of *keep* and *cool,* a very clear difference to a speaker of Arabic. Human beings are capable of uttering hundreds of different sounds, but only a relative few are meaningful in any individual language; in English, the number is approximately 44.

Phonological knowledge also includes the stress patterns in a language. Where we place stress or accent, as well as the rising and falling intonation in different words, conveys meaning. Contrast the following sentences:

- *You* wore that sweater? (As opposed to Mary, who was supposed to have worn it instead of you.)
- You wore *that* sweater? (The sweater was really too ugly, tattered, or out-of-style to be seen in public.)
- You wore that *sweater*? (Instead of the lighter jacket, because it really wasn't all that cold outside.)

Stress patterns within words also signal differences: Compare *pres*ent (the kind you give) with pres*ent* (the act of giving something to someone).

Semantic Knowledge

Semantic knowledge refers to the relationship between words and the concepts they label. Let's push aside the labels for just a moment to plumb the underlying concepts. Decades of psychological research reveal that, whether we are aware of it or not, in our brains human beings tend to organize our experiences and our world in terms of networks of interrelated concepts that are arranged *hierarchically.* Within this hierarchical network, there are superordinate, subordinate, and coordinate relationships. The ways we organize and teach concepts often reflect this type of organization. Consider the periodic table in chemistry, the taxonomic classification system in biology, and the classic outline format that may be applied to any subject area. As Chapter 4 will discuss, this may be why—if we use them effectively—*graphic organizers* can be so effective in our vocabulary instruction.

Syntactic Knowledge

We all have knowledge of the *syntactic* categories or families in our language. We know how to arrange words into expressions, and our knowledge for each word or concept we know includes information about where it fits within sentences. All words have meaning, of course, and psychologists believe that the "dictionary entries" for each word in our head also include syntactic information about words.

A simple distinction between the different syntactic categories of words involves content words versus function words. *Content words* have a clear, imageable meaning and are therefore easier to learn, comprising things, actions, and attributes of things and actions, with words freely added to a language as new meanings arise (e.g., *astronaut, google*). In contrast, *function words* (e.g., *of, the*) do not have a clear meaning on their own but serve rather a binding or structural role in a sentence. Function words are often described as the "glue" words that hold concrete words together in expressions. Take *the* and *a,* for example. Unlike content words that represent more tangible concepts, it is difficult to point to an example of *the* or *a* in the real world; the meaning of both words is to specify a type of word that will follow. The word *the* signals that the noun to follow is a specific example of something—a particular cat, a particular quotient, or a particular molecule—while the word *a* signals that a less specific noun will follow—any old cat, quotient, or molecule. Most linguists partition content words into nouns, verbs, and words that modify nouns and verbs. They use the term *particle* to refer to the function words, which most commonly go by the terms *conjunctions* (*and, but, because*), *articles* (*the, an*), and *prepositions* (*in, on, over*).

Morphological Knowledge

We've said that *morphological knowledge* refers to how words are put together. More specifically, we're dealing with meaningful chunks of language and how they combine. Meaningful chunks are referred to as *morphemes,* defined as the smallest units of meaning in a language. There are two types of morphemes. *Free* morphemes can occur by themselves (words) whereas *bound* morphemes cannot occur by themselves. Bound morphemes are word parts, prefixes and suffixes such as *un-* and *-ible,* and many Latin and Greek word roots such as *dic* (*dictate*) and *phon* (*phonics*). Psychologists have revealed that our brains establish relationships not only between individual words—free morphemes—and underlying concepts, but also between word parts or bound morphemes such as *anti-* and *-ment* and underlying concepts. Our vocabulary instruction can both facilitate these relationships and build on them.

Because most words in English are created through processes of word formation or morphology, knowledge of morphology is a critical part of your repertoire for teaching vocabulary. Let's examine it more closely.

Have you ever noticed how, when we're tired or under stress, we make errors such as "I dranked the whole bottle"? Such slips of the tongue reveal our morphological knowledge at work. In this example, the underlying rule for creating past tense verbs overrides the irregular forms of these verbs—and the fact that our brains can generate these kinds of errors reveals just how pervasive our morphological knowledge is. Just as our brains have tacit rules that enable us to arrange words into sentences, our brains have rules for arranging meaningful word parts into words.

Using as an example the word *predict,* let's examine morphology at work:

predict (verb): If Holly disagrees with Jim, I can *predict* his reaction.
predictable (adjective): Uh, oh! Holly disagreed with Jim and his reaction is perfectly *predictable.*
predictably (adverb): Jim *predictably* bit his pencil in two.
unpredictable (adjective): This time of year the weather is *unpredictable.*
unpredictability (noun): The *unpredictability* of this weather is driving me nuts!

By adding different suffixes and prefixes onto the base word *predict,* in other words, we can derive quite a number of related words. Suffixes very often determine the role the word plays in the sentence—its part of speech. This is the way most English words are constructed, and this is why most linguists refer to English as a *morphological* language.

There is one more level of analysis to which we can take *predict:* It may be broken down into the prefix *pre-* and the Latin root *dict,* meaning "say or speak." Literally, then, *predict* means "to say or speak before" something happens. Our students do not need to become linguists to understand morphology, but we *do* intend to help them become aware of morphology and understand how this awareness can help them learn, remember, and grow their understandings about words. "Getting language awareness of this kind helps establish nodes in verbal memory," David Corson notes, and this makes the words "semantically and morphologically transparent for ease of activation and future use" (1995, p. 182).

Linguists have identified three components or "families" of morphology: compounding, inflectional morphology, and derivational morphology. *Compounding* is the process from which we get compound words such as *seagull* and *strawberry.* It unites two or three words that represent a single concept, even when the words remain separate, as in *high school. Inflectional morphology* indicates verb tense and number; inflectional suffixes, also termed *inflectional morphemes,* are most commonly referred to as *inflectional endings,* such as adding *-ed* to a verb to indicate action occurring in the past. And as we will see, *derivational morphology* is the richest of the three components. Derivational suffixes, also termed *derivational morphemes,* often change the syntactic role of a base, though the core meaning is usually retained.

Derivational suffixes are really the "workhorses" of morphology. There aren't many of them, but they allow us to derive any number of additional words from a single base or root. Because of this, we often tell our students that if they know one word, they know ten! By exploring how suffixes such as *-ive, -ize, -ate,* or *-ion* affect the base words to which they are attached and how they usually change the part of speech of the word, students grow their understanding of English morphology.

At the same time students develop a foundation for learning the Greek and Latin components of English. A number of educators and researchers have noted that learning basic morphological processes supports the learning of the Greek and Latin forms in the academic vocabulary of particular content areas, such as, for example, *sol* (sun) in *sol*ar and *sol*stice, *gon* (angle) in poly*gon* and tri*gon*ometry, and *jud* (judge) in *jud*icial and pre*jud*ice.

HOW WORDS ARE WRITTEN: SPELLING MAKES SENSE!

A scholar once observed that a writing or spelling system is really a set of directions for thinking about language (Olson, 1996). In some East Asian writing systems, words are written with one sound represented in the middle of the word and the other sounds arranged around it; these nonlinear writing systems reflect, the scholars say, the way these cultures make sense of and organize their knowledge about the world. The fact that most Western spelling or writing systems are linear may reflect the fact that Western societies tend to organize their worlds in a linear fashion: *beginning, middle, end; first, next, last; cause–effect;* and so forth. These are intriguing notions, if oversimplified. Still, we encode or write our language from left to right and we talk about the beginnings, middles, and ends of words, sentences, paragraphs, and genres.

A classic poem bewailing the shortcomings of the English spelling system includes the lines "Beware of heard, a dreadful word/That looks like beard and sounds like bird" and "I think you already know/Of tough and bough and cough and dough." We're going to address the spelling system for two reasons. First, contrary to the poem's suggestions, spelling makes much more sense than we have traditionally believed (Ehri, 1997; Templeton, 2003b; Venezky, 1999). Second, our understanding of how the spelling system works will help us better teach vocabulary.

What does it mean to say that spelling makes more sense than most of us have grown up believing? The common impression is quite the opposite: The system is inconsistent, illogical, and incomprehensible! What most people see as a problem of English spelling is the fact that it does not have a consistent one-letter/one-sound relationship. The same sounds may often be spelled different ways (/f/ may be spelled *f* as in *f*ace and *ph* as in *ph*ase) and the same spellings may often stand for different sounds (the words in our poem, for example, and the *gh* in *gh*ost, tou*gh,* and throu*gh*out). Chapter 3 explains many of these discrepancies in terms of how spellings and sounds have historically evolved in English. However, most of these apparent discrepancies may be explained by looking more closely at the type of information the spellings are representing.

Let's assume for a moment it's possible to wave a wand and spell words more in line with how they sound. You can probably figure out the following three words:

kumpeet
kumpetitiv
komputishun

At first glance, this might seem pretty attractive. But now let's consider how these words are *actually* spelled:

*compe*te
*compe*titive
*compe*tition

What do you notice that is the same across all three words? You've been given a hint, of course, by the italics. The spellings of these three words share many letters in common, having the effect of making these words *look* similar. This is no coincidence, because these words are related in meaning. Because of the way morphology works in English, as we have seen, the words *competitive* and *competition* are derived from the base word *compete*. While the pronunciation of the base changes when suffixes are added, the spelling does not change to reflect this; instead, the spelling of the base remains strikingly consistent.

This, then, is the bargain English spelling has struck with the English language. It may not represent individual sounds as consistently as one might wish, but this is because it serves to spell *meaning* more consistently. Words that are similar in meaning are very often similar in spelling as well, despite changes in sound. This is what is termed the *spelling–meaning connection* (Templeton, 1983, 2004b), and you will teach your students how it works as we help them expand their vocabulary. The cartoon in Figure 2.1 helps to illustrate this point.

Like most of us, this gentleman probably thinks that we should spell words the way they sound, and this leads him to ponder why there is a silent *n* in *autumn*. We can solve this deep conundrum for him, however, by pointing out how the spelling–meaning connection works in English. We show him the word *autumnal* and talk about how it is related in meaning to *autumn*. Interestingly, the *n* does stand for a sound in *autumnal*.

FIGURE 2.1

Traditionally, we have been used to looking at and thinking about words in isolation—like *autumn*—rather than in spelling–meaning families, and this inevitably leads to questions about why letters don't consistently represent sounds. When we *do* look at words together in spelling–meaning families, which is just another label for morphological groupings, the meaning relationships become apparent. Your students' awareness of these types of relationships will not only help them improve their spelling, but their awareness will also help expand their vocabulary as well. And once students become aware of and understand this relationship when you point it out to them, they begin to see these patterns quite a bit—which makes sense, because they are apparent in the vast majority of words in English.

In English spelling, there is an intricate interplay among sound, pattern, and meaning in representing words in print. As noted in Chapter 1, learners develop knowledge of this interplay developmentally, over time, with the guidance of knowledgeable teachers. We've begun by looking at the representation of *meaning* for two reasons—first, to get your attention. It usually is somewhat startling to realize how "regular" spelling can be when we attend to meaning as opposed to sound. Second, because spelling can represent meaning directly, knowledge about spelling can facilitate vocabulary development.

What is meant by sound and pattern in word formation? Suspend disbelief for a moment or two and pretend you do not know how to read and spell. This may give you a sense of how spelling knowledge develops from the *sound* or alphabetic level to the *pattern* level and how it supports writing and reading. You are now a beginning reader/ writer; how will you go about learning the spelling system?

First of all, you assume that print somehow captures sounds, and it does so with letters. Moreover, these letters somehow match up in a linear, left-to-right way. You expect this because knowledgeable adults have shown you how writing "works" left to right.

You have learned about these letters—their names and their sounds. As you are writing and you want to spell a word, knowing there aren't many words that you know how to spell the way they appear in books, you gamely pronounce, slowly, what you want to write down. You listen for sounds, thinking of letters that make those sounds. You get quite good at this, and these efforts are important, because they really get you thinking about words, their sounds, and their spellings. What is helping you with this are the words you see in print. If your teacher has chosen wisely, you are seeing lots of words, especially words with simple spelling patterns that match your expectation of how letters and sounds match up. She or he is helping you read and learn about words that have a simple consonant-vowel-consonant structure; these are important because they make sense in terms of your own ideas about how the system works: *c-a-t*. She is also, however, helping you learn to read words that do *not* match up with your theory, words such as *cake*, which you've been spelling KAK or CAK because this matches your left-to-right letter–sound matchup theory. (There is a silent letter at the end of *cake*; what's *that* about? Letters make sounds, after all!)

After awhile, however, you've learned to read quite a few of these words that end in *e*, as well as those that have long vowel sounds spelled with other silent letters, like *ai* in *rain*. You start using these spelling patterns in your writing; you're getting to the point where it makes sense to you that some letters do not make sounds. Your spelling looks like this: SNAIK for *snake* and CAOM for *comb* (you're trying out the *oa* spelling you've noticed in words like *boat* and *coat*, and on occasion you'll switch the letters). You have achieved a very important insight. Chunks or groups of letters can work together to correspond to sound. You have discovered the *pattern principle* in English spelling. You have also moved beyond the grip of the one-letter/one-sound expectation. Words that you have learned to read correctly have become words you are now learning to spell correctly.

Another challenge awaits, however. How do you learn that sometimes long *a* is spelled like *sail* and sometimes like *sale*? How do you sort it out? Your teacher will guide you through the following understandings:

- *Is the word a homophone?* Homophones are words that sound the same but are spelled differently. Though generations have despaired that such words exist, this knowledge actually helps determine *which* spelling students select. Yes, although the long vowel sound in /pān/ may be spelled *a*-consonant-*e* or *ai*, the appropriate spelling is determined by *meaning*. Are you writing about the glass in a window or extreme discomfort? The meaning carries with it a consistent spelling. The glass in a window will always be spelled *pane* and the extreme discomfort will always be spelled *pain*. The /sāl/ on a boat will always be spelled *sail*; the /sāl/ where products are sold will always be spelled *sale*. For these types of words, we hang our memory for spelling on a meaning hook.
- *How sounds are spelled very often depends on their position within a word.* Words such as *say* and *rain* reveal that, in single-syllable words, long *a* is usually spelled *ay* at the end of a word (but rarely in the middle) and often *ai* in the middle (but never at the end).
- *How sounds are spelled very often depends on other sounds they are adjacent to.* Words such as *ridge* and *cage* reveal that the /j/ sound is usually spelled *dge* when it follows a short vowel but usually spelled *ge* when it follows a long vowel.
- *Some spelling patterns are far more likely to occur than others.* For example, there are more instances of the *a*-consonant-*e* pattern for the long *a* sound in the middle of a syllable than for any of the other patterns. It is important to know that there just aren't that many words in which long *a* is spelled *ea* as in *great*.

As your teacher supports your learning of spelling patterns in single-syllable words, she is showing you how to use that knowledge to decode longer words that you encounter in your reading. Learning about *ai* in *paint* and *train* helps you figure out *contain* and *exclaim*.

Over time, your spelling begins to reflect characteristics of those longer words you are decoding in your reading—for example, MIDDEL for *middle* and ALOW for *allow*. A significant feature of English spelling is this "doubling" phenomenon: When do we double and when don't we? You'll first learn how this works with words such as *gripped/gripping* and *griped/griping.* In these types of words, we tend to double a consonant if it follows a short vowel and we don't double the consonant if it follows a long vowel. You'll learn that this pattern applies not only to words to which endings are added, such as *grip* and *gripe,* but to words such as *human* and *pattern* as well. Does it always apply? No; we have both *rabbit* and *habit.* Over time, however, the apparent exceptions to the rule become explained as we learn more about how words work—and usually, as we will see in Chapter 3, these explanations have to do with the meaning and origin of the word.

As you continue to explore how spelling works, most of the errors you make occur in the more complex and polysyllabic words you have encountered in your reading and are trying out in your writing—for example, OPPISITON for *opposition,* IRRELEVENT for *irrelevant,* and BENEFITTED for *benefited.* Even adults will still occasionally, or even commonly, make such errors.

This concludes this little experiment in helping you appreciate the fact that learning to spell is not simply a matter of memorizing words, but that it is a process that follows a developmental arc and reflects the types of words learners encounter in their reading and then attempt to use in their writing, based on an understanding of word structure (Invernizzi & Hayes, 2004). Your students exhibit a range of spelling ability; as discussed in Chapter 8, you can assess their developmental spelling levels, inferring their reading abilities as well, and adjust instruction accordingly.

While email, instant messaging, and websites such as MySpace, Facebook, and Twitter allow subscribers to spell—and to write—pretty much as they wish, this phenomenon will probably not lead to the end of the need to spell conventionally. In spite of spellcheck and increasingly sophisticated voice recognition software, the need to spell correctly in different contexts will remain for the foreseeable future (Templeton, 2006). Just like informal and formal registers of speech, there are registers of writing. The formal registers will continue to require conventional spelling. But stepping back to look at spelling or orthographic knowledge more broadly, as described in Chapter 1, the abilities to read and to spell words are two sides of the same orthographic coin. If one is not familiar with the spelling system, then fluent and meaningful reading cannot occur.

"SPECIALTY" WORDS AND PHRASES

There are many ways that language scholars have categorized words over the years. In this section, we share examples of the most common categories.

The "H" Words

Over the years, homophone, homonym, homograph, and heteronym have been used in different ways, and though there is still some fuzziness at the definitional borders of a couple of them, we'll share their most common applications with you, as well as showing the Greek or Latin roots that form their names (Templeton, 2003a).

Homophones (*homo*, same + *phone*, sound). We've already been introduced to *homophones,* which are words that sound the same but are spelled differently and have different meanings: *lone/loan, faint/feint, morning/mourning, compliment/complement.*

Homonyms (*homo*, same + *nym*, name). Words that are spelled *and* pronounced the same but have different meanings are called *homonyms.* For example, *bear* may refer to the animal or to the act of supporting something, as in *bear* a burden, or of bringing forth, as in *bearing* a child. Often, these types of words are also referred to as *multiple meaning words.* To add to the confusion, you will also see this term used interchangeably with homophones. (How these confusions get started is anyone's guess; probably, someone simply started using the term incorrectly and it stuck.)

Homographs (*homo*, same + *graph*, writing) and Heteronyms (*hetero*, different + *nym*, name).   Both *homographs* and *heteronyms* are words that have the same spellings but different pronunciations and meanings: a *tear* drop or a *tear* in a fabric; *refuse* to do something or the *refuse* from a cleanup operation; a birthday *present* or being *present* at a meeting. Which term you use depends on whether you're thinking about a different pronunciation or the same spelling—slightly confusing. *Homograph,* however, is more commonly used.

The following list is a small sampling of resources that are excellent for exploring homophones, homographs, and homonyms. Although Gwynne's and Terban's books are targeted at younger readers, older readers also enjoy them—the illustrations are often as much of a "groaner" as the puns!

Gwynne, F. (1988). *A chocolate moose for dinner.* New York: Simon and Schuster.
Gwynne, F. (1988). *The king who rained.* New York: Simon and Schuster.
Lederer, R. (1996). *Pun and games.* Chicago: Chicago Review Press.
Lederer, R. (n.d.) *Language sites on the internet.* http://pw1.netcom.com/~rlederer/rllink.htm
Pryle, M. (2000). Peek, peak, pique: Using homophones to teach vocabulary (and spelling!). *Voices from the Middle, 7*(4), 38–43.
Terban, M. (1982). *Eight ate: A feast of homonym riddles.* Boston: Houghton Mifflin.
Terban, M. (1988). *The dove dove: Funny homograph riddles.* Boston: Houghton Mifflin.

The Rest of the "Nyms"

As we've noted above, *nym* means "word," and it is intriguing to explore these additional "nym" words: acronym, eponym, toponym, and aptronym.

Acronyms.   *Acronyms* "economize" the language by combining several words into one word; they combine the initial letter or letters of the words in a term or phrase. *Acro* is from the Greek, meaning "tip"—the "tip" of the word.

LASER: Light Amplification by Stimulated Emission of Radiation
NIMBY: Not In My Backyard
AIDS: Acquired Immune Deficiency Syndrome

Eponyms.   An *eponym* is a word derived from a person's name. The person may be real or fictional or a name from a myth or legend. All of the major disciplines have eponyms, and they represent ideas, theories, inventions, and so forth. The following list gives a handful of eponyms:

aphrodisiac: Aphrodite, the Greek goddess of love and beauty
boycott: Charles Boycott, whose servants and staff refused to work for him because he would not lower rents
guillotine: Joseph Guillotin, a French physician and the inventor of the device
pasteurize: Louis Pasteur, who developed the process whereby bacteria are killed in food and drink
sax: Antoine Joseph Sax, Belgian instrument maker, designer and builder of the first saxophone

Toponyms.   From the Greek word *topos,* meaning "place," *toponyms* are words that derived from place names.

champagne: From the Champagne region of France
bikini: Named for the island of Bikini
tuxedo: Named for Tuxedo Park, the location in New York City where this type of suit was first worn
bayonet: Probably based on Bayonne, the French city where they were first made

Aptronyms.   A relatively recent category, these are names of individuals that are "apt," because they fit what the individuals do (and just for clarification and emphasis, these are real individuals):

> *C. Sharpe Minor:* an organist
> *Dan Druff:* a barber
> *Dr. Fingers:* Australian gynecologist
> *Linda Toot:* Former principal flautist with the Milwaukee Symphony Orchestra
> *James Bugg:* Exterminator
> *Bill Headline:* Washington DC station chief for CNN

More Economizing

Portmanteau or Blended Words.   The term *portmanteau* was coined by Lewis Carroll in *Through the Looking Glass.* Parts of different words are blended together to form a new word; occasionally whole words are blended with parts of another word: Carroll describes Humpty Dumpty explaining to Alice, "You see it's like a portmanteau—there are two meanings packed up into one word." The term *portmanteau* comes from French and refers to a suitcase with two hinged compartments that are folded or blended together. *Port* comes from the Latin root meaning "carry," and *manteau* comes from a Latin word meaning "cloak."

> **Portmanteau Words**
> *smog: sm*oke + f*og*
> *chortle: ch*uckle + sn*ort*
> *cyborg: cyb*ernetic *org*anism
> *genderlects: gender* + dia*lect*

> **Clipped Words (Part of a longer word is "clipped" off)**
> *memo: memo*randum
> *gym: gym*nasium
> *cab:* taxi *cab* (*cab* is a clipped form of *cabriolet,* the original word)
> *quack* (a medical charlatan or pretender): originally *quack*salver

Contractions.   Contractions are separate words that have been *pulled together* (the Latin root *tract,* pull + the prefix *con-,* together). Specifically, a contraction pulls a verb plus *not* together, with an apostrophe standing in place of letters that have been deleted: *can + not = can't, does + not = doesn't.* There is a long historical tradition in English spelling of using apostrophes to indicate where letters and sounds have been dropped, but with the exception of contractions the practice has fallen away over the last couple of centuries.

LOOKING AHEAD

Before moving more directly to the "how to" of teaching vocabulary, some intriguing mysteries about words remain to be explored. Chapter 3, by exploring the historical processes that have worked on languages and words, will provide some answers to questions your students often raise. For example, when they look up the prefix *in-* in the dictionary and it says "also spelled *il-, im-, ir-,*" what is *that* about? Why does the word *dumb* end in a *b*? Why is *ough* pronounced so many different ways? And just when your students understand what word roots are and how they work, they wonder why spellings sometimes change—as, for example, in *video/vis*ual, ex*plain/*ex*plan*ation, and re*ceive/*re*cep*tion.

3 CHAPTER

Where Words Come From and Where They're Going

Dave Barry, the humor columnist, once wrote that "Our language is a rich verbal tapestry woven together from the tongues of the Greeks, the Latins, the Angles, the Klaxtons, the Celtics, the 76ers and many other ancient peoples, all of whom had severe drinking problems." With a mischievous twist, Barry captures the fairly hazy understanding that a lot of us have about the history of English. However, even this vague knowledge understands that English has been shaped by many influences. While a legacy of many languages has been a source of enrichment, this polyglot heritage has also been seen by many as a cause for confusion in the spelling system and clutter in the vocabulary with the number of odd irregular verbs. Why examine this history at all?

The English language we speak today is indeed a rich tapestry, with very deep and interconnected threads, and a little bit of knowledge about this tapestry on our part can be a good thing as we work to develop our students' vocabulary. Sharing this knowledge with our students, when appropriate, can help to develop their sense of control over the vocabulary and the language, and this sense of control leads to a sense of ownership. And if we come to understand more about how words "work" and how they have evolved over time, words will yield insights to understanding other times, people, and places—not to mention all the subject areas teachers are responsible for teaching. Fundamentally, this knowledge leads to students' *word consciousness*—their understanding and appreciation of words and (we hope) the lifelong motivation to continually learn more (Lubliner & Scott, 2008; Stahl & Nagy, 2006).

For the moment, let's pretend to conduct a common experiment—actually, a common party game more than an experiment, but it will help prove a very important point. Referred to as "broken telephone," this experiment involves one person thinking of something to say and writing it down. She then whispers it to someone else, who in turn whispers the message to another person, and on it goes from person to person until the last person says the message out loud. This final version is then compared to the original. For example, after being passed along through 20 individuals, the sentence "I am dying to vacation in Cancun" emerges as "Slime the ragin' cannon," quite a different message altogether. This game illustrates a fundamental and very important understanding: The sounds and meanings of words change over time as they are filtered through individual speakers. Knowing this prepares students for much that they will learn about the meanings and spellings of words.

Another quick experiment: Is a *preeblie* large or small? How about a *gowster?* Even though they have not heard or seen these words before, most people will say a *preeblie* is small and a *gowster* is large. There is something in the roots of our language—indeed, in the roots of a great many languages the world over—that tells us certain vowel sounds like /ē/ are often associated with small, diminutive things. Other vowel sounds like /ow/ are deep, full-bodied, and are often associated with large things.

Now consider some real words. Why did *gnarly* never really catch on, but *dude* definitely did? Why does *nice*, which once meant "stupid," now mean "agreeable"? Or why does *meat*, which once referred to any solid food, now have a much narrower definition? And how about *citizen*, which once meant "city dweller," but now extends to a state, nation, and the whole world? Words, and language in general, exist in *social* contexts: How, when, why, and where we use words in communicating with one another affects their meanings and their uses. And as *nice, meat, citizen, gnarly,* and *dude* illustrate, the passage of time also affects the popularity, importance, usage, and usefulness of words. Words lend themselves to all of these influences, and in doing so become the marvelous tools we use to help us think and communicate at this moment in time and across time.

After briefly considering etymology as a topic, our exploration of the history of the language will include the Indo-European language, the development of writing, the influence of Greek and Latin, and the phases of the English language: Old, Middle, and Modern English.

ETYMOLOGY

Examples such as *citizen, meat, gnarly, dude,* and *nice* move us into thinking about etymology, a word introduced in Chapter 2 meaning "study of the history of words." *Etymology* comes from the Greek word *etymon,* meaning "the true sense of a word." When we explore the etymology of a word—its history—we are indeed getting to the true sense or core of its meaning. Linguists use different terms to describe how meaning develops; we find the following terms most helpful (Claiborne, 1989; Robinson, 1989): Over time, the meanings of words and word parts may widen or generalize (*citizen*), narrow or specialize (*meat*), drift (*nice*), and extend through metaphor. An example of this metaphorical extension is the word *heart*; it may refer to the actual organ or, metaphorically, to someone who "has a heart," meaning someone who is kindly.

Robert Claiborne observed that words and word parts grow by a sort of "linguistic free association, in which one idea suggests others more or less akin to it. . . . Sometimes the connection in meaning is obvious, sometimes there is no traceable connection at all" (1989, p. 16). Consider *kerd,* for example, a word meaning "heart" in Indo-European, a seminal language we will consider in the next section. Throughout seven millennia, through its migrations within and across different languages, *kerd* arrived in English, giving us not only *heart* but *creed* and *courage* as well. Vowels and consonants change, meaning changes subtly and significantly, but the core meaning of "heart" lives on in these words. In addition to the organ and the kindly disposition, we may talk about a *creed,* a belief that is felt in the heart, and *courage,* a righteous boldness that is felt in the heart—from *coeur,* the French word for "heart," which also evolved from the earlier *kerd.*

One other, perhaps more light*heart*ed example: Where in the world did the word *manure* come from? It came from a Latin root meaning "hand," and by metaphorical extension, *working* with one's hands—*manual* labor, *manufacturing* or making something by *hand,* and in the case of *manure*—yes, literally spreading barnyard dung by hand.

These examples may provide a sense of how word meanings may evolve. Much of the balance of this chapter explores this process more extensively, homing in on how the language and the words of English have developed and grown.

THE GRAND ANCESTOR OF ENGLISH: THE INDO-EUROPEAN LANGUAGE

English—and dozens of other languages including Spanish, Icelandic, Romanian, Hindi, Bengali, and Persian—all began as *one* language, *Indo-European.* Linguists chose this term to represent the geographic reach of the languages that arose from this single language—from the Indus valley to the far reaches of Europe and beyond (see Figure 3.1). The most recent scholarship exploring the origins of Indo-European suggests that it arose over 7,000 years ago in the region between the eastern part of present-day Turkey

FIGURE 3.1   Languages That Developed from Indo-European

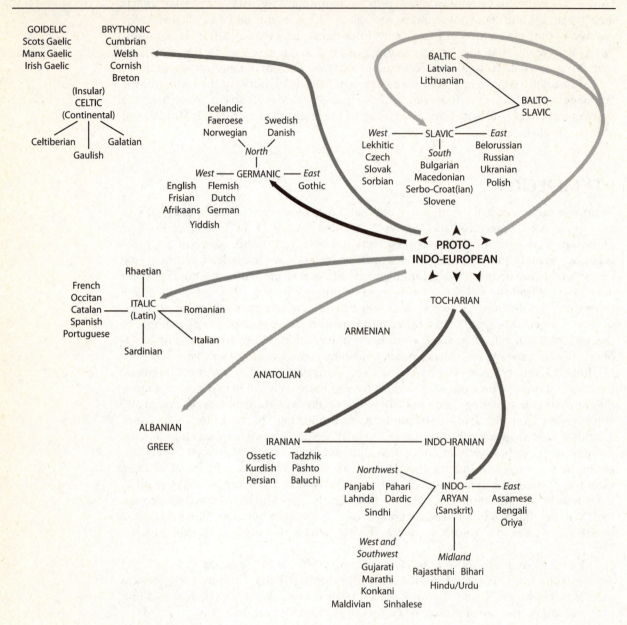

and Georgia, Armenia, and Azerbaijan to the east. How did it turn up thousands of years later in so many different languages?

The Indo-Europeans didn't stay at home. Over hundreds if not thousands of years, small groups would strike out on their own, traveling literally in all different directions. Over time, their language changed in many ways—remember the broken telephone game?—as well as mixing with the languages of the peoples they encountered. And if there is one constant in language, it is change.

Let's explore a couple of examples of Indo-European vocabulary. Look up the common word *ball* in the *American Heritage Dictionary*. The entry for *ball* describes round, spherical objects, some of which are used in athletic events, as well as a "vulgar slang" usage. At the end of the entry we are invited to "see *bhel* in Appendix I." Appendix I is actually an entire dictionary of Indo-European roots. Turning to the entry for *bhel* (or clicking on *bhel* in the online entry of the *American Heritage Dictionary*), we find this information: "To blow, swell; with derivatives referring to various round objects and to the notion of tumescent masculinity." This single root, spoken over 7,000 years ago, evolved into words such as *ball, balloon, boulder, bold, fool,* and *phallus.* At its core, each of these words has the meaning of swelling—a *balloon* by literally swelling, a *boulder* by its shape, *bold* by the feeling of swelling when confronting danger. Exploring a more specialized word, *architect,* we find in its dictionary entry that it comes from two Greek roots, *arkhi* meaning "chief, most important," and *tekton,* meaning "builder." At the end of the entry, we are invited to see *teks* in the Indo-European dictionary; this root meant "to weave, fabricate." Reading further in this entry, we see that other words such as *technology, polytechnic,* and *technical* all came from a word spoken some 7,000 years ago. The core meaning of these terms, then, carries the sense of "making" something. We also see that words as apparently diverse as *text, tissue,* and *subtle* came from this root as well.

While vowels changed radically from the original Indo-European (IE) roots, the initial consonants didn't change as much. When they did change, they did so predictably. In the following list, the words for *father* and *mother* across five different languages are presented. Interestingly, for reasons not really understood, among Indo-Europeans who migrated to the north and northwest the sound of initial /p/ changed to /f/. Among Indo-Europeans who migrated to the west, into the Mediterranean region, the sound of /p/ did not change:

Indo-European:	*mater*	*pater*
Latin:	mater	pater
Spanish:	madre	padre
French:	mère	père
German:	Mutter	Vater*
English:	mother	father

*In German, the /f/ sound is spelled with the letter *v.*

Sometimes a sound changed predictably *within* the same migrating group. For example, while many words retained their initial /b/ sound from the root *bhel—ball, balloon, boulder*—a number changed to an initial /f/ sound in many words, such as *fool* and *phallus.* This change to /f/ in many words occurred among the Indo-Europeans who went west and settled in either the Greek or the Italian peninsulas. In Latin the /f/ sound is spelled with the letter *f;* in Greek words absorbed into Latin the /f/ sound is spelled *ph.*

To give you a fuller example of this sound change, please refer to the IE root *bha* and some of its descendants in Figure 3.2. In Indo-European, *bha* meant "to speak." As the root later evolved into Latin and Greek, we see the /b/ to /f/ sound change and the different spellings for the sound in Latin and Greek. Don't be thrown by the initial /b/ sound in *blasphemus;* the root is now spelled with *ph* and the *blas* part came from a root that meant "evil"—literally, "evil speech" (present-day *blasphemy*—to speak contemptuously or irreverently about something that is sacred). In Latin, the root evolved to *fat,* giving rise to the word *fate;* for the Romans, *fate* referred to that which was spoken by the gods. In French, the root evolved into the word *affable,* an adjective with the sense of being easy to *speak* to.

Other examples include *fabula,* which meant a spoken story; it evolved into the Middle English words *fable* and *fabulous,* which originally meant "celebrated in a fable." The word *infant* meant "no speech," which makes sense, but what about *infantry?* Traditionally, the infantry are the youngest in the military—the word *infant* became extended metaphorically to young soldiers. Indeed, Italian cavalrymen referred to the infantry as "the babies" (Templeton, 1991). The words on the right-hand side in Figure 3.2 are, of course, present-day English words. They all retain the meaning of "speak" or "sound." *Preface* literally means "to speak before" a book, and *prophet* literally means to speak before others speak.

We're getting into later phases of language history, of course, and we will turn to these soon. Before doing so, however, it will be helpful if we first look at the development of writing.

FIGURE 3.2   **Evolution of the Indo-European Root** *Bha*

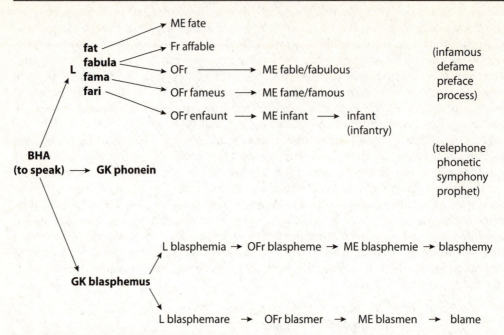

Source: From Templeton, S. (1991). *Teaching the Integrated Language Arts*, 2e. © 1991 Wadsworth, a part of Cengage Learning, Inc. Reproduced by permission. www.cengage.com/permissions

THE DEVELOPMENT OF WRITING

Indo-European did not have a writing system. For that matter, 7,000 years ago the only type of writing system that existed was quite different than what we have today. A writing system that corresponded to sound didn't develop until around 3,000 B.C.E. among the Sumerians in Mesopotamia. Evolutions of writing systems are usually described as *logographic* or *ideographic, syllabic,* and *alphabetic.* The predecessor to these systems was a *pictographic* form of representation.

The drawings on cave walls represent early peoples' desire to understand and control their world. In the beginning, these may simply have represented important events—a hunt, for example. The following simplified example represents "Man catches fish" (Templeton, 1991):

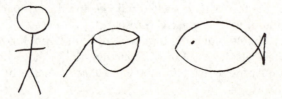

Over time, pictographs evolved into representing ideas in a particular language—they became *ideographs* or *logographs* (*logo* comes from the Greek term for "word"):

This "writing" means "Man catches cow." Obviously one can't use a net to catch a cow, so the representation for "net" has become a logograph, standing for the idea of

catching something—not just fish, but cows and any number of other creatures and things as well. With the passing of even more time, these representations have lost almost all pictorial correspondence, although the following may still represent "Man catches cow":

Around 3,000 B.C.E., the Sumerians developed a logographic system that evolved into the first system that represented sound (Gelb, 1963). Termed *cuneiform* from the Latin word for "wedge," this system evolved from wedgelike marks that were made on soft clay tablets (Figure 3.3).

In ideographic or logographic systems, *context* played an important role in helping the reader determine the meaning of the logograph: The sign for "sun," for example, could also mean "bright" or "day." This led to the representation of sounds apart from the meaning of the logographs. For example, Gelb describes this process using a modern-day word: The sign meaning "to kneel" would be combined with the sign meaning "sun" to produce "Neilson." When this begins to happen the signs lose their original ideographic meaning and are now becoming a system that represents sound. This is a tremendous advance, because linking characters to sound reduces the number of characters that must be learned—although this still left about 600 characters in Sumerian, which had 600 separate syllables. The *syllabic* writing that evolved in Sumeria eventually stimulated the development of syllabaries in Egypt, which in turn influenced Phoenician and Greek, examples of which are presented in Figure 3.4.

FIGURE 3.3   Cuneiform Writing

FIGURE 3.4   **Examples of Scripts from Syllable-Based Writing Systems**

Egyptian   Phoenician   Early Greek

Notice how similar the characters in Phoenician and Greek appear? This is because the Greeks borrowed the Phoenician alphabet. Spoken Greek was quite different from spoken Phoenician, however: the syllable structure of Phoenician was fairly simple when compared to the syllable structure of Greek, so the Greeks made the Phoenician characters "fit" their own language by matching characters not to individual syllables but to individual sounds *within* the syllables. Representing sounds in writing turned out to be, as some have argued, the first great technological invention of humankind (Havelock, 1982). While the "invention" of an alphabet—a writing system that established a one letter/one sound correspondence—may not be the "first" great invention, it certainly ranks toward the top of the list. Why? Because most of the guesswork—the reliance on context—was taken out of reading. We can illustrate this with an example using our own alphabet: Can you read the four-word sentence represented by the letters JKNBX? It may be a bit easier to read when *all* of the sounds are represented, as with JACKINTHEBOX. Having more letters—especially letters that represent vowels—provides much more context for print, making it possible to "decode" anything that is written down. (By the way, JACKINTHEBOX is deliberately written without spaces—it was still some time before spaces were introduced between words. The Greeks used the metaphor of a flowing river for language—ongoing, unbroken, without interruption.)

This description is quite simplified, of course. As we saw in Chapter 2, any one language actually has a lot more "sounds" in it than are represented by an alphabet or a spelling system. Still, for languages that are complex syllabically—as was Classical Greek and present-day English—if both consonants and vowels are represented that's a lot more information than if only consonants are represented. And if you've got more information represented in the writing system, it is potentially easier to teach and to learn. Literacy is therefore more accessible, and the need and demand for reading material expands phenomenally. Literacy is no longer the exclusive domain of priests and potentates, but is accessible to the people. Havelock expressed the strong form of this point of view when he observed that the Greeks "did not just invent an alphabet; they invented literacy and the literate basis of modern thought"; moreover, their alphabet "made possible the production of novel or unexpected statement, previously unfamiliar and even 'unthought'" (1982, pp. 87, 88). The Romans adapted the Greek alphabet and subsequently spread it far and wide throughout their empire, and the rest, as they say, is history.

One last thought before we leave our brief overview of the development of writing: The understanding that language can potentially be segmented into sounds is, as we've seen, a relatively late historical development. Over thousands of years, writing systems evolved from pictographs/ideographs to representing syllables, only recently evolving into systems representing consonants and vowels. This should give us pause when we try to "teach" young children in kindergarten—not to mention preschool—how to segment speech and learn that letters can map to individual sounds. It's not nearly as easy or transparent as most noneducators assume—and because of those well-intentioned but misdirected efforts, many young children who have struggled with this aspect of literacy in kindergarten and first grade wind up being struggling readers in the middle and secondary grades.

THE ORIGINS OF ENGLISH

On occasion, you've probably watched a movie from the 1950s, 1940s, or earlier. You have seen excerpts from speeches by John F. Kennedy, Franklin Delano Roosevelt, perhaps Eleanor Roosevelt, or heard a recording of W. E. B. Du Bois. The farther back you go, decade by decade, the more you notice that the English that is spoken sounds different—subtly so; it's difficult to put your finger on it. Keep going back, and the language becomes less and less intelligible. You'd need to go back hundreds of years, however, before you would have considerable difficulty understanding a native speaker of English. Even plopped down in the middle of Shakespeare's London in the late 1500s and early 1600s, you'd recognize the language you hear as English. Go further back another 100 to 150 years, however, and you'd have considerable difficulty—flickers, glimmers of words that sound vaguely familiar, but that's all. Another few hundred years and you wouldn't recognize the language as English.

It's an interesting fact that English, along with most other languages spoken today, has not changed all that much for several hundred years. Go back further, however, and the pace and nature of change accelerates considerably. In the balance of this chapter we will explore the nature of this change and how knowledge of it may support learning present-day vocabulary.

The Influence of Greek and Latin

Why begin with Greek and Latin when we're focusing on English? Because most English vocabulary comes either from Classical Greek and Latin, or from Greek and Latin word parts that were assembled to form new words centuries after the Greek and Roman civilizations had declined. In Chapters 1 and 2 we referred to generative vocabulary knowledge and the importance of Greek and Latin word parts in developing this knowledge. This knowledge is a critical aspect of every student's *strategy* for independent word learning, involving the examination of words for Greek and Latin roots, thinking about their meanings and the possible meanings of the English words they are associated with, and plugging that meaning back into the context in which the words occur. It is a critical part of the knowledge that helps students learn and retain the meanings of words. Interestingly and importantly, this understanding also helps students' *spelling* knowledge considerably, by explaining a number of otherwise odd and difficult-to-remember spellings.

As we will see later in the sections on Old, Middle, and Modern English, many words in English have come from words that were used in Greek and Roman times: for example, *symmetry* from Greek *symmetria, construct* from Latin *construere,* and *liberty* from Latin *libertas.* Many more words with Greek and Latin word parts, however, never existed in Classical times but have been created more recently. For example, while telescopes and microscopes obviously didn't exist over 2,000 years ago, the Greek word parts *tele* (far off), *micros* (small), and *skopos* (watch, look at) did. These word parts were readily available for assembling into words that named new inventions long after the Classical Greek civilization had passed from the scene.

Greek and Latin roots combine with one another and with prefixes and suffixes to form literally tens of thousands of words in the English language. For example, the word *inspect* contains the Latin root *spect,* meaning "to look," and the prefix *in-,* meaning "into." Putting these two word parts together we get the meaning "to look into," which is literally what *inspect* means. The word *inspection* can similarly be taken apart and analyzed: the suffix *-ion,* meaning "the act or result" is connected to *inspect,* which we already know means "to look into." Thus, *inspection* literally means "the act or result of looking into" something.

As will be explored in Chapter 4, we first introduce students to Greek and Latin roots using words they know and in which the meaning of the roots in combination with the prefixes and suffixes is literal and straightforward—words like *inspect* and *inspection.* Later on, we can explore how the combinations have extended metaphorically and are less literal. For example, the combination of *spect* with *circum,* another Latin root, results in *circumspect.* By combining *spect* (to look) with *circum* (around) we get the literal meaning "to look around." The word has grown metaphorically to mean that you are cautious in what you do and say and you do not take risks—you "look around," so to speak, and are careful. Sharing such examples with our students helps us talk through how current meanings can evolve from the original literal meanings.

At the end of Chapter 2 we left you with some mysteries about words that have to do with spelling, pronunciation, and meaning. Most of them can be explained by looking at Greek and Latin word roots and by thinking about their combinations and changes over time. A few answers will be revealed here; the rest will be addressed when we look at the history of the English language. In our examples of roots so far, the spelling of the root remains constant and does not change when combining with other roots and affixes: *inspect, inspection, circumspect.* Sometimes the spelling does change, however; the root *vid* (to see) in *video* and *evidence* becomes *vis* in *visual* and *televise.* The root *scrib* (to write) in *inscribe* and *scribal* becomes *script* in *inscription* and *prescription.* Why does this happen? In Roman times, when certain endings were added to a root the pronunciation of the root would change, and the spelling usually changed as well to represent this change in pronunciation. Why? You may get a feel for this when you try pronouncing *inscri̲b̲tion* or *prescri̲b̲tion* rapidly several times. Unavoidably, you will hear and feel how the /b/ sound becomes a /p/ sound as it blends into the /sh/ sound that begins the suffix. This is exactly what happened, over time, as people pronounced these words. Eventually, the spelling changed to reflect the sound changes.

As many of these words and word parts filtered down to English through the centuries, the various spellings of the roots were kept intact. In many other words, the spelling of a root changed because the pronunciation in a later language—usually French or Middle English—changed. And, on occasion, the spelling changed to fit existing spelling–sound patterns in English. For example, the words *provoke/provocation* and *invoke/invocation* have the Latin root *voc* (to call). Why don't we have the spellings *provoce* and *invoce?* Because these words would have to be pronounced /provōse/ and /invōse/, given the "rule" in English that a *c* followed by an *e* has a soft sound. The *voc* spelling works in the related words *provocation* and *invocation* because *c* followed by an *a* has a hard sound. And we simply can't have a spelling such as *invoc.* Word-final syllables with long vowels in them do not end with a single consonant. So, we're back to the reason for *provoke* and *invoke:* The spelling has to change in the root to fit the spelling–sound patterns in English.

While the spelling of roots was often changed depending on the ending or suffix that was added, a similar phenomenon occurred with the spelling of prefixes when they were affixed to a root. For example, look up the dictionary entry for the prefix *in-* and you will find that it is also spelled *il-*, *ir-*, and *im-*. Look up the prefix *ad-*, meaning "to" or "toward," and you will find that it is also spelled *ac-*, *af-*, *ag-*, *al-*, *ap-*, *as-*, or *at-*. What is happening in these situations? Why is *ad-* spelled so many different ways? These spelling changes are not arbitrary. In the case of *in-*, when this prefix was first affixed to a word such as *mobile* to mean "not mobile," it was pronounced i<u>n</u>mobile. Try saying i<u>n</u>mobile rapidly, several times. It's difficult, isn't it? Switching from the /n/ to the /m/ sound rapidly is somewhat awkward. It was for the Romans, too. So, over time, the /n/ sound became slurred or absorbed into the /m/ sound. Eventually, the spelling changed to reflect this sound change. The same phenomenon occurred with *in-* + *relevant*—it's easier to say *irrelevant*—and *in-* + *mediate*—it's easier to say *immediate*. The prefix *ad-* works the same way: *ad-* + *count* becomes blended into *account*; *ad-* + *company* becomes *accompany*; and *ad-* + *tack* becomes *attack*. (Try saying *adcount, adcompany,* and *adtack* rapidly several times; yet again, you can see how the /d/ sound slurs into the sound at the beginning of the word to which it was being affixed.)

You will find that these absorbed prefixes seem to be everywhere. In the word *support,* for example, the root is *port* (carry). The prefix originally was *sub-*, meaning "beneath, under, below"; in terms of meaning, put them together and *support* literally means "to carry from below." In terms of sound, put them together and the /b/ of *sub-* slurs into, is absorbed by, the /p/ at the beginning of *port*. To prove this, try our rapid blending experiment again: say su<u>b</u>port rapidly several times.

Connecting vowels are another legacy from Greek and Latin. Connecting vowels do not represent meaning, but naturally resulted when people coined words by putting morphemes together—which continues to the present day. All of the following words have a connecting vowel inserted, indicated by the letter in parentheses: *equ(i)valent, petr(i)fy, chrom(o)some,* and *cosm(o)naut.* As an experiment, try pronouncing each of these words without the connecting vowel—it's just about impossible. So it was for the Greeks and the Romans, and when they spelled the words they included these connecting vowels. This also explains the lack of agreement, on occasion, between different dictionaries in indicating the spelling of an affix or a root. Some will include the connecting vowel as part of the morpheme; others will not (*cosmo* vs. *cosm*; *heter* vs. *hetero*; *ology* vs. *logy*). So why do we discuss this phenomenon with students? In general, knowing the how and why of connecting vowels furthers their understanding of how words work and how words have evolved. More specifically, this understanding helps students when they are analyzing the structure of an unknown word in order to figure out its meaning—they can better determine what's a morpheme and what isn't. Finally, this awareness and understanding prevents confusion when they see that different resources—dictionaries, word history books, websites—have slight differences in their spellings of affixes and roots.

Chapters 5 and 6 provide examples of how to "walk through" words with two or more morphemes, explaining for students how the meaningful parts combine to produce the meaning of the word. When a connecting vowel is involved in the process, these explanations will point it out.

To sum up these effects of sound and spelling, Ayers (1986) provides an apt comment: "None of these sound changes were hit or miss, nor were they thought out; they were completely natural. They are the result of things that take place in our mouths when we talk" (p. 71). And for so many words that later came down to us in English, these changes had already occurred in Greek, or later in Latin.

Historically, Latin first influenced the British Isles, if not the English language, beginning over 2,000 years ago. It began with Julius Caesar's invasion in 54 B.C.E. *Vini, vidi, vici,* the famous phrase he uttered on another occasion ("I came, I saw, I conquered"), would certainly have been appropriate here. He did not stay long, however; he had bigger plans and his ambitions lay back in Rome. After he left, the Romans did not return and really settle in for another hundred years. When they did return, however, they stayed for over three centuries. They took the name *Brittania* for the lands they ruled, adapting it from the earlier *Britt-os,* the Celtic name for the native inhabitants. They grew a small trading village named Londinium into a large urban area. When the Romans left, however, Brittania was defenseless against the ensuing bloody and devastating invasion that gave birth to the English language.

Old English (A.D. 450–1066)

The Romans left in the first half of the fifth century when Germanic tribes from the north were invading the Italian heartland of the Roman Empire. In the second half of the fifth century Brittania was vulnerable to waves of different Germanic tribes from northern Europe, primarily the Angles, the Jutes, and the Saxons. The onslaught was brutal. As Winston Churchill once wrote, the English language was brought to the Britons on the bloody edge of a sword. Some Britons escaped, fleeing to the west and north. In the west, in present-day Wales, the Welsh language contains roots of what was spoken before the Germanic tribes invaded, as in the sentence *Y meant yr mynyddoedd yn canu, ac y mae'r arglwyddes yn dod* (translation: "The mountains are singing, and the lady comes"; Cooper, 1986, p. 44). Susan Cooper's *The Dark is Rising* series, appropriate for intermediate grade students and above, engagingly blends in snippets of Welsh, spinning wordplay and legends reflecting Arthur and Merlin—legendary figures who arose from this period when native kings and their legions fought valiantly yet in vain against the invading Germanic tribes. Some linguists suggest the sounds and cadences of those who built Stonehenge linger still in the Welsh language.

Over the ensuing years in *Angle*land, the invaders blended in with those who had not escaped but had nonetheless survived. The Old English language, also referred to as Anglo-Saxon, grew. Although only a few words have survived into Modern English, they are critical. All of the 100 most frequently used words in English come directly from Old English—*the, is, on, in, for, go, run, I, we, me, he, she.* Some of the earliest words have to do with the land and making a living from the land: *sheep, earth, wood, work, dirt, tree.*

In Chapter 2 we noted that inflectional morphology is not a very large morphological category in modern English: *-ed/-ing, -s/-es, -er/-est,* and that's about it. In Old English, in contrast, inflectional morphology played a much more significant role. Rather than using word order to specify who did what to whom and when, word endings did most of the job: Today we would say "Hagar bit Prince Valiant in the leg" or "Prince Valiant bit Hagar in the leg"—switching the names *Hagar* and *Prince Valiant,* depending on who did the biting. In Old English, the inflectional endings took care of this; the places that Hagar and Prince Valiant held in the sentence stayed the same, and inflectional suffixes took care of the rest by indicating who did the biting. Over several hundred years these inflectional endings fell away, and just a handful from Old English remain today; for example, *-en* as in *fallen*.

About A.D. 597 the Christian missionary Augustine arrived in Angleland (for history buffs, this is not the same St. Augustine from almost two centuries earlier who is recognized as a Doctor of the Christian church—although, for his efforts in Angleland, this second Augustine eventually became sainted as well). As Church Latin spread, words such as *psalm, angel,* and *temple* entered Old English. Quite a few Greek words entered as well, having been "latinized," or changed in spelling to conform to Latin. This process of borrowing from Greek continues up to the present day, but almost always the Greek words and word parts are latinized when they are added. For example, *school* entered as *scol*, from the Greek word for leisure, *skhole*. The meaning of the term drifted: If there is time for leisure, there is time for discussion, and time for discussion eventually leads to someone who tends to monopolize, and eventually . . . well, you have a lecture! And lectures, as we well know, have been mainstays of education ever since.

The cycle of invasion and conquest, however, had only begun. Norsemen, whose name contains the root meaning "north," swept in from Scandinavia and Denmark. *Scandinavia*, by the way, comes from an Old Norse word for "south end of Sweden." For some time the Norsemen's path was unchecked. Their advance moved in all directions, and were it not for one man much of the world might today be speaking Scandinavian rather than English. Without an army, with no weapons, in the midst of a raging storm—or so the story goes—the Anglish king Alfred was taken in by an elderly couple living on the edge of a heath and given food and shelter. With spirit renewed, he rallied. He slowly rebuilt and refortified his army, and over the next few years beat back the Norse onslaught. Eventually, a truce was struck and the invaders settled to the north of Angleland. Alfred not only saved Angleland; during his reign he ushered in a time of sound governance and a commitment to religion, scholarship, and expanding education and literacy. It is noteworthy that, of the dozens of British monarchs in over a thousand years of English history, Alfred (849–899) is the only one who is referred to as "the Great."

As years went by and as such things go, children who spoke the native language and children who spoke the language of the invaders inevitably began to play with one another, and before long words were moving back and forth. This is a process that usually occurs when different languages intermingle for a period of time. As we will see, because of the many significant contacts the language has made with other languages, this process is particularly pronounced in English. As English and Danish intermingled, words that meant the same thing in Danish as in English gradually took hold. This had the effect of making possible finer and finer conceptual distinctions within the language. For example, where first there were two words for the *same* thing, there later were two words for two *separate* things. In Old English the word *shirt* met the Danish *skirt*—both words originally referred to a single type of garment—but with time, *shirt* came to refer to a garment worn above the waist; *skirt* to a garment worn below the waist. Old English *rear* and Danish *raise* shared the same meaning, and in fact are often used interchangeably today, but the primary meaning of *rear* has come to refer specifically to bringing up a child, whereas *raise* refers more generally to movement or lifting up.

Old English spelling was primarily *alphabetic*, although some short vowel sounds in two-syllable words were indicated by doubling a consonant. We've been using modern English spelling to represent the words from Old English; here are some actual spellings (Venezky, 1999): *hloh*/laugh, *hræfn*/raven, *hnute*/nut, *hwæt*/what. The initial /h/ sound in each of these words fell away over the years, as did the *h* spelling—except in the case of *hwæt*, in which the /h/ sound remains in Standard English today. Interestingly, the *hw* was reversed centuries later, probably to look similar to other words spelled with initial /wh/. In contrast to words such as *hlæfn*, other spellings did not fall away as the sounds disappeared from the language. In words such as *dumb, knot, knee, gnat,* and *gnaw*, the underlined letter was pronounced. In Old English, *dumb* was spelled *dumbr* and the *b* was pronounced. The *k* at the beginning of *knot* and *knee* was once pronounced (and spelled with a *c*). With *gnaw*, the initial /g/ + /n/ sounds were what linguists call *imitative* and English teachers call *onomatopoeia*—they actually represented the sound of biting and chewing. And what about *gnat*? It was an insect that *bit*.

Figure 3.5 offers an example of orthography from the Old English classic *Beowulf*, which was first written down around A.D. 1000, although it had been shared orally for hundreds of years. By A.D. 900, the English language was the language of scholarship throughout medieval Europe. Most books were produced in "scriptoriums" in England. In another 150 years, however, this all changed. What happened?

Middle English (1066–1500)

In 1066 the Norman French crossed the English Channel from Normandy in what is now northeastern France and defeated the English at the Battle of Hastings. You are perceptive if you noticed the *Nor* in *Norman* and *Normandy*—yes, this area of France was settled by Norsemen a century earlier. It seems the Norsemen had a penchant for invading and conquering. As they settled in Normandy, the Norsemen incorporated the French lan-

FIGURE 3.5   **Old English: *Beowulf* (c. A.D. 1000)**

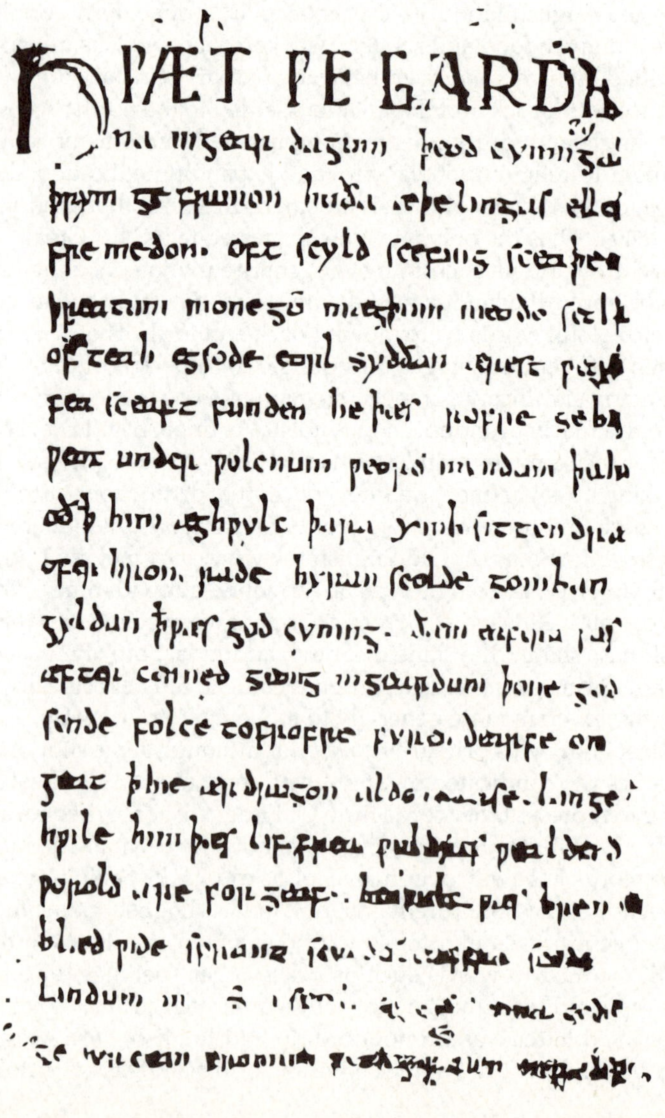

guage, and when they invaded Britain they brought the vocabulary with them. For the English language, the long-term consequence of this invasion and defeat was the infusion into Old English of a large component of French vocabulary. Over the next several centuries, this infusion was to have a considerable impact on the language.

A significant proportion of Latinate vocabulary that had been incorporated into French now passed into English. The language of the church, of government, and of legal affairs was now largely Norman French. And as happened when the earlier Norsemen invaded in A.D. 750, words that represented the same thing were usually kept, leading to finer conceptual distinctions over time. The language scholar Jesperson (1938) wrote, "While the names of several animals in their lifetimes are English, they appear on the table with French names" (p. 92). Compare English *swine, sheep,* and *deer* to French *pork, mutton,* and *venison.* Some other examples reflect the distinction in language usage between more common versus more elevated social registers. Contrast English and French *begin/commence, feed/nourish,* and *hide/conceal.* The more specialized Latinate vocabulary often introduced a third distinction: consider English *ask,* French *question,* and Latin *interrogate*—each evolving into slightly different shades of meaning.

The language was changing in other ways as well. For example, a number of phrases became condensed into words throughout this period: *break the fast = breakfast; God be with you = goodbye; All hallow's eve = Hallowe'en = Halloween.* Surnames also probably arose in the 1300s, determined by characteristics of lineage, as in the "son of" someone (John*son,* Thom*son*), by where one lived (*Rivers, Brooks*), or by one's occupation (*Hunter, Miller, Cooper*).

In the latter part of the fourteenth century, Chaucer's *Canterbury Tales* was published. Chaucer could have written in French or Latin, but he chose English, and his *Tales* represent the finest expression of Middle English. Figure 3.6 shows the first several lines from the *Prologue* to the *Canterbury Tales;* contrast the spelling with Old English and then early Modern English.

Spelling in Middle English evolved from alphabet to pattern. By 1200, some consonants were doubled between syllables to indicate short vowels. Over the next 300 years the occurrence of these *between*-syllable patterns (see Chapter 2) expanded so that by Shakespeare's time it was quite widespread: The French *manere* became *manner* and in Old English *scateren* and *hlæder* became *scatter* and *ladder.*

With the introduction of the printing press in England by Thomas Caxton in 1475, a process began in which the dialect spoken in London became the "standard" dialect of English, and spelling more consistently represented this dialect. This standard spread through the proliferation of printed texts that became available to a much larger segment of the population than before. At about the same time, cultural events on the Continent were affecting England significantly. The Renaissance, beginning in Italy in the 1400s, had spread to England. One of the defining characteristics of the Renaissance was the rediscovery or "rebirth" (French *renaissance*) of Classical Greek and Latin. These languages were thought to be the finest expression of human thought and the "standard" to which all languages should aspire. A number of scholars even undertook the respelling of a large number of words in a way to reflect the real or imagined classical origins of the words. You can get a feel for the work of these scholars by trying to match the words in the left-hand column with their revised or "etymologized" versions in the right-hand column, which were based on the Latin terms in the middle column (Templeton, 1980):

dette	*debere,* "to owe"	receipt
sisoures	*scindere,* "to cut"	admonish
doute	*dubitare,* "to waver in opinion, hesitate"	debt
amonest	*admonere,* "to warn"	verdict
receite	*recapare,* "to take"	doubt
verdit	*dicere,* "to say"	scissors

FIGURE 3.6   *Prologue* to the *Canterbury Tales* (c. 1387–1400)

Whan that Aprill with his shoures sote
the droghte of Marche hath perced to the rote,
And bathed every veyne in swich licour,
Of which vertu engendred is the flour;
Whan Zephirus eek with his swete breeth
Inspired hath in every holt and heeth
The tendre croppes, and the yonge sonne
Hath in the Ram his halfe course yronne,
And smale fowles maken melodye,
That slepen al the night with open yë—
So priketh hem Nature in hir corages—
Than longen folk to goon on pilgrimages,
And palmeres for to seken straunge strondes,
To ferne halwes, couthe in sondry londes;
And specially, from every shires ende
Of Engelond to Caunterbury they wende,
The holy blissful martir for to seke,
That hem hath holpen, whan that they were seke.

In a great many words—such as *debt, receipt, scissors,* and *doubt*—this etymologizing movement led to the addition of silent letters to the spellings (Johnston, 2000/2001).

Up until this period, the primary role of literacy and reading in the cultural lives and experiences of most people had been religious, and most religious writings were intended to be read aloud. So, the role of spelling had been more in support of reading aloud—a closer match between letters and their sounds. Beginning in the 1500s, however, the role of spelling was changed significantly (Scragg, 1974; Venezky, 1999). Because the printing press made more reading material available, the content of that material increasingly addressed secular rather than religious topics, and at the same time, education for the middle classes expanded significantly. Given these two developments, the role of spelling changed from that of primarily supporting correct pronunciation of words in oral reading to primarily supporting thinking and reflection in silent reading. As part of the larger movement to spell words to reflect their classical origins, words that tended to be related in meaning came to be spelled similarly, so that *bome* took the spelling *bomb* to connect meaningfully, and visually, with *bombard.* Other examples include *nacion* and *national* (*nation/national*) and *directe* and *dyreccyon* (*direct/direction*).

The representation of sound was not, however, left totally behind, though its role had been diminished. For some related words such as *explain/explanation* and *exclaim/ exclamation* the match could not be as direct. Words with vowel digraphs such as *explain* and *exclaim* had to retain their spellings to indicate their long vowel pronunciations. They couldn't be respelled *explan* and *exclam* because the vowel would then be short—and changing their spelling to *explane* and *exclame* would have been too radical a change.

In Middle English, a rather remarkable phenomenon occurred over a period of approximately 150 to 200 years: the Great Vowel Shift. Linguists get quite excited about the Great Vowel Shift because they believe it's one of the most important linguistic events since the consonants changed in Indo-European—but it only occurred in English, not in other languages spoken in geographically close proximity. Moreover, there is no single agreed-on theory about why it occurred, and to this day linguists argue about what caused it. Probably beginning during the 1300s and completed by about 1500, the Great Vowel Shift applied primarily to long vowels:

	Middle English			*Modern English*	
pro*f*ane	/ah/	pro-*fah*-nuh	→	/ā/	pro-*fān*
serene	/ā/	se-*rā*-nuh	→	/ē/	sae-*rēn*
div*i*ne	/ē/	di-*vē*-nuh	→	/ī/	di-*vīn*

These examples illustrate what happened to long *a,* long *e,* and long *i.* Using the phonetic respellings as a guide, try pronouncing *profane, serene,* and *divine* as they were pronounced in Chaucer's time: pro-*fah*-nuh, se-*rā*-nuh, di-*vē*-nuh. (Yes, the final *e* was not silent in Middle English.) Now pronounce the stressed vowel sound in the second syllable of pro-*fah*-nuh and pro-*fān,* paying attention to what your tongue does as it shifts from *ah* to *ā.* Do you notice that your tongue moves or shifts from a lower position in your mouth to a higher position? Do the same for se-*rā*-nuh and se-*rēn.* Do you notice how your tongue shifts in the same way from a lower to a higher position? That's exactly what happened to these vowels toward the end of the Middle English period. Now do the same for di-*vē*-nuh and di-*vīn.* The *ē* in di-*vē*-nuh is already as high as it can go in your mouth, so what's left for it to do? It falls all the way down and back, to an "ah" sound that you make when you begin to pronounce the long *i* sound.

The vowels we have mentioned here are all termed *front* vowels, because we articulate them toward the front of our mouths. The Great Vowel Shift applied to *back* vowels, too—referring to the long *o* and the long *u* sounds. In Middle English, *boot* was pronounced /bōt/; *hous* (present-day *house*) was pronounced /hūs/. In *boot* the long *o* sound shifted up to a long *u* sound, and the long *u* sound in *hous* had no place to go so it fell down to a sound that begins the pronunciation of the modern-day /ow/ sound, as in *cow.* With all this shifting of the long vowel sounds, what happened to the short vowel sounds? They pretty much stayed the same. And as for that final *e:* Although the sound it once represented dropped out, it remained in the spellings of these words primarily for two reasons. First, printers kept it because they could add it or drop it to justify a line of print; second, and more significant, it served to indicate a preceding long vowel sound as opposed to a short vowel sound.

With all of these sound changes, however, it's important to remember that the role of the spelling system was changing significantly toward representing classical origins and maintaining visual similarities among words that were related in meaning. For many words in English that did not lend themselves to these influences, however, their spellings still reflected the history of their changing pronunciations over the centuries. For example, Cummings (1988) observes that "we have sounds and spellings from close to a dozen Old English, Old Scandinavian, and Old French sources converging into three Middle English sounds, which then converged into two Early Modern English, which finally converged into . . . one sound . . . long a" (p. 251). Venezky (1999) describes this type of development that occurred with all of the primary vowel sounds and spellings as a "soap opera" sustained over 1,000 years (p. 118). What remains from the long *a* soap opera, therefore, are 14 separate spellings for this sound. However, as we pointed out in Chapter 2, they are not all equally probable. For example, *au* for long *a* occurs in only one word, *gauge; ae* occurs in only two words, *Gaelic* and *usquabae* (and how often are you going to be using *those* words?).

While historical linguists may enjoy the soap opera, there's really no need for the rest of us to get involved. What most students are capable of learning by the end of the primary grades is that there really are only three common spellings for the one long *a* sound: *a, ai,* and *ay.* And as we also saw in Chapter 2, which spelling we choose often depends on the position of long *a* in a word and whether we are dealing with a homophone. These same conditions apply to other vowel spellings (Cummings, 1988; Johnston, 2001).

Because of the Great Vowel Shift, we now have *line* pronounced /līn/ and *lice* pronounced /līs/—but what's going on with words such as *marine* and *police,* in which the same spelling pattern stands for a long *e* sound? They still have a spelling–sound correspondence that looks and sounds like Middle English. The answer is that words that have come into English *after* the Great Vowel Shift usually bring their native pronunciations with them; some are anglicized, but we tend to retain the original pronunciation of most. So we now have words such as *caprice,* which was borrowed from Italian after the Great Vowel Shift, and in which the *i* stands for the long *e* sound. More recently, as Spanish has become the language with the most influence on English, we have *mesa* and *armadillo,* in which the letters, just as in French and Italian, represent sounds that had previously shifted in English. It is interesting that such words are returning Middle English vowel spellings to our spelling system. In fact, in addition to Spanish, French, and Italian, the spelling–sound correspondences in many other languages reflect the patterns that existed in Middle English—Italian, Romanian, German, and Dutch, to name just a few. What excites linguists is that English was the only one of these languages in which the vowels shifted. However, it is significant that the spelling remained fairly constant.

Modern English (1500–Present)

Present-day English contains hundreds of thousands of words. Our literate vocabularies contain tens of thousands. Obviously, most of us use only a fraction of the possibilities, because so many of the words are highly specialized words such as *batrachomyomachy, phitolithologist,* and *geosyncline.* English has wound up as the repository of most of these highly specialized terms, primarily as a result of the spread of English throughout the British Empire from the seventeenth century on, and more recently, the ascendance of American English throughout much of the world since the Second World War.

The processes through which the numbers of words grew into the tens of thousands began with the effects of the Renaissance in the late Middle English period and continued in the early Modern English period. As Europeans undertook voyages of discovery and economic expansion they encountered many new things—flora and fauna—and when the local populations could not provide a term the roots of Greek and Latin lent themselves perfectly to the task. Using these roots captured much of what these novel worlds revealed. Quite a few Native American terms also entered the language; many were kept as they were (*moccasin, hominy*) and others changed with usage (*raughroughouns* became *raccoon; isquontersquash* became, simply, *squash*). Aboriginal terms from the continent of Australia entered the lexicon, such as *koala* and *boomerang.*

Beginning in the sixteenth century, the scientific revolution revealed insights into ourselves, quite literally, as well as into the world around us. New ideas, new organisms, and new parts of things all required naming. Scientists drew from Greek and Latin affixes and roots—*geography, circulatory, technology, barometer,* and *pterodactyl,* for example—and of course do so to this day.

While Chaucer represented the loftiest usage of Middle English, Shakespeare was the epitome of early Modern English. Blending the language of the aristocracy and the language of the "groundlings"—working-class folk who paid admission to sit on the ground in front of the stage because they could not afford to sit in the sheltered area set farther back—he spoke to all audiences, and his influence on the vocabulary of English is well documented. Although the number of words he is alleged to have coined may be exaggerated, such as by Lehr (2007), who confidently estimates the number to be around 6,000, the words and turns of phrase attributed to him that remain current in the language are impressive. A few examples: *countless, premeditated, courtship,* and *assassination.* And as we pointed out at the beginning of this section, were we to magically materialize in Shakespeare's England we would definitely recognize and probably even be able to get about in the milieu of early Modern English.

While scribes and printers had been working toward a consistent spelling system, it was still acceptable throughout the sixteenth century to spell pretty much as you wished. Elizabeth I spelled the same words differently at different times, and Shakespeare, in fact, spelled his own name several different ways. Toward the end of the sixteenth century, a number of scholars and educators were calling for a dictionary of the language that would standardize English spelling. Quite a number were written, but they were very different from our modern conception of a dictionary. None of the early dictionaries applied a systematic approach to analyzing the vocabulary of English; rather, the authors followed their own whims, inclinations, and prejudices. One of the more laudable attempts was published by Richard Mulcaster in 1582, in which he argued for stabilization of the spelling system and recommended standardized spellings for hundreds of words. It took another century, however, before the spelling system was much closer to stabilization.

In 1755 Samuel Johnson published his *Dictionary of the English Language,* the first major, systematic effort to include as many words as possible that existed in the English language. Johnson couldn't resist a personal touch, however, and many of his definitions are thinly disguised editorials on the politics and the personalities of his day. His suggested spellings completed the standardization that was almost complete decades earlier. He definitely sided with those reformers, stretching back over two centuries, who wanted to spell words to reflect *meaning* rather than trying to represent *sound* consistently. When given a choice of representing sound or representing morphology, he clearly opted for morphology (Pinker, 1999).

The second major dictionary of English that attempted a comprehensive analysis was published by Noah Webster in 1828, with a decided twist. His dictionary was titled the *American Dictionary of the English Language.* He strongly believed that Americans spoke American English, and American English was very different from British English. His commitment was tied to the nationalistic pride felt by many Americans in the decades following the American Revolution and the War of 1812. When all is said and done, however, there is a lot that American English and British English share when compared to their differences. Although we chuckle when we hear it, the adage that Americans and British are separated by a common language may not be all that true. Webster deliberately set about the work, however, of ensuring that American and British English were different, at least with respect to their spelling. In America, Webster proclaimed, we do not spell words like *valour, honour,* and *behaviour* with a *u;* we spell them *valor, honor,* and *behavior.* In America, Webster further proclaimed, we do not end words in *re* as in *centre* and *theatre.* Rather, we end them in *er* as in *center* and *theater.* And indeed, Americans did—at least, after Webster published his dictionary! He decided what was to go and what would stay—he was, after all, writing the first dictionary of American English.

Webster instituted a peculiarly American spelling convention in his efforts to distinguish American spelling from British spelling—one that, unfortunately, is the bane of many American students and adults to this day. Whereas the British simply double the final consonant whenever they add inflectional endings to words that end in a single consonant—as in *benefitted, channelled,* and *occurring*—Americans do not always do so, as the following list makes clear. See if you can figure out Webster's rule for doubling the final consonant when adding *-ed* or *-ing:*

omitting	orbited
propelled	traveled
compelling	leveled
occurred	equaling

Have you divined Webster's rule? It has to do with where the accent falls in the word to which you're adding the prefix: In the left-hand column, does the accent fall on the first or second syllable in *omit, propel, compel,* and *occur?* In the right-hand column, does the accent fall on the first or second syllable in *orbit, travel, occur,* and *equal?* Now that you've thought about where the accent falls, do you see how that determines whether the final consonant is doubled or not? If the accent falls on the second syllable, we double; if it does not, we do not double.

As is apparent from this "to double or not to double" example, Noah Webster worked very hard to prove that American English was indeed different from British English. When we look at the vast corpus of words in the language, however, we see that he did not change all that much. The examples above stand out because they are interesting; they prove the rule, however, that there is far more in common between British and English than there is different.

Modern English continues to develop, of course. Some scholars, only half in jest, ask when we will leave the Modern English phase of the language and enter the "Postmodern" English phase. And every generation, as it matures and grows older, becomes convinced that the English it speaks is the way English is *supposed* to be spoken, and that the younger generations are destroying the language. (We can find language mavens writing centuries ago about the youth destroying the language, but English is still here and in quite good shape.) We do wonder, though, at how digital literacy and its associated technology will affect language and words and our students' conception of them.

WHERE ARE WORDS GOING?

We are concluding this chapter by turning at last to the second half of the title of this chapter: Where, indeed, are words going? You have probably divined the method in our madness of waiting until now to address this. We have actually been addressing this question all throughout this chapter. Where words are going is where they have been going for thousands of years. Their fundamental work will remain the same—providing labels for and keys to unlocking our underlying conceptual worlds—as will the processes according to which they change in meaning and representation. Their work and the processes they undergo will continue to occur, of course, in contexts that will change in ways that are, right now, the stuff of fantasy. The World Wide Web and how we access it are, of course, changing our world and our literacies in ways we are only beginning to fathom.

How will digital literacy change language in general? We now hold access to the world—ourselves, others, libraries the world over, all types of media—literally in the palms of our hands. The Web and the wireless world continue to evolve, as well as our methods of access. As Lanham observed, "The long reign of black-and-white textual truth has ended" (1993, p. x). Language—sounds, words, meanings—will inevitably continue to change and evolve. So much of our students' understanding and ability to negotiate the changing cyberspace world and the real world it reflects and influences, however, will depend on the type of critical reflection on words and how they work that you will be teaching (Templeton, 2006). Yes, so much of it all comes back to how you approach your vocabulary instruction. How you guide your students' exploration of words and the worlds they represent will significantly influence how they explore and think about their world.

RESOURCES FOR LANGUAGE HISTORY, WORD ORIGINS, AND GREEK AND LATIN ROOTS

History of English

Bryson, B. (1990). *The mother tongue: English and how it got that way.* New York: Avon.

Bryson, B. (2001). *Made in America: An informal history of the English language in the United States.* New York: Perennial.

Crystal, D. (2005). *The stories of English.* Woodstock, NY: The Overlook Press.

Lehr, S. (2007). *Inventing English: A portable history of the language.* New York: Columbia University Press.

Resources for Word Origins

Ayto, J. (1990). *Dictionary of word origins.* New York: Arcade.

Merriam-Webster new book of word histories. (1991). Springfield, MA: Merriam-Webster.

Templeton, S., Johnston, F., Bear, D., & Invernizzi, M. (2009). *Word sorts for derivational relations spellers* (2nd ed.). Boston: Allyn & Bacon.

While both of the following books are based on Indo-European roots, they provide excellent etymologies for hundreds of English words:

Claiborne, R. (1989). *The roots of English: A reader's handbook of word origins.* New York: Times Books.

Shipley, J. (1984). *The origins of English words.* Baltimore: Johns Hopkins University Press. (For truly dedicated wordsmiths, Shipley's book is the ultimate source.)

History of Dictionaries

Winchester, S. (1999). *The professor and the madman: A tale of murder, insanity, and the making of the Oxford English Dictionary.* New York: Harper Perennial.

Winchester, S. (2003). *The meaning of everything: The story of the Oxford English Dictionary.* Oxford, GB: Oxford University Press.

Nature and History of the Spelling System of English

Cummings, D. (1989). *American English spelling.* Baltimore: Johns Hopkins University Press.

Venezky, R. (1999). *The American way of spelling: The structure and origins of American English orthography.* New York: Guilford Press.

Latin and Greek Roots: For Students and Teachers

Ayers, D. M. (1986). *English words from Latin and Greek elements* (2nd ed.; revised by Thomas Worthen). Tucson: The University of Arizona Press.

Crutchfield, R. (1998). *English vocabulary quick reference: A comprehensive dictionary arranged by word roots.* Leesburg, VA: LexaDyne Publishing, Inc.

Danner, H., & Noel, R. (1996). *Discover it! A better vocabulary the better way.* Occoquan, VA: Imprimis Books.

Kennedy, J. (1996). *Word stems: A dictionary.* New York: Soho Press.

Moore, B., & Moore, M. (1997). *NTC's dictionary of Latin and Greek origins: A comprehensive guide to the classical origins of English words.* Chicago: NTC Publishing Group.

Schleifer, R. (1995). *Grow your vocabulary by learning the roots of English words.* New York: Random House.

LOOKING AHEAD

With the conclusion of this chapter, we are ready to apply the foundational information of the first three chapters toward truly effective daily vocabulary instruction that will lead to a lifetime of learning, enjoyment, and appreciation for your students. The subsequent chapters address the "how-to's" of this application, including the needs of English language learners and how to assess and organize for effective and engaging vocabulary instruction and learning.

4 Essential Vocabulary Strategies and Activities

CHAPTER

Educational and developmental psychologists agree on the importance of background knowledge in developing new understandings. Background knowledge provides the context for students to achieve conceptual insights and to learn the terms that represent these new ideas. You picked this up early in your educational studies, and like most of us, probably continue to find ways to access your students' background knowledge and grow their new understandings. Depending on the topic, you may set up a number of concrete, hands-on experiences. Often, however, this is not possible, and you rely on virtual or indirect experience (Marzano, 2004). This includes reading, discussion, categorization of words and concepts, and video, software, and Web-based experiences.

Building on background knowledge, vocabulary instruction should occur before, during, and after units of study, including the reading that accompanies those units.

1. Vocabulary instruction before reading and study should explore concepts in terms already familiar to the learner, connecting directly with their background knowledge.
2. Encountering words previously discussed during reading and study enhances word knowledge and enriches reading comprehension.
3. Revisiting and working with words after reading and study assimilates new terms into students' existing knowledge structure and solidifies new understandings with new vocabulary.

The strategies and activities presented in this chapter and illustrated in Chapters 5 and 6 may be used at any point in reading and study: before, during, and after. They also lend themselves to a variety of contexts, whether students already have a fair amount of background knowledge about a topic, just a little background knowledge, or even no background knowledge at all. For the words you select, these strategies and activities will provide the multiple encounters and variety of experiences that are absolutely necessary for students to learn and be able to apply knowledge of these words.

Regardless of the subject you teach, at least once a week you should read to your students from an example of good writing. If you teach specific content areas, your own passion for your subject will come across, of course, but so will your conveyance of a sense of the rhythm and flow of the language of your subject and its specialized vocabulary. A friend of ours, a high school biology teacher, shares with her students the following excerpt from *The Dragons of Eden* by Carl Sagan (1977) during the first week of school:

> While our behavior is still significantly controlled by our genetic inheritance, we have, through our brains, a much richer opportunity to blaze new behavioral and cultural pathways on short time scales. We have made a kind of bargain with nature: our children will be difficult to raise, but their capacity for new learning will greatly enhance the chances of survival of the human species. In addition, human beings have, in the most recent few tenths of a percent of our existence, invented not only extragenetic but also extrasomatic knowledge: information stored outside our bodies, of which writing is the most notable example. (pp. 3–4)

Our friend comments that Sagan pulls her students in with his prose and his observations. Along the way, this passage offers up two intriguing and probably unfamiliar words, *extragenetic* and *extrasomatic.* One of these, *extragenetic,* contains a basic form (*genetic*) that is central to an understanding of biology. These words, their component parts, and words that are similar in structure and meaning are also briefly discussed following this read-aloud. She guides her students through thinking about words not because the students will encounter these particular words in the future, but because they illustrate how words can be constructed from other word roots and affixes—a critical understanding that we work to help all our students acquire.

GUIDELINES FOR TEACHING CORE ACADEMIC AND CONTENT-SPECIFIC ACADEMIC VOCABULARY

As noted in Chapter 1, core academic vocabulary includes words that students may encounter frequently in their reading across a wide range of subjects and genres, including many that they should be able to use in their writing. Although words like *infuriated* and *lackadaisical* may initially be unfamiliar to the students, they probably already have an underlying concept for these words. Although some words occur across most content areas, responsibility for teaching them usually falls to English/language arts teachers. On the other hand, academic or content area vocabulary usually represents new concepts and new words from science, mathematics, history, and social science as well as the arts, geography, economics, technology, and physical education—words such as *impressionism, alluvial, anarchy, covalent, osmosis,* and *omnivores.* Familiar words that represent different concepts in specific content areas also fall in this category, as for example *product* in math and *cell* in science. Similar instructional guidelines (Beck et al., 2008; Diamond & Gutlohn, 2007; Marzano, 2004; Nilsen & Nilsen, 2004; Stahl & Nagy, 2006; Templeton, 2004b) support the teaching of core academic and content-specific academic vocabulary:

* Activate background knowledge. Through discussion, determine what your students already know about the terms and concepts and relate this to familiar concepts and newer concepts they have recently learned. Usually there is a range of understandings among your students, so getting them involved in discussion is very important.
* Use a variety of activities that involve students in using words and thinking about their meanings. Activities include sorting the words, thinking of related words, and discussion and explanation of the words including examples and non-examples. Graphic organizers and charts or diagrams, such as those shown in this chapter, support these explanations and discussions. Ask students what they learned that is new and interesting, what they have questions about, what has confirmed knowledge they already have. As students read and discuss, pose questions that include new vocabulary: "What did you find out about the *lithosphere?*" Ask students to turn to each other to answer questions and make comments so that many more students are involved in language use and not just one child in the typical question, recite, and evaluate mode. For example, "Turn to your neighbor and discuss how the crust and the mantle are similar and how they are different."
* When necessary, you may explain the meaning and give examples of how the words are used.
* Teach *generatively.* Reinforce how the structures of the words—affixes, bases, and roots—provide clues to their meanings.
* Periodically review the words, and most important, make a point of using the words yourself.

From this point on, you will see an emphasis on discussion for both generative and word-specific strategies and activities. This is deliberate and imperative, because words and larger dialogue in general become internalized over time, and in turn drive intellectual growth. Focused teacher–student and student–student dialogue is a courtesy that ensures this growth (cited in Corson, 1996, p. 191).

TOOLS FOR TEACHING

You will want resources on hand to make teaching vocabulary easier and more meaningful. Students can use word and concept sorts, dictionaries, and a variety of technologies to help them along.

Word Sorts and Concept Sorts

Word sorts and *concept sorts* have justifiably become a popular approach to vocabulary as well as spelling instruction and learning. Word sorting or word categorization activities engage students in comparing and contrasting words according to different features and characteristics. Sometimes you will tell the students the categories into which they will sort the words (a *teacher-directed* sort); other times the students will examine the words to come up with their own categories (an *open* sort). Word sorts may be done in a variety of ways—by manipulating words on separate individual cards, sticky notes, or slips of paper, or by writing in vocabulary notebooks. Probably the most engaging and effective procedure is sorting words that are each written on separate cards. Conducting sorts that focus on generative word knowledge early in the school year—using words that share common bases, roots, and affixes—will powerfully support student word learning and word decoding throughout the year.

Following is an example of a sort in which the students know most but perhaps not all of the words. It focuses on generative knowledge as it helps students understand something about the spelling–meaning connection and how they may use spelling to learn meanings. The teacher has the students match up a base word (*column*) with its suffixed or derived form (*columnist*). Teachers and students then work through another sample pair of words:

    column   resign
    columnist   resignation

He then has the students pair the remaining words:

    sign   muscle
    signature   muscular

    bomb   autumn
    bombard   autumnal

He asks them to discuss what they notice about the words: Are there clues to the meaning of words that are perhaps unfamiliar, such as *autumnal?*

Concept sorts follow the same format as do word sorts, but here the focus is on word *meaning* rather than structure, though on occasion the two may overlap. Usually, however, the words to be sorted are the key vocabulary and important related words for a topic of study. In a unit on "Producers and Consumers" in an earth science class, Amy Harway presents examples and has the students work in pairs to sort them according to whether they have to do with producers or with consumers. Afterward, the sorts will be compared. Amy may have the students do this same sort at the conclusion of the unit as one means of assessing their learning. The completed sort is shown below.

Producers	*Consumers*
autotrophs	heterotrophs
(*auto*, self + *troph*, nutrition)	(*hetero*, other + *troph*, nutrition)
photosynthesis	herbivores
solar energy	carnivores
chemosynthesis	omnivores
plants	detrivores
biomass	decomposers
	animals

More examples of word sorts and concept sorts are provided in this chapter, as well as in Chapters 5 and 6. See also Appendixes B, D, E, F, and G. The power of word sorting and concept sorting activities lies in student engagement in the comparing, contrasting, and discussing based on what they know and what they are learning. In the process, they are actively applying what they are learning—in the case of word sorts, about how word parts function within words, as well as how the meanings of these word parts work within particular words. Sometimes the meaning is straightforward as in *export* and *import;* other times it is more subtle and abstract, as in *protract.* Students can come to understand these subtleties and nuances through this active examination and discussion—all of which leads to deeper understanding of specific words and of generative processes of word formation.

The Dictionary

The classic instruction to "look it up in the dictionary" doesn't often work. You get caught in a circular process of looking words up in the definition of the word you don't know, often to be confused about yet more unfamiliar words in the additional definitions.

Still, dictionaries should be an important tool in students' vocabulary growth. As they think about meaningful word parts in an unfamiliar word and about the context in which the unfamiliar word occurs, dictionaries provide a third resource for checking and elaborating on word meanings. In so doing, dictionaries provide generative as well as word-specific information. You open up this powerful resource for your students by demonstrating how to read dictionaries and how they can confirm or extend the hunch they have about an unfamiliar word encountered in reading, while pointing out the other types of information that are included—usage, history, meaningful constituent parts, and pronunciation. A related tool, the glossary, may provide considerable help when using textbooks in specific content areas.

Technology

Chapter 3 observed that the nature of literacy itself—what it is and how it is used—is undergoing a revolutionary transformation. Most of our students are living that transformation. Theirs is a post-typographic world (Reinking, 1998), while most of their teachers still live in a print-based world. Teachers turn pages; their students skim screens.

Applications of new technology continue to evolve almost exponentially, and they can certainly support both teachers and students in teaching and learning vocabulary. From your perspective, for example, the publishing company from whom your district has adopted your subject matter texts—science, social studies, English/language arts, math—usually provides access to an ever-evolving array of online resources on its website. In addition, the digital world also offers an incredible array of other online sites, including online dictionaries and vocabulary websites, that provide you and your students information and resources about words. These will be discussed in Chapters 5 and 6.

Classroom-based technologies such as interactive whiteboards offer quite exciting opportunities for presenting information and engaging students in contributing to that information. Interactive whiteboards can be used as chalkboards—saving information you and your students have written from day to day that can be revised whenever you wish. Interactive whiteboards also allow you to use any of your Microsoft- and Mac-based applications more interactively, including vocabulary sorting or categorization activities (discussed below). Most students love coming up to the interactive whiteboard to add information and re-sort words. This is because the interactive whiteboard screen functions just like a laptop or desktop computer screen—rather than using a mouse, however, students have the appealing "big sweep" engagement where they may tap the screen, mark text or an image, and then drag and drop this information into different categories. You can save these co-constructed presentations—as well as the "chalkboard"-type presentations—as PDF files, placing them on your website so that your students may later access them and use them as a basis for extension activities.

While websites, classroom-based technology, and software all offer remarkable possibilities and virtual realities, remember that you remain the critical guide to your students' negotiation of these experiences.

GUIDELINES FOR SELECTING WHICH WORDS TO TEACH DIRECTLY

"So many words, so little time." This is a common lament among teachers at all levels. Remember, however, that most of our students' vocabularies grow through wide reading and discussion about that reading. This may be a bit reassuring, but you still feel the responsibility of choosing those words that *should* be directly addressed, and choosing wisely. This section provides guidelines for your selection of core academic or content area academic vocabulary to teach directly. Importantly, your selection will powerfully reinforce your students' comprehension of what they read and their understanding of academic subjects more broadly.

Guidelines for Selecting Core Academic Vocabulary

Publishers of the core texts that you may be required to use are increasingly paying attention to criteria for selecting and highlighting vocabulary that students probably need to know, but it's important not to assume that there's nothing else you'll need to do. Based on the particular selection to be read, a number of educators agree that you should apply the following criteria to your selection of which words to teach (e.g., Graves, 2006; Stahl & Nagy, 2006):

- Is the word significantly important for understanding the selection?
- Is the word likely to occur across all academic domains?
- Does the word lend itself to generative instruction—is it one of a larger family of morphologically related words?

A word does not have to meet all three of these criteria for selection but should usually meet at least two of them. It is important to keep in mind, however, that while a word may indeed meet these criteria, you may decide not to teach it if you decide that students may be able to determine its meaning on their own by applying their structural analysis strategy together with help from the context.

A number of researchers have applied the criteria of frequency of occurrence and application across all academic domains in order to identify a set of core academic vocabulary words that should be taught over the course of grades 4 through 12. The Academic Word List (Coxhead, 2000) and the General Service List and its adaptations (West, 1953) are widely used in ESL instruction, but they also have direct application for all learners. Both of these lists include, for each basic word, morphologically related words. English/language arts teachers in particular may wish to refer to these.

Guidelines for Selecting Content-Specific Academic Vocabulary

With regard to specific chapters to be read or units to be taught, you should apply the following criteria to your selection of which words to teach (Flanigan & Greenwood, 2007; Stahl & Nagy, 2006):

- Reading through the chapter and thinking about your unit as a whole, what are the words that represent major concepts and for which students will need to develop a deep understanding? You will introduce and develop these at the beginning of the unit of study and before the reading, as well as during and after. Examples from math are *proof* and *algebraic expression;* from science, *organ* and *cell;* from social studies, *civil rights.*

- What words are necessary to know for the specific reading assignment but do not require deep understanding? You may mention these, providing definitions, but not exploring further unless it becomes necessary for some students.
- And, as with core academic vocabulary, what words are important but may be figured out by the students through application of their structural analysis strategy together with help from the context?

GENERATIVE STRATEGIES

Wide reading is absolutely critical for vocabulary growth. As pointed out in Chapter 1, however, your students' vocabulary will grow more significantly if they understand the generative characteristic of most English words—those processes of word formation that govern how prefixes, suffixes, base words, and Greek and Latin roots combine. By adding prefixes and suffixes to bases and roots, we are able to generate many other words, and more important, understand them as well. This process is often referred to as *morphological problem solving* (Anglin, 1994; Carlisle & Stone, 2005). Our example of the word *courage* in Chapter 1 illustrates this: If you know *courage* you should also be able to learn *courageous, courageously, encourage, encouragingly, discourage,* and *discouragingly.* Possessing this knowledge about the generative nature of English vocabulary also powerfully supports decoding unfamiliar multisyllable words students encounter in their reading.

Students who are wide readers in the intermediate grades already know the word *relation,* and when they run into the words *relations, related, relating,* and *unrelated,* they should know them immediately if they are able to apply what they already know about how word parts combine. Here's where you come in, however. They may not be explicitly aware of the relationships among *relate* and *relation, relative, relationship, relational, correlate, correlational,* and *correlative* unless a teacher points these out, explicitly noting the relationships among the words and talking with the students about how these words all have the base *relate* and therefore share a core meaning. (Most adults, for that matter, have probably not reasoned through where the word *correlate* comes from; if two things or events *correlate,* they literally relate together or with each other—the prefix *cor-* means "with, together"). Beyond the level of adding simple prefixes and suffixes, most students are not spontaneously aware of how words work at the level of derivational relationships. It is up to us to show them. This is also the time to explore the spelling–meaning connection in depth. Words that are related in spelling are usually related in meaning as well. For example, notice the change in the pronunciation of the base word *relate* (re-*late*) when the suffix *-ive* is added (*rel*-ative) and in the base word *courage* (*cour*-age) when the suffix *-ous* is added (cour-*age*-ous).

You saw in Chapter 2 that linguists describe two types of morphology: inflectional and derivational. Derivational morphology is the richer of the two, and it's the powerhouse underlying generative vocabulary growth. While many students enjoy learning the term *derivational morphology,* using the label *spelling–meaning connection* may be a bit less off-putting for a number of students. The spellings of words and their component parts is a powerful clue to their meanings, and that's why these two aspects are often discussed together.

Which morphological elements should be taught across the grades? The appendix at the end of this chapter presents a sequence for the most common core prefixes, suffixes, and Greek and Latin roots (Templeton, 2004b). These core elements will be found across all content areas and should be addressed by English/language arts teachers from the intermediate grades on up. Sample lessons for many of these elements are provided in Appendix A for the intermediate/middle grades and Appendix B for the secondary grades. In addition, Appendix E contains a number of games that will reinforce understanding of word formation processes and specific words. Specific games will be mentioned in later sections. In Chapter 6, tables of content-specific roots and affixes are provided; these elements will be addressed by content area teachers from the intermediate grades on up. While these elements may not occur frequently across all academic domains, they usually do occur with considerable frequency within a subject area.

Word Formation with Base Words and Affixes

We rely primarily on two criteria when determining the variables that underlie the selection and presentation of affixes: first, the frequency of these elements in written texts and second, their conceptual clarity—that is, the ease of understanding the words that result from their combination with base words. For example, the prefixes *un-*, *re-*, *in-/im-/il-/ir-*, *dis-*, and *non-* are addressed early on. This is because these prefixes occur in the majority of all prefixed words in analyses of written texts in grades 3 through 9 (White, Sowell, & Yanagihara, 1989) or, as another analysis found, in first grade through college (Zeno, Ivens, Millard, & Duvvuri, 1995). When these prefixes combine with most base words their sense—usually "not" or "the opposite"—results in words whose meanings are straightforward and transparent (for example, *inflexible, incomplete, illiterate*). As another example, the suffix *-ly*, meaning "like," is one of three suffixes that occur in almost 20 percent of suffixed words in written texts (the other two are *-er* and *-or*). When this suffix combines with most base words the resulting meaning is also usually straightforward (for example, *slowly, dangerously, solemnly*).

Even though most of these affixes are addressed in instructional materials by fourth grade, this does not guarantee that all or even most students will know them or be able to apply them in decoding longer words in reading and in supporting memory for new words. It is important to address them again at the intermediate grades and above, in words that are appropriate for those grade levels, and whenever possible, in groups such that the common meanings of the targeted affixes are the same or similar—for example, the prefixes *un-* and *in-* (Baumann et al., 2002).

Strategy for Decoding Longer Words.   Students should apply knowledge of the prefixes and suffixes they are learning—and later, Greek and Latin roots—to decoding unfamiliar words in their reading. Here is the basic strategy to teach them:

1. Examine the word for meaningful parts—base word, prefixes, or suffixes.

   - If there is a prefix or a suffix, take them off so you can find the base.
   - Look at the base to see if you know it or if you can think of a related word (a word that has the same base).
   - Reassemble the word, thinking about the meaning contributed by the base, the suffix, and the prefix. This should give you a more specific idea of what the word is.

2. Try out the meaning of the word in the sentence; check if it makes sense in the context of the sentence and the larger context of the text that is being read.
3. If the word still does not make sense and is critical to the meaning of the overall passage, look it up in the dictionary. To illustrate, the teacher underlines the word *ungovernable* in the following sentence:

The country reached the point where it was <u>ungovernable.</u>

Pointing to *ungovernable*, the teacher asks the students, "If you ran into this word in your reading, how would you figure it out? Here's our strategy: First, are there any prefixes or suffixes? If so, take them off." The teacher erases *un-* and *-able*.

govern

"What's left? Right, the base word *govern*. Do you know it? Now, put the affixes back on—the suffix and the prefix—think about the meaning, and try out that meaning in the context of the sentence. Sometimes, you need more than just the sentence—you may need to think about the paragraph or even the topic or main idea of the whole text."

Principles of Teaching Morphology: Base Words and Affixes.   The following two principles guide instruction:

- Teach prefixes and suffixes first in the context of familiar base words. Begin with words in which a spelling change does not occur when the affix is added, then examine words in which a spelling change *does* occur.
- Model how to apply knowledge of the new affix in context, and model flexibility— what to do when the expected meaning of the element does not seem to apply.

Let's apply these principles in some examples:

- *Teach prefixes and suffixes first in the context of familiar base words.* Beginning with familiar base words not only helps students focus on the process of word formation, it also ensures that the function of the affix will be clearer and more transparent to your students.

For example, teach *-ly* by affixing it to words such as *quiet* and *delicate*: "Let's look at the word *quietly* in the following sentence."

Susan quietly tiptoed upstairs when she got home an hour and a half after her curfew.

"What is the base word in *quietly*?" (*quiet*) "Correct! What's the suffix? Right; it has to be *-ly,* doesn't it? Now let's look at the word *delicately* in the following sentence."

Josh delicately lifted the boiling test tube out of the rack.

"What is the base word in *delicately?*" (*delicate*) "Right again! What's the suffix? Yes, once again it's *-ly.* I wonder what the suffix *-ly* means or tells us when we see it attached to a base word?" (With the familiar base words and derived words, students are led to the awareness that *-ly* has the general meaning of "like" whatever it is affixed to.) "It serves as an adverb that describes how something is done."

When adding an affix results in a spelling change in the base word, here's how the lesson may go: "Let's look at the word *indication* in the following sentence."

There was no indication that we would have an early release day.

"What is the base word in *indication?*" (*indicate*) "Correct! What's the suffix? Right! It's *-ion.* Now let's look at the word *illustration* in the following sentence."

Which illustration best captures the theme in this story?

"What is the base word in *illustration?*" (*illustrate*) "Right again! What's the suffix? Yes, once again it's *-ion.* So, what do you think the suffix *-ion* means or tells us when we see it attached to a base word?"

The students may not come up with the exact meaning, such as "the act or result" of the base word, but their discussion will lead in that direction. You can either use this definition to summarize for them or have them check the dictionary. Then, ask students about the spelling change when *-ion* is added to each of the words. If they note that suffixes may change the part of speech of a word, terrific! If not you can point out that the verb *illustrate* becomes the noun *illustration*—the result of illustrating—with the addition of *-ion.* That is something you will be exploring with them explicitly.

In both of these examples, make sure that students understand that the base words and derived words share the same *core* meaning. Often students have learned from the definition of a suffix that "it changes the meaning of a word" and that gets in the way of seeing the common meaning. Most suffixes subtly affect the meaning but usually do not significantly change the core meaning.

This type of explicit walk-through of how the suffix works with the base word in a sentence may often be followed by word sort activities (discussed next).

- *Model how to apply knowledge of the new affix in context, while also modeling flexibility when the expected meaning of the element does not seem to apply.* For example, after teaching the most common meaning of the prefix *in-* with familiar words (to mean "the opposite" of whatever it is added to), discuss the following sentence:

> I never felt as <u>incompetent</u> as when I played in a pickup game with three of the first-string varsity.

"Okay, we see *in-*, don't we? If we cover it, what's left? Right—*competent*. When you are *competent* in doing something, what does that mean . . . ? So when we add *in-* back on, would the meaning 'not' work in this sentence?"

Next, present a counterexample:

> Many scientists believe that these higher-than-average summer temperatures are <u>indices</u> of a genuine climate change.

The teacher's discussion may go something like this: "Do the letters *in-* seem to be a prefix? If we cover them, what is left? Would *dices* make any sense? We may not even be sure how to *pronounce* this word. And even if we pronounce it correctly, if we haven't heard of it before we wouldn't get any clue to the meaning. We've got to think about how the word fits in the sentence, the paragraph, and the overall topic of what we're reading about."

How do you help students learn how to use *context* as a decoding strategy? It's important to help them understand that an unfamiliar word's structure, together with thinking about the meaning of what they are reading, will usually help them identify the possible meaning of the word. When it doesn't, however—as with *indices*—model your thinking for them:

"Okay, this sentence with the word *indices* in it occurs in an article on global warming. Keeping that in mind, and thinking about the word in this specific sentence, it seems to me that the word could either mean the temperatures are causing the genuine climate change or are telling or letting us know something about genuine climate change. But as we've been learning, higher temperatures are caused by other things—they don't just happen by themselves. So, that's probably not the meaning in this sentence. On the other hand, the meaning of telling or letting us know might work here. Those words seem to substitute nicely in the sentence. Let's look it up to check my hypothesis."

Along the way, students may realize—or you will point out—that *indices* is a plural form of *index*.

Here's another example, using the unknown word *allude* (meaning an indirect rather than a direct reference to something) and modeling the use of questions to support students' thinking about the unknown word in context (Templeton, Johnston, Bear, & Invernizzi, 2009). On an overhead, you display the following sentences:

> Brent wanted Allison to know that he realized he had acted immaturely when they went to the movie together. He didn't want to refer directly to his flipping popcorn at the screen, so instead he planned to <u>allude</u> to it by saying something like "There probably are better ways to impress a girl!"

Next, ask the following questions:

- "Did Brent want to mention the fact that he was flipping popcorn at the screen?"
- "How did he decide he would let Allison know he wasn't going to behave like that again?"
- "So, what do you think *allude* means?"

This type of modeling or think-aloud and questioning has as much to do with teaching about comprehension as it does vocabulary (Beck & McKeown, 2008). This is important to keep in mind, and researchers tell us that it is difficult to separate the two. When you're modeling how context—the overall sense of the meaning you're getting when you read something—is helping you figure out a word, you're in the land of comprehension.

After modeling a time or two, engage the students in talking about how they are trying to figure out some additional unfamiliar words. What information are they using to try to provide clues to a word's meaning? This type of discussion is very effective in helping students apply both knowledge of word structure with context, or context alone, in decoding unfamiliar words (Goerss, Beck, & McKeown, 1999; Stahl & Nagy, 2006).

Word Sort Activities to Support Word Formation with Base Words and Affixes. Using base words and affixes as the focus, the following sort is an example of how the common suffix *-ion* and its various forms such as *-sion* and *-tion* affect the meaning of the base to which it is attached. Along the way, students learn why the form of the suffix changes, which reinforces the spellings of these patterns as well. Prefixes and suffixes with the same or similar meanings are clustered together in the appendix to this chapter. It is helpful to teach them in clusters. Suffixes are often presented as if they are separate and distinct—for example *-tion, -ation,* and *-ition*—when they are actually different forms of the same suffix, in this case *-ion.* In such instances, they should be taught together.

Explain to students that you're going to examine the suffix *-ion* and its effect on base words. Begin by pairing the base word *elect* with *election* in one column and *possess* with *possession* in the other column. Next, have students pair up bases with their derivatives, in the following manner:

elect	possess	predict	oppress
election	possession	prediction	oppression
extinct	confess	detect	
extinction	confession	detection	

Ask students what they notice about the words in each grouping. What happens to the base words when the suffix is added? How are the base word and its derivative alike? How are they different? These questions will move the students toward thinking about meaning and about the role each word plays in a sentence—the *act* in comparison to the *result* of the act—*verb* versus *noun.* Encourage students to cast the words into sentences; this will also highlight the similarities and differences.

Word Formation with Greek/Latin Roots and Affixes. Why is a focus on word formation with Greek and Latin roots and affixes so critical? As Figure 4.1 illustrates, knowledge of Latin and Greek word roots is potentially a very powerful aspect of generative vocabulary knowledge. As students learn meanings for the most frequently occurring roots in core academic vocabulary—such as *struct* ("build")—and in content-specific academic vocabulary, they may generate an exponential boost in their vocabulary

FIGURE 4.1   **A Selection of Words Containing the Latin Root *struct***

construct	reconstruction	structure	instruct	microinstruction
construction	reconstructionism	structural	instructible	obstruct
constructive	misconstruction	restructure	instruction	obstructer
unconstructive	destruct	unstructured	instructional	obstruction
constructively	destruction	infrastructure	instructive	unobstructed
constructiveness	destructibility	nonstructural	instructively	reconstructive
constructor	destructible	substructure	instructor	obstructionism
constructivism	destructive	superstructure	preinstruct	obstructionist
constructivist	destructively	technostructure	uninstructed	obstructive
deconstruct	destructiveness	understructure	uninstructive	obstructively
deconstruction	indestructibility	structurally	misinstruct	
reconstruct	indestructible	macrostructure		
unreconstructed		microstructure		

growth. As an additional benefit and byproduct, this knowledge should help high school students significantly on the vocabulary components of the *Scholastic Aptitude Test* and the *American College Test.*

Chapter 3 presented a walk-through of how the root *spec* combines with the prefix *in-* and the suffix *-ion.* These word parts were chosen with care. The meaning of the root is straightforward, and in combination with these particular affixes the resulting meaning is also straightforward. This is how instruction with Greek and Latin roots is approached. In this sense, the criteria for the elements that are presented in the appendix on pages 72–76 are similar to the criteria in the last section. Begin with roots whose meanings are clear and direct, and examine how their combination with affixes results in words whose meanings are clear and transparent. In addition, examine how these elements combine to result in the meanings of words that students already know. Once students understand these straightforward relationships, we move to examination of less obvious combinations of elements within words.

It must be emphasized that the sequence in the appendix provides general guidelines only and is not hard and fast. Remember, there should be a degree of serendipity in the exploration of words—words will pop up on many different occasions and teachers will want to puzzle about why they work the way they do and do the things they do. Teachers who do wish a more structured sequence and presentation of roots, either to get instruction in roots underway or from which to occasionally pull, should find the lessons in Appendixes A and B helpful (see also Templeton et al., 2009). The first set is appropriate for the intermediate and middle grades, while the second set is appropriate for secondary grades. While there is overlap between the two sets for the most frequently occurring roots and affixes, the words that illustrate the roots and affixes vocabulary, however, are appropriate for the different levels. Secondary teachers who wish to differentiate instruction for some students or classes will find that the intermediate/middle lessons present less content than the secondary lessons and are paced more slowly.

Principles of Teaching Morphology: Greek/Latin Roots and Affixes.   The following principles guide instruction:

- When first teaching a new Greek or Latin root, use words that students are likely already to know, containing affixes they have already learned.
- Then move to examination of unfamiliar words whose meanings, when affixes and roots are examined, are more conceptually transparent.
- Next examine words whose meanings, when affixes and roots are examined, are more conceptually opaque or challenging.

Let's apply these principles in the following examples.

- *When first teaching a new Greek or Latin root, use words that students are likely already to know, containing affixes they have already learned.* Science teachers may list the following words and ask students what they think each word part means:

microscope   telescope   microphone   telephone

If necessary, this exploration may be facilitated by the following type of explanation. Start by discussing how the two parts of *microscope* give a sense of viewing (pointing to *scope*) something that is very small (pointing to *micro*); if something is very small we say it is *microscopic.* A *telescope* is used to view (pointing to *scope*) something that is far (pointing to *tele*) away. *Microphone* literally means "small sound," so discuss how a microphone is not itself a small sound but helps us hear sounds that are close by that would otherwise not be heard very well. How is that different from a *telephone*?

English/language arts teachers may write the words *tractor* and *contraction* and underline the root *tract* in each. Tell the students that these words contain the Latin word root *tract*, meaning "to pull." Ask them how a *tractor* has to do with pulling something—they may think of a tractor pulling a combine or a tractor/trailer combination. Ask students to call out examples of contractions and write them on the board. Assume you have the words *can't, didn't, wouldn't,* and *don't.* Discuss how they each came from two words: *can not, did not, would not,* and *do not.* What happened to these two-word pairs? They were each *pulled together* into one word. Pointing to each element in the word *contraction,* mention that it literally means the act (*ion*) of pulling (*tract*) together (*con*).

This examination of the root *tract* in the word *contraction* may be followed by having the students examine and discuss how the meaning of *tract* combines with affixes to result in the words *retract, distract,* and *extract.* The Latin root *rupt* also works well for this type of exploration. Write the words *erupt* and *interrupt* on the board and underline *rupt.* Explain that this root means "to break," and that when a volcano *erupts* it literally *breaks* (point to the root *rupt*) *out* (point to the prefix *e-*). Ask the students to think about the word *interrupt.* What happens when you *interrupt* a conversation? They will come to realize that you literally *break* (point to *rupt*) *in between* (point to the prefix *inter-*) the words another is speaking.

• *Then move to examination of unfamiliar words whose meanings, when affixes and roots are examined, are more conceptually transparent.* For example, walk through the word *intractable.* With *intractable, in-* is probably a prefix so take that off. What's left? *Tractable.* Knowing the meaning of *tract,* if we say that someone is *tractable* what might that mean? They are easily pulled along or influenced. If someone is *intractable* they are not easily pulled along; they are sticking to their position.

• *Next, examine words whose meanings, when affixes and roots are examined, are more conceptually opaque or challenging.* Consider the sentence "Understanding Avogadro's number is a really *abstract* concept for me." If it is difficult or challenging to understand something, we are *pulled* (point to *tract*) *away* (point to *abs-*) from understanding the concept rather than being pulled toward understanding. If individuals are *corrupt* or are engaged in *corruption,* they are *breaking* (*rupt*) *with* (*cor*). The meaning of the word evolved from the fact that more than one individual may often be involved in *breaking* the law; individuals *break* the law *together.*

This type of thinking about words is challenging, of course. But as Donald Ayers observed, "When you find a word which is capable of analysis but which means something quite different from the sum of its parts, plug in your curiosity and try to determine how its present sense developed" (1985, p. 66). When you model this way of thinking about words—plugging in *your curiosity*—you help your students develop a sensitivity to words that applies well beyond the particular word being analyzed. This sensitivity will help them develop a whole new level and habit of thinking about words in general.

Figure 4.2 is a Progressive Root Web transparency in which the teacher walks through the processes of generating words from the single root *spect.* This model can then be used with other roots by students working in pairs or small groups. Again, these are not locksteps. They describe a general sequence from concrete to abstract. While discussing *rupt* for the first time, for example, a student

FIGURE 4.2   Progressive Root Web

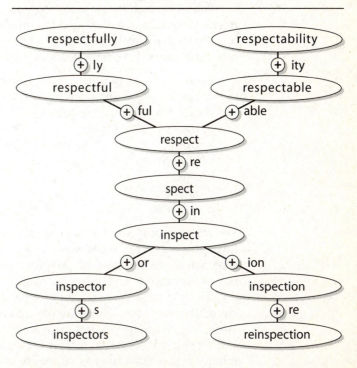

may well ask "but what about *corrupt?*" Go ahead and walk through it with the students; in doing so, you're planting the seed for their systematic thinking about words later on. As always, try to think about the context in which the word occurs as well. Once students have thought about the meaning of "the sum of the parts," putting this meaning to work in the word's usual contexts leads to more in-depth understanding of the word. For example, the following sentence provides one context for a discussion of *corrupt:*

The <u>corrupt</u> politicians had grown rich by selling their votes.

Word Sort Activities to Support Word Formation with Greek/Latin Roots and Affixes.   After beginning an exploration of common Latin roots, for example, the teacher could present a number of words such as *dictate, audible, contradict,* and *audience* and ask students to sort them according to their common root. This could either be done individually or in pairs. The students' completed sort would look like the following:

dictate	audible
contradict	auditorium
verdict	auditory
diction	audience
edict	audiotape
dictionary	inaudible
dictator	audiology
benediction	audition
indict	

The teacher then engages the students in discussing what they think the roots might mean. Because there is a mix of known and unknown words, students discuss—given the possible meaning of the roots—what they think the unknown words might mean. For *dict,* the sense of "having something to do with talking or speaking" usually emerges—although *dictionary* may be a puzzler at first. Depending on the students' background knowledge, some may have a sense of *indict* and *benediction,* but these might need to be checked against the dictionary. The meaning of *aud* is pretty straightforward in *audible* and *auditory,* for example, but how does the meaning "to hear" work in the words *audition* and *auditorium?* As with *indict* and *benediction,* the dictionary may be the final arbiter.

Following is an example of a more advanced sort involving words in which the roots refer to language or to the mind (adapted from Templeton et al., 2009). The teacher first has the students work in pairs to sort words by what they believe are their common roots; the completed sort appears as follows:

vocal	linguist	memory	psychology
vocalic	linguaphile	immemorial	psychiatry
vocabulary	sociolinguist	remembrance	psychopathology
advocate	linguini	commemorate	psycholinguistics
invoke	multilingual	memorandum	
invocation			
provoke			
provocation			
provocative			

The students may share what they think each root means; the teacher will then walk through a number of the words—in this case, providing more information. Alternately, each pair of students could be responsible for tracking down one root and later sharing how it functions in each of the words.

Begin with *voc* and words in which the meaning of the root and its function is straightforward; *vocal,* for example, refers to characterizing or having to do with the voice, and *vocabulary* also has to do with "voice" in a way—specifically, with words. The teacher shares with the students that *advocate* literally means speaking *to* or *toward* something, which is what an *advocate* does to *advocate* for someone. Walk students through the parts of each word and help them see how these parts fit together to define each word.

Remind students of the words *bilingual* and *monolingual;* what, then, does *multilingual* mean? The root *ling* refers to "language," but the teacher points out that it originally meant "tongue" in Latin; the extension to language more generally was quite natural. The words with *ling* offer some good possibilities for exploration. A *linguist* is one who studies language, and a *sociolinguist* studies how language is used in a social context. The teacher reminds students that they learned the word *philosophy* means "lover of wisdom," so the word *linguaphile* means "one who loves language." After discussing these *ling* words, the teacher asks the students why they think *linguini* has the *ling* root in it; if necessary, she reminds them of the original Latin meaning for *ling*—"tongue"—so the meaning of *linguini,* therefore, returns us to "having to do with the tongue."

The appendix at the end of this chapter presents some of the most frequently occurring Latin and Greek roots in core academic vocabulary. Students may learn them and revisit them through the intermediate, middle, and secondary grades. Chapter 6 will present additional generative roots and affixes for each of the major content areas.

WORD-SPECIFIC STRATEGIES

As you have seen, most of the words in English can be decomposed into identifiable affixes, bases, and roots. One of the most powerful means of learning, remembering, and using new words is by attending to these meaningful elements. In this section, additional ways of introducing, developing, and extending these understandings of specific words are examined.

Concept Sorts.   Just as with word sorts, in concept sorts students categorize words into different groups. The focus is usually on meaning, however, and the words to be sorted are the key vocabulary and important related words for a topic of study. Concept sorts help to activate background knowledge and generate interest in and questions about the topic. Depending on the students' level of background knowledge, concept sorts may be closed—meaning that the teacher determines the categories—or open—meaning the students choose their own categories. In either case, a "not sure" category is useful. Consider the following vocabulary for a science unit focusing on "Heavenly Bodies":

planet   star   sun   moon   asteroid   comet   meteorite   meteoroid

nebula   white dwarf   supernova   black hole   neutron star   galaxy

The terms the teacher has selected include words the students will know (*planet, star, moon, sun*) as well as some of the new terms used in the unit (*asteroid, neutron star, white dwarf*). Because the students have a fair degree of background knowledge in space and astronomy, the teacher asks them to buddy up in an open sort and see how many different ways they can think of to sort the concepts, as in the following possible categories that might emerge:

* They are in our solar system or out of it
* They are a single body or members of a group
* They generate light or reflect light

Here is one possible Single Body/Member of a Group concept sort.

Single Body	Member of a Group	Not Sure
sun	planet	meteoroid
star	moon	nebula
asteroid	meteorite	
comet		
supernova		
black hole		
galaxy		
neutron star		

As students discuss this sort, concepts in one category may be moved to any of the other two categories. More background information is brought out, and uncertainties are clarified or kept in the "not sure" category.

Early in his unit on poetry, Corbett Ballard engages his students in a *closed* sort; he knows most of the students have little or no background knowledge of the structure and purpose underlying this form. He has the students sort the following terms according to whether they have to do with "sound" or "structure" of poetry:

iambic pentameter couplet euphony rhyme sonnet ballad

alliteration haiku meter stanza onomatopoeia epic

After the students sort and discuss, Corbett shares short examples of each. The objective is not for the students to learn all of the unfamiliar concepts that particular day, but to get an initial sense of them. Their understanding will grow and become secure as the unit progresses.

Teachers may offer different degrees of support for open concept sorts. In addition to the "wide open" sort, students may be told there are two or three categories, or that there are a certain number of terms in one category and a certain number in the other category. Most of the time, however—if you have chosen the terms carefully and considered your students' background knowledge—"wide open" provides the most productive context.

Students may record one or two sorts in their Vocabulary Notebooks (see pp. 61–62). As students move along through the unit of study, they may re-sort as well as come up with new categories and new words to add. They may also create a *power map* from their concept sort (see pp. 67–69). All of these sorts also serve as good preassessments, allowing both students and teachers an opportunity to revisit during and after the unit of study to reflect on and confirm learning and understanding.

Vocab-O-Grams.   A *vocab-o-gram*, occasionally referred to as a *predict-o-gram*, is a classification activity most often based on the structure or elements of a story (Blachowicz, 1986; Blachowicz & Fisher, 2009). The activity engages students in making predictions about how particular key vocabulary words will be used by the author in developing the narrative. It may also be adapted for use with content material (see Chapter 6, p. 125). As with concept sorts, vocab-o-grams help to activate background knowledge and generate interest in and questions about the story or topic. To introduce this activity, a secondary English teacher might prepare a vocab-o-gram similar to Figure 4.3, based on Cynthia Rylant's short story "Checkouts" (1990), and then pass out copies of the activity to student groups. Once students understand how to use a vocab-o-gram, the teacher may in the future simply write the vocabulary words on an overhead and ask the students to sketch the vocab-o-gram chart in their Vocabulary Notebooks and then fill in the words.

To begin the activity, the teacher arranges the class into groups of three to five students each. She then announces that they will be reading a short story by Cynthia Rylant (students may remember reading Rylant's work in elementary school). The teacher tells them that this particular story may be quite different from those elementary school narratives. This story, "Checkouts," is from a collection of short stories titled *A Couple of Kooks and Other Stories about Love*. The teacher then passes a vocab-o-gram out to each group. She reads and discusses the directions with them and then has them turn to their groups to do the following activity:

1. Discuss what they think each word means.
2. Discuss how they think the author will use each word to develop the story. In the left-hand column, classify the words according to the story element each word may be used to develop; words may be classified into more than one category. Unfamiliar words they may have never heard or seen before are listed in the "Mystery Words" category.

FIGURE 4.3   **Vocab-O-Gram for Cynthia Rylant's "Checkouts"**

Discuss what you know about each of the words. Think about how Cynthia Rylant might be using the words to develop her story and write the words where you think they will be used to develop each story element. The words may be used more than once. If there are words that your group is not sure about, list them as Mystery Words. Use the vocabulary words to make predictions about "Checkouts," and write your predictions in the right-hand column next to the words.

intuition solitary distract lapse impulse bland shards deftly	
reverie meditation depression witty grocery cocky dishevelment	
Setting	
Characters	
Problem or Goal	
Actions	
Resolution	
What Question(s) Do You Have?	
Mystery Words	

3. Based on the words they have placed in each category, make predictions about how they believe the narrative will develop. Their predictions will be written in the right-hand column.
4. List questions that they may have about the narrative. These questions will emerge from the discussions about word meanings and how the words might be used to develop different elements of the story, as well as from their predictions. Questions become, in effect, *purposes* for reading.
5. Groups share out their classifications, predictions, and questions. Based on this discussion, the teacher decides whether any of the vocabulary words she selected need further discussion or whether any uncertainties may be resolved as students read the words in the context of the story. Often, words that a particular group listed as Mystery Words become clarified in the whole-class discussion.
6. Students read the story. Afterward, predictions and questions are revisited and perhaps revised, and vocabulary words are revisited and discussed.

Vocabulary Cards.   As shown in Figure 4.4, vocabulary cards may be used for the most important key vocabulary in a selection or unit of study—those words that represent the "big ideas." Teachers model how to make these cards so that students will subsequently be able to make their own. The basic format has the target vocabulary word on the front and the definition on the back.

As students construct their own cards, they should select the definition from the text itself, include a sentence in the text that uses the word, or both. For informational texts this is fairly straightforward; for narrative texts students may need to refer to a glossary (if the selection is in an anthology) or to a good dictionary. *Susceptible* in Figure 4.4 is from a unit based on Dickens's *Oliver Twist*. As students learn and use different types of graphic aids, they may also include these formats on cards—for example, the back of the cards may be a "4-Square" design (see p. 65).

FIGURE 4.4   Vocabulary Cards

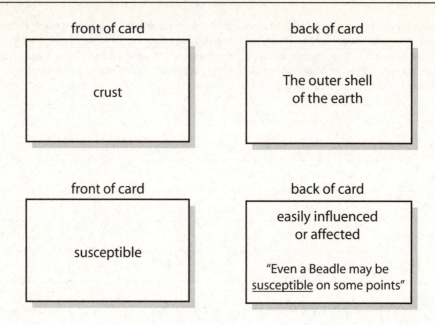

List/Group/Label. *List/group/label* activities are effective before, during, and after reading or a unit of study:

- *List.* Students are presented with key vocabulary and related terms or brainstorm all the words they can think of having to do with a particular topic.
- *Group.* Students suggest logical ways to group the words.
- *Label.* Students suggest a label for each group.

When conducted before a unit of study, this activity is very similar to the "concept map" graphic organizer discussed later (see p. 65). The main difference is that the groups are not visually arranged to suggest the relationships among them. For this reason, list/group/label may be an effective activity to use before moving to the use of the graphic aid. When used after a unit of study or a reading assignment, the only adjustment is that students brainstorm all the words they can recall from the reading selection or unit of study. Then they will group and label them. As with the preceding activities, the content of the lists and the nature of the groups and labels will evolve and change when comparing "before" and "after," and offer excellent opportunities for teachers and students to reflect on and assess their learning.

For example, after students have read and discussed a selection addressing the dangers of living in the shadow of the volcano Mt. Rainier (see Chapter 6), the teacher asks the students to brainstorm, in small groups, all the terms they can recall. The selection focused on *lahars,* which are landslides or mudflows of volcanic fragments that flow down the sides of a volcano. The students then share as a whole class. The sharing ensures that a term or terms not recalled in a particular group will be added when the whole class compares notes. This is the *list* step of the procedure; following are the terms that were recalled from the Mt. Rainier selection:

mudflow   geothermal aquifers   percolating   glacier
hydrothermal alterations   cohesive lahar   sulfuric acid clay
geothermal fluids   fumaroles   semiliquid mud   slurry

Next, the students *group* the terms and then discuss and decide on a *label* for each group:

What Lahars Are Made of and What They Look Like	*How Lahars Occur*
mudflow	geothermal aquifers
slurry	percolating
cohesive lahar	glacier
semiliquid mud	hydrothermal alterations
sulfuric acid clay	geothermal fluids
	fumaroles

Exploring Antonyms and Synonyms.   When students explore antonyms and synonyms, they attend to the finer distinctions or gradations among words. This leads to deeper understanding of concepts and the relationships among concepts. The common definition of *antonym* is "opposite in meaning," though there are different degrees of opposite. For example, *hot* and *cold* seem clearly opposite, but when students begin to explore terms that may fall between these polar opposites, they realize they may have to make subtler distinctions—and they wind up making distinctions among *synonyms* as well. Along a continuum with *hot* and *cold* at each end, for example, where would you place *warm, cool, frigid, tepid,* and *crisp?* Involve students in this type of discussion. Make the connection to writing by mentioning *word choice* and how attending to these types of distinctions helps students become more sensitive to finding and using the most appropriate and effective words in their writing.

Figure 4.5 is an example of a continuum you could use to introduce the idea of how to arrange terms between two polar opposites.

Analogies.   Analogical reasoning is a powerful means of thinking critically and of developing deeper understanding of specific words. Students also develop understanding of complex relationships and logical reasoning by examining *analogies,* as in the following sequence (Templeton, 1997):

1. To teach the form of analogies, begin with simple analogies such as *hot* is to *cold* as *strong* is to *weak.*
2. Present analogies in which one of the words is omitted and possibilities for completion are offered: *ice* is to *cold* as *fire* is to _____ (*fireplace, hot, water*). At this level and the next two levels, you can include target vocabulary words.
3. Analogies are presented without possible choices.
4. Present analogies in which the missing word or term occurs in places other than the final slot.

Vocabulary Notebooks.   *Vocabulary Notebooks* are an integral part of students' word learning, used to record word sorts, concept sorts, and other appropriate vocabulary activities, as well as to record information about new words encountered in their reading. Composition books, spiral-bound notebooks, or three-ring binders work well for Vocabulary Notebooks, which are used for recording resources like the following:

- Weekly word sorts and their explanations as well as extensions of these sorts, such as word hunts for related words and homework based on these words
- Collaborative word study activities, including concept sorts, interesting collections of words, and key vocabulary for unit or theme study
- New and interesting words students encounter in their reading

FIGURE 4.5   Continuum for Opaque/Clear Distinction

Opaque	Murky	Foggy	Translucent	Visible	Clear

When students do word or concept sorts with target words, they may write these in columns, just as they sorted them. At the bottom of their sorts and in their own words, they write what they learned about the words and their features: meanings of words, meanings of roots, affixes, and spelling features. When there are spelling rules that may be generated from the words—such as the rule about whether or not to double the final consonant when adding *-ed* and *-ing* to words such as *benefit* and *occur*—students may write these rules in their own words.

Just as students are encouraged to write down "golden lines" from their reading—examples of language that reached out and grabbed them as they were reading—they are encouraged to record new and interesting words they encounter. We encourage them to be alert to "golden words"—words that really catch their fancy. They write the sentence in which the word occurs, underline the word, and include any other information about it that may be helpful. While this is often a new word, it may also be a familiar word used in a new, engaging way. The following steps are commonly used for entering new and interesting words in the Vocabulary Notebook:

1. While reading, place a question mark above words you find difficult and cannot figure out using your structural analysis plus context strategy. Place a question mark in the margin for easy reference. If you cannot mark in a book, use a sticky note. When you are through reading, go back to your question marks or sticky notes.
2. Write the word in your notebook, followed by the sentence in which it was used, the page number, and an abbreviation for the title of the book. (Sometimes the sentence will be too long, so write enough of it to give a clue to meaning.)
3. Record related words. Think of other words that are like this word, and write them underneath the part of the word that is similar.
4. Look the word up in the dictionary, read the various definitions, and in a few words record the meaning (the one that applies to the word in the book you are reading). Look for similar words (both in form and meaning) above and below the target word, and add them to the list you started in step 3. Look at the origin of the word, and add it to your entry if it is interesting.
5. Review the words.

A realistic goal is to collect 10 words a week. These words may be brought up in class and shared. Following is an example of the entry for the word *orthography*:

1. Record the word and sentence: *orthography*—"English orthography is not crazy, and it carries the history of the word with it." p. 22, *Sounds of Language*
2. Look at word parts and think about their meaning: *ortho graph* ("may have something to do with writing")
3. Record possible related words: *orthodontist, orthodox, graphics*
4. Study the word in the dictionary, and record interesting information: "A method of representing the sounds of a language by letters; spelling." Origin: *ortho,* "correct" + *graph,* "something written"

Note. The third definition fits most nearly the meaning of *orthography* as it was used in the sentence. The first two meanings are "1. the art or study of standard spelling; 2. the aspect of language study concerned with letters and spelling" (*The American Heritage College Dictionary,* 2000, p. 965).

Students should collect examples of the word and its use outside of the classroom—where they have seen it and heard it—and enter their findings in their Vocabulary Notebooks.

Graphic Organizers.   *Graphic organizers* may be a very effective means of revealing the architecture of students' minds to them, as was noted in Chapter 2. The several examples of graphic organizers presented here effectively support your explorations of both core academic and content-specific academic vocabulary. More examples and applications will be provided in Chapters 5 and 6.

FIGURE 4.6 Venn Diagram

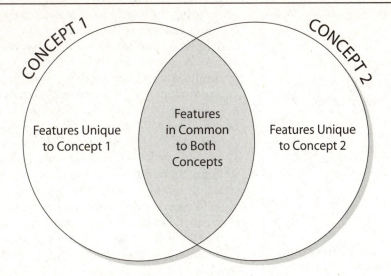

Venn Diagram and an Adaptation.   You are probably familiar with the classic *Venn diagram,* perhaps the most frequently used graphic organizer in education. As Figure 4.6 shows, it concretely presents comparisons and contrasts between concepts.

In working with his middle grade reading classes, David Smith found that a table adaptation of a Venn diagram provided more flexibility in comparing and contrasting. Figure 4.7 presents an example from his class.

Concept of Definition.   A graphic organizer that works well for teaching how dictionary definitions are constructed (Stahl & Nagy, 2006), a *concept of definition* is useful for generating discussion and deeper understanding of new and important vocabulary (see Figure 4.8).

As discussed at the beginning of this chapter, unless students already have some understanding of the general domain into which a word fits—some background knowledge—then dictionary definitions may not be of much help. To help them learn how to read and think about dictionary definitions, begin with a word with which students are fairly familiar. Explain to them that most definitions have two main parts. The first tells you the category to which the word or concept belongs, and the second

FIGURE 4.7 Comparison and Contrast: Asian versus African Elephants

African Elephant	Feature Being Contrasted	Asian Elephant
4–7 tons	Weight	3–5 tons
9–13 feet	Height to shoulder	6–11 feet
Two "fingers" on tip	Trunks	One "finger" on tip
Larger	Ears	Smaller
Features in Common		
In general, elephants are the largest land mammal with the biggest brains.		
Elephants have extremely dexterous trunks made up of over 100,000 muscles.		
Elephants have acute hearing, superior to humans.		

FIGURE 4.8   Concept of Definition

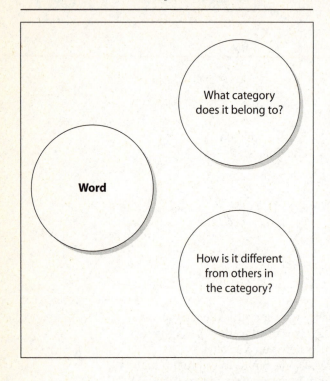

part describes how the word or concept is different from other words or concepts in the same category. Then, using the word *telephone* as an example, map it with a concept of definition format. A *telephone* is defined as "an instrument that converts voice and other sound signals into a form that can be transmitted to remote locations and that receives and reconverts waves into sound signals" (*American Heritage Dictionary of the English Language*). It belongs to the category *instrument*. How does the definition differentiate it from other instruments? The teacher gets the students to discuss this, and in so doing, phrase the dictionary definition in more straightforward or accessible language: Converting and reconverting voice signals has to do with changing them in some way, and a remote location is one that is far away. This more straightforward description is entered in the concept of definition (see Figure 4.9a).

Such teacher-led discussions should be followed by students working collaboratively with familiar words to look up, discuss, and try to understand the category/differentiation distinction. For example, in the context of an earth science unit, *tectonic* is discussed by the class and then the dictionary definition is reworded from "a branch of geology concerned with the structure of the crust of a planet (as earth) or moon and especially with the formation of folds and faults in it" to be recast as in Figure 4.9b.

FIGURE 4.9   Concept of Definition: Telephone and Tectonic

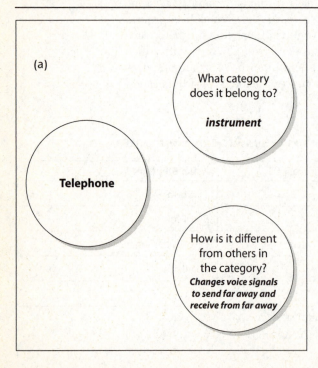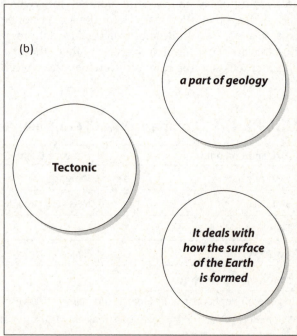

FIGURE 4.10   **Concept of Definition: Schwartz and Raphael**

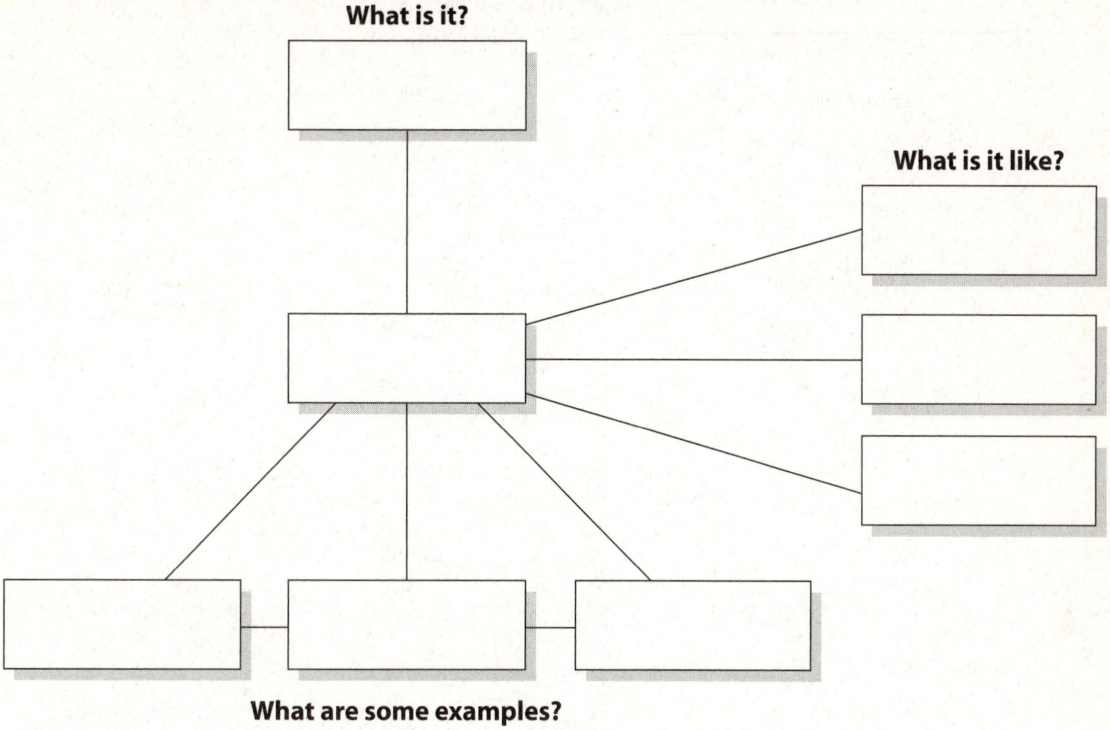

What is it?

What is it like?

What are some examples?

Source: Adapted from Schwartz, R. E., and Raphael, T. E. (1985). Concept of definition: A key to improving students' vocabulary. *Reading Teacher, 39,* 198–205.

Schwartz and Raphael (1985) offer a slightly different graphic organizer for concept of definition that allows for a more explicit and elaborated presentation of examples and characteristics (Figure 4.10).

Concept or Word Map.   A *concept map* (or *word map*) is similar in format to the concept of a definition. Figure 4.11 presents a concept map for the term *colony* that was constructed with a class of sixth graders.

4-Square Concept Map.   Also referred to as the "Frayer Model" (Frayer, Frederick, and Klausmeier, 1969), a *4-square concept map* may be used in different ways. Sometimes you will read a definition of a word, discuss it, perhaps give examples, and then have students fill in the four blocks themselves. Other times you will not provide a definition but let the students generate their own given the examples and experiences you have provided. Figure 4.12 is an example generated by a group of students in a sophomore English class for *abstract.* On completion, these should be kept in the students' Vocabulary Notebooks.

Semantic Map.   A *semantic map* provides support throughout a unit of study. Focusing on the main word or concept, the steps in collaboratively constructing a semantic map with students are as follows:

• Students brainstorm words/concepts that come to mind when they think of the main concept—for example, volcanoes.

FIGURE 4.11   Concept Map: Colony

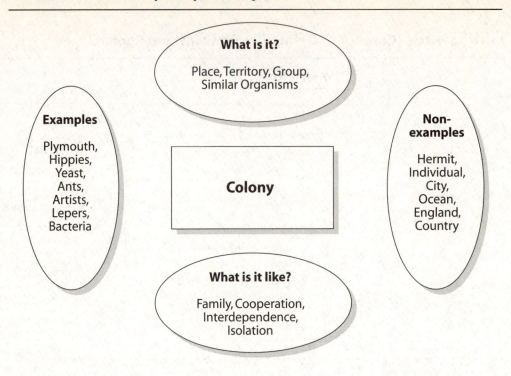

FIGURE 4.12   4-Square Concept Map: Abstract

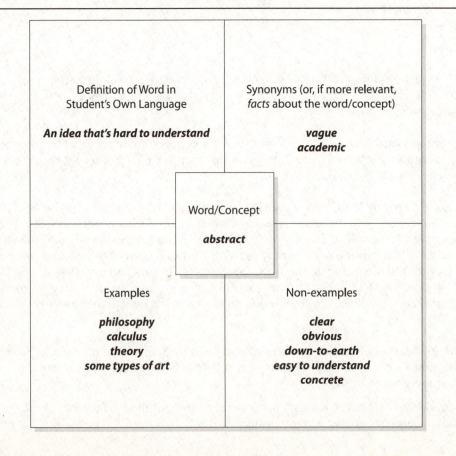

- The teacher adds words to the brainstormed list that are important related terms in the unit.
- The teacher guides the students in discussing how to map and categorize the terms on the list; those added by the teacher are indicated in parentheses.
- As students read and discuss the content of the unit over several days, they may change or add categories to the map.

Figure 4.13 illustrates a semantic map for "Volcanoes" in a unit from an earth science class.

Power Maps.   Some students initially have difficulty understanding the implied hierarchical relationships among words/concepts in concept sorts and in graphic organizers. Based on the technique of "power thinking" (Santa, Havens, & Valdes, 2004), *power maps* offer additional support for students who may not as readily see these hierarchical relationships among the big ideas, subtopics, and details or examples (see Flanigan, Hayes, et al., in press, for a fuller discussion with several examples of power thinking and power mapping). To construct a power map, different levels of importance are assigned to the words/concepts in a unit. The Power 1 level is vocabulary related to the "main" or "big idea" level; the Power 2 level is vocabulary related to subtopics; the Power 3 level is vocabulary that represents supporting details or examples. The terms Power 1, Power 2, and Power 3 are used to help students make more explicit the nature and the level of the relationships among main ideas or topics, supporting details or defining features, and examples. The strategy is introduced with topics the students know well, such as movies or sports. Shapes or colors should consistently be used to differentiate Power 1, 2, and 3 vocabulary; for example, circles are

FIGURE 4.13   Semantic Map

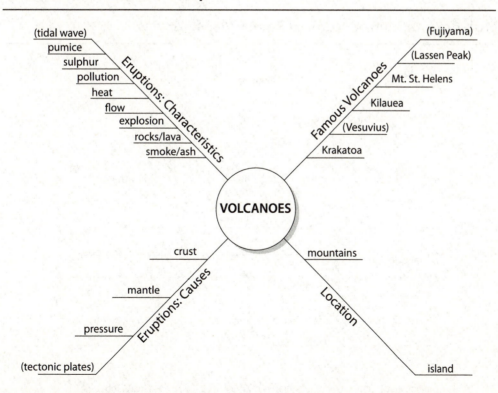

Power 1, triangles Power 2, and rectangles or straight lines are Power 3. Figure 4.14 shows a "Movie" power map that Kevin Flanigan used to introduce and walk through this strategy with his seventh- and eighth-graders; students inevitably join in with him and that, of course, is excellent.

Once you have selected the key vocabulary terms for a unit of study, determine the power level of each term or concept. Biology teachers, for example, often begin study of biological classification—kingdom, phylum, class, order, family, genus, species—with three of the six kingdoms that are more obvious to students and about which they have more background knowledge. Power 1 is kingdom; Power 2 is examples of specific kingdoms; Power 3 is examples of each specific kingdom. (Figure 4.15 illustrates this simple map.) Then write these vocabulary terms on sorting cards.

1. In pairs or groups, ask the students to sort the terms into categories based on common features. In this case, the students are not aware of the power levels of the vocabulary words; they must figure them out during the sort. Encourage students to use the Power 1, 2, and 3 language as they sort. We have found this simple addition of asking the student to use "power language" goes a long way in helping make explicit the structure of the information and in clarifying their own thinking. It also gives students a common language to communicate with peers and the teacher.

2. For additional support, you might tell the students that there is one Power 1 and three Power 2s, but not tell them what they are. For more support, you might tell your students what the Power 1s and 2s are (for example, "*Kingdom* is your Power 1, and *Fungi, Plantae,* and *Animalia* are your Power 2s"), but not the Power 3s. Or you might give them the Power 1s and 3s, but not the Power 2s. In this case, they will need to label each Power 2, or each category, themselves. This variation is similar to the list/group/label strategy described on pages 60–61.

FIGURE 4.14   Introduction to Power Maps: Movies

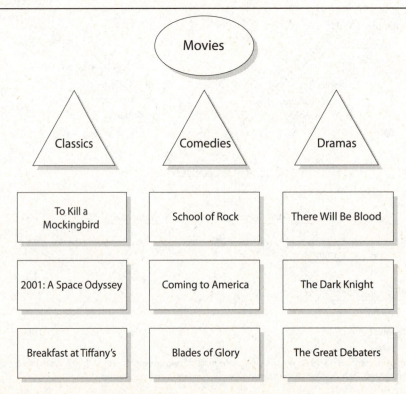

FIGURE 4.15 **Completed Biology Power Map**

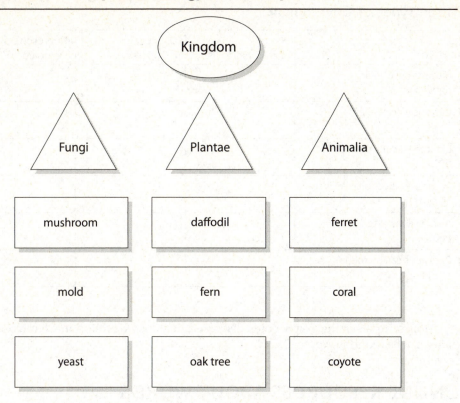

3. Circulate around the room during the support session to guide student discussion.
4. If appropriate to your content, be prepared if students come up with a different placement of terms than you have planned and are able to justify it—such results reveal the need for clarification and at other times demonstrate the essence of critical thinking.
5. Have groups share with the whole class at the end of the sort.

Have students record their power maps in their Vocabulary Notebooks. Again, as with word sorts and concept sorts, revisiting and rearranging these sorts and maps during a unit of study helps students reflect on and confirm their understanding.

Semantic Feature Analysis. A *semantic feature analysis* explicitly highlights similarities and differences among target words/concepts and helps students identify what they know, what they don't know, and what they may be a bit fuzzy about or only have a partial understanding of. You may first construct one to present to your class, but as your students understand how this type of graphic organizer works they may become involved in constructing them and sharing. Figure 4.16 presents a semantic feature analysis that supports comparison and contrast of three types of government (Flanigan & Greenwood, 2007). First, the teacher writes the target words—the three types of government—across the top and the specific features down the left-hand side. Next, the teacher displays the feature analysis grid on a transparency or interactive whiteboard and discusses the first term with the class; writing either *yes* or a plus sign indicates the feature is a characteristic of the government, writing either *no* or a minus sign indicates a feature is not a characteristic, and a question mark indicates uncertainty—further investigation is necessary. As the students move through a unit, additional characteristics and words/terms may be added to the grid.

FIGURE 4.16   **Semantic Feature Analysis: Comparing and Contrasting Three Types of Government**

	Dictatorship	Direct Democracy	Representative Democracy
Citizens have voting rights			
Citizens elect leaders			
Limit to leaders' term of office			
Representatives are elected by citizens			
All decisions voted on by people			
Decisions can be made quickly			

More samples of the graphic aids discussed here may be found in Chapter 6. Templates can be found in Appendix H.

ONLINE RESOURCES ABOUT WORDS

In addition to the resource books for word study that are offered throughout this text, there are a number of online resources that are invaluable. At the time of this writing, there are literally hundreds of sites available, and most are interesting and may be helpful. Depending on your purposes—basic dictionary information, word histories, translations of specific words, or finding cognates in other languages for English words (see Chapter 7), you should find the sites listed below very helpful. As is the case in general where the Internet is concerned, more sites seem to appear almost daily. Those we have included here are sites we have found to be very helpful in our teaching and in our research and which have enjoyed a fairly long life online:

> *www.onelook.com* A comprehensive dictionary website. Most of the major, well-respected dictionaries are available; the link to the *American Heritage Dictionary* also includes an additional link to a dictionary of Indo-European Roots, which greatly simplifies etymological searches for you and your students. The onelook.com site also features excellent search capabilities that allow you to search for words that contain specific roots and affixes, spelling patterns, words as they occur in specific phrases (very helpful for English learners—see Chapter 7), and words that relate to a particular concept.
>
> *www.americancorpus.org* The Corpus of American English, created by Michael Davies, is an invaluable online resource for locating related words in English. It requires that you register, but registration is free. It may be used to search for the occurrence of words in different contexts—for example, spoken language, magazines, fiction, and academic texts.
>
> *www.etymonline.com* Very useful for exploring word histories, this site includes much of the etymological information you would find in the Oxford English Dictionary.

http://dictionary.reference.com/languages This site accesses the *Kernerman English Multilingual Dictionary* which provides, for any word in English, words in a number of other languages that have the same or similar meaning. It is an excellent resource for finding cognates (see Chapter 7).

www.wordsmith.org You may subscribe for free and receive a new word in your inbox every day. Words follow a theme each week, and the categories of words discussed in this book—for example *toponyms, eponyms, sesquipedalian* words, and more—will be represented.

www.verbivore.com/rllink.htm An especially good site for wordplay and word consciousness with innumerable links to excellent and informative language and word sites.

GAMES

The primary importance of word games is to reinforce word-specific and generative vocabulary learning as well as word consciousness more generally. Games are still a valuable way to review words not only for a test, but also over time. Appendix E provides a number of games that accomplish these objectives. Students may also create many games themselves based on popular favorites such as Concentration, Rummy, War, Slap Jack, Uno, and Trivial Pursuit.

LOOKING AHEAD

This chapter has suggested basic strategies and activities for developing students' generative and word-specific knowledge. The next two chapters provide examples of applying these routines in specific instructional domains. Chapter 5 addresses the teaching of core academic vocabulary, which is most often the responsibility of English/language arts teachers. Chapter 6 addresses the teaching of content-specific academic vocabulary, and teachers of different content areas will find examples of instruction for their specific domains. Both chapters offer ideas for all teachers, however, and we hope the examination of strategies and activities across grades and content areas will help lead toward more unified efforts at the middle and secondary grades to teach vocabulary more effectively and collaboratively.

APPENDIX   Sequence of Instruction for Core Affixes and Roots: Intermediate, Middle, and Secondary Levels

The following prefixes and suffixes have usually been introduced in the primary grades, but they should be addressed in the intermediate and middle grades as they combine with the words that are appropriate at these levels:

Prefixes[1]			Suffixes		
un-	not, opposite	*un*lock	*-y*	like	lac*y*
in-	not, without	*in*correct	*-ly*		glad*ly*
im-		*im*possible	*-er*	comparative	cold*er*
il-		*il*legible	*-est*	superlative	cold*est*
ir-		*ir*responsible	*-less*	without	penni*less*
re-	again, back	*re*make	*-ness*	condition	happi*ness*
dis-	opposite, not, apart	*dis*agree	*-ful*	full of, like	hope*ful*
		*dis*like	*-er*	people who	teach*er*
		*dis*connect	*-or*	do things	act*or*
non-	not	*non*fiction	*-ist*		pian*ist*
mis-	badly, wrongly	*mis*fortune			
		*mis*fire			
pre-	before	*pre*view			
		*pre*season			
uni-	one	*uni*cycle			
bi-	two	*bi*cycle			
tri-	three	*tri*cycle			

The following prefixes and suffixes have usually been introduced in the intermediate grades, but they should be addressed in the middle grades and beyond as they combine with the words that are appropriate at these levels:

Prefixes			Suffixes		
com-	together, with	*com*press	*-al*	like, characterized by	nation*al*
sub-	under	*sub*marine			natur*al*
		*sub*urban	*-ous*	possessing, full of	courage*ous*
de-	remove, opposite	*de*fuse	*-ment*	result, action, or	develop*ment*
		*de*tract		condition	excite*ment*
post-	after	*post*game	*-ion*[2]	action, process of, or	inspec*tion*
		*post*season		result	
inter-	between	*inter*continental	*-ic*	of, relating to, or	angel*ic*
		*inter*rupt		characterized by	formula*ic*
		*inter*act	*-able*	capable of, likely to	profit*able*
		*inter*vene	*-ible*		flamm*able*
intra-	within	*intra*state			cred*ible*
		*intra*mural	*-ant*	performing or causing	observ*ant*
trans-	across	*trans*port	*-ent*	an action	confid*ent*
		*trans*continental	*-ance*	action or process	observ*ance*
anti-	against	*anti*freeze	*-ence*		confid*ence*
		*anti*prejudice	*-ity*	quality, condition	acid*ity*
					moral*ity*
			-an	relating to, specializing	Chicago*an*
			-ian	in, belonging to	musici*an*
					Canad*ian*
					dietici*an*

APPENDIX   Continued

As students read within and across different genres and content areas, they encounter an increasingly larger number of bases and roots that combine with the following prefixes and suffixes:

Prefixes

super-	over; greater	*super*vise
		*super*natural
counter-	opposing	*counter*act
		*counter*factual
contra-		*contra*dict
		*contra*indicate
ex-	out	*ex*it
		*ex*communicate
		*ex*cise
e-		*e*normous
		*e*rupt
		*e*mit
ex-	former	*ex*-president
fore-	before	*fore*word
		*fore*knowledge
pro-	in front of, forward; in favor of	*pro*active
		*pro*spect
		pro-American
		pro-development
in-	in, into	*in*dent
im-		*im*plode
il-		*il*luminate
ir-		*ir*radiate
en-	cause to be, in, on	*en*courage
		*en*able
		*en*circle

Suffixes

-logy	science of, scientist	geo*logy*
-logist		geo*logist*
-phobia	abnormal fear	claustro*phobia*
-phobic		aqua*phobic*
-ism	condition, belief	aut*ism*
		capital*ism*
-ist	one who does, believes, specializes	pian*ist*
		capital*ist*
		podiatr*ist*
-crat	rule	auto*crat*
-cracy		demo*cracy*

Absorbed Prefixes

The process of "absorbing" prefixes is examined explicitly:

in-	not, in/into	i*n* + *l*iterate = i*ll*iterate
		i*n* + *p*ort = i*m*port
		i*n* + *r*ational = i*rr*ational
		i*n* + *m*ediate = i*mm*ediate

The following roots are usually introduced in the upper elementary grades, but they should be addressed in the middle grades and beyond as they combine with the words that are appropriate at these levels.

Greek Roots

tele	far, distant	*tele*vision
		*tele*graph
		*tele*gram
		*tele*scope
		*tele*photo
therm	heat	*therm*ometer
		*therm*ostat
		*therm*al
		exo*therm*ic

Latin Roots

aud	hear	*aud*ible	*aud*itorium
		*aud*ience	*aud*io
		*aud*itory	*aud*ition
spec	look	*spec*tator	pro*spect*
spic		in*spect*	su*spect*
		*spec*tacle	suspi*c*ious

continued

APPENDIX   Continued

Greek Roots (continued)

photo	light	photograph	
		telephoto	
gram	thing written	diagram	
		monogram	
		telegram	
		grammar	
		program	
graph	writing	telegraph	
		autograph	
		biography	
		photography	
		telegraph	
		graphic	
		calligraphy	
		polygraph	
		digraph	
micro	small	microscope	
		micrometer	
		microfilm	
		microwave	
scop	target, view, see	microscope	
		microscopic	
		telescope	
		telescopic	
		periscope	
		kaleidoscope	
phon	sound	telephone	
		phonics	
		symphonic	
		euphony	
		homophone	
bio	life	biology	
		biography	
		biome	
		biopsy	
auto	self	autograph	
		autobiography	

Latin Roots (continued)

port	carry	import	portable
		export	portfolio
		transport	report
rupt	break[3]	bankrupt	rupture
		eruption	abrupt
		disrupt	corrupt
		interrupt	
fract	break[3]	fracture	
		fraction	
		refract	
tract	drag, pull	distract	contract
		tractor	retract
		tractable	attract
		extract	traction
		detract	protract
		trace	
mot	move	motion	promotion
		motivate	emotion
scrib	write	inscribe	inscription
script		transcript	transcription
		prescribe	prescription
		manuscript	
		transcribe	
		describe	
dict	say	dictate	indict
		diction	dictator
		predict	benediction
		edict	jurisdiction
		contradict	
vis	see	vision	vista
vid		invisible	visit
		television	supervise
		revise	video
		advise	provide
struct	build	construct	instruct
		structure	destruction
gress	go	progress	digression
		regress	aggressive

If not taught earlier, the following affixes and roots should be addressed in the middle and secondary grades:

Middle and High School Latin Affixes and Roots

pos	put, place	compose	cred	believe	credo
pon		expose			credible
		oppose			incredible
		position			credence
		component			incredulous
		exponent			creditable
		opponent			

APPENDIX   Continued

Middle and High School Latin Affixes and Roots *(continued)*

duc	lead	pro*duc*e	*ced*	go	pro*ceed*
duct		re*duc*e	*ceed*		pro*cess*
		con*duct*	*cess*		ex*ceed*
		e*duc*ate			ex*cess*
		se*duc*e			inter*cede*
		pro*duct*			con*cede*
		re*duc*tion	*ven*	to come	inter*ven*e
vers	turn	re*vert*	*vent*		circum*vent*
vert		di*vert*			cove*nan*t
		intro*vert*			*ven*ue
		ad*vers*e	*clud*	close	ex*clud*e
		*vers*atile	*clus*		con*clud*e
		contro*vers*y			in*clud*e
ject	throw	pro*ject*			ex*clus*ion
		re*ject*			con*clus*ion
		in*ject*			in*clus*ion
		e*ject*	*jud*	judge	pre*jud*ice
		inter*ject*			*jud*icious
		ob*ject*			ad*jud*icate
leg	law	*leg*al	*fac*	make	*fac*tory
		*leg*islate			*fac*simile
		*leg*itimate			*fac*tor
		privi*lege*			satis*fac*tion
	read	*leg*ible			*fac*ilitate
fer	bear, carry	trans*fer*	*fec*	make	in*fec*t
		in*fer*			ef*fec*t
		acqui*fer*			af*fec*t
		de*fer*	*fic*	make	*fic*tion
		af*fer*ent			ef*fic*ient
		ef*fer*ent			bene*fic*ial
bene	good, well	*bene*fit			de*fic*ient
		*bene*ficial	*fy*	make	beauti*fy*
		*bene*factor			falsi*fy*
		*bene*volent			satis*fy*
corp	body	*corp*oration			personi*fy*
		in*corp*orate			objecti*fy*
		*corp*ulent			classi*fy*
		*corp*se	*man*	hand	*man*ual
		*corp*oreal			*man*age
sta	stand	*sta*ble			*man*ufacture
stat		*stat*ic			e*man*cipate
stit		*stat*istics			*man*acle
		con*sta*nt			*man*e
		con*stit*ution	*mis*	send	*mis*sion
		di*sta*nt	*mit*		*mis*sile
					dis*mis*s
					pro*mis*e
					trans*mit*
					e*mit*
					re*mit*

continued

APPENDIX Continued

Middle and High School Latin Affixes and Roots *(continued)*

Prefixes			Absorbed Prefixes		
mal-	bad	*mal*function	*ad-*	to, toward	*ad* + count = a*c*count
		*mal*adjusted			*ad* + firm = a*f*firm
		*mal*content			*ad* + gress = a*g*gress(ion)
		*mal*efactor			*ad* + locate = a*l*locate
		*mal*aria			*ad* + null = a*n*null
a-	without, not	*a*part			*ad* + point = a*p*point
		*a*moral			*ad* + rest = a*r*rest
an-		*an*emia			*ad* + sign = a*s*sign
		*an*archy			*ad* + tend = a*t*tend
retro-	backward, past	*retro*spect	*syn-*	together,	*syn* + bol = sy*m*bol
		*retro*active	*syl-*	with	*syn* + drome = syndrome
		*retro*rocket	*sym-*		*syn* + agogue = sy*n*agogue
		*retro*gressive			*syn* + chronic = synchronic
per-	through,	*per*vasive			*syn* + logistic = sy*l*logistic
	thoroughly	*per*ennial			*syn* + metrical = sy*m*metrical
Additional Prefixes					*syn* + phonic = sy*m*phonic
epi-	upon, on,	*epi*center	*com-*	together,	*com* + active = *co*active
	over, near,	*epi*demic	*con-*	with	*com* + note = *con*note
	at, before,	*epi*dermis	*co-*		*com* + duct = *con*duct
	after	*epi*phenomenon	*cor-*		*com* + clude = *con*clude
dia-	through	*dia*gnose			*com* + gress = *con*gress
	across	*dia*gram			*com* + locate = *col*locate
		*dia*rrhea			*com* + quest = *con*quest
		*dia*meter			*com* + rupt = *cor*rupt
		*dia*chronic			*com* + spire = *con*spire
		*dia*spora			*com* + tract = *con*tract
ana-	up	*ana*tomy			*com* + vene = *con*vene
		*ana*lyze (loosen *up*)			*com* + operate = *co*operate
	back/backward	*ana*chronism			*com* + educate = *co*educate
		*ana*phora			*com* + motion = *com*motion
		*ana*thema			*com* + passion = *com*passion
	again	*Ana*baptist (baptize *again*)			*com* + incidence = *co*incidence
ab-	off,	*ab*sent			
	away	*ab*duct			
		*ab*stract			
		*ab*normal			
		*ab*hor *ab*dicate			
meta-	change,	*meta*morphosis			
	beyond	*meta*phor			
		*meta*cognitive			

[1]Most prefixes have more than one meaning. In this scope and sequence, notice that the meanings of prefixes are not all taught at the same time. Students need time to learn, explore, and understand how a particular meaning for the prefix consistently performs. For example, the most common meaning of *in-* is "not"; it is important that students explore, understand, and appreciate how the meaning of "not" is consistently represented across a wide range of words before later introducing the next most common meaning of *in-*: "in, into." (From a developmental perspective, it is similar to trying to teach a first- or second-grader all of the spellings of long *a* at once and expecting the student to be confident about learning all of them at the same time and being able to use the correct spelling in writing.)

[2]*-ation, -ition, -sion,* and *-tion* are all variations of *-ion.* Which spelling is used depends on the base or root to which the suffix is attached.

[3]Occasionally, more than one root from Latin with a similar meaning has come down to us, as is the case with *rupt* and *fract.* More often, however, it is the case that a root from Latin and a root from Greek have come to us with the same meaning; Appendix C presents a comprehensive table of Greek and Latin roots paired according to their meanings.

5 CHAPTER

Vocabulary for Narrative Texts

> There is a life cycle to cool, a kind of evolution: From poor to edgy and arty, to funky to established.

Anita Romero, who teaches junior and senior English classes, writes this sentence, excerpted from a newspaper article (Booth, 2007), on the board. She asks her students why they think *cool* begins as "poor." If necessary, she shares with them how many *cool* phenomena began in poor, often marginalized, communities. "Take music," she suggests, "whether it's hip-hop, salsa, the Beatles in Liverpool, jazz—or take art, whether it's van Gogh or Picasso—so many trends came from outside the economic and social mainstream." She continues, "How about styles in physical appearance—clothing, hairstyles, makeup?"

A lot of examples are out on the conversational table, and Anita's students begin to respond. She continues: "What about the 'edgy and arty' part? What does that mean?" Anita and her students continue the discussion, wrapping up with talking about how *cool* ends up "established"—and suggesting examples. Along the way, a number of the students decide that many "Gangsta" and "Goth" styles, for example, are "established"—and they earnestly debate whether *cool,* once it becomes established, is even "cool" anymore. They find themselves discussing popular culture—once *cool* becomes popular and moves into popular culture, is it still cool—or something else? Can popular culture even be said to be *cool?* Does *cool* always begin "poor"? Does it always move from "edgy" to "arty" or can it skip directly to "established"?

After the discussion has taken off, occasionally with some heat, Anita has to exercise her "benevolent dictator" rights—as she has jokingly described her role to the students—and bring matters, at least for this period, to a close. She wraps up by sharing with them that the original sense of *cool* as they have been discussing it first appeared in *Beowulf,* meaning "not heated by passion or emotion," "undisturbed," and "calm" (*Oxford English Dictionary Online,* 2009). Hundreds of years later, in 1440, Chaucer also used it in this sense in his *Canterbury Tales.* "And then," Anita concludes, "amazingly, there is no record of *cool* being used in this way again until the African American writer Zora Neale Hurston used it in the early 1930s. And, of course, we've been using it ever since!"

By design, Anita is able to address several objectives in this discussion: With respect to vocabulary development, she is developing *word consciousness* through facilitating students' reflection on language, and doing so in an engaging and motivating way. She is setting the stage for talking explicitly about the *etymology* of words—how their meanings evolve over decades and centuries (one of her state's vocabulary standards)—and doing so with a topic that is immediately relevant to her students. With respect to the broader literature curriculum, Anita is able to tie the immediacy of the topic back to two classics in the canon of the high school English curriculum, *Beowulf* and Chaucer's *Canterbury Tales.*

Developing word consciousness helps students become aware of words in ways that go beyond a specific set of particular words. Like developing an appreciation for art or music, developing an appreciation for word choice and nuances of meaning provides the foundation for better communication. We all want our students to understand what they hear and read, and we also want them to be able to use words effectively when they talk and write. Because words are the building blocks of communication, receptive vocabulary and productive vocabulary are as important in reading and writing as they are in listening and speaking. While teaching *core academic vocabulary* is the charge of the English teacher, this instruction is often characterized as teaching a new word for a familiar concept. This is true, but a subtler and quite important type of learning still occurs: When a new word becomes associated with it, the familiar concept does not remain unchanged. The new word engages the student in reexamining the existing concept, and the result of this reexamination is a subtly altered, richer underlying concept, reconnected to some other concepts in refreshed and new ways.

Language in general, and new words in particular, nourish conceptual growth. In addition to core academic vocabulary instruction, the English language arts must accommodate *content-specific* academic vocabulary. The words and phrases Gary Paulsen juxtaposes in *Hatchet* to highlight the conflict and advance the story line are core vocabulary because they are based in universal human experiences of hope and despair: *new hope, hissing madness,* and the like. But to describe the author's point of view as *limited omniscient* brings us into the territory of content-specific academic vocabulary in English, which often involves introducing a new label for a new concept—specifically, that authors write stories from different points of view, depending on their purpose.

Specialized academic words like *alliteration, assonance, consonance,* or *rhyme* might be specifically tied to a unit on the use of sound to achieve meaning in poetry, but simple word choices in literature such as "weep and wail," or "roiling and boiling," also contribute to the depth and richness of our understanding (Yolen, 1988). Unlike other content areas, it is particularly difficult for the English/language arts teacher to separate these two kinds of vocabulary. While it is usually the responsibility of the English teacher to teach the core academic vocabulary, which we have defined as high utility words that occur across all content areas, the English language arts have their own content-specific academic vocabulary, such as *conflict, protagonist, antagonist,* and the like. In teaching these literary terms, teachers unavoidably use words that occur across all content areas. In thinking about how to teach vocabulary in the English language arts, it is helpful to remember that word knowledge is closely aligned to world knowledge, and that world knowledge includes one's personal experience in the world. This is an important point in considering the English language arts, a discipline that has its own content related to universal themes of human experience and its own academic vocabulary related to literary terminology. This chapter concerns both types of vocabulary instruction in the English language arts.

In the sections that follow, the activities and strategies presented in Chapter 4 are illustrated through some examples that afford English/language arts teachers and their students many ways in which new words can be categorized or sorted, organized, and discussed. Since most English teachers are required to teach "the canon," we draw on these classics to contextualize vocabulary instruction.

CORE ACADEMIC VOCABULARY IN THE ENGLISH LANGUAGE ARTS

Teaching New Words

Denotative/Connotative Meanings: "The Naming of Parts."   As discussed in Chapter 2, words have two types of meaning: a *denotative,* or literal meaning, and a *connotative,* or implied meaning, that has to do with past history and associations linking that word

to certain situations that are loaded with feelings and emotions. For example, while the denotative meaning of the word *weak* is "lacking in physical strength," its implied meaning may connote a lack of backbone, character, or willpower, making the word *weak* an apt choice to refer to those of us who easily yield to the temptation of chocolate. Dictionaries typically present the literal, denotative meaning of a word first, followed by its connotative meanings when used in certain ways (Templeton, 1997).

Writers take advantage of the fact that words have more than one meaning and deliberately choose words to mean two things at once. This is particularly true of poets who seek to use only the most meaningful words in the sparse economy of a poem. The distinction between denotative and connotative word meanings allows them to create *contrast.* Consider, for example, "Naming of Parts," a poem by Henry Reed, a World War II British poet who wrote about the "Lessons of War." In the poem, Reed is being taught how to handle firearms, but his mind wanders elsewhere: He thinks about life, spring, and renewal, concepts that wartime now prohibits and that he himself, the soldier-poet, is being taught how to annihilate. Students can easily see the contrast in his word choice by categorizing his word choices into his contrasting themes:

Weapon Parts	*Life/Spring*
bolt	Japonica (a flowering plant)
sling swivel	gardens
piling swivel	branches
safety-catch	blossoms
breech	bees
upper sling swivel	flowers
lower sling swivel	spring
spring	almond blossoms
cocking piece	

In discussing these contrasting word choices, the conversation will inevitably lead to the climactic line "easing the spring," which opens the last stanza of "Naming of Parts." Literally, the denotative meaning of this line refers to opening the breech, the cocking of the weapon. In association with Reed's other word choices, however, "easing the spring" has a very different implied meaning. The same is true for the phrase "point of balance," which refers literally to balancing the spring on the weapon and connotatively to the fragile balance between life and death.

Characterization: *Romeo and Juliet*.   Traditionally taught in ninth grade, *Romeo and Juliet* potentially resonates with students because the main characters are experiencing what most ninth-graders are convinced they are themselves experiencing, or have already experienced: overwhelming, uncompromising, and unarguably eternal love for another. Sandra Whitaker (2008) describes her approach to the play, which includes several concept sorts related to character allegiances and character development over the course of her unit. The words/concepts to be sorted are the characters' names: Romeo, Juliet, Friar Laurence, Mercutio, Montague, Capulet, Benvolio, Tybalt, Friar John, Balthasar, Abraham, Lady Montague, Lady Capulet, Nurse to Juliet, Paris, Prince Escalus, the Apothecary, the Chorus, Sampson, and Gregory.

The first sort in which Sandra engages her students uses the categories *Capulet, Montague,* and *Other.* By having students sort the characters into the houses they are associated with, Sandra is ensuring that the students "become familiar with the characters' outward allegiances" (p. 103). Later, she has the students sort the characters by their personalities: *Peacekeepers, Troublemakers,* and *Neither.* As the unit moves along, students realize that different characters may be recategorized: for example, a *peacekeeper*— Friar Laurence—may later be reconceptualized as a *troublemaker.* Another sort Sandra uses includes the categories *For the Marriage, Against the Marriage,* and *Neutral.* Again, characters initially categorized *against the marriage* may later emerge as being *for the marriage*. Sandra observes that these different concept sorts "afford kids opportunities to deepen their understanding of the nuances, connotations, and multiple meanings of words" (p. 105).

Conflict: *Grapes of Wrath.*   In her English class, Kara Moloney begins her unit on John Steinbeck's *The Grapes of Wrath* by helping her students develop a sense of the world of the 1930s, the drought and economics of the time conspiring to uproot a proud people and send them to a place they did not know and which was no better—and probably worse—than the place they left. All of the universal themes of human love and conflict are here, as well as similarities to present-day situations that share to varying degrees aspects of the world of the 1930s. In addition, Kara wants to develop further her students' understanding of *internal* versus *external* conflict. These two types of conflict are content area academic concepts that she has already introduced and explored in a short story. As part of her introductory activities before getting into the book, Kara plans a vocab-o-gram (Figure 5.1).

To establish the tone for the unit, Kara begins with a read-aloud from the first chapter of *The Grapes of Wrath.* She then partitions the class into groups of four or five, assigned the following tasks:

1. Discuss the meaning of the words and terms and decide how Steinbeck might have used them to develop different types of external conflict or to develop internal conflict. Then write the words next to the appropriate type of conflict.
2. Make predictions, based on the words they have placed in each category, about how they believe the narrative will develop.
3. List questions that they may have about the narrative. These questions will emerge from discussions about word meanings and their role in developing different types of conflict, as well as from the predictions they generated.

Students may refer to their initial vocab-o-grams throughout the unit, using them as aids for reflection and revision of their developing perspectives and impressions. The vocab-o-grams may also serve as effective springboards for writing activities exploring the elements of narrative (for example, *characterization, rising/falling action, resolution*), summarization (Allen, 2007), and the various writing traits.

The objective of the vocab-o-gram activity is not to be "correct" right from the start, but to apply the developing understanding of the content area academic vocabulary terms *internal conflict* and *external conflict* while learning and elaborating the concepts underlying important core academic vocabulary. Most of the words Kara has selected for the vocab-o-gram fall into this latter category; a handful, such as *Hoovervilles, dust bowl, tenant farmer,* and *pellagra* are technically content area academic vocabulary in other subjects. Kara has included them, however, because they represent concepts and understandings that are important in grasping the overall setting and background of the novel. In selecting the core academic words, Kara has applied the criteria listed in Chapter 4 (p. 48). She is well aware that there will be additional words throughout the book that reflect core academic vocabulary; some she will briefly explain as they arise, while others will be presented as vocabulary words to be explored more deeply and tested over the remainder of the unit.

Concept sorts can also be used to teach students academic vocabulary such as *conflict,* a major literary technique for advancing plot in narrative prose. Students learn early on that stories often develop around a conflict or struggle between opposing sides or forces. In stories, the plot can develop from conflict between characters, as between the main character in Jack London's *The King of Mazy May* and the other older gold diggers with nefarious intentions, or plot can develop from conflict experienced within a character who may be struggling with right and wrong, or, as in *Greyling* by Jane Yolen,

FIGURE 5.1   **Vocab-O-Gram for *The Grapes of Wrath*:
Internal versus External Conflict**

Discuss what you know about each of the words. Think about how Steinbeck may use the words to represent *external* and *internal* conflict. The words may be used more than once. If there are words that your group is not sure about, list them as Mystery Words. Use the vocabulary words to make predictions about *The Grapes of Wrath*.	
Oklahoma dust bowl California banks tenant farmer pellagra rape truculent quest monster Hoovervilles disconsolate perplexed union 1930s prodigal migrant misfortune animosity tarpaulin contractor wrath paradox vigilante	
Internal Conflict: Person vs. Self	
External Conflict: Person vs. Person	
External Conflict: Person vs. Society	
External Conflict: Person vs. Elements	
What Question(s) Do You Have?	
Mystery Words	

with what the character "tries" to be versus his "true nature." In other stories, conflict exists between man and nature, as in Paulsen's *Hatchet*. Later on, usually in the upper grades, students learn to look for word choices in the author's craft that highlight these conflicts, word choices that create parallel *contrasts*.

It is often helpful to have students deconstruct an author's choice of words and even sort them into contrasting categories. Consider, for example, the juxtaposition of the following words and phrases from *Hatchet*: *green carpet, new hope, celebration of being alive, green willow, turtle eggs, nourishment* versus *breath-tightening rip of terror, moment of fear, hissing madness, terrified, without hope. Hope, celebration,* and *nourishment* might go in one category associated with staying alive, while *hissing madness, fear,* and *terror* might go in another category associated with death. These are "golden" words and phrases that Paulsen juxtaposes to illustrate the clash of hope and despair as Brian struggles to survive in the Canadian wilderness. Relating these words and phrases to students' own personal conflicts with hope and despair is the first step toward building word consciousness and expanding vocabulary knowledge through the medium of this classic tale of courage and determination.

Theme: *I Know Why the Caged Bird Sings*.   One of the guiding principles for selecting words for instruction that we presented in Chapter 4 was to look for words representing the "big ideas" underlying the literary work. *Themes* are those unifying big ideas and they become the recurring refrain in a work of poetry or prose. As a result, thematic discussions present a ripe opportunity for relevant vocabulary instruction.

Maya Angelou's *I Know Why the Caged Bird Sings* is a classic example of two traditional themes in autobiographical literature: the triumph over obstacles and the search for identity. Core words related to these themes in *I Know Why the Caged Bird Sings* might include *assail, tribulation, maim, desiccate, torturous, violator, berate, belligerent, ostracize, heinous,* or *unscrupulous.* These words could be contrasted with other words related to Maya's survival and ultimate self-respect in concept sorts, or they could be used to predict future outcomes through the use of vocab-o-grams. By searching for those golden words related to recurring themes and motifs, teachers can move students from specific words that are variations on a theme to words that have the power to articulate *why* the caged bird sings. Of course, two parallel and often contrasting subthemes of *I Know Why the Caged Bird Sings* relate to the Black gospel tradition represented by Grandmother Henderson, who is always stoical in the face of trouble, and the Black blues/jazz motif, represented by Maya's mother. Which of the following words would lend themselves to these contrasting motifs: *brimstone, jitterbug, deacon, swagger, pulpit, jaunty,* and *dauntless?*

Antonyms and Contrast: *The Scarlet Letter*.

Antonyms are words that are the opposite in meaning of other words, though there are different types of oppositional relationships (Templeton, 1991). There are antonyms that are truly oppositional and have no middle ground, such as *right* versus *wrong,* or *yes* versus *no.* But there are also antonyms that are more relational and represent points along a continuum. Although words such as *hot* and *cold* might lie on opposite ends of a continuum, there are many other words suggesting degrees of warmth or chilliness that could appear in between. Combined with words that are similar in meaning, synonyms (*syn,* "alike, with, or together" + *nym,* "name"), a study of antonyms (*anti,* "opposite, against, over, or counter to" + *nym,* "name") gives students the opportunity to make fine distinctions among relationships and improve critical thinking. A study of antonyms can also lead to the study of *contrast,* a literary technique that pervades all the elements of literature.

The juxtaposition of light and darkness in *The Scarlet Letter* plays a major role in Hawthorne's presentation of the novel's background, setting, and character development, where antonyms often set the tone and suggest which side of good and evil the characters may fall. Students might be encouraged to locate and pair up Hawthorne's antonyms and match them with aspects of the novel's scenery, or aspects of the characters themselves.

Ms. Eye began sensitizing her English students to Hawthorne's use of antonyms to create contrast by writing the following sentence on the blackboard and inviting her students to find two words that could be considered opposites: "The scarlet letter threw a lurid gleam along the dark passageway of the interior." After some discussion of the word *lurid* (denotatively and connotatively!), the students quickly focused on the words *gleam* and *dark.* Thereafter, the class began to compile a list of words that Hawthorne used to refer to light or darkness: *midnight, glowing, sombre, noon, grey, daylight, blazing darksome, nighttime, shaded, sunshine, fire, ablaze, meteor, bright, dusky moonlight, dawn, dull, shadows, alight, dim, gleaming, lighting, dark, gloomy, dusk, radiance, black, darkened, burning,* and *aglow.* Ms. Eye had already taken the first step of a list/group/label routine—brainstorming or compiling lists.

In step two, her students sorted their lists into categories. Most chose categories corresponding to *light* and *dark,* but others made finer classifications to accommodate the shadowy, gloomy words or to illuminate the fiery ones. What was most important in this activity, however, was not the number of categories but the rationale for forming them, and this is accomplished in the third step of the list/group/label process. Ms. Eye asked her students to label their categories and then to defend their labels based on the applicability of the words in each group to a character, scene, or thematic issue in the novel. Some students labeled their gloomy, dim, and shadowy category as *Dimmesdale.* Others with the same classification and rationale labeled that group of words as *Divided* and were able to explain the moral conflict undergirding Dimmesdale's motives.

Working with the same list of words, Ms. Eye engaged her students in another vocabulary activity on the following day. This time, Ms. Eye asked her students to choose two words from their list that they felt were furthest apart in meaning, such as *noon* and *midnight*, or *day* and *night*. This required some tough thinking as students struggled to articulate how *dull* might be the opposite of *bright* or *gleaming*. Then Ms. Eye asked students to rank order words in the categories from their list/group/label activity two days earlier—from *shadow* to *black*, for example, or from *sunshine* to *ablaze*. Why is *darksome* darker than *dusky*? Why do you think *radiant* is brighter than *gleaming*? In these discussions, Ms. Eye's students discussed the denotative and connotative meaning of the words, and once again, related them to Hawthorne's setting, characters, and themes.

Not all the words Hawthorne used in *The Scarlet Letter* have to do with light and darkness, of course, so in selecting words for core academic vocabulary instruction it is important to look for words that are essential to understanding the underlying themes of the reading selection and that are likely to occur in other literate contexts. Ideally, the words we select not only meet these two important criteria but will also meet a third: vocabulary instruction should lead to generative word study.

Ms. Eye wants her students to be able to discuss the major characters of *The Scarlet Letter* in terms of the distinctive qualities that Hawthorne has given them to advance his themes. She chooses her words carefully and economically so that they not only describe each of the main characters aptly, but also so she can generate additional vocabulary study using the spelling–meaning connections contained in the words she selected. To achieve this, Ms. Eye used the 4-square approach. Each student divided a notebook page into four equal squares. In the top left square, they wrote the word *hypocrisy*. They repeated this with two more words: *sympathetic* and *fiendish*. Their charge was to complete each 4-square by writing synonyms to the right of each word, examples in the bottom square below it, and non-examples in the bottom square to the right. Finally, after sharing and discussing, students wrote the definition of the word in the top left square below the word. Figure 5.2 shows three 4-squares that were produced by Ms. Eye's students.

FIGURE 5.2   Three 4-Squares for Vocabulary from *The Scarlet Letter*

Hypocrisy: pretending to have beliefs, feelings, or virtues that one doesn't really possess	**Synonyms:** deceitfulness; insincerity; duplicity; two-facedness
Example: A preacher who sins; Dimmesdale	**Non-examples:** Martin Luther King; Gandhi; sincerity; honesty

Sympathetic: understanding of relationships between people; understanding that whatever affects one affects others	**Synonyms:** compassionate; understanding; kindhearted
Example: Hester Prynne	**Non-example:** Chillingworth

Fiendish: diabolical; evil spirited	**Synonyms:** wicked; evil; cruel
Example: Chillingworth	**Non-example:** Mother Teresa

Notice the examples for each word ended up being the character exemplifying that trait.

After a fervent discussion of these three vocabulary words in relation to Hawthorne's characters and themes, Ms. Eye takes the opportunity to extend their understanding of these core vocabulary words to other words that share the same spelling–meaning connections, such as *sym* in *sympathetic* and *hypo* in *hypocrisy*. She points out *hypo* in *hypocrisy* and asks if anyone knows any other words that start with the root *hypo*. Students volunteer the following: *hypodermis, hypoglycemic, hypothermal,* and *hypochondriac*. Ms. Eye calls on students to define the words, using the dictionary as needed, and then asks students what the prefix means. Dictionaries with etymologies will confirm their idea.

They conclude that in each of these words, *hypo* means "under, below, or beneath." *Hypodermis* means under or beneath the dermis or skin. *Hypoglycemic* means levels of glycerin (or sugar) below acceptable levels. *Hypothermal* refers to mineral deposits formed at great depths and high temperatures. Some students volunteer similar sounding words that start with a different root, such as *hyperactive, hyperventilation,* and *hypnotize*. Ms. Eye suggests that they contrast *hyperthermia* and *hypothermia* to find the meaning of *hyper*. They conclude that while the root *hypo* means "under or beneath," *hyper* means the opposite: "over, above, or beyond." A *hyperactive* child has an activity level over and above what is considered a normal activity level. Someone who is *hyperventilating* is someone whose breathing (ventilating) rate is over and above the normal breathing rate, and so on. *Hypno* has yet another meaning and is associated with sleep, as in *hypnotic, hypnosis,* and *hypnotize*.

To follow up with these spelling–meaning connections, Ms. Eye has her students sort these words by their roots and then discuss their probable meanings, as shown in Figure 5.3. These word sorts are recorded in the word study section of their notebooks and other words are added to each column as they find them in their reading.

Returning to the word *hypocrisy*, students use their knowledge of Dimmesdale to articulate his essential "underhandedness" and duplicity. With a little help from the dictionary to find the origin of *crisy*, derived from *krinein*, "to separate," Ms. Eye's students observe how Dimmesdale separated his feelings underneath from his espoused beliefs on the surface.

Ms. Eye adopts a similar approach with *sympathetic*. Students generate other words starting with the *sym* root, such as *symphony, symmetric, symbiosis,* and other similar sounding words starting with *syn*, such as *synchrony, synchromesh,* and so on. After learning that the *sym* root means "together, with, alike, or similar," students guess the meanings of known words like *symphony* (sound together or with sound), *symmetric* (similar metric or measure), and *symbiosis* (living together). Using the dictionary of Indo-European roots, students discover that *syn* is a variant of the root *sym* and begin to guess the meaning of *synchrony* (same time). After sorting words beginning with the root *syn* and its variant *sym*, the class returns to *sympathetic*, and using their knowledge of Hester

FIGURE 5.3   Word Sort Comparing *hypo*, *hyper*, and *hypno*

hypo	hyper	hypno
hypodermis	hyperactive	hypnotic
hypochondria	hypercritical	hypnosis
hypoglycemic	hyperventilate	hypnotist
hypothermal	hypersensitive	hypnotism
hyposensitive		

Prynne and a little more help from the dictionary to find the origin of *pathetic* (pathos, or feeling), students are able to articulate why Hester is so able to feel everyone's pain. These words could be added to others with the same root to create a different word sort (see Appendix D).

Combining the study of synonyms and antonyms with sorting words into categories provides a powerful bridge between what students already know and what they don't know, between the familiar and the unfamiliar, and between old and new vocabulary (Johnson & Pearson, 1984). From the supported study of three core words carefully selected to epitomize each of the three main characters from *The Scarlet Letter,* Ms. Eye was able to elaborate and then expand her students' vocabulary knowledge to include other words that share the same root. Effective vocabulary instruction is generative.

CONTENT-SPECIFIC ACADEMIC VOCABULARY IN THE ENGLISH LANGUAGE ARTS

Teaching Academic Terms Related to Literary Genres

The English language arts is filled with literary terms that comprise their own content area, and teaching the meaning of these content-specific academic words must build on students' existing knowledge. Knowing the word *verse,* for example, involves a network of related words from all kinds of sources including songs, the Qu'ran, the Bible, rap, nursery rhymes, hip-hop, and networking protocols for real-time communication between computer graphics software. The more students read, talk, hear, and experience things related to *verse,* the more likely they will understand the content-specific academic senses of the word *verse.*

The content-specific academic vocabulary of literary elements forms a taxonomy of terms much like the biological classification systems of kingdom, phylum, class, order, family, and genus. The taxonomy of literary elements has two major kingdoms: poetry and prose. Within the kingdom of poetry, there are several different phyla: narrative poetry (poetry that tells a story) and nonnarrative poetry are two of the major ones. Within the phylum of narrative poetry, there are different classes—for example, ballads, limericks, sonnets, and free verse. Within the class of sonnets, there are different orders: Petrarchan and Shakespearean sonnets, and so on. Dictionaries help little in teaching these terms because dictionaries are poor tools for learning the meanings of new words representing new concepts within new domains of knowledge. Students will need first-hand experiences with this new domain of poetry as well as conversational exchanges with other students and their teachers as they grapple with the content-specific academic vocabulary of poetry in the context of what they are reading. Exposure to these different poetic forms is the first step. As poems are read and discussed, they can be classified according to the taxonomy shown in Figure 5.4. Where would you place Nikki Giovanni's "Balances," for example? Narrative or nonnarrative? Why? What class? Why? As more poems are read, their titles can be sorted and recorded into the categories of poetic forms.

Within the kingdom of prose there are two major phyla: *narrative* and *expository.* Within the phylum of narrative prose, there are different classes, such as *escape* and *interpretive.* Within escape literature, there are different genres or orders: fantasy, mysteries, adventure, and so on. Within the genre of fantasy there are different families: science fiction (*The Golden Compass*), allegorical (*The Lion, the Witch and the Wardrobe; The Hobbit*), and satirical (*The Giver*). Once again, the dictionary will be a poor tool in differentiating these narrative types and their labels. Students must be marinated in hearing, seeing, and using these terms in response to specific books and short stories heard, read, and written. Wide reading is the first step. Engaging discussions is the second. In the

FIGURE 5.4   A Taxonomy of Literary Genres

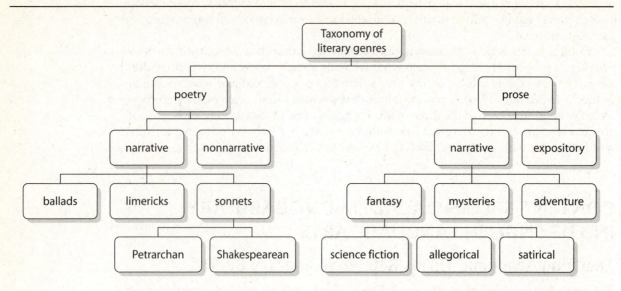

taxonomy above, where would you place Walter Dean Myers's *Somewhere in the Darkness?* Laurie Anderson's *Speak?* And why? Through wide reading and teachers' coaching about the characteristics of different types of literature, students will acquire the content-specific academic vocabulary needed to learn more within the English language arts.

In teaching the content-specific word meanings related to poetry and prose, it is helpful to further categorize concepts related to surface-level text structures that organize the text in visible segments, such as paragraphs or stanzas, versus internal structures related to specific genres. For example, in Western literature the most common narrative structure includes a setting, a protagonist and antagonist, a problem or conflict, rising action that attempts to resolve the problem, a climax or denouement, and a resolution. Other cultures have different narrative structures, and through a study of multicultural literature these can be compared and contrasted. Regardless of which culture a narrative comes from, teachers will need to teach academic terms like *protagonist* and *antagonist* directly. Understanding the meanings of these terms will not only advance student understanding of narrative structures, but deconstructing these terms into their morphological roots will increase their vocabulary knowledge as well.

Teachers might begin by asking students what parts of the words *protagonist* and *antagonist* are the same. Once *agonist* is identified, teachers might ask students if they know any other words that sound similar: *agony* or *agonize*, for example. A little dictionary exploration will reveal that both of these words are related to struggle. Once the similar word parts are identified, teachers might call attention to the parts of the words *protagonist* and *antagonist* that are different: *prot* and *ant*. Again, a little dictionary excursion will reveal that the *prot* in *protagonist* comes from *proto*, meaning "first, leading, principal, or in front of or forward." Brainstorming other words that contain the root *proto* might lead to *protozoa* (first animals), *protoplasm* (principal living matter of plant and animal cells), or *prototype* (first form). A brief consult with the dictionary will likewise reveal that the meaning of the *ant* in *antagonist* comes from *anti*, meaning "against, or in opposition to." Putting *anti* and *agonist* together yields a sense of struggling against or in opposition to. In many narrative structures, both plot and theme can be advanced by the *protagonist* or leading character who is often in competition with the *antagonist*, or foil. Students can reflect on the meaning of these academic terms as they sort related words according to the *proto* or *anti* roots—words like *protolanguage* or *Proto-Indo-European* versus words like

FIGURE 5.5   Core Vocabulary from Freedman's Photobiography of Lincoln—Arranged Chronographically

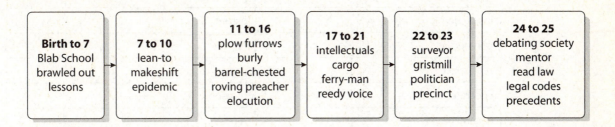

Birth to 7	7 to 10	11 to 16	17 to 21	22 to 23	24 to 25
Blab School brawled out lessons	lean-to makeshift epidemic	plow furrows burly barrel-chested roving preacher elocution	intellectuals cargo ferry-man reedy voice	surveyor gristmill politician precinct	debating society mentor read law legal codes precedents

antithesis and *antarctic.* Thus, the meanings of content-specific academic words can be generalized to other core vocabulary.

Internal structures for expository texts differ from narrative structures. Expository texts are often organized by chronological order, causes and then effects, or in a compare and contrast fashion. Direct instruction in these text structures can also include academic vocabulary. In fact, by sorting familiar, known core academic words into categories of text structure, students can expand their understanding of text structures to accommodate new concepts and their labels. The words and phrases depicted in the concept sort in Figure 5.5 classifies core vocabulary and names from Russell Freedman's *Lincoln: A Photobiography.* The result is a chronological summary of Abraham Lincoln's early life.

In discussing the chronological presentation of Freedman's text, the word *chronological* serves as a catalyst for some academic word study. For example, *Chronus*, the Greek titan ironically mislabeled the god of time, has become known as "Father Time." Some derivatives worth studying include *chronic* (all the time), *chronicle* (a record of events over time), and our academic vocabulary word: *chronological.*

GENERATIVE ROOTS AND AFFIXES

Over the course of several years, English/language arts teachers can guide students' exploration of many core academic words to understand how their meaningful parts— prefixes, suffixes, bases, and roots—can combine to create meaning. The principles for teaching roots and affixes presented in Chapter 4 are a good guide for moving from concrete to more abstract relationships, and the core list of roots and affixes presented in the appendix to Chapter 4 provides a guide to those that may be addressed over the course of the middle and secondary grades.

The following is an example of a sort with which to begin the exploration of Latin word roots, allowing you to walk through explanations of how the root and affixes combine to result in the meaning of the word. Begin by having the students sort the words into two categories according to their root, *spect* or *port*, as shown in Figure 5.6. The meaning of these Latin roots is straightforward, as are the meanings of most of the words in which they combine with other affixes and roots. Because of this, you may wish to begin by asking students to speculate about the meaning of the roots. Then you can walk the students through two or three words, explaining how the elements combine to produce the meaning of the word:

Begin by writing the word *inspection* on the board or overhead. Ask the students to explain the meaning of *inspection* and use it in a sentence. Then tell them that the word is made up of the suffix *-ion* (the "act or result" of something), the Latin root *spec*, "to look at," and the prefix *in-*, "into." Now think about it. Given their explanation and definition of *inspection,* do they see that putting these words parts together literally means "the act of looking into" something?

FIGURE 5.6   **Word Sort for the Word Roots *spect* and *port***

spect	*port*
inspection	export
perspective	deport
retrospect	import
spectator	transport
circumspect	report
prospect	portfolio
introspect	heliport
spectacle	portage
spectacular	importune
spectrum	opportune
	supportable

Repeat this process with *export*. After students discuss what it means, show them that the word comes from the Latin root *port*, "to carry," and the prefix *ex-*, "out." Now think about it. Given their explanation and definition of *export*, do they see that putting the root *port* together with the prefix *ex-* literally means "carrying out"? (You may mention *import* as well here. Tell them the prefix *im-* means "in, into." Is it clear how *export* and *import* are related?)

After sorting the words by root, follow up by having students discuss, in pairs, how they think the word parts combine to produce the meaning of each word. *Circumspect* is one word in this sort whose precise meaning is more connotative than literal; putting the word parts together yields the meaning "to look around." Discuss the connotative meaning of the word—the meaning that is *suggested* by the word and the *associations* that may be made with it. When you behave in a *circumspect* manner, you look around and are careful because you are thinking of the possible results of what you might do.

Another word you might walk through with the students is *perspective*, "look through." When you talk about your *perspective* on an issue or on life you are actually talking about how you have *looked through* that issue. This may lead to a similar word, *prospect*, "look forward." Point out to the students that the vast majority of words that appear to contain a word root can best be analyzed by beginning at the end of the word. Reflect on how you analyzed the words *inspect, circumspect,* and *export. Important* may at first be hard to reconcile with other *port* words since it literally means "carry into." Metaphorically, it might mean "carrying weight into." This lesson may be extended in other directions as follows:

- Take time to discuss the prefix *trans-*, "across," and brainstorm other words that start with it: *transfer, transplant, transmit,* and *transcontinental.* If you have a prefix chart on the wall, add *trans-*.
- Several words offer possibilities for generating additional words by adding *-ion* or *-ation*. Have students see how many derived words they can generate, first by discussing whether the derived words really exist or not, and then by checking the dictionary to confirm or not. Examples include *transportation, transformation, reformation, importation,* and *retrospection.*

- Another spelling of the root *spec* is *spic,* as in *conspicuous.* Have students explore the meanings of the following words, discussing how they each have to do with "seeing": *conspicuous, perspicacious, auspicious.*
- Additional words that may be explored are *expect, expectation, introspective, retrospective, spectacles, specimen, suspect; airport, seaport, comportment, deport, heliport, portmanteau,* and *rapport.*

Another example of how to walk through word formation processes and meanings is offered by the root sort on p. 56 in Chapter 4. Discussing the root *mem* in this sort is fairly straightforward. *Memory* has to do, obviously, with the mind. *Remembrance,* of course, is derived from *remember*—literally, bringing the mind "back"; *commemorate* has to do with honoring the memory of someone—remembering "with" (*com*) others. The teacher discusses *immemorial* by introducing this sentence: "Since time immemorial, people have said that dogs are humans' best friend." She discusses how the meaning "without memory" literally refers to a time beyond anyone's memory.

The *psych* root provides a good opportunity to tie in to mythology (see below). *Psyche* was the young Greek woman who fell in love with Eros and became the personification of the soul. The teacher discusses with the students why they think *psych* then came to represent the "mind"—and also acknowledges the *Eros–erotic* link because a student asked about it! In discussing *psychiatry,* the teacher pointed out the suffix *-iatry,* "healing," and asked them what they then thought the literal meaning of *psychiatry* is.

Morphological and Contextual Analysis

In this section we grow the strategy presented in Chapter 4 for decoding unfamiliar words in context (pp. 50–51). When your students have a foundation in how bases, roots, and affixes work within words, they can apply their growing sophistication in morphological awareness to their decoding and remembering a large number of the new words they encounter in their reading. We encourage them to open up and become more flexible in their thinking about words that are morphologically related.

Modeling the Analysis: George Orwell's *Animal Farm*.   In her freshman English classes, Sara Jones systematically teaches about word formation processes during the first several weeks of the school year. Throughout the rest of the year she draws on this knowledge and the strategy for applying it when introducing new vocabulary. The following examples, based on Sara's unit on George Orwell's *Animal Farm,* illustrate how Sara walks her students through new vocabulary. Sometimes she will begin with the word in context and then move to the morphological analysis, and other times she begins with the morphological analysis and then looks at the word in context. This flexibility helps strengthen her students' awareness and use of morphological analysis in unison with contextual analysis.

First, Sara writes the new term *apathy* on the board and asks the students if they can think of any words that may be related in spelling to *apathy.* If they don't mention *sympathy,* she writes it below *apathy.* She discusses how the root *path* works with the prefix *sym-* literally to mean "feeling with" someone. "If you have sympathy for someone you are 'feeling their pain' with them, so to speak. With the word *apathy,* the prefix *a-* means 'without,' so *apathy* means literally 'without feeling.'"

Sara then has students turn to the first couple of pages of Chapter 2 in *Animal Farm* and directs them to look at the third paragraph. She reads the following sentence aloud: "Several nights a week, after Mr. Jones was asleep, they held secret meetings in the barn and expounded the principles of Animalism to the others. At the beginning they met with much stupidity and apathy." She then discusses with the students how the meaning of "without feeling" works in the context of the sentence. What Sara has done is help students become aware of how they can combine morphological analysis with thinking about the context in which the unfamiliar word occurs to generate a possible meaning for the word.

Sara addresses *tractable* similarly. She has the students turn to the passage with the excerpt "throughout that year a wave of rebelliousness ran through the countryside. Bulls which had always been tractable suddenly turned savage." She reminds the students of their examination earlier in the year of the word *attract*, in which the root *tract* meaning "pull" combines with the prefix *at-*, meaning "toward," to mean literally "pull toward." She solidifies this understanding for her students when she asks them, "If you are attracted to someone, do you feel 'pulled toward' them?" The students get the point! Returning to the sentence "Bulls which had always been tractable suddenly turned savage," she asks the students to turn to a partner and discuss how the structure of *tractable—tract* plus *-able*—works in the context of this excerpt. Can they come up with a probable meaning for *tractable*?

As students understand more about the strategy and content of morphological analysis, they will become more adept at flexibly applying this knowledge to figuring out and remembering new words. Sara walks her students through an example of this flexible perspective with the following words, underlining *amor* in each word:

amorous
enamored
amoral
glamorous
metamorphic

Sara helps her students understand that *amor* means "love" in the first two words. She asks her students if it means "love" in *amoral*. Of course, it doesn't—if the students don't mention it, Sara notes that *moral* is the base word, and *a-* is the prefix meaning "not." They continue the discussion with *glamorous* and *metamorphic*. What the students now explicitly understand is that you can have the same letter sequence—as with *amor*—but it may stand for different morphemes. When analyzing a new word, be flexible. If one analysis doesn't result in a meaningful word in the context in which it occurs, try another analysis. An excellent follow-up is to check etymological information in a dictionary.

Modeling the Analysis: Literature from Earlier Historical Periods. From the middle grades on through senior honors English classes, teachers should model this approach combining morphological and contextual analysis, showing students how it "grows up" as they read more challenging literature from earlier historical periods. Often, they will encounter words whose meanings and connotations vary significantly from the contemporary senses. There are two steps English teachers can take to help students understand this process. First, share a number of examples to alert students to this phenomenon and help them think through how the meanings and connotations have evolved. Second, remind them that when they are reading independently they should apply a morphological analysis of a word, together with the context in which it occurs, to reassure themselves that they will often be able to reconstruct the original meaning.

The following examples from Anita Romero's *Hamlet* unit are model minilessons that Anita uses to walk through and model these two important steps for her students.

In Act I, Scene i, Hamlet learns that the ghost of his father may have appeared to Marcellus and Bernardo. He tells them:

If you have hitherto conceal'd this sight
Let it be tenable in your silence still.

Anita explains, "In other words, if Marcellus and Bernardo haven't told anyone else about this, they should continue to keep it to themselves. Now, let's look at the word *tenable*. Today, what does it mean—or can anyone use it in a sentence?" After a brief discussion in which students talk about a point of view being *tenable*, Anita continues: "Can you think of other words with this same root? We have talked about the root *ten*, meaning 'hold,' as in *attend*—to hold your focus on something, and *tenacious*—to hold strongly to and fight for your point of view, for example. In this scene, if Marcellus and Bernardo have until now hidden from others the possibility that they have seen the dead king, Hamlet encourages them to continue to *hold* it in their silence, to keep it to themselves."

In Act IV, Scene v, Laertes laments Ophelia's descent into madness when he describes her as "a *document* in madness." Anita points out that the root *doc* means "teach"—as in the original meaning of *doctor* and in the words *indoctrinate* and *doctrine*. In the sense in which Shakespeare uses the word *document* it retains its earlier meaning of "teach," describing how Ophelia becomes a "lesson" in madness. Anita reminds her students:

"When you encounter a word that does not seem to have its present-day meaning, look at its structure—affixes and base or root—and think about the meaning of those parts in the overall context in which the word occurs. Very often, you will find that you have discovered Shakespeare's meaning!" (Or, depending on the text, Chaucer's meaning, or Donne's, or Hawthorne's, and so on.)

On occasion, of course, students will encounter a word that is rarely or never used in contemporary English. For example, in Act I, Scene iii of *Hamlet*, Laertes is cautioning Ophelia about the consequences of her coming to believe Hamlet's expressions of love. He tells her:

Then weigh what loss your honour may sustain
If with too <u>credent</u> ear you list his songs.

Anita discusses with the class what Laertes is trying to tell Ophelia here. The students have the sense that he is trying to warn her not to take what Hamlet might say as revealing what he really feels or believes. Anita then asks the students to think about the word *credent:* "We don't really see this word in English anymore, but are there any other words you can think of that are similar to *credent?*" They come up with *credible* and *credence* and discuss how both of these words have to do with something that is believable. One of the students remembers that these words have the root *cred,* which means "belief." Anita asks them to discuss with their partner if that meaning seems to work for the word *credent* in the context of Laertes's caution.

A Little Bit of Latin.   While they rarely occur in textbooks or in most narrative literature middle and secondary students read, a number of Latin terms and phrases pop up from time to time in articles and online publications that students will be reading. For students moving on to college, they will discover that these terms and phrases will occur with more frequency in their readings. It is helpful to walk through the literal meanings of these and help students understand how the terms and phrases function in context. Of course, students may always refer to a dictionary for the meaning of such terms and phrases when they run into them, but they are more likely to remember them and learn a bit about how they work if you have shown them how and why they are used. The following are presented in the order of how often they seem to occur in texts:

- *etc.* (and the rest) Students are very familiar with this abbreviation but rarely have seen the original Latin term *et cetera: et* (and) *cetera* (the rest). A minor but beneficial consequence of attending to the original Latin is that students who have been mispronouncing *etc.* as "ekcetera" will remember the correct pronunciation!
- *a priori* (from what is before) "A lot of political analysts seem to be wrapped up in a priori reasoning rather than stepping back and looking at the facts on the ground." The term has to do with an argument or a reason that is based on an existing

assumption or point of view—the "former" or "prior" part of the definition—rather than on observable facts. Teachers ask students if they see a familiar word in this term (*prior*). They usually do, and it is the key to remembering what *a priori* means.

- *ad hoc* (to this) "Our committee will meet on an ad hoc basis." The term refers to something that is not planned in advance but rather based on the situation at hand, for a particular purpose.

- *non sequitur* (not following) "So many advertisements are non sequiturs and appeal to our emotions—'If you don't subscribe to this Internet provider you are missing all of the online excitement!'" The conclusion does not logically follow from the first statement or premise. Note the similarity in spelling and meaning between *sequitur* and *sequence*.

- *ad nauseam* (to sickness) This term means "to the point of nausea"—often used to describe someone talking about something and going on and on. "Barry talks about his bug collection ad nauseam—he really needs to get a life!"

- *per capita* (by the head) When we determine the amount of food consumed *per capita* each year, this refers to "per person." *Capita*, "head," is another way of referring to a person. Note the similarity in spelling and meaning between *capita* and *capital* (a city that is the "head" of a state or nation).

- *per diem* (by the day) When we hear or read of someone being paid on a *per diem* basis, they are paid on a daily basis, not on a weekly or monthly basis. In this term, *di* means "day," as in *diary* and *diurnal*. This is a good opportunity to do a minilesson on *di*, noting that letter sequences often stand for different meanings (see p. 90). *Di* may also mean "two," as in *digraph*. In addition, it is also a form of *dis-*, as in words such as *digest* (to carry *away*). Sara Jones explains it this way to her students: "Latin word parts are kind of like the *multiple meaning* words we've talked about. The same spelling can occasionally stand for different meanings—like *bear* the animal and *bear* meaning 'carrying a burden.' Latin word parts often work the same way—the same spelling, like *di*, can represent different meanings, so we have to look at the context in which the word containing such a word part occurs."

- *et al.* As with *et cetera*, the abbreviation for *et alii* (and others) is more common. The spelling *alii* is the plural form of *alium*, which means "other," so *alii* means "others." The next bullet explains this phenomenon.

- *Latin Plurals* Throughout their academic careers, older students will encounter a number of situations requiring them to read or spell words of Latin origin in which the singular and plural forms follow some very precise and predictable rules. Here are the most common:

    Singular -*us* becomes plural -*i*: alumn*us*/alumn*i*
    Feminine singular -*a* becomes plural -*ae*: alumn*a*/alumn*ae*
        (*ae* is pronounced like a long *e*)
    Singular -*um* becomes plural -*a*: medi*um*/medi*a*, bacteri*um*/bacteri*a*
    Singular -*ex* and -*ix* become plural -*ices*: ind*ex*/ind*ices*, vort*ex*/vort*ices*,
        matr*ix*/matr*ices*, append*ix*/append*ices*

The following word sort explores Latin singular and plural forms with words known by most secondary students. Students match singular and plural forms and discuss the different singular/plural patterns that they see. For middle school students, any unknown words may also be an opportunity to expand vocabulary; the sort is presented in its completed form below:

analysis	analyses	alga	algae	alumnus	alumni	datum	data
synthesis	syntheses	vertebra	vertebrae	radius	radii	bacterium	bacteria
basis	bases	formula	formulae	stimulus	stimuli	curriculum	curricula
				octopus	octopi		

GREEK AND ROMAN MYTHOLOGY: A VERY BRIEF PRIMER

The importance of a familiarity with Greek mythology and the related mythology of the Romans is widely acknowledged. Their themes, their psychology, and their deities and characters pervade much of the culture and the literature of English-speaking America. And literature, from the real-world standpoint of the English/language arts teacher, inevitably includes what is out there in the popular culture. In both literature and popular culture, for example, consider how often we encounter references to a "Trojan horse," a "siren song," and a "Pandora's box." Students are often astonished to realize that the quests, the battles, and the characters that live in the pages of graphic novels (for example, *Watchmen*), the architecture of videogames, and on the screen in popular films are so often latter-day reflections of ideas, issues, and challenges that the ancient Greeks explored. They will discover similarities in myths across different cultures as well, including those as geographically and historically disparate as the Norse, East Asian, Middle East, and Anasazi of the American Southwest. Words from the myths, with their connotations and their allusions, are a significant part of the core academic vocabulary our students will learn.

This brief "primer" provides some background information to get your stories and conversations about mythology and its role in generating vocabulary underway, as well as serving to pique students' interest in the role of Greek and Latin in English. Once they have a certain level of awareness, they will notice and better understand in literature the innumerable allusions to gods, characters, and contexts of classical Greece and Rome. In fact, students often come to realize that these allusions seem to be almost everywhere—not only in the eternal "canon" which includes, for example, Chaucer, Shakespeare, Keats, Shelley, and Yeats, but the more recent works of writers such as Eugene O'Neill, Lorraine Hansberry, Truman Capote, and Richard Rodriguez.

There are many different versions and interpretations of the myths, and the Resource List at the end of this section provides well-grounded and interesting text and Web-based resources. In addition, Table 5.1 presents some of the most significant deities and individuals in Greek mythology; many of their names remained the same when the Romans assimilated them. When the names *did* change, the Roman counterparts are listed second in this table.

Most of the myths and much of the study of the Greek myths—*mythology*—have been based on oral accounts originating with Homer and Hesiod. The Homeric epics and the poems of Hesiod, most notably the *Theogony* (*theo*, god + *gony*, genesis) and *Works and Days*, offer insight into the world and the minds of both the ancient Greeks and the later Classical Greeks who wrote down these works and interpreted them. The Romans later interpreted and reinterpreted these myths; Vergil's *Aeneid* and Ovid's *Metamorphoses* provide the most extensive account (*meta*, beyond + *morph*, structure, "changing structure")—both gods and monsters were always changing their form. Table 5.1 lists some of the words derived from these mythological characters.

According to the ancient Greeks, in the beginning there was Chaos, no form or order. The Greeks believed that Gaia (earth) and Uranus (sky) came out of chaos. Gaia and Uranus had many children, the first of whom were the Titans. Oceanus, the oldest Titan, became a river that encircled the world. Another Titan, Cronus, eventually led the other Titans in overthrowing Uranus. Interestingly, his mother, Gaia, helped him in this effort by giving him a sickle-shaped sword to use—with which he literally castrated his father (foreshadowing the tragedy of *Oedipus* as well as Jim Morrison and the Doors' lyrics in "The End" and Kurt Cobain's cover of the same song years later). When Uranus's blood hit the ground it gave birth to the Erinyes, known by their more common Roman name, the Furies; when it splashed on the waters, it gave birth to Aphrodite, the goddess of love.

The Titans then pretty much ruled the world. The children of Uranus and his wife Rhea, however, would also rise up against their parents, led by Zeus (a recurrent theme in mythology and in life—your students may come to realize that their struggles to move beyond their parents have very deep historical and literary roots). After Zeus and his siblings were victorious, they set up living arrangements on Mt. Olympus. One of the Titans, Atlas, was condemned for eternity to hold up the earth on his shoulders.

Zeus becomes the most important god, but shared rule of the cosmos with his brothers Poseidon (Roman Neptune), who ruled the sea, and Hades (Roman Pluto), who ruled the underworld—the world of the dead. The gods, however, were not all-powerful. The Fates, who may also be the offspring of Uranus, play an important role in ruling the universe, for only they could affect an individual's fate. There were three fates: Clotho (Roman Nona), who spun the thread of life; Lachesis (Roman Decima), who determined the length of the thread; and Atropos (Roman Morta), who cut the thread. Morta was explicitly referred to in Roman mythology as the goddess of death (*mortal, immortal, mortician*).

Zeus and his wife, Hera, had many children, including Hephaestus (Roman Vulcan), the god of the forge; and Ares (Roman Mars), the god of war, who in turn had two sons, Phobos ("fear") and Deimos ("terror"). Zeus had children by mortals as well (students are usually fascinated by the promiscuity of the gods and their offspring): Dionysus, who is most notable for his responsibility for the grape harvest, also known as Bacchus, from which we get *bacchanalia* (extremely festive celebrations). His followers would fly into extreme revelries; they were known as Maenads, a word with the same root as *mania*.

Two other "lesser" deities in the Greek pantheon were Iris and Pan. Iris, a winged messenger from Zeus, was the goddess of the rainbow. (The *iris* in the eye can be many different colors; *iridescent* refers to "many colors.") Pan was the god of woodlands and the patron of shepherds and their flocks. Often attending the revels held by Dionysus, he was unpredictable—he could inspire fear or *panic* among groups of people or animals.

A handful of mortals are listed in Table 5.1, such as Heracles and Odysseus. They are the primary characters in *legends,* which differ from myths in that they are based on individuals who either once lived, or archetypes of such individuals. Over time, their exploits became enhanced and they often were credited with superhuman accomplishments.

Resource List: Greek and Roman Myths and Legends

Asimov, I. (1961). *Words from the myths.* Boston: Houghton Mifflin.

Parada, C. (1993). *Genealogical guide to Greek mythology.* Jonsered, Sweden: Paul Astroms. Carlos Parada's more accessible resource, however, is online. This is a truly comprehensive and easily navigable resource—truly one of the very best available on the Web: http://homepage.mac.com/cparada/GML/index.html

Rosenberg, D. (1998). *World mythology: An anthology of the great myths and epics* (3rd ed.). Lincolnwood, IL: NTC Publishing Group. An excellent ancillary text for high school students.

www.perseus.tufts.edu   This site includes many of the primary works in translation, in addition to the original Greek.

WORD CHOICE IN WRITING

As part of our efforts to help students develop word consciousness, we point out those instances in which a writer has used language effectively to help develop students' sensitivity to "words that illustrate the power and beauty of effective word choice in writing" (Stahl & Nagy, 2006). Throughout this chapter, *word choice* has been examined in the context of the narratives that students are reading. This type of exploration of words, of course, relates directly to students' word choice in their *own* writing, and teachers help students make these explicit connections—not only in the narrative genre but in informational writing as well.

TABLE 5.1 Words from Greek and Roman Myths and Legends*

Chaos The raw material of the universe—a great, dark, confused mass in which air, earth, and water were all mixed together.
chaos • chaotic • chasm

Cosmos The opposite of chaos—things with form and shape; in order, good arrangement.
cosmic • cosmopolitan • cosmetic

Gaia (GAY-uh), also **Gaea** (JEE-uh) Goddess of earth; Greek word for earth.
geography • geology • geometry • geode

Terra
territory • terrain • terrestrial • terrace • terrarium

Uranus God of sky, heaven.
uranium • Uranus (the planet)

Gigantes Children of Uranus and Gaea, ferocious beings of tremendous size and power.
giants • gigantic

Cyclops Children of Uranus and Gaea, they lived on the island of Sicily and made thunderbolts for Zeus; from a Greek word meaning "round-eyed"—monstrous giants with one eye in the forehead.
cycle • cyclone

Titans/Titanesses Offspring of Uranus and Gaea, these were a race of giants who ruled the world before the Greek gods and goddesses took over. They warred with the gods and lost; their fate was eternal punishment of some type or another.
Titanic • titanium

Cronus Most powerful of Titans; because of the similarity to the Greek word *chronos,* he is often mistakenly referred to as the god of time.
chronological • synchrony • synchronous

Oceanus (oh-*see*-uh-nus) Oldest of the Titans; symbolized water that encircled the land of the world.
ocean • oceanic

Atlas One of the Titans, Atlas's punishment was to support the world on his shoulders. A picture of this was often included in early books of maps, so over time such books came to be called atlases.
atlas • Atlantic • Atlanta • Atlas Mountains (the god Atlas turned to stone)

Zeus God of the sky, king of the gods.
Jupiter or **Jove**
jovian • jovial

Luna Goddess of the moon. At one time people believed the moon had the power to drive some people out of their minds.
lunar • lunacy • lunatic

Hypnos God of sleep.
hypnosis • hypnotic • hypnotism
Somnus
insomnia • somnambulate

Mt. Olympus Where the Greek gods and goddesses lived.
Olympian

Aphrodite Goddess of beauty and love.
aphrodisiac
Venus Her symbol, a looking glass, became the symbol for female.
Venus (the planet) • venusian • venerate • venerable

Eros God of young love.
erotic
Cupid
cupidity

Psyche A maiden who fell in love with Eros. Her name means "soul."
psychology • psychiatrist

Nyx From Chaos, goddess of darkness or night.
Nox
nocturnal • nocturne

Lethe Daughter of Eris, the goddess of discord. Her name means "forgetfulness." Lethe is the river in Hades where the spirits of the dead drink and then forget their former life and become listless ghosts.
lethargic • lethal

Europa She lived on the Asiatic coast of the Mediterranean and was the first person on the continent of Europe. Zeus turned himself into a white bull and Europa jumped on his back. She rode him to the continent of present-day Europe.
Europe • European

Apollo God of prophecy, poetry, medicine, and music.
Apollo Theater (in Harlem) • Apollo (moon program) • Apollonian

Athena Daughter of Zeus, goddess of wisdom, knowledge, arts, war and peace.
Athens • Athenian
Minerva

Ares God of war.
Mars His symbols, the shield and the spear, became the universal symbol for "male"; also means "bloody."
Mars (the red planet) • March • martial arts

Phobos Son of Ares, the god of war. His name means "fear."
phobia • phobic

Demeter Goddess of grain and the harvest.
Ceres
Cereal

Pan God of fields, forests, wild animals. Part man/part goat, he often caused serious trouble. The belief that he was nearby often caused people to run in terror.
panic • pandemonium • pandemic
Faunus God of woodland life.
fauna

Iris Goddess of rainbows, she was also Zeus's messenger.
iris (the flower, part of the eye) • iridescence

continued

TABLE 5.1 Continued

Helios God of the sun.
*heli*um • *helio*centric
Sol
*sol*ar • *sol*ar system • *sol*arium • para*sol*

Hermes Messenger of the gods; was also thought to be related to Thoth, the Egyptian god of astrology and magic.
*herm*etic (sealed off) • *herm*it (one who is "sealed off" from society)
Mercury
Mercury (the planet) • *mercur*ial

Mnemosyne Mother of muses, goddess of memory.
*mnem*onic • a*mnes*ia • a*mnes*ty

Hygeia Goddess of health.
*hygi*ene • *hygi*enist
Salus
*salu*te • *salu*tation • *salu*tory • *salu*brious

Charites The Graces, three sisters who were goddesses of all that is charming in women.
*char*ity
Gratiae
*grac*e • *grac*eful • *grac*ious

The Muses Nine daughters of Zeus; they are the goddesses primarily of the arts.
*mus*ic • *mus*eum

Nemesis Goddess of retribution, justice, or vengeance
nemesis

Tantalus Human son of Zeus. He boasted of his friendship with the gods, so Nemesis followed him and had him punished by a lifetime of standing in water up to his neck with grapes not quite within reach; when he bent to drink the water receded.
*tantal*ize

Echo A mountain nymph, she offended Zeus' wife, Hera, because she talked so much. Hera condemned Echo to haunt the mountainsides, being able only to repeat the last few words of the person speaking. Echo was in love with Narcissus; after he died, she wasted away until nothing was left but her voice.
echo

Narcissus A young man who fell in love with his own reflection in a pool of water.
*narciss*ism

Heracles The strongest of the Greek heroes. Heracles had to perform several seemingly impossible tasks (for example, one was the slaying of a nine-headed monster, the Hydra; when one of its heads was severed, two grew in its place).
Hercules We often speak of *hercul*ean tasks, which means they are very difficult and trying.

Hydra A water serpent that was slain by Heracles.
*hydr*aulics • *hydr*ophobia • *hydr*ant

Odysseus The Greek king whose attempts to sail home after the Trojan War took him far away from home.
odyssey
Ulysses

Orpheus Poet-musician with magic musical powers.
*orph*an • *orph*ic

Ambrosia The food of the gods.
ambrosia

Nectar The drink of the gods.
nectar • *nectar*ine

Marathon A plain located 25 miles from Athens on which a battle was fought between the Greeks and the Persians. A Greek courier ran to Athens to tell the city of the Greek victory and then died.
marathon

Romulus and **Remus** Twin brothers who were raised by a she-wolf. Romulus was the legendary founder of Rome.
Roman • *roman*tic • *roman*ce

Janus Roman god of doors—entrance and exit—who had two faces.
*Janu*ary • *jan*itor

Laconia A part of Greece where the Spartans lived. The Spartans were warlike but not given to boasting. They spoke few words and in few sentences.
laconic

*Greek name listed first, Roman (when different) listed second

Developing Students' Sensitivity and Awareness

Regardless of the genre and format, students' awareness of and sensitivity to word choice will serve them well when they are considering and selecting the particular nouns, verbs, adjectives, and adverbs that will help them convey most appropriately whatever message and meaning they intend. Older students are becoming aware of language in power relationships, and they certainly apply this knowledge in their *oral* communication (Moloney, 2008). It's a small but significant step to apply this same awareness to how they are choosing words in their *written* communication.

The Double-Entry Draft (DED). A *double-entry draft* may be an ongoing feature of students' Vocabulary Notebooks or writing/response journals. On a weekly basis, they keep

FIGURE 5.7   **Student's Double-Entry Draft (DED)**

Text	Student's Response
But he still had dignity, and he would not let those deputies push him out the door. He led them. (*Farewell to Manzanar*, p. 6)	This made me stop, and I read it a couple more times. I know what "dignity" means, but this really hit me. I pictured how the father left his own home. He didn't know if he'd see his family again—this just really got to me.

track of a sentence or sentences in their reading that really grabbed their attention. At the beginning of the year, you may model the process of keeping the double-entry draft, or DED. Students draw a line down the center of a single journal page; on the left-hand side, they write a sentence or sentences that really grab their attention in the narrative or expository selection they have been reading, along with the title and page number of the selection on which their sentence or sentences occur. On the right-hand side, they will write their explanation of *why* they were struck by those lines. It may be a particular idea, word, phrase, or word use in general that makes them stop and think, "Wow! That's powerful!" Occasionally, it may not be the language itself but an idea suggested by the narrative or expository text. At least once a week, students who wish to do so share their entries with the class. Teachers may respond in writing, individually, to the students' DEDs.

Figure 5.7 shows part of a DED written by a freshman while reading *Farewell to Manzanar* (Houston & Houston, 1973), a narrative based on an actual Japanese American family's internment in a concentration camp in the high desert in southern California during World War II. The student had just finished reading the first chapter in which the narrator, a young girl, describes how two deputies came to the family's house near Long Beach, California, several days after the attack on Pearl Harbor. They arrest her father, a fisherman, who had known as soon as he learned of the attack that he would eventually be arrested. Clearly, a well-known word—*dignity*—took on an even deeper, more enriched meaning for this student. Over time, this type of awareness and insight about words will guide students' choices about the most appropriate words to use for particular purposes.

Remaking a Passage.   Select a passage from a narrative and rewrite it, substituting more common and less vibrant words. Depending on your instructional focus, you may target nouns, verbs, adjectives, adverbs, or all of these. Then have students work in groups to discuss and substitute livelier words. The groups then share the passages.

Applying Students' Sensitivity and Awareness

In your own writing over the years, you have probably had teachers who wrote comments such as "awkward" or "vague" in the margin of your paper. These comments usually meant that your word choice or your sentence construction was not as effective as you may have wished (Hacker, 2008; Lunsford, 2006). Help support your students' selection of appropriate words by having them question themselves:

- Is this what I mean?
- Does this sound good?
- Will a reader understand this?

The following strategies support students' reflection on these questions:

- As students are taking risks with their developing word knowledge, it is not unusual for words to be used in slightly inappropriate ways. Kevin Flanigan, a former middle school teacher, shares a delightful example from a sixth-grade student's composition: "The climate of the Sahara Desert is such that the inhabitants had to live elsewhere, so certain areas of the desert were cultivated by irritation" (Flanigan, personal communication).

Certain word choices and expressions may inadvertently result in unanticipated connotations, as in Strunk and White's classic example, "He sat with his head in his hands and his eyes on the floor." When students are "trying on" new core or content area academic vocabulary, they are often inclined to overuse it, believing that their teachers will be more impressed with their word choices. It is better to be clear and direct, using the most appropriate word in a particular context, than to throw down the new vocabulary in unnecessarily long sentences that do more to obscure than to clarify the message.

By sharing such examples with students and getting them to dig into the reasons why such choices and constructions may not work, we are helping them fine tune their sensitivity to how words work and the effects they may have.

- Share with students that very often, as they are writing, the "perfect" word may not occur to them in a particular context. Model for them how, whenever that happens, they can go ahead and write whatever words *do* occur to them, putting a slash in between the words. Later, they can go back and either select from the list or work to find another word.

- Demonstrate how to use a thesaurus. With the spread of word processing, it is easy to click on a word to see suggestions from the thesaurus for possible synonyms. The advantage of using a hard copy of a thesaurus or an online version of the hard copy is that additional information about the context and use of synonyms is provided. Even then, however, students should really think about the appropriateness of the synonym they are tempted to use. As is the case with unabridged dictionaries, students' comfort with and facility in using a thesaurus will grow as their volume of reading and writing grows.

- Beginning with Strunk and White, all style and usage manuals counsel the following: If you find that you're taking a lot of time trying to "fix" a particular sentence by working on different word choices, phrasing, and order—drop it and start that sentence over. Many students become wedded to a particular structure or word choice and keep trying to make it work, when the better plan is to begin anew.

- In working on word choice within a sentence, first look at your nouns and verbs. Are they strong and precise? If they are, *then* your attention to strong and interesting adjectives and adverbs will be more effective.

- Check your pronouns. Is it clear to whom or what they refer? If may be obvious to you, but not to your reader.

Style and Usage Resources

While the classic style manual is Strunk & White's *A Manual of Style*, the examples often cited to illustrate preferred usage assume a fairly advanced level of literacy. More accessible for students are the following:

Hacker, D. (2008). *A pocket style manual* (5th ed.). Boston: Bedford/St. Martin's.
Lunsford, A. A. (2006). *Easy writer: A pocket reference* (3rd ed.). Boston: Bedford/St. Martin's.

An excellent online site is "Grammar Girl"—http://grammar.quickanddirtytips.com.

One of our favorite sites, both for style and usage information as well as for writing tips in general, is http://writingfix.com, a resource of the Northern Nevada Writing Project.

ETYMOLOGICAL NARRATIVES: STORIES ABOUT WORD HISTORIES

Oliver Wendell Holmes, Sr., observed: "The poetry of words is quite as beautiful as the poetry of sentences. The author may arrange the gems effectively, but their shape and lustre have been given by the attrition of ages." The more that our students are aware of this "attrition of ages"—another way of talking about the *etymology* of words—the more they are able to bring to and take away from their engagements with poetry and prose. Teachers may facilitate this awareness through the type of activity illustrated by the example of *cool* at the beginning of this chapter and through the stories we tell our students about words, such as the *decimate* narrative Tamara Baren shared with her students in Chapter 1. (Please also see the "Resources for Language History, Word Origins, and Greek and Latin Roots" in Chapter 3, pp. 42–43). In Chapter 6, a number of narratives are shared across the different content areas. In English classes, teachers can support this perspective through the etymological narratives they share with their students, two examples of which follow, and through the "Word Museum" activity. Remember that there are many sources for these stories.

- Where did the word *English* come from? Easy enough, of course; from *England.* But where did the word *England* come from? From the word *Angleland,* so named for one of the invading Germanic tribes, the Angles, in the fifth century A.D. You may wish to share with students the rest of the story, the more complete background, presented in Chapter 3.
- A student, applying his new awareness of morphological relatedness and spelling–meaning connections, once asked "What was so *romantic* about the *Romans?*" Not really knowing himself, the teacher saw this as an opportunity to explore *with* the students. Using a couple of word history books in the classroom, they discovered that, in the Middle Ages, some works were written in local dialects in Europe that had grown out of the Latin that was originally spoken hundreds of years earlier. Because these dialects came from the language originally spoken by the Romans, they came to be called *Romance.* Over time, these dialects became languages in their own right, and today we refer to them as the Romance languages—French, Spanish, Italian. The most popular works written in these Romance languages involved the knight who met all kinds of challenges, eventually rescuing the proverbial "damsel in distress"—and that's where the "falling in love" meaning of *romance* came from. The teacher then wrote the following on the board, underlining the common element *roman* shared by each term:

<u>Roman</u>s > Latin =
<u>roman</u>ce dialects =
<u>Roman</u>ce languages =
Tales of <u>roman</u>ce

Teachers often voice reservations about sharing these stories, picturing the inevitable student rolling of the eyes and slouching halfway out of desks. Used judiciously, however, these stories can have the desirable effect. As Stahl and Nagy (2006, p. 155) commented, "Even though students rolled their eyes when they saw a story coming on (and do so to this very day), these are the teachers whom students remember. Be one of those teachers."

For their freshman English classes, Sara Jones and Kara Moloney assign a semester project, the "Word Museum" (Jones, personal communication, 2007; Moloney, 2008; Thomas & Tchudi, 1998). Originally designed for college undergraduates, the assignment has been adapted by Sara and Kara to help younger students develop a deep consciousness of a word, its etymology and evolution, and its denotative and connotative meanings over time. Each student investigates a word, creates a display, and the displays are shared in a culminating whole-class event—the Word Museum. Students are provided the handout shown in Figure 5.8, and Sara and Kara talk them through it, addressing any questions they may have.

The "word wall" to which the teachers refer comprises a number of core academic vocabulary words, and it will evolve and grow over the course of the year. Sara and

FIGURE 5.8   Word Museum Handout

Word Museum Assignment

A "Word Museum" is a celebration of words, word histories, and the diversity of the English language. On November 21st, we will construct a Word Museum in class. You are **each** responsible for creating **your own** display for our museum.

The Word Museum—Research

I will assign you a word from the word wall. If you love a particular word and want to work on it, please let me know BEFORE I hand out the words to the class.

Read about the history and origins of your word in *The Oxford English Dictionary*. **Copy** your word's entry in the dictionary. **Answer** these questions:

1. From which language did your word derive?
2. What is the first recorded instance of its use in the English language?
3. Write down some of the most interesting or surprising citations recorded over the years.

Find and copy an encyclopedia article that helps to explain what your word means or meant in the past. **Write** 1–3 sentences that explains why this information is important.

Find and copy a poem that helps to explain what your word means. **Write** 1–3 sentences that explain what your poem has to do with your word.

In Google, type your word into the search bar. **Write a paragraph** that tells how many sites use your word and explains how at least three of the sites use your word differently.

Collect evidence of your word in print, on TV, or another public source like a billboard. Simply write down how your word was used; then cite your source. **Do this** WITHOUT USING A COMPUTER. Your goal here is to find out about how the word has been used in the past, how it is used today, its different connotations, and its evolution.

Interview three people of varying ages **outside class** to find out what the word's current meaning is. Use these data to develop your own conclusions about what this word means in current and common usage. Ask your interviewees to

1. Define the word
2. Describe the word's connotations, overtones, innuendoes, and slang meanings
3. Use it as they would in ordinary conversation

The Word Museum—The Display

Create a display that shows the origin, evolution, and current meaning of your word. There are only a few requirements:

Your word is multifaceted. Your display should be, too. Therefore, the display should be **multidimensional.** Think about appealing to **all the senses.**

Make sure that the display shows ALL of your research—you won't receive credit for research that I can't see. Pack as much information into your display as possible.

Write a **1-page narrative** about your word. Incorporate your research (printed sources and interviews), course readings, and your own views on language usage and change.

An important part of your display is the **citing of sources.** Attach a completed bibliography to your display.

Have fun!

Kara show the students how to access the *Oxford English Dictionary* online. Teachers in school districts that do not subscribe to the *OED* online or have it in hard copy may have students instead go to the *Online Etymology Dictionary* (www.etymonline.com).

SPELLING–MEANING CONNECTIONS

Why talk about spelling when our focus is on vocabulary? Because, as pointed out in Chapters 2 and 4, helping students understand the connection between spelling and meaning develops vocabulary as well as improving students' spelling. Exploring this connection helps to emphasize word formation processes—the generative, morphological aspects of English vocabulary. In this section, this connection between spelling and meaning is examined more closely and in more depth.

The English/language arts teacher will be the guide to students' learning of the spelling–meaning connection, explicitly showing them how their understanding of this connection can support their vocabulary learning not only in English but in their other content areas as well. In exploring the spelling–meaning connection, we move from familiar words, through the less familiar, to the unknown. Students initially explore words that they know but often do not realize also share meaning relationships, words such as *type/typical* and *mine/mineral*. Over time, teachers support students' extending this understanding of spelling–meaning relationships to unfamiliar vocabulary terrain—exploring spelling–meaning families such as *punish/punitive/impunity* and *impugn/pugnacious/pugnacity*—in which the word root rather than a base word is the core unifying element in a spelling–meaning family.

Of course this is a book about vocabulary instruction, specifically about teaching vocabulary *their* way. And of course you've picked up on our recurring refrain: Teaching students about the many spelling–meaning connections in English orthography expands their vocabulary. And since English *is* the content area of the English teacher, it falls to us to sensitize students to the connection between the spellings of words and their meanings. The word sorts presented in Appendix D illustrate how your students can become aware of the connection between the spelling of a word and its meaning and how an understanding and appreciation of these spelling–meaning connections can expand their vocabulary by establishing links between known and new words.

LOOKING AHEAD

For English/language arts teachers, this chapter has extended the strategies and activities presented in Chapter 4 that support students' generative and word-specific knowledge. While it is the responsibility of English/language arts teachers to teach a *core academic vocabulary*, it is clear that this fundamental goal may be addressed in ways that develop and sustain students' curiosity about and enjoyment of words—their *word consciousness*. Chapter 6 will explore how students' word consciousness can extend to all content areas, while addressing the goal of teaching the specific academic vocabulary within each content area. In addition, students will come to understand and appreciate the significant role that their generative knowledge will play in supporting their learning of content-specific academic vocabulary.

6 Teaching Content-Specific Academic Vocabulary

CHAPTER

Remember the first time you saw a video of a dung beetle in action? Or a photograph showing the microscopic mites that thrive in our pillows and mattresses by the tens of millions? As your teacher intended, those images definitely got your attention and drew you into the subject at hand. That engagement also supported your learning of the appropriate vocabulary. What your teacher may not have shared with you, however, are the meanings and connotations couched within the structures of the words (see Figure 6.1). For example, the Latin term for one family of dung beetle is *trox horridus*, a name that immediately signifies something horrid. The literal meaning is even creepier; *trox* means "to gnaw," so this type of beetle is literally a "horrid gnawer." Another Latin term, *dermatophagoides,* for a family of mites, literally means "skin eating."

Both of these terms include word parts that most students may recognize in other more familiar words such as *horrid* and *dermatologist*. And *this* is where much of the value lies in sharing and examining the structures or spellings of the words themselves that represent concepts large and small. Connections are made within content area concepts—such as dung beetles, mites, and their functions—and concepts and general experience. A specific dung beetle (*horridus*, "scary") leads to associations with *horrid* and *horrible*. The *concept* that the word represents and the *spelling* of the word itself work together to deepen students' understanding.

Lemke observed that "the mastery of academic subjects is the mastery of their specialized patterns of language use" (1988, p. 81). As you help students construct knowledge of your discipline, you're also helping them learn the *language* of your discipline: the words that historians, mathematicians, or scientists use to talk about their worlds. Toward this end, this chapter uses the following organizational framework:

- *An overall instructional emphasis on generative and word-specific strategies and activities for each content area*. Examples are grouped together to encourage thinking across the subject matter areas and to underscore the similarities among ways of approaching different

FIGURE 6.1 *Trox Horridus* and *Dermatophagoides*

trox horridus   **dermatophagoides**

strategies and activities across all disciplines. As you read and think about each of the content areas, please keep in mind how activities may also be used, with different content, at any level of instruction for that subject. In addition, it is important to keep in mind that most activities work *before, during,* and *after* reading or exploring a unit. The examples provided in this chapter should help to illustrate this. Because prior misconceptions held by students are often difficult to break even in the face of new facts (cited in Pearson, Hiebert, & Kamil, 2007), by returning to earlier activities in a unit such as concept sorts and graphic organizers, students are much better able to determine what has been learned and is now understood that might have been unknown or confused before.

• *Tables of generative Greek and Latin roots and affixes for each content area.* These tables include only those roots and affixes that occur most often in a particular discipline. Becoming familiar with these generative elements, therefore, should provide students with a leg up on learning much of the vocabulary in that content area. As an additional generative element, many of these roots and affixes occur in other areas.

• *Methods to become comfortable talking about how roots and affixes combine to create meaning.* Examples are provided throughout the chapter for each content area, illustrating the ways that teachers can discuss the meanings that result from combining generative elements. Some of these "word narratives" are straightforward and literal—an *equilateral triangle* has three (*tri,* "three") sides that are equal (*equ,* "equal" + *later,* "side"). Some are more general—*endogenous* is the quality of being produced from within (*gen,* "produce" + *endo,* "within"). Students will still need to learn many specific examples of this process. An understanding of the general meanings produced by combining the word parts, however, will be a strong memory hook on which students can hang the specifics.

For the vast majority of words and their parts, however, we leave the narratives to you. You understand the nuances of the language of your content area. What we hope to do is help you realize the potential for these narratives to enhance content area study. The more you think about specific words and the generative elements of the words in your discipline, the more confident and comfortable you become talking about the words and language of your discipline.

VOCABULARY AND THE CONTENT AREA TEXTBOOK

The core resource for most content area teachers is the textbook. Together with continually evolving Web support, textbooks reflect the content standards for the subject and grade level. These standards are established by each state, usually with close attention to the standards developed by the professional organization of each discipline, such as the National Council for the Social Studies (www.socialstudies.org), the National Council for Teachers of Mathematics (www.nctm.org), and the National Science Teachers Association (www.nsta.org). Though textbooks may be the core resource, however, they should not be the sole resource. Content teachers supplement, elaborate, and extend instruction in many ways, and these should include the approach to and types of vocabulary instruction presented in this chapter. The concepts and vocabulary that are presented in your district's adopted curriculum, represented by the core textbook, should be a very good guide to your vocabulary selection and focus.

Understanding the structure of the textbook is an important part of developing the necessary background for a content area, scaffolding knowledge for exploring the discipline and its language and vocabulary. The organization of the textbook usually reflects the structure of the discipline. In algebra, for example, simple operations and equations precede and are necessary for understanding polynomials and factoring. History usually follows a chronological structure, though this is not an imperative, and innovative history teachers often complement this structure with other perspectives.

There are strategies for using textbooks effectively that have stood the test of time and of research (e.g., Blachowicz & Ogle, 2008; Fisher & Frey, 2007; Vacca & Vacca, 2007). They all incorporate aspects of basic educational psychology—*preview, read,* and *reflect:*

- Prior to the preview, help students get a sense of what they may already know about the topic, becoming aware of their own level of background knowledge.
- Then, as they preview, help them think about how the organization and presentation of information can provide support in thinking about important ideas and supporting information. Note and discuss titles and headers, boldfaced words, charts, and diagrams. Let them in on an important psychological trick: If it isn't already framed as such, turn each heading into a question. This simple adjustment "primes" their brain to be more attentive when they return to read in more depth.
- As students read, suggest that they keep prior questions and information in mind, make notes as necessary, and on reaching the end of a section, take a minute or two to reflect and think back on the information presented and how it fit with their prior understandings.

However, there are so many new vocabulary terms—and so little time, it seems—that you may have to streamline your approach by adapting the steps first presented in Chapter 4 in your selection of vocabulary. In general, as a subject matter teacher—or a teacher of several subjects in the intermediate grades—you will want to apply the following criteria:

- What are the "big ideas" that you will want to emphasize and develop throughout the year? As you plan for each unit or chapter, think about how these overall ideas are reflected by the vocabulary and concepts in each chapter or unit.
- Reading through the chapter and thinking about your unit as a whole, what are the words that represent the "big ideas"—the major concepts for which students will need to develop a deep understanding? Introduce and develop these at the beginning of the unit of study and before the reading, as well as during and after. Examples from math are *proof* and *algebraic expression;* from science, *organ* and *cell;* from social studies, *civil rights.*
- Which words are necessary for the specific reading assignment but do not require deep understanding? You may mention these, providing definitions, without exploring further unless it becomes necessary for some students.
- As with core academic vocabulary, which words are important but may be figured out by the students through application of their structural analysis strategy together with help from the context?
- Which of these words or ideas may be developed by walking students through the constituent roots and affixes?

New and important vocabulary in textbooks is likely to be shown in bold letters, italics, or treated in some way so as to draw attention to it. In addition, these highlighted terms are usually defined either in context, in a sidebar note, or in some other way right on the page where they first appear, as well as in the glossary of the book. Students need to be explicitly taught to use these sources of information and to pay attention to new vocabulary. While it may be possible to skip over unfamiliar words and still easily comprehend a piece of fiction, this is often not true when reading expository text whose very purpose is to introduce new concepts and the labels for those concepts. Teachers should preview texts to look for vocabulary that is not bolded but may present a challenge to their students. While new vocabulary is often listed in the teacher's edition or guide, the list may not be comprehensive.

Rare words, like those encountered in the sciences, are likely to have single meanings (Nagy & Scott, 2000). There will be words with multiple meanings like *organ* and *tissue* that will be used in new ways in the study of body systems, but words like *pathogen, loess,* and *epidermis* will only mean one thing. Teachers may find that textbook glossaries are more helpful than standard dictionaries both to supply the subject-specific meanings of words with multiple meanings like *front* and *resistance* and to offer well-developed definitions of new vocabulary. Some textbook glossaries have both English and Spanish. Glossaries will get heavy use when teaching vocabulary and they should be examined carefully as part of any textbook review process. Glossaries should include pronunciation guides but often do not.

GENERATIVE INSTRUCTION

It is especially important in the content areas for students to understand the ways in which meaningful word parts combine. This understanding will help them learn the key vocabulary of each content area, and understanding the roots and affixes that frequently occur in each discipline can generate an understanding of quite literally hundreds of additional words in each discipline.

To dramatize this effect, Sonia Gretzky, a secondary science teacher, talks about the root *struct* and discusses how its meaning, "to build," functions to contribute to the meaning of many words. She shares a complete list of *struct* words she obtained from www.onelook.com (similar to Figure 4.1 on p. 53) and comments, "Pretty impressive, isn't it? This one root occurs in well over 300 words in English! Now let's look at the root *hydr*—we don't see it too often, do we? Any ideas what it means?"

If there's no response, Sonia may ask "If you have to *hydrate* someone after a long soccer practice on a hot day, what does that mean?" She helps the students understand that *hydr* usually means "water" or "fluid." She then asks, "How many of you think this root will occur in more words than *struct?* Fewer words?" Sonia then shares the results of her Onelook search for **hydr**, and students are usually quite surprised to see that this root occurs in almost 900 words in English—more than three times as many words as *struct.*

Sonia continues: "Wow! We've got a lot of curious-looking words in these lists! Check them out: *dehydrochlorinase, hydrocephalous, sterhydraulic*—not exactly everyday words, are they? But somewhere inside of them, you know they've got something to do with 'water' or 'fluid.' And although you're not going to run into the word *dehydrochlorinase* very often, you *are* going to run into the root *hydr* quite a bit in science. In fact, you're not going to run into this root in many places *other* than in the sciences, such as biology and chemistry. So, for us, it's an important root to learn—as are a few others we'll be exploring this year!"

Conducting word sorts and exploring roots and affixes are those aspects of *generative* instruction that best develop students' awareness and application of generative learning.

Word Sorts

The word sorts from different content areas illustrated in this section illustrate how comparing and contrasting words and their *structures* can unlock and reinforce word *meanings.* Word sorts also offer opportunities for teachers to bring in interesting, often historical background information relating to the origins of many of the words and word parts. Our hope is that, over time, students begin to internalize these dialogues and modes of thinking about words, becoming motivated to explore further. Additional sorting activities with base words, affixes, and roots are provided in the lessons found in Appendixes A and B.

History/Social Studies.   The following sort focuses on the roots *crat/cracy* (rule, government) and *arch/archy* (rule), both of which originated in Greek. Related words may be matched and discussed. Have students work in pairs to match up the base and derived forms, then discuss their possible meanings. Most students will have at least heard most of these words, though they may be uncertain about the meanings, which can easily be checked in dictionaries.

cracy	*crat*	*archy*	*arch*
autocracy	autocrat	monarchy	monarch
democracy	democrat	oligarchy	oligarch
plutocracy	plutocrat	anarchy	anarchist
aristocracy	aristocrat	hierarchy	hierarchical
bureaucracy	bureaucrat	matriarchy	matriarch
technocracy	technocrat	patriarchy	patriarch

In follow-up discussion, the teacher explores with students their ideas about the meanings of *crat/cracy* and *arch/archy*, along with the dictionary information they found. For example, *plutocrat/plutocracy* refers to wealth and government or rule by the wealthy or rich. Although they realize it probably doesn't apply, on occasion students joke about Pluto, the beloved Disney dog, ruling. Actually, teachers may share with students that the Disney dog was indeed named after the planet Pluto (long before the planet was demoted to just a ball of ice). In Roman mythology, Pluto was the god of the underworld, and the underworld was not as scary as it later became in the Western mind. *Pluto* meant "wealth" in Roman mythology, because it was believed that the underworld was the source of wealth that comes from the ground—grain, gold, and so forth. The teacher shares a quote from Theodore Roosevelt: "Of all the forms of tyranny, the least attractive and most vulgar is the tyranny of mere wealth, the tyranny of plutocracy."

Following are additional morphological analyses that may be discussed:

- *aristocrat/aristocracy.* Literally, rule by "the best," though this has come to mean rule by the nobility and the rich.
- *bureaucrat/bureaucracy.* Literally, rule from "an office."
- *theocrat/theocracy.* Literally, rule by "God"—though in fact it is humans who are ruling, but claiming to do so in the name of a god, following his or her precepts.
- *oligarch/oligarchy.* Rule by "a few."
- *anarchy/anarchist.* In these words, *an-* is a prefix meaning "without" (as in *amoral*). Literally, *anarchy* is "without rule"—there is no government in control.

An excellent follow-up to this type of sort is the game "It's All Greek to Us" in Appendix E.

Science.   The following sort explores the suffixes *-phobia/-phobic* (fear), *-ine* (like; chemical substance), *-itis* (disease of; inflammation of), and *-ide* (chemical substance). These suffixes apply to a very large number of words in the sciences and might best be approached through an explicit walk-through before students sort the words that contain them.

First discuss the meanings of each of the suffixes in the words. The suffixes *-phobia/-phobic* come from Phobos, the name of the Greek god of fear and also the name of one of the moons of Mars (see "Greek and Roman Myths and Legends" in Chapter 5). (*Note:* If students mention that *-ia* and *-ic* are also suffixes, good! These suffixes have the meaning "relating to," so literally *phobia* and *phobic* both mean "relating to fear.") The suffix *-ine* can also mean "of or relating to," as in *serpentine*, *crystalline*, and *medicine*, or indicate a chemical substance. Prior to taking a course in chemistry or biology, understanding that the suffix *-ide* refers to a chemical substance is sufficient.

Discuss which of the words in this sort fall into the category "I've heard of it but am not sure of the meaning." You may wish to discuss some of them. After discussing the meaning of *claustrophobia*, for example, tell the students that the root *claustr* comes from the Latin word for an enclosed space—the same word that also generated *cloister* and *closet*. Or you may simply direct the students to look them up and study the etymologies before discussing with the rest of the group how the words have come to have their current meanings. Students may know that *arachnophobia* means "a fear of spiders" but may not know the myth of Arachne. *Xeno* comes from Greek and means "stranger"; illustrate its meaning with the sentence "During the war the nation was gripped by a wave of xenophobia."

-phobia/-phobic	*-ine*	*-itis*	*-ide*
claustrophobia	adrenaline	tonsillitis	monoxide
arachnophobia	alkaline	laryngitis	peroxide
technophobic	medicine	arthritis	bromide
xenophobia	chlorine	sinusitis	hydroxide
	crystalline		fluoride
	figurine		chloride
	antihistamine		
	serpentine		

This sort may be extended by generating other words that share spelling–meaning relationships with the words in the sort: For example, *arthritis/arthritic*; *tonsillitis/ tonsillectomy* (literally, *ec,* "out" + *tomy,* "cutting" of the tonsils). Note a link with Indo-European, by the way: *arth* comes from *ar,* the Indo-European root meaning "joint"; this Indo-European root is still evident in the word *arm.*

Math. This sort engages students in exploring the number prefixes *quadr-* (four), *tetra-* (four), *quint-* (five), *penta-* (five), and *deca-* (ten). An earlier sort would have addressed *uni-*, *mono-*, *bi-*, and *tri-* (for example, *mono*pod, *uni*lateral, *bi*ceps, *tri*athlon; see Greek Number Prefixes in Appendix B).

First, students will sort the words according to number prefix. Have them discuss any words they know or have at least seen or heard. Speculate as to their meaning: If *triad* refers to a group of three, for example, what does a *tetrad* refer to? If *tripod* refers to three feet, what does *tetrapod* refer to? Share the following sentence with students: "Scientists reported today that they discovered the leg bone of the oldest amphibian, a tetrapod that lived 360 million years ago." If *monarchy* refers to rule by a single person—a king or a queen—then what might a *tetrarchy* refer to? A *pentarchy*? While students may know *quintuplets* refers to five, share with them that the word *quintessence*, which refers to the purest or highest essence of something—"She was the quintessence of gymnastic ability"—historically and literally means from the fifth and highest "essence" after the essences of air, earth, fire, and water. The sentence "We now have the quintessential recipe for tacos" means that the recipe is the most representative one for tacos.

quadr-	*tetra-*	*quint-*	*pent-*	*dec-*
quadruple	tetrad	quintuple	pentagon	decimal
quadruplets	tetrarchy	quintuplets	pentangle	decathlon
quadrangle	tetralogy	quintessence	pentathlon	decathlete
quadruped	tetrapod	quintessential	pentathlete	decimate
quadrennial			pentarchy	

After several number prefixes have been explored, share with the students *why* there are different prefixes for one, two, four, five, and so forth: Greek had its own words for these elements; Latin had other words for them. Both sets of number elements survived and were passed down through other languages without significant change.

This sort may be extended by discussing why there seem to be so many Greek-derived words and elements that refer to *athletics.* This may evolve into an exploration of the value the Greeks placed on physical prowess and beauty.

Generative Roots and Affixes

As noted earlier, learning and understanding how the generative roots and affixes function within a content area will support learning of specific concepts as well as help students access new concepts. Note that terms appear as they represent concepts to be taught at different levels; this does not mean that they cannot be addressed earlier as they arise or as you feel appropriate.

We have shared many examples of how to talk about the generative aspects of words with students. As we've seen, much of this discussion occurs in the context of word sorts. But there are other, more focused walk-throughs of words, targeting structural relationships and discussing how meaning is created by combining morphemes—bases and affixes or roots in general. For each content area, examples of these walk-throughs are offered.

Mathematics.   The vocabulary of *geometry* (*geo*, "earth" + *metr*, "measure") lends itself quite obviously and transparently to the combination of Greek and of some Latin elements—for example, *sphere, diameter, hypotenuse,* and *symmetry.* Geometry has a long history going back to the Egyptians and Babylonians, who knew the Pythagorean theorem 1,000 years before the Greek mathematician for whom it is named. However, the ancient Greek Euclid wrote the first definitive book on geometry so it should come as no surprise that the study of geometry is full of vocabulary terms whose origins are Greek.

Algebraic terms are often not so transparent. Nevertheless, there is a sequence for exploring Latin roots in mathematics, and it begins with some simpler terms and concepts. Often, even Algebra II students are surprised when they learn how Latin elements contribute to the meaning of the simpler terms and concepts that they learned years earlier in elementary school.

For older students, share with them how the structures of the words they learned in elementary school hold within them the key to their meaning, as in the following examples:

- *Fraction* comes from the Latin word part *fract*, meaning "to break." If you break a bone into two or more pieces, you have a *fracture. Fractions* are a way of talking about breaking things into smaller pieces (like bones).
- *Circumference* may be broken down as
    ence—the result
    fer—of carrying
    circum—around
  which is literally what *circumference* means!
- A *triangle* is a figure with three (*tri*) angles. A *rectangle* is a figure with all right (*rect*) angles (yes, *rect* is the root of the common word *correct*, meaning "right").
- A triangle that has equal sides is an *equilateral* triangle, from the Latin *equ*, meaning "equal," and *lat*, meaning "side." (What other words do the students know that have *lat* in them? When you *lateral* a football you throw it to the side; *latitude* is literally a measurement around the *side* of the earth.)

Students' understanding about word structure with these more simple, familiar concepts can be extended to newer words and concepts.

- The prefix *com-*, meaning "together, with," appears in a number of terms assimilated as *con-* and *cor-*, and suggests "with" or "togetherness":
    *con*verse—"turn (*vers*) with," suggesting "opposite"
    *cor*respond—"respond or answer together"
    *con*centric—"circle together" or common center

- *Trans,* meaning "across," shows up in many words:
    *trans*late—"to remove from one place to another"
    *trans*verse—"turn across" (*vers*)
    *trans*form—"form across" or change shape
- *Parallel* and *perpendicular* are often confused by students. The prefix *para-* means "beside," as suggested in *paraphrase*—a phrasing that is "beside" or close to the original phrasing. It is commonly used to label various assistants who would work "beside" experts as in *paraprofessional, paralegal,* and *paramedic. Parallel* is composed of *para + allel* (from a Greek word meaning "other"); literally, one line that is "beside the other" line. *Perpendicular* is built around the root *pend* (to hang) and refers to a plumb line that would hang vertically or perpendicularly to the ground. *Pendant, pendulum, appendage, appendix, dependent,* and *pending* are also derived from the same root and all suggest hanging of some kind.
- After the formal definition and examples of a *tangent* have been provided, the teacher tells the students, "When something is tangible we say we can touch it. What do you think: Do tangents in math have anything to do with touching something?"

Table 6.1 presents generative roots and affixes for mathematics.

TABLE 6.1 *Generative Roots and Affixes in Mathematics*

	Intermediate/Middle Grades	Secondary
a- (L) not		*a*symptote ("not converging")
ab- (L) away		*ab*scissa ("cut away")
co-/cor- (L) with, together	*co*ordinate ("ordered together")	*cor*relation ("relate together")
circum- (L) round	*circum*ference	
syn-/sym- (L) together, with	*sym*bolic/*sym*metry/axis of *sym*metry/ rotation *sym*metry/line of *sym*metry	*syn*thetic geometry/a*sym*ptote
iso- (G) same, equal	*iso*sceles triangle ("equal legs")/*iso*metry	
equ- (L) equal	*equi*lateral triangle ("equal sides")/ *equ*ation/*equi*distant	
ex- (L) out	*ex*ponent ("to put out")	*ex*ponential notation
trans- (L) across	*trans*formation	*trans*verse/*trans*pose/*trans*lation
poly (L) many	*poly*gon	
cycl/cyl (G) circle	*cyl*inder	
fract (L) break	*fract*ion	
log (L) reason		*log*arithm ("arithmetic reason")
med (L) middle	*med*ian	
hedron (G) face	tetra*hedron*	
nom (L) name	mono*nom*ial	poly*nom*ial
quadr/quar (L) four	*quadr*ant/*quadr*ilateral ("four sides")	*quadr*atic/*quar*tile
cent (L) hundred	*cent*imeter/per*cent*	

continued

TABLE 6.1   Continued

	Intermediate/Middle Grades	Secondary
mill (L) thousand	*mill*ion	
kilo (G) thousand	*kilo*gram/*kilo*meter	
deci (L) ten *deca* (G) ten	*deci*mal/*deca*de/*deca*gon *deci*meter/(1/10th of a meter) *deca*meter/(ten meters) *deci*liter/(1/10th of a liter) *deca*liter/(10 liters)	*deci*bel (after Alexander Graham Bell) non*deci*mal numeration
liter (G) unit of weight	*liter*/milli*liter*/deci*liter*/deca*liter*	
gon (G) angle	penta*gon*/octa*gon*/hexa*gon*/deca*gon*/ poly*gon*/irregular poly*gon*/diago*n*al	trigo*n*ometry trigo*n*ometric ratio trigo*n*ometric relation
lat (L) side	quadri*lat*eral	
angle (L) angle	right *angle*/equilateral tri*angle*/scalene tri*angle*/isosceles tri*angle* ("equal legs")/ rect*angle* ("right [*rect*] *angle*s")/acute *angle*/obtuse *angle*/complementary *angle*/corresponding *angle*s	central *angle*/right tri*angle* geometry/ interior *angle*/*angle* bisector/*angle* of depression/supplementary *angle*
metr/*meter* (L) measure	dia*meter* ("measure across")/ peri*meter* ("measure around")/ sym*metr*y ("measure together")/ geo*metr*y ("measure the earth")	para*meter* ("measure/beside")
rad (L) root		*rad*ical/*rad*ical expressions
ratio (L) relation (reason)	*ratio*	*ratio*nal number
sect (L) cut	bi*sect*/inter*sect*	
pl(ic)/*pl*(y) (L) fold	multi*pl*y/multi*pl*ication	
sinus (L) bend curve		
		sine/arc*sine*/co*sine*
tang (L) touch		*tang*ent/line of *tang*ency

Science.   Once students have been shown how to explore words for Greek and Latin roots and affixes, the type of lesson shown here is very effective (Invernizzi, 2007). The example is similar in some ways to a vocab-o-gram in that students are making predictions prior to reading a selection, but it is different in that their predictions are based on only *one* term—notice how the teacher gets them to think about that term and other structurally related words.

Before reading and discussing an article based on the potential dangers of living close to Mt. Rainier in Washington, students make predictions based on the term *hydrothermal alteration*. The teacher asks them, "What would a passage about hydrothermal alteration on Mt. Rainier contain? What makes you think that?"

The teacher then guides the students in an examination of the word. "Look at the word roots."

hydrothermal   *alteration*
hydro   alter
thermal

"Now let's think of some related forms."

hydro	thermal	alter
hydrogen	thermal	alter
hydrant	thermos	alter ego
hydraulic	thermometer	alterable
hydrate	thermostat	alternate
		alternative

"Now, what do you think *hydrothermal alteration* might be in relation to an active volcano?" The teacher has helped students explore networks of words they already know that contain these roots, thereby activating and energizing their underlying understandings of meanings represented by *hydro*, *thermal*, and *alter*. She then helps them bring those understandings to bear on their thinking about the characteristics of an active volcano.

Biology. In the context of studying angiosperms and gymnosperms—plants whose seeds are enclosed within an ovary versus plants whose seeds are not so enclosed—the teacher walks students through an analysis of two words, *conifer* and *gymnospermous*. The science teacher presents the following display:

- *Conifer* is a combination of *fer* (bearing) and *con* (cones). The dictionary definition of *conifer* is given: "Any of various mostly needle-leaved or scale-leaved, chiefly evergreen, cone-bearing gymnospermous trees or shrubs such as pines, spruces, and firs" (*American Heritage Dictionary*).
- *Gymnospermous* is a new but critical term, so the science teacher reminds the students that they've already learned in English class the origin of *gymnasium* and *gymnast*—*gym* means "naked." They have learned in biology that *sperm* literally means "seed," so putting the parts together and reading right to left in *gymnospermous*: "containing" (*ous*) "seeds" (*sperm*) that are "naked" (*gymn*). (This usually brings hoots of laughter from adolescents—but they are certainly paying attention!) The teacher explains that the *o* is just a connecting vowel; it doesn't attach to either of the roots but makes the word easier to pronounce when the parts are blended together. When the students then examine pinecones that the teacher has distributed, they observe how the seeds are exposed. The concept that the word represents, and the spelling of the word itself, work together to deepen students' understanding.

Cellular Biology. New vocabulary terms presented in the reading material are usually key to understanding the concepts involved. Even rather intimidating words can be related to other words and word parts that students may already know to become easier to understand, read, and spell.

Before delving into the lesson "Homeostasis and Transport," the teacher guides the examination of the following important words:

hypertonic	endocytosis
hypotonic	exocytosis
isotonic	pinocytosis
	phagocytosis

The teacher guides the students into the terms by exploring roots in the more familiar terms *hyperactive, hyperventilate, hypertension, hypothermia,* and *hypodermic*.

She asks them to speculate as to the meaning of *hyper* and *hypo* in these words, and the students come to the conclusion that *hypo* has to do with "under" (as in *hypodermic* needle) and *hyper* with "over" (*hyper* or "over excited"). The students realize that *hyper* has in fact come to be used by itself to refer to someone's behavior or personality.

Returning to the new terms *hypertonic* and *hypotonic,* the teacher tells the students that *tonic* has to do with "stretching." So, the students conclude that the terms are dealing with "under"-stretching and "over"-stretching with regard to cells. The teacher points out that *iso* means "equal," as in *isometric,* so the students conclude "equal" stretching must somehow mean that a cell is "just right."

Sketching the outlines of cells on the board, the teacher goes on to explain that cells transport fluids through the cell walls. Three conditions are possible, she tells the students. "So if a cell had just the right amount of fluid inside the cell as there was outside the cell, how would we describe it? What if it was almost ready to burst because it had a great deal of water? What if the cell lost fluid and became shrunken and limp or pressure from outside caused it to shrink?" She then writes the definitions next to each term:

> *hypertonic*—excessive stretching due to too much fluid
> *hypotonic*—lack of stretching or the opposite of stretching due to too little fluid
> *isotonic*—equal stretching due to a balance of fluids inside and outside the cell

Next, the teacher discusses the root *cyt,* "cell or vessel," as in *cytoplasm,* and the suffix *-osis,* "process," as in *metamorphosis* and *osmosis.* She introduces *endo* and *exo,* and if the students do not know them she mentions that they are opposites like *hyper* and *hypo: endo* means "within," as in *endoplasm;* and *exo* means "out of, away from" as in *exoskeleton* and *exorcise,* which literally means "cut out."

Writing the following terms on the board, the teacher explains that they involve transporting substances in and out of cells; the students discuss them and decide which term applies to which process and arrive at a definition:

> *endocytosis*—"inside–cell–process" (the process of transporting into a cell)
> *exocytosis*—"out of–cell–process" (the process of transporting out of a cell)

The teacher and students talk about what kinds of things cells would need to transport in and out, such as water, oxygen, and nutrients.

The last two terms are presented:

> *pinocytosis*—pino = "drink" (*pino* does not show up as a root in many other words)
> *phagocytosis*—phago = "eat" (many words have the root *phag* including *esophagus* and *sarcophagus,* literally "eating flesh")

The teacher asks, "Which one of these involves the transportation of fluids? Of solids?"

Table 6.2 presents generative roots and affixes for science.

TABLE 6.2 *Generative Roots and Affixes in Science*

	Intermediate/Middle Grades	Secondary
amphi- (G) both	*amphi*bian	
cata- (G) down, reverse, thoroughly	*cata*clysm	*cata*lyst (loosen thoroughly)
endo- (G) within	*endo*thermic	*endo*genous
equ- (L) equal	*equ*ator	*equ*ilibrium of ecosystems
iso- (G) same, equal	*iso*metric	*iso*tope
syn-/sym- (L) together, with	photo*syn*thesis	molecular *syn*thesis/organic compound *syn*thesis/protein *syn*thesis

TABLE 6.2   Continued

	Intermediate/Middle Grades	Secondary
trans- (L) across	*trans*form/*trans*port/*trans*fer ("carry across")/*trans*parent	neuro*trans*mitter
proto- (G) first	*proto*type	*proto*lithic
quadr (L) four	*quadr*ant	
cent (L) hundred	*cent*imeter/per*cent*	
dec (L) ten	*dec*imal/*dec*imeter	
mill (L) thousand	*mill*ipede/*mill*imeter	
kilo (G) thousand	*kilo*gram/*kilo*meter	*kilo*watt/*kilo*hertz
anthr (L) man	*anthr*opologist	*anthr*opology/*anthr*opoid
cult (L) cultivate	*cult*ure	*cult*ure/*cult*ivate
cyto/cyte (G) cell		*cyto*plasm/lympho*cyte*
eco (G) house	*eco*system/*eco*logy	equilibrium of *eco*systems
hered/herit (L) heir	*hered*ity	*herit*ability
gen (L) producing	*gen*e/*gen*etics/*gen*eration	*gen*e encoding/*gen*etic diversity/ phylo*gen*etics/phylo*gen*y
ign (L) fire	*ign*ite/*ign*eous rock	
hydro (G) water, liquid	*hydro*gen/*hydr*aulic	*hydro*gen ion/*hydro*ponics
aqu (L) water	*aqu*arium/*aqu*ifer	
chrom/chrome (G) color	*chrom*osome/mono*chrome*	*chrom*atography
chlor (G) green	*chlor*ophyll	
leuko/leuco (G) white *alb* (L)	*leuk*emia *alb*umin	*leuk*ocyte
magn (L) great, large	*magn*ify/*magn*ification	
meta (G) beyond	*meta*morphic/*meta*morphosis	
morph (G) form, shape, structure	meta*morph*ic/meta*morph*osis	*morph*ology
plasm (G) to shape, mold	*plasm*a/cyto*plasm*/*plas*tic	
plast (G) small body, structure, particle	chloro*plast*	leuco*plast*
som (G) body	chromo*som*e	
ceph (G) head	*ceph*aplic	
card (G) heart	*card*iovascular	
derm (G) skin	*derm*atology	
neuro (L) nerve	*neuro*n/*neuro*transmitter	

continued

TABLE 6.2   Continued

	Intermediate/Middle Grades	Secondary
ichthy (G) fish	*ichthy*ology/*ichthy*osaur	
flu (L) flow *rrhea* (G)	*flu*id/*flu*vial/*flu*ctuate/in*flu*enza/ dia*rrhea*	
radi (L) ray	*radi*ate/*radi*ation/*radi*o (clipped form; originally *radiography*)	*radi*o wave/*radi*oactive
zym (G) fermentation *ferm* (L)		en*zym*e/lyso*zym*e *ferm*ent
phen (G) show, display	*phen*omenon	*phen*otype
phyll (G) leaf *foli* (L)	chloro*phyll* *foli*age	hetero*phyll*ous ex*foli*ate
dent (L) tooth *dont* (G)	*dent*al ortho*dont*ist/pterano*don*	
pter (G) wing	*pter*odactyl	
phy (G) natural		*phy*sics/*phy*siology
phyl (G) class		*phyl*um/*phyl*ogenetic
tom (G) cut	a*tom*	ana*tom*ical
sect (L) cut	in*sect*/dis*sect*	
pathy/path (G) disease, one who suffers from a disease	osteo*pathy*/osteo*path*	*path*ogen
sol (L) sun	*sol*ar system/*sol*stice	
stel (L) star *aster/astr* (G)	*stel*lar/conste*l*lation/inter*stel*lar *aster*oid/*astr*onomy	*stel*liform
therm (G) heat *calor* (L)	*therm*ometer/geo*therm*al/endo*therm*ic *calor*ie	
pyr (G) fire, heat	*pyr*ite	
phag (G) eat *vor* (L)	carni*vor*e/herbi*vor*e/omni*vor*e	bacterio*phag*e
algia/alg (G) pain	neur*algia*/an*alg*esic	
emia (G) blood, condition of the blood		leuk*emia*
-ician (L) specialist in	physi*cian*/dieti*cian*	
ate (L) having, characterized by	vertebr*ate*/invertebr*ate*/hydr*ate*	
-ide (L) related or similar chemical compounds or elements		monosacchar*ide*/ sodium chlor*ide*
-ine (L) chemical substance		chlor*ine*

TABLE 6.2   Continued

	Intermediate/Middle Grades	Secondary
-ite (G) rock, mineral, fossil	hema*tite*/trilob*ite*	
-itis (G) inflammation		appendic*itis*/bronch*itis*
-ic (G) the higher of two valences		stan*nic* chloride ($SnCl_4$)
-ous (L) the lower of two possible valences		stann*ous* chloride ($SnCl_2$)
-on (G) unit of	electr*on*/prot*on*/neutr*on*	phot*on*
-logy/-logist (G) science of, scientist	*geology* (science of the earth, studying the earth)/*geologist* (one who studies the earth)	
-phobia (G) abnormal fear	claustro*phobia*	

History/Social Studies.   The following two examples illustrate walk-throughs of several important generative roots.

The teacher begins a discussion about prejudice by writing the word on the board and asking the students what it means. Most students usually offer examples of prejudice before thinking about a "dictionary"-type definition. If no one points it out, the teacher then asks them if they notice which word *prejudice* comes from. Most students have never made this link, and if no one responds, the teacher writes the word *prejudge* underneath *prejudice*. He comments that all of their examples of prejudice involve situations in which a person, group, or idea has been *prejudged* by another person or group.

The teacher then writes the following words in a column:

    judge
prejudge
prejudice
prejudicial

The teacher asks the students to offer examples of how *prejudicial* may be used in a sentence. Then, working off of the base word *judge,* the teacher writes the following words on the board, underlining the root *jud* in each:

    judge
judicial
judiciary
adjudicate

Students discuss how these words are related, but many may not be sure about *adjudicate.* Using a sentence such as "The sports commissioner will adjudicate the disagreement between the coach and players," the teacher asks the students to discuss possible meanings based on the context and the root *jud* of the word. The teacher may then follow up by having students check in a dictionary or briefly explaining that when a judge or person in authority adjudicates a case, she "hears and settles" the case; literally, the word *adjudicate* means "to judge to or toward" something (*ad-*, the prefix, means "to or toward").

In the next example, the teacher discusses the roots of *politics* and *civics*. She writes the following words on the board:

politics
political
politician

She explains that the words come from the Greek word *polis*, meaning "city." In classical Greece, the city was the primary organizing form of government, and inhabitants of Athens, for example, considered themselves citizens of the city, not of a nation or country (concepts that would evolve centuries later). She asks the students to turn to a partner and think of other words that have the root *poli* in them; after about a minute, they share *police, policy, metropolitan,* and *cosmopolitan.* The teacher writes these on the board, discussing with the students what each of these words has to do with a city and which terms can apply beyond the idea of a city (*policy, cosmopolitan*). She adds *Minneapolis, Annapolis,* and *acropolis,* commenting that the students can figure these out on their own. (She knows that *acropolis* is unfamiliar; later in the unit, she will follow up and discuss with them the etymology they found in the dictionary: *acropolis* literally means the "tip" or highest point of the *polis*. In ancient Athens, the Acropolis was built on the hill above the surrounding city.) There are, in fact, hundreds of towns in North America with *polis* in their names—many students have never analyzed the meaning or origin of their town's name, and this awareness can begin the investigation.

The natural progression of this walk-through involves exploration of the word *city*. The teacher continues the discussion by pointing out that, while the Greeks had the word *polis* to represent the concept of "city," the Romans had the word *civis*, meaning "citizen" and *civitas,* meaning "city." The word *civil* is derived from these words and has to do with citizens and citizenship, including the civil rights that all citizens are entitled to in a democracy.

As she shares this information, the teacher writes the words in a column, underscoring the common element in each:

<u>ci</u>ty
<u>ci</u>tizen
<u>ci</u>vic
<u>ci</u>vil
<u>ci</u>vil rights

The teacher draws the discussion to a close by noting that, for the Classical Greeks, the concept of the *polis* or city was in many ways the equivalent of the later concept of a nation. And while the Romans eventually developed the most extensive empire up until that time in history, they began as a small agricultural community that evolved into a city, and as with the Greeks, this city was the core of their form of government.

Table 6.3 presents generative roots and affixes for history and social studies.

TABLE 6.3   *Generative Roots and Affixes in History/Social Studies*

	Intermediate/Middle Grades	Secondary
trans- (L) across	*trans*portation	
neo- (G) new	*Neo*lithic	*neo*classical
arche (G) ancient	*arche*ology/*arch*aic	
anthr (L) man	*anthr*opology/*anthr*opologist/ phil*anthr*opist ("love for mankind")	

TABLE 6.3   Continued

	Intermediate/Middle Grades	Secondary
nat (L) to be born	*nat*ion/inter*nat*ional/*nat*ional	
bel (L) war	re*bel*/re*bel*lion	ante*bel*lum period
cap (L) head	*cap*ital/*cap*italism/per *cap*ita	
civ (L) citizen	*civ*ic/*civ*il rights/*civ*il war/*cit*y	*civ*ilization
crit (G) judge	*crit*ic/*crit*ique	
cult (L) cultivate	*cult*ure/multi*cult*ural/agri*cult*ure ("cultivate a field")	*cult*ure/*cult*ivate
demo (G) people	*demo*cracy	*demo*graphic
ethn (G) people	*ethn*ic/*ethn*ography	
popul/pub (L) people	*popul*ation/*popul*ace/*pub*lic/re*pub*lic	
dic (L) say, speak	*dic*tator	
dom (L) home	*dom*estic	
eco (G) house	*eco*nomy/*eco*nomics	
eval (L) age	medi*eval*	prim*eval*
greg (L) gather	se*greg*ation/inte*gr*ate	
jud (L) judge	*jud*icial/pre*jud*ice/*jud*icial	
jur/jus (L) law, just	*jur*y/*jus*tice	
leg (L) law	*leg*al/*leg*islate	
liber (L) free	*liber*ty/*liber*ate/*liber*ation	
mono (G) one	*mono*narchy/*mono*nastery	
urb (L) city	*urb*an/sub*urb*/ex*urb*	
poli (G) city	metro*poli*s/cosmo*poli*tan/*poli*tics	
port (L) carry	trans*port*ation/im*port*/ex*port*	
*sen** (L) old	*sen*ate/*sen*ator	
soc (L) companion	*soc*ial/*soc*iety	*soc*iology
terra (L) earth	*terr*itory	
geo (G)	*geo*graphy	
vol (L) roll, turn	American Re*vol*ution	French Re*vol*ution/ Russian Re*vol*ution
-crat/-cracy (G) rule	demo*cracy*	auto*crat*/auto*cracy*
-ism/-ist (L) belief in/ one who believes		commun*ism*/commun*ist*/ capital*ism*/capital*ist*

*In Roman times, the meaning of the root *sen* also connoted "elder," which the word *senator* more directly meant.

FIGURE 6.2   Explore-a-Root: *sal*

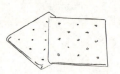

-sal-

Comes from Latin: salt

salinate: to make salty

saline: containing salt

desalinate: remove salt

salimeter: something that measures
salt content

salami: salted pork

salary: Roman soldiers were paid in salt

Others: salad, saltines, sauce (French),
salsa (Spanish)

Explore-a-Root: All Subjects.   Another way to investigate root meanings while turning responsibility for researching them over to students is with the *explore-a-root* process. Assign one root to each student with the challenge to find out its meaning, origin, and as many words as possible that are derived from it. They can be asked to each create a small visual display that can become part of a bulletin board and take turns reporting their findings to a classmate. Students might also enjoy creating a PowerPoint slide for each root so that all the slides could be compiled into a class effort. This way everyone could have a copy. Figures 6.2 and 6.3 provide two student-created examples.

A good dictionary with word origins like the *American Heritage Dictionary* or *Merriam-Webster Intermediate* in either hard copy form or on the Web is a good starting point for students. Students can search electronically for words using asterisks before and after the root (*sal* and *pter*) but need to understand that not all the words that turn up are related in meaning. Provide several books about the origins of words (see "Resources for Language History, Word Origins, and Greek and Latin Roots" on pp. 42–43 in Chapter 3).

WORD-SPECIFIC INSTRUCTION

As you read and think about each of the activities focusing on teaching specific word concepts, recall the suggestion at the beginning of the chapter: Please keep in mind how activities within each example may be used, with different content, at any level, and before, during, or after reading or exploring a unit. These activities very often include an assessment aspect that will help to focus and ground the learning that will occur. In addition, content inventories should help you assess the overall levels of students' familiarity with the subject that you teach. These are discussed in Chapter 8.

Concept Sorts

A *concept sort* will activate students' prior knowledge and raise questions about the topic they will be studying. They also afford possibilities for reviewing vocabulary and can be revisited at the end of a unit of study as a summative assessment. See Chapter 8 for more information about using concept sorts diagnostically. Following the guidelines presented in Chapter 4 for preparing a concept sort, key words are selected as well as characteristics and examples of each.

FIGURE 6.3   **Explore-a-Root:** *pter*

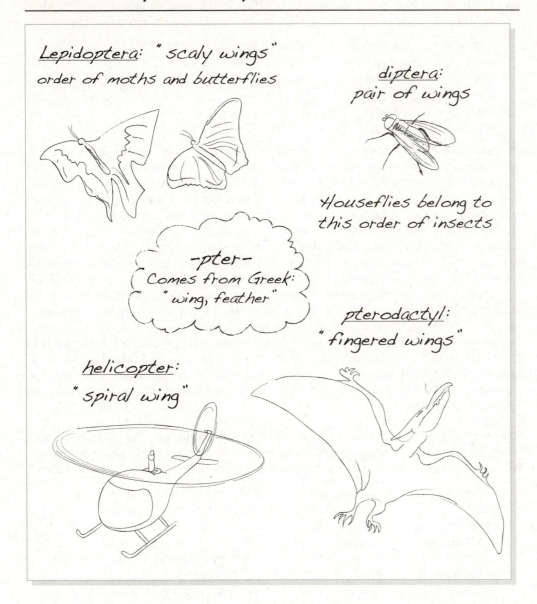

Earth Science: The Four Earth Systems.   For a unit on the four earth systems—atmosphere, biosphere, hydrosphere, and lithosphere—a concept sort could be created based on collecting terms from the chapter (for example, *mantle, organisms*) and also including a number of words that students already know (*gas, animals*).

Introduce the four category headers—atmosphere, biosphere, hydrosphere, and lithosphere—by writing them on the board. Students will probably know the word *atmosphere*—the air surrounding the earth. Have them speculate about *hydrosphere* (what do *hydro* and *sphere* mean?). This is an opportunity to apply students' work with word roots:

hydrosphere: *hydro* = "water," as in *hydroplane*
biosphere: *bio* = "life," as in *biology*

Lithosphere may elude them, but students may be able to figure it out a bit later from the characteristics and examples they discover.

Give each student a page with the words all scrambled up and have them cut it apart. Put up the four headers and ask them to sort the words under the appropriate header. They may work with a partner. The sort will look like the following list:

atmosphere	*biosphere*	*hydrosphere*	*lithosphere*
gases	organisms	water	crust
hydrogen	humans	glaciers	mantle
water vapor	animals	oceans	granite
oxygen	plants	groundwater	basalt
air	living things	icebergs	rocks

After the students have completed the sort, discuss it with them and try to reach agreement about where the terms are categorized. If there are words students do not know where to sort, set them aside in a "Don't Know" pile. For example, if they are uncertain about *lithosphere,* ask them to speculate about what it might mean—most or all of the words that could not be sorted under the other three headers have to do with the lithosphere, and that may give students a clue. The teacher may ask, "If granite and rocks are not living things, are not in the air, and are not floating in water, where might they be found? How would you describe the *sphere* where granite and rocks might be found?" The teacher or students would then follow up by checking the Online Etymology Dictionary or an unabridged dictionary, discovering that *litho* means "rock." Art students might have heard of *lithographs,* which are prints made with stones. The teacher may ask for definitions of other words such as *basalt* or *mantle.*

Wrap up the activity by explaining that the students will encounter these words in their reading in the chapter and throughout the unit, and they should pay careful attention to them. Students may save the words for additional activities in an envelope stapled inside their Vocabulary Notebooks (see the discussion of Vocabulary Notebooks later in this chapter).

Chemistry: Elements, Compounds, and Mixtures or Solutions.   As with the previous example, this concept sort is created using terms from the chapter (*covalent bonds, ionic bonds, isotopes*) as well as a number of words that students already know (*air, soil, water*).

Elements	*Compounds*	*Mixtures/Solutions*
gold	different atoms	seawater
pure	molecule H_2O	soil
one kind of atom	water	air
isotope	covalent bond	parts retain identities
molecule H_2	ionic bond	can be separated
hydrogen	metallic bond	made of elements and compounds
oxygen	salt	

Earth Science: Geological Forces That Shape the Earth.   Ideas and word lists for content-specific concept sorts are available in Appendix F. The words have been selected to represent significant concepts specified in the national standards for the different content areas.

Mass Movements	*Wind*	*Water*	*Ice*
creep	abrasion	runoff	glacier
mudflow	sand dune	delta	cirque
landslide	deflation	load	moraine
avalanche	ventifact	meander	drumlin
slump	loess	oxbow	eskers
earthquake	drought	flood	U-shaped valley
		alluvial plain	
		V-shaped valley	

Geometry: Planes and Solids.   Often, this sort is best begun with pictures or actual figures, which are particularly helpful with English learners. In addition to classifying according to planes and solids, the terms can be classified in other ways. For example, triangles could be classified according to lengths of sides or sizes of angles. The following sort classifies figures as planes or solids.

Plane   *Solid*

_____   _____

_____   _____

_____   _____

cube   triangular prism   rectangle   rectangular prism   cylinder   triangle

Geometry: Points, Lines, and Planes.   Terms to be sorted are words that represent the characteristics and examples of points, lines, and planes. The completed concept sort would appear as follows:

Points	*Lines*	*Planes*
pen point	edge of a ruler	piece of paper
collinear	parallel	desktop
A	A–B	floor
intersection of	intersection of	coplanar
two lines	two planes	3 points
	skew	
	segment	
	ray	

History/Social Studies.   As students move through a unit titled "Reformation and Counterreformation," they might conduct concept sorts with the words and concepts associated with either or both movements. One possible "target" sort is represented in the following list:

Reformation	*Counterreformation*	*Both*
self-government	Jesuits	New World colonization
indulgences	Council of Trent	Erasmus
Martin Luther	St. Ignatius of Loyola	
John Calvin	Catholic Church	
95 theses		

Graphic Organizers

Graphic organizers can be used before, during, or after a unit of study to capture related ideas. Teachers can use them to find out how much background knowledge students have about a topic and students can use them as a study tool. See Chapter 8 for ideas about using graphic organizers for assessment purposes.

Concept Map: Mathematics.   The example in Figure 6.4 would be appropriate for illustrating the characteristics of a concept map for older students, as well as for providing a review of some simple concepts often forgotten. "Adding with Mental Math" is the topic of one section in a unit. Different *properties*, the focus term or concept, illustrate how to add with mental math, and different property types are arrayed below the major focus, together with their definitions and examples. The related concepts of "breaking apart" and "compensation" are arrayed to the side. Alternatively, these two concepts could be addressed lower on the page, where examples could be shown.

FIGURE 6.4 **Concept Map for Addition Properties**

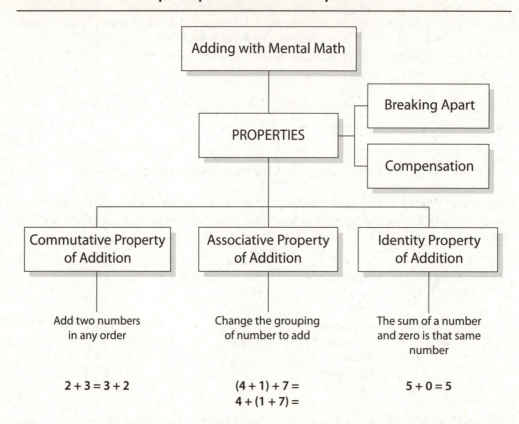

4-Square Concept Map: Algebra. The textbook definition of the target concept *linear function* is provided in the upper left quadrant of Figure 6.5. Students may also, in their own words, write a definition underneath the textbook definition if they wish. Examples and counterexamples will be discussed and entered. Constructing this 4-square should be a whole-class or small-group activity, so that the concept of rational numbers can be explored, discussed, and applied.

Semantic Feature Analysis: Earth Science. A semantic feature analysis as shown in Figure 6.6 offers another way to think about terms that might have been introduced in discussions or concept sorts such as the one described earlier for geology. Talk about the words across the top and the fact that many of them end in *-ologist*. Determine what that means (one who studies something) and then ask students which of the four earth systems each of the scientists would need to study. Use two plus signs for things they would need to study well and only one for related areas. A variation is to have students write a written reflection of why they marked the grid as they did.

Semantic Map: Science. In a unit on environmental issues the teacher writes the term *Population Density* and then brainstorms with students which factors might influence population density. They might explore both human populations and animal populations. Terms that students might suggest are *food supply, water, births, deaths, predators,* and *pollution.* The teacher then introduces some key vocabulary words—*dispersion, immigration,* and *emigration*—and guides students in categorizing the terms. As students read and discuss the content of the unit over several days, the categories may change with additional words added to the map.

FIGURE 6.5   4-Square Concept Map

Presenting Rational Numbers Conceptually

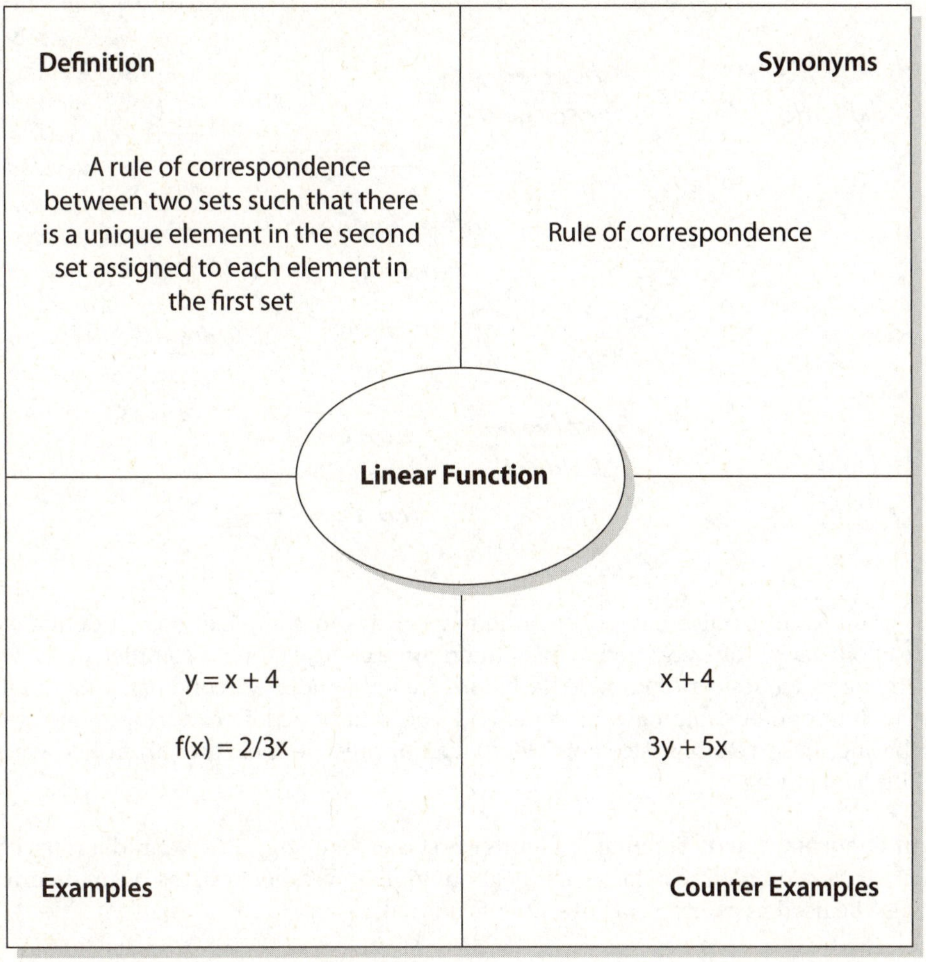

Definition	Synonyms
A rule of correspondence between two sets such that there is a unique element in the second set assigned to each element in the first set	Rule of correspondence

Linear Function

Examples	Counter Examples
$y = x + 4$ $f(x) = 2/3x$	$x + 4$ $3y + 5x$

Source: © David Chard 2006. Used by permission.

FIGURE 6.6   Semantic Feature Analysis—Earth Science

	geologist	biologist	ecologist	meteorologist	paleontologist	oceanographer
lithosphere	++		+		++	
atmosphere			++	++		
hydrosphere	+	+	++	+	+	++
biosphere		++	++		+	+

FIGURE 6.7   Student-Constructed Semantic Maps—Before and After

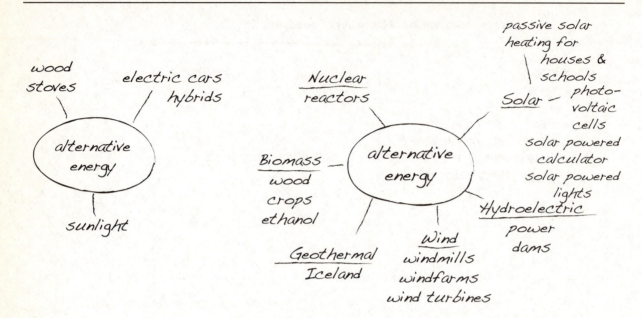

Figure 6.7 illustrates how a semantic map grows in complexity as students learn more about a topic of study, in this case "alternative energy." One is completed as a way to activate and assess prior knowledge before the unit, and the second one is completed as a way to demonstrate new concepts and vocabulary acquired during the unit. By comparing these versions, students clearly can appreciate their growth in knowledge and understanding.

Venn Diagram: Earth Science.   Figure 6.8 shows one student's Venn diagram constructed after completing a unit of study about violent weather systems. Venn diagrams can also be used as assessments of students' knowledge.

FIGURE 6.8   Student-Constructed Venn Diagram Comparing Tornadoes and Hurricanes

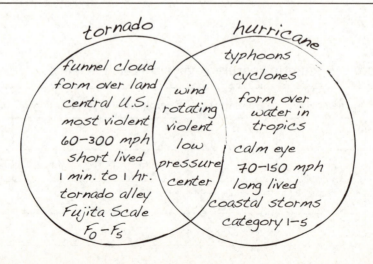

Venn Diagram: Mathematics. Given the following characteristics and examples, students can work in groups to construct a Venn diagram with one circle labeled *Triangle*, the other circle labeled *Quadrilateral*, and the overlap labeled *Both*:

Triangle	*Both*	*Quadrilateral*
3 sides and angles	equilateral	4 sides and angles
scalene	equiangular	parallelogram
isosceles	acute angles	rectangle
right	right angles	rhombus
sum of angles = 180°	obtuse angles	square
		trapezoid
		sum of angles = 360°

Vocab-o-Gram: Biology. A vocab-o-gram can be used to introduce a unit of study. For the following terms, students should make some guesses about what the words suggest and how they are related to the topic of blood. They may note, for example, that two words start with *anti*, which suggests "against." Three words end with *cytes* and students will already have learned that these have to do with cells. They have probably heard of white blood cells and red blood cells to link to these words. *Plasma* and *platelets* might also be familiar.

plasma   erythrocytes   hemoglobin   leukocytes   phagocytes

antibodies   platelets   fibrin   antigen   Rh factor   agglutinate

Vocabulary Notebooks: All Subject Areas. Chapter 4 described how Vocabulary Notebooks may generally be used; they are certainly a mainstay in English/language arts instruction. They should, however, also be a mainstay in other content areas—in whichever form works better for students, as either a single spiral-bound notebook tabbed for each different subject or as a tabbed section within the notebook for each separate subject. In addition to the guidelines provided in Chapter 4, here are some additional ways in which they may be used across subject areas:

1. As a follow-up to a concept sort, students write a sentence for each category:
   - "The biosphere includes all the living things on earth such as humans, animals, plants and other organisms."
   - "The lithosphere is the surface of the earth and includes the crust, which is made up of granite and basalt as well as the mantle that lies below the crust."
2. Students write using the target words in context:
   - Students write definitions in their own words.
   - Students write a summary of what they learned using posted vocabulary words (this may also be part of a learning log).
   - Students write questions for each other using the new vocabulary. The questions have to be in a form that indicates an understanding of the term. One way to do this is to challenge them to use two new words in one question. "Why would a geologist need to study the *hydrosphere?*" In "what part of the *lithosphere* is *granite* likely to be found?" Students can work in groups to answer each other's questions.
3. Vocabulary Notebooks may be the "home" for graphic organizers containing new vocabulary that students create on their own.
4. Ongoing word sorts are recorded in Vocabulary Notebooks. As existing words are used and additional ones are introduced throughout the unit, word sorts develop, maintain, and extend word and conceptual knowledge.
5. Students illustrate terms. For example, if you are studying coastal landforms students may create their own drawings to show *estuary*, *barrier island*, and *lagoon*.

FIGURE 6.9   **Power Map: Mexican-American War**

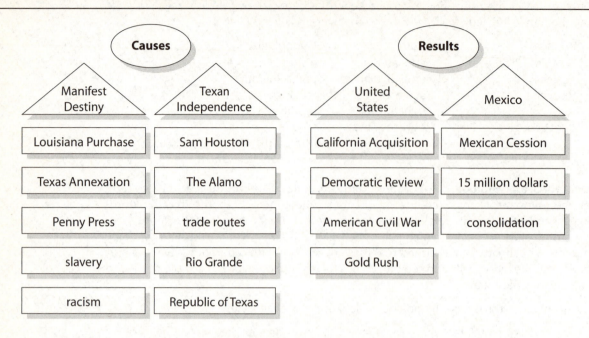

Power Map: History/Social Studies.   Power maps help students consider the relative importance of ideas. Echoing a theme of professional historians, Kevin Flanigan approaches his unit on the Mexican-American War with the objective of supporting his students' awareness and understanding that "many truths constitute the past" (Weber, 2006). Both the U.S. and the Mexican perspectives leading up to the war and after the war are examined. Figure 6.9 shows the completed power map based on main ideas (Power 1), subtopics (Power 2), and supporting details (Power 3) in the textbook section addressing the war. Kevin determined that his students had enough background to do the power map prior to moving into the unit; for another class, he may have determined that the map would be constructed after the unit had been underway for a couple of days.

Vocabulary Cards: Mathematics.   Vocabulary cards are especially good for related, straightforward definitions—more complex concepts lend themselves to other types of graphic organizers. Teachers should walk students through the process of using these cards:

• The term is written on one side and the definition, examples, or formulas on the back.
• Students can work with a partner; one student reads or shows a word for the other student to define.
• Show students how to sort words into two piles, *Known* and *Unknown*. Unknown words get reviewed until they are moved to the known pile.

Figure 6.10 provides an example for the term *exponent* in an algebra class.

FIGURE 6.10   **Vocabulary Card: Exponent**

---

front of card

> **exponent**

back of card

> The number of times a base number is multiplied. The superscript in an exponential expression.
>
> base 5^4 exponent
>
> $5 \times 5 \times 5 \times 5$

ETYMOLOGICAL NARRATIVES: STORIES ABOUT WORD HISTORIES

Many new words in the humanities and the sciences and mathematics are "big words," but breaking them into meaningful parts is in many ways like finding the episodes in a narrative. Let's return to Sonia Gretzky, our secondary science teacher.

Selecting a word that she knows many of her students are already familiar with, Sonia breaks *hydraulic* into its "episodes" for her students: *hydr*, which means "water, fluid" plus a Greek word, *aulos*, which means "pipe, flute." Literally, the early meaning of our present-day word *hydraulic* was "relating to a water organ"—an organ powered by controlling the water running through its pipes. She then asks for a volunteer to explain how hydraulic brakes work. They're not running on water flowing through pipes, but is the basic principle the same?

Exploring an academic domain or content area is really a narrative of inquiry. Words have stories about where they come from and why they have come to have the meanings they now represent. *Etymology*, as noted in Chapter 3, comes from Greek and means "the true sense of a word." Stories usually have both word-specific and generative characteristics. Teachers may plan to tell more in-depth narratives about some of the interesting vocabulary in their content areas, as well as providing shorter "mentionings," where appropriate, along the way.

At the beginning of the year, you might wish to share with students narratives about the origins of the important terms for your subject area. You will be able to build on this narrative as the months go by, but it's an engaging hook up front. The origins of the labels for the following academic domains are quite literal indeed:

- *Geometry* literally means "measuring" (*metry*) the earth (*geo*). A long time ago, farmers in the Mideast needed a way to reliably determine how much land that their plots covered so they wouldn't be continually bickering over what belonged to whom.
- *Mathematics* comes from the Greek meaning "to learn." A *polymath* is a person who has learned or become knowledgeable about many different academic domains.
- *Arithmetic* was first used by Archimedes, the mathematician who is credited with so many insights, including the potential of the lever—he uttered the phrase "Give me a place to stand and I will move the earth." *Arithmetic* describes operations with numbers and comes from the same root as *arm* and *arthritis*, meaning "to fit" or "join"—*arithmetic* literally means to fit and join numbers together.
- *History* comes from a root meaning "to inquire," from an earlier meaning of "wise, learned."
- *Science* comes from the root "to know"—students are often intrigued to learn how *science* works in the word *conscience:* Literally, *conscience* means "knowing with" oneself—it's not a far leap to realize how our present understanding of conscience has to do with knowing oneself.

- *Art* is a distant relative of *arithmetic*, in that art involves "fitting together" colors, shapes, and materials.
- *Music* comes from the *Muses*, mythological Greek goddesses who presided over the arts and sciences.

Following are some examples of how content teachers can use the structure of words in their respective content areas to share intriguing etymological narratives with their students.

History/Social Studies

How does the word *Mesopotamia* figure into a middle grade social studies teacher's lesson? Because the social studies/world history content standards for his state specify that students be introduced to the Babylonian Empire in the middle grades and study it in more depth in high school, Derek Tarleton helps to frame his students' understanding by beginning with a discussion of the Iraq War. He then tells them that part of modern-day Iraq includes what is known as "the cradle of civilization"; thousands of years ago, between the Tigris and Euphrates rivers in Iraq, a number of civilizations and empires developed, the most famous being the Babylonian Empire. Because this area was between two rivers, it became known as Mesopotamia, from the Greek words for "river" (underlining *pot*) and "middle" or "in-between" (underlining *meso*). Before he finishes his lesson with the students, Derek writes the word *hippopotamus* on the board, underneath *Mesopotamia,* and asks them to turn to their neighbor and discuss whether they notice any similarities between the two words. After a minute, the students share out; many will notice the similar letters *potam.* Reminding the students that *pot* means "river," he asks them, "Do hippopotami have anything to do with rivers?" The students agree that they do, and then Derek underlines *hippo* and tells them it comes from a Greek word meaning *horse;* "the Greeks referred to hippopotami as 'river horses'!"

Pointing to a map, he indicates the location of Baghdad, the capital of Iraq. He then points to two rivers, the Tigris and the Euphrates, and notes that Baghdad lies along the Tigris River: "Thousands of years ago, this area in between these two rivers, which includes Baghdad, was called Mesopotamia. It is often referred to as the 'cradle of civilization' because of the advanced civilizations that began and developed there. The most well known is the Babylonian Empire, whose capital was Babylon, down here about 50 miles south of Baghdad, on the Euphrates River. These civilizations all lay between these two rivers, the Tigris and Euphrates. And this is where the word *Mesopotamia* comes in, from the Greek words for "river" and "middle." (Later in the year, when students are learning about Meso-American and Andean cultures, they can make a connection by realizing how the name of the *Meso-American* culture describes its location.)

Here are two additional examples from history:

- In discussing the Pax Romana with her world history class, a teacher shares that *pax* is the Latin word for "peace." *Pax* can take the form *pace*, from which come our words *pacify, pacifist, pacification,* and *Pacific.*
- This teacher also shares with her students the origin of a famous phrase, *Veni, vidi, vici,* which they might encounter at some time. Supposedly posted in a letter sent home by Julius Caesar after defeating the Parthians in 47 B.C.E. (Parthia is modern Iran), it means "I came, I saw, I conquered." For a teacher, much of the power of this utterance lies in the related words that spring from the roots of *veni, vidi, vici.*

    veni = con*ven*e, con*ven*tion (come together)
    vidi = *vid*eo
    vic = *vic*tor, *vic*tory

Science

Chemistry teachers may share a brief narrative about the atom. While the existence of atoms was not confirmed until the late nineteenth century, their existence was first hypothesized approximately 2,500 years ago by the Greek philosopher Democritus. He was thinking about what happens when you keep cutting something up and reach a point where you cannot cut it up any smaller. He believed that whatever you have at that point must be the smallest unit of matter, and he referred to that unit as an atom, from the Greek word *atomos*—"that which cannot be cut." The word *atom* is made up of the root *tom*, meaning "cut," and the prefix *a-*, meaning "not." Of course, we have known for some time now that it *is* possible to "cut up" an atom into smaller particles, but when we do that we no longer have the element of matter we began with—if we began with copper or bismuth, we no longer have copper or bismuth. At that level, we have a lot of *sub*atomic particles, many of which may in turn be broken down even further. While *electrons* can't be broken down further, *protons* and *neutrons* can, and the resulting "sub-" subatomic particles reveal the universe of *hadrons*, showing even more interesting words worthy of exploration.

The origin of *chemistry* is intriguing. The word comes from Middle English *alkamie*, which came originally from Medieval Latin *alchymia*, which in turn came from an Arabic word *al-kimiy*. *Al* means "the" in Arabic, and *kimiy* refers to *chemistry*. Going way back, this term probably came from *Khemia*, the Greek name for Egypt. In a way, modern-day chemists are descendants of medieval alchemists, who believed a process could be found that changed ordinary metals into gold. Newton practiced alchemy throughout most of his life, and most alchemists also practiced what we would consider "legitimate" chemistry. Their desire to learn how to turn metals into gold was hardly a belief in magic; based on their understanding of chemistry at that time, this seemed a possibility.

Mathematics

Origin of the Calendar.   Discussing how the calendar evolved is of interest to students from the intermediate grades on, in part because it explains why the ninth month in the year, September, has the root *sept* (seven), the tenth month the root *oct* (eight), and so on. The early Roman calendar was supposed to have been introduced by Romulus, who according to legend was the founder of Rome. This calendar, which in reality was borrowed from the Greeks, who in turn borrowed it from the Babylonians, was based on the phases of the moon. It had ten months that covered 304 days. From a solar year perspective, that left 61 days kind of floating out there in the middle of winter. The first month of the year was March, the fifth month was named *Quintilis*, the sixth *Sextilis*, so *Sept*ember was indeed the seventh month, *Oct*ober the eighth month, *Nov*ember the ninth month, and *Dec*ember the tenth month. A calendar that did not match up to the solar year, however, became quite awkward, so Numa Pompilius, another legendary figure and supposed successor to Romulus, added the months of January and February, which brought the calendar to 355 days, closer to the solar year. *January* came from *Janus*, the god of doors who had two faces, one looking forward and one looking backward (new year/old year). This addition threw off the months that were named for numbers. As time went on, Roman politicians began playing around with the months, extending the days for some, subtracting days for others, all on a whim. Julius Caesar decided to change all that, and introduced the Julian calendar, substituting his own name (*July*) for *Quintilis*. His great nephew's name, Caesar *August*us (considered the greatest of the Roman emperors), was later substituted for the month of *Sextilis*.

Caesar's calendar worked rather well for many centuries, but by the late sixteenth century it was about 10 days off, so for this reason—as well as political reasons—Pope

Gregory modified the Julian calendar, and his version is the one used to this day among Western cultures.

Origin of *Multiply*.   The root *ply*/*pli* means "fold," as in *ply*wood and *pli*able. In mathematics, the word *multiply* literally means "to fold many times." The sense of "folding" may be illustrated by walking students through the process of folding a piece of paper two, three, four, and five times. What happens each time you fold the paper into another square? (Each time you fold into an additional square you are doubling by 2 the number of squares.)

> 1 fold = 2
> 2 folds = 4 (then take 4 and fold it into another square, you get 8—$2 \times 2 \times 2 = 8$)
> 3 folds = 8 (then take 8 and fold or "square" it, you get 16—$2 \times 2 \times 2 \times 2 = 16$)
> 4 folds = 16
> 5 folds = 32

You always have two halves to the paper, as it were, but when the paper is unfolded, you see twice as many squares as before.

Trigonometry.   Share with students that a "trigon" was originally a musical instrument in Greece. How many sides did it have? We still have the word *trigon* in *trigonometry*. So, we're literally measuring—*metr*—in terms of three. Trigonometry is, at its heart, the exploration of the angles and sides of triangles. The *o* between *trigon* and *metry* is a connecting vowel—it's there because it makes trigonometry easier to say.

Further Exploration

In this section, we have shared just a few examples to illustrate the possibilities of exploring etymological narratives. As we shared at the beginning of this chapter, we leave the rest of the narratives to you. The "Resources for Language History, Word Origins, and Greek and Latin Roots" on pp. 42–43 in Chapter 3 provides information for sources that provide some of the best etymological information available.

LOOKING AHEAD

For both generative and word-specific vocabulary instruction, teachers will be able to apply the strategies and activities presented thus far to students who are learning English as a new language. This is the terrain to be explored in Chapter 7, and that examination will complete our investigation of teaching vocabulary *their* way. Chapter 8 will round out that picture by examining assessment of our students' vocabulary knowledge, seeking to discern their underlying knowledge *their* way. Assessment to determine our students' word and concept knowledge and their generative or morphological understanding can provide the foundation for organizing supportive vocabulary instruction.

7 Vocabulary Instruction with English Learners

CHAPTER

In education, the term "English learners" is used specifically to refer to students who have learned a first language other than English and whose competence with English has not reached a level at which they can be taught exclusively in English. Of course, at some level we are *all* English learners. However, teachers at all levels are working with increasing numbers of English learners (ELs) who reflect an increasing diversity of languages, and there has been considerable emphasis in recent years on how best to accommodate this broad diversity. Approximately 180 different languages are spoken by students in American classrooms, and English learners enter classrooms with various levels of proficiency in English and reflecting diverse educational and socioeconomic backgrounds. While many teachers may at least be conversant in a second language, they probably will encounter students who speak one of those 179 other languages. Although the definition of English learners is very specific with respect to students who have "not reached a level at which they can be taught exclusively in English," all too often in contemporary classrooms the reality is that these students will in fact be receiving little if any instruction in their native language. Realizing this, a central theme of this chapter will be on establishing a supportive social context for lots of focused discussion in every classroom.

The preceding chapters in this book have presented the foundation, strategies, and activities for vocabulary instruction for our older students. All of these strategies and activities work equally well for English learners with just a few adjustments from time to time. For a number of reasons, students who are recent immigrants usually learn quickly the norms, vocabulary, and syntax of conversational English. Their challenge, and yours, lies with the more specialized academic vocabulary that is essential to success in school and in life. Accommodating English learners, however, is not a one-way street. Before focusing primarily on this rapidly growing population of students, the following observation about language learning in general must be noted.

English has been a universal language since the heyday of the British Empire and the international rise of American influence after World War II. This is why students in so many other countries study English and why many Americans whose first language is English believe that they have no need to learn a language other than English. The world, however, is becoming increasingly interconnected—"flat," in a popular characterization (Friedman, 2007). The necessity of native-English-speaking American students learning other languages is becoming increasingly important, if not critical. In this new context, therefore, effective instruction for English learners in the intermediate grades and beyond is a two-way street: At the same time English learners are acquiring knowledge of English, native speakers will be learning about the languages that English learners bring with them into the classroom. Guided by knowledgeable teachers, students traveling this two-way street will be more aware of the perspectives and experiences of others, more knowledgeable, and, it is to be hoped, better able to negotiate the challenges of this emerging interconnectedness in the twenty-first century.

In her freshman English class, Sara Jones plans to have her students explore different words that may be used to describe characters (as well as themselves). She writes the following words on the overhead:

elegant euphoric hyperactivity inquisitive artístico melancholic

eufórico creativo ambitious vanity melancólico generoso elegante

artistic generous ambicioso hiperactividad creative inquisitivo vanidad

Sara has the students work in pairs; she matches native-English-speaking students with students who speak Spanish at home, although they are all at intermediate or advanced levels of proficiency in English. She passes out a sheet to each pair with the words printed on it and asks the students to match words they think go together: the English word in one column and the Spanish word next to it in the second column. She expects that their finished word sort will look something like the following:

euphoric	eufórico
artistic	artístico
melancholic	melancólico
ambitious	ambicioso
generous	generoso
inquisitive	inquisitivo
creative	creativo
elegant	elegante
vanity	vanidad
hyperactivity	hiperactividad

Sara then guides the students in a discussion about how the words are alike and different. The students note the similar spellings and meanings. She asks them about the endings or *suffixes:* For example, words that end in *-ic* in English seem to end in *-ico* in Spanish. She asks them what Spanish suffixes appear to correspond to *-ous, -ive,* and *-ity.* She poses other questions as well: Do the suffixes have the same meaning in Spanish that they do in English? Do they mark the same types of speech? Which suffixes in English identify adjectives? Nouns? Which suffixes in Spanish identify adjectives? Nouns?

Next, Sara shows the students the following words:

mélancolique élégant artistique euphorique

généreux ambitieux créateur inquisiteur

She asks the students if they would have any problems in matching these words to the English and Spanish words. One of the students says that the words look like they are French; if no student had mentioned this Sara would have noted it. She then asks volunteers to write the French words in a third column next to their English and Spanish counterparts. She concludes this lesson as follows:

"We're going to be finding an awful lot of words in different languages that look a lot alike. They usually have a similar meaning or exactly the same meaning, and they're called *cognates.*" She writes the term on the board. "The term *cognate* originally meant 'born together.' Many cognates in different languages and the word parts they came from—like our examples from English, Spanish, and French—were truly 'born together' in a language spoken thousands of years ago."

On another day, Sara asks the students—if they haven't already brought this up themselves—about the diacritical marks or accents above certain letters in Spanish and French. What's their purpose? Students who are native speakers of Spanish and are literate in Spanish—or who are learning Spanish as a new language—can explain that these marks tell us which syllable is most strongly stressed or emphasized in speech. The marks may also be used to distinguish between homophones, as in *qué* (what) versus *que* (that). Students who are learning French may share that this mark does not show stress or accent but is only used with the letter *e* to show that it stands for a different sound than do other instances of the letter *e.*

THE CONTEXT FOR INSTRUCTION

In all classrooms, word learning most effectively and efficiently occurs when students are active members of a learning community (Bear, Helman, Templeton, Invernizzi, & Johnston, 2007; Echevarria, Vogt, & Short, 2004) and are engaged in purposeful talk (Bailey, 2006; Corson, 1995; Schleppegrell, 2004). Regardless of their levels of competence with English, English learners must be in the social situations—teacher–student and student–student—that support learning about the important concepts teachers are addressing. Research investigating the most effective *context* for this instruction supports the following:

- *A low-anxiety environment,* in which student interaction and learning activities allow students the opportunity to make mistakes.
- *Student-to-student interactions* involving peer discussions, cooperative learning teams, and other small-group activities. For students with more limited English, teachers should include working with a partner or having a peer translator if available.
- *Positive expectations for students* based on appropriate assessment of where the students fall along a developmental continuum (see Chapter 8).
- *Strong student-to-teacher connections*—these create the bond that supports learning; teachers at the middle and secondary grades have more of a challenge in this regard than teachers at the intermediate level, but it is a goal well worth striving for.

Research investigating the most effective instructional practices for English learners supports integrating the following characteristics (Bear et al., 2007; Echevarria et al., 2004; Freeman & Freeman, 2002):

- *Instructional-level teaching.* Match tasks and instructional materials to the developmental level of the students and to their background knowledge.
- *Modeling and think-alouds.* Provide examples of whatever task or activity is to be undertaken. Depending on the degree of abstractness, this often involves a multisensory input for English learners. As teachers "walk through" a task or activity, they "talk through" their thinking, making it explicit.
- *Modifying language.* Make the input comprehensible (Krashen, 1985) by talking more slowly, facing the students, emphasizing key words, and avoiding idioms. In addition, teachers can modify their language by the use of paraphrase, by providing examples and analogies, and by elaborating on student responses. Questions may be adapted so that student response can vary from pointing to simple yes/no or one- or two-word responses to a sentence response or even a more elaborate response.
- *Contextualize instruction.* Use real-life objects, expressive body language, and role playing.
- *Move from simple to complex.* Break down tasks and activities into sequenced steps, gradually moving to more complex formats. Along the way, guide students in the application of whatever is being learned, providing appropriate feedback.

When applied to vocabulary instruction specifically, the following practices ensure that these characteristics will be realized.

Wide Reading

Reading nurtures students' background knowledge, so essential in supporting vocabulary growth and development as well as being a source of new vocabulary (see Chapter 4). To the extent possible, English learners should also have access to texts in their home language, particularly if they are already literate in that language. The Internet is rapidly becoming a rich source for this access as digital libraries evolve and become more comprehensive (see, for example, the website of the International Children's Digital Library: www.childrenslibrary.org). Bit by bit, digital libraries are providing texts not only in Spanish but in a number of other languages as well, such as Arabic, Farsi, Swahili, Croatian, Russian, and Japanese. Although at present the International Children's Digital Library includes texts only appropriate through the middle grades, even older English learners will enjoy seeing these texts and sharing them with younger family members—as well as using them to help native English speakers appreciate and perhaps learn a bit about a different language.

It is also critical that you provide your English learners with texts in English that are on their reading instructional levels. Many publishers are now working to accommodate this need, so that teachers don't have to rely solely on a textbook or a single literary selection. This is commonly addressed through *text sets*, selections at different reading levels that address a single topic (Flanigan, Hayes, Templeton, Bear, Johnston, & Invernizzi, in press). Such an adjustment allows all students to be involved in exploring and discussing a topic or theme. The "primary" text or selection may also be made accessible through teachers reading aloud to students, as well as through audiotape, CD, or MP3 player and iPod downloads. The read-aloud is important, providing opportunities to scaffold further vocabulary and content instruction (see below).

Purposeful Writing

Purposeful writing of course addresses a broad range of objectives, and with respect to vocabulary development it provides students the opportunity to try out and exercise their developing word knowledge. Teachers should share and invite student involvement in online writing communities in which students with similar topic or writing interests meet and share ideas and writing. Similar in feel and collegiality to the MySpace, Facebook, and Twitter online environments, these writing communities usually are not school-related but invariably involve important learning objectives. Black (2005) provides a compelling and practical description of one such archetypal community (www.fanfiction.net) and its popularity among adolescent English learners.

Your students' independent writing will provide insights into their application of developing word knowledge as well as sentence structure and overall organization. For English/language arts teachers in particular, these insights will help in the planning of appropriate minilessons for individuals and small groups.

Reading to Your EL Students

During read-alouds, English learners hear the rhythm and cadence of written English. Because they may not comprehend and process the text as fully as native speakers, take the opportunity to explain, elaborate, and talk specifically about particular words, idiomatic expressions, or turns of phrase that may be unfamiliar to the students. In content areas, reading to the students can also be a means of creating instructional-level reading materials in a process called "Content Dictations" (Bear et al., 2007). In this process, if your textbook or content resource material is too difficult for students to read on their own, read it to them. Take time to clarify confusing vocabulary, answer questions, and share visuals relating to the topic. After your reading, have students then dictate to you what they learned from the material. If you have a TV monitor or LCD projector hooked up to your classroom computer, you can type what the students dictate and they can see it clearly on the screen as you do so. Afterward, print copies of the dictation for the students; these dictations then serve as additional "instructional-level" reading selections. The dictations reflect the students' vocabulary, sentence structure, and understanding of the topic or theme. As their English language proficiency develops, the dictations will also reflect their growing skills of description and summarization. The content dictation experience also allows teachers to help students clarify their understandings of the content and of the vocabulary that represents the important concepts or ideas, providing rich small-group discussion opportunities.

Ongoing Word Study Activities

The social and language context that supports word study activities, as well as the nature of the activities themselves, are critical for your English learners' vocabulary development. Word sorting activities with a partner, word games with small groups, word hunts, brainstorming and creating words from bases and roots, and recording information about words and word families in Vocabulary Notebooks are all important (Chapter 4).

DETERMINING ENGLISH LEARNERS' LEVELS OF ENGLISH PROFICIENCY

As much as is possible, teachers attempt to determine their English learners' development of English language proficiency. This development is described by the following levels (Bear et al., 2007):

- *Level 1—Emergent/Early Receptive Language.* English learners have little or no understanding of oral English. They usually attempt to communicate in their home language or with body language, gestures, and one- or two-word phrases.
- *Level 2—Beginning.* Students begin to show some understanding of oral English and are able to communicate expressively in short phrases, in contrast to the one- and two-word utterances of Level 1.
- *Level 3—Early Intermediate.* Students are able to respond with more understanding and comfort to a variety of communication situations. In their expressive language, they are becoming more fluent in phrasal expression.
- *Level 4—Intermediate.* Students have a large receptive vocabulary, they use most verb tenses correctly in conversation, and they understand and use most fundamental academic language. Their core academic and content-specific academic vocabulary, however, is still limited.
- *Level 5—Advanced.* Students demonstrate a high level of understanding and use of core academic and content-specific academic vocabulary, and their command of phrasing and syntax approaches that of native English speakers. They are able to learn content-specific information through English.

In addition to getting a sense of where your English learners fall along this proficiency continuum, you should find the following questions helpful as you and your fellow teachers gather more specific information to help guide your instruction (Bear, 2005; Bear et al., 2007; Dickinson, McCabe, & Sprague, 2003):

1. What language or languages does the student speak?
2. How often does the student use the primary language?
3. How common is the student's language in your school?
4. What is the student's preferred language when viewing television?
5. How long has the student been learning English?
6. How willing is the student to start a conversation?
7. Is the student understandable when speaking in English?
8. How often does the student attempt to use a variety of English words or try out new words heard or encountered in texts or from the teacher?
9. Does the student speak in connected phrases?

10. Is the student expressive in his or her speech, or does she or he speak haltingly and with little fluency?
11. Are there sounds in English that you notice are difficult for the student to pronounce?
12. How many years did the student receive formal education in her or his primary language? What is the level of literacy development of the student in the primary language?
13. Does the student read text in the primary language with accuracy, fluency, and expression?
14. Does the student use the primary language for writing in classroom activities?
15. In writing, does the student blend the primary language with English?

Several of these questions explore students' knowledge and language experiences in their primary language. Others explore their educational experiences. Students who have had rich educational experiences in their primary language have a strong foundation for acquiring English and for learning to read and write in English and have most likely already developed strong academic vocabularies in their home language.

WORD-SPECIFIC CHALLENGES FOR ENGLISH LEARNERS: HOMOPHONES, HOMOGRAPHS, HOMONYMS, AND IDIOMS

The concepts of homophones, homographs, homonyms, and idioms may be particularly challenging for English learners. Understanding and exploring the "H" words may not only facilitate vocabulary and reading comprehension, but spelling as well.

As noted in Chapter 2, the "H" words share the Greek root *homo*, meaning "same." Teachers can use the structure of these words themselves to help students learn what they stand for: same *name* (homo*nym*), same *sound* (homo*phone*), same *writing* or spelling (homo*graph*).

Students best understand how these "H" words work when the words occur in context and as students learn to read these words and gain an understanding of their meaning (Templeton, 2003). A simple *homophone* pair with which to begin instruction is *eye/I;* then, discuss the meaning of the homophones in sentences, such as the following:

> Emma is *merry* when she thinks about the man she will *marry.*
> The bird is going to *bury* the *berry.*
> The doctor must have *patience* to see so many *patients.*

Other homophones that could be discussed are *allowed/aloud, flour/flower, wait/weight, presents/presence,* and *they're/there/their.* In these discussions, take time to talk about the meanings of the words and how they are used in sentences—their functions. For example, *patience* describes a quality or characteristic of a person, while *patients* are a group of people who go to see a doctor. Draw out and encourage the students' use of their English skills in discussing these distinctions in homophones.

What do you do with the consistently confusable homophones such as the classic *there/their/they're?* Emphasize *meaning,* talk about how each word functions, and reinforce the correct usage of each during students' writing, particularly in the editing phase. The emphasis on spelling is secondary to understanding meaning and function, but as students think about the appropriate spelling in their writing, they will reinforce the connection to meaning and function. (By the way, students for whom misspellings of particular homophones persist—or other easily confused words such as *advise/advice*—may be encouraged first to edit a composition *only* for these particular words, before going back through with their editorial eye turned to other conventions.)

It isn't possible to know which pronunciation of a *homograph* is correct until its role in a sentence is clear. For example, share with students the sentence "Will you contest the contest?" Talk about the different pronunciations of *contest* and why this difference might occur. What distinguishes two-syllable homographs is where the accent or stress is placed within them, and this is determined by their function in a sentence. After discussing the meaning of homographs in the context of sentences, teachers may have students conduct a word sort in which the homographs are sorted according to their part of speech; the accented syllable in each word would be underlined:

Noun	*Verb*		*Noun*	*Verb*
pre̱sent	pre̱se̱nt		re̱play	repla̱y
pro̱ject	pro̱je̱ct		pro̱duce	produ̱ce
re̱cord	reco̱rd		su̱spect	suspe̱ct
pe̱rmit	permi̱t		tra̱nsport	transpo̱rt
co̱ntest	conte̱st		u̱pset	upse̱t
i̱nsult	insu̱lt		su̱bject	subje̱ct
re̱fill	refi̱ll			

When all the words have been sorted, teachers should read down each column with the students, placing extra emphasis on the accented syllable. This type of sort makes clear the role that part of speech plays with many homographs. If they function as nouns, the accent falls on the first syllable; in verbs, the accent falls on the second syllable. At a tacit level, native English speakers are sensitive to accent because it is an important feature in understanding spoken English, but even they may have some difficulty consciously attending to this feature. An emphasis on two-syllable homographs, therefore, will help them as well as English learners.

Homonyms are more often referred to as "multiple meaning" words, as in the following examples: *What do you mean by saying that? He is a very mean and angry person. The mean temperature here in the summertime is 87 degrees.* As with homophones and homographs, homonyms are best understood by examining their use in context, including their function in sentences.

The verbal art form of *puns* depends on homophones, homographs, and homonyms (Chapter 2). Such wordplay develops students' word consciousness, including their enjoyment of words: Which would you rather have in your side—a *pane* or a *pain*? Did you hear about the glassblower who accidentally inhaled? He ended up with a *pane* in his stomach (Lederer, 1996).

All languages have *idioms* and *idiomatic expressions* (Chapter 2). For English learners, these expressions are understood through continuous exposure, over time, and with some targeted instruction. After explaining the meaning of some common idiomatic expressions in English such as "to hit the jackpot" and "you're playing with fire," teachers may invite English learners to share some idiomatic expressions from their respective languages. The English translations will start cropping up in the conversations of native-speaking students! For example, *Cada quien tiene su manera de matar pulgas* is a Spanish idiomatic expression; its English translation is "Each has his way to kill fleas." The expression in English that captures this same sense is "There's more than one way to skin a cat." The Spanish equivalent of "Fools rush in where angels fear to tread" is *No hay nada tan atrevido como la ignorancia* and translates as "There is nothing more bold than ignorance." Hmong students of immigrant parents may be familiar with the expression *Ua sieb ntev,* which parents often use in teaching young children appropriate behavior. It literally means "make, do, or act with a long liver" but as an idiomatic expression refers to the patient endurance of wrongs or difficulties (Fadiman, 2006, p. 90).

GENERATIVE INSTRUCTION: EXPLORING THE STRUCTURE OF WORDS AS CUES TO THEIR MEANINGS

The vast majority of the most frequently occurring words in academic English are constructed by combining meaningful parts of words, so it is important for English learners to understand the nature of this process. While this process was covered in depth in several preceding chapters, the examples that follow illustrate how this process may be adjusted and introduced for English learners who are at least at the intermediate level of proficiency (see also the intermediate/middle grades sample lessons in Appendix A). The lessons presented in this section offer different ways and different levels of guiding English learners' understanding of the generative aspects of word structure or *morphology*.

Compound Words

Compounding, in which new words are created by combining existing words, is a universal language process. In Chinese, for example, compounding is the primary means by which new words are created. The activity below focuses on a collection of compound words that are fairly common in English (adapted from Bear et al., 2007). Show your English learners the following words and ask them if they see parts that are related. Have them work in pairs or small groups to sort the words into categories based on these similar parts. You may need to model two or three categories and sort a few words into each if necessary (see Chapter 4); for example, *airsick, airfare, airport / snowball, snowstorm, snowfall*.

> firelight   airsick   backpack   haircut   airfare   snowball   bookshelf
> backbreaking   fireplace   bookstore   scrapbook   hairbrush   firewood
> hairstyle   snowstorm   hairline   airport   backyard   airhead   snowfall

After sorting, discuss the meaning of some of the words and how the meaning relates to the two words that make up each compound word: *fireplace* is a specific *place* for a *fire*; *firewood* is *wood* for a *fire*; a *snowstorm* is a *storm* with *snow*; and so forth. On the face of it, these relationships seem so obvious that one might wonder why bother discussing them. Such discussion engages the language of relationships; as thinking about relationships among concepts becomes more precise, vocabulary grows. Later on, relationships among more abstract concepts represented in compound words will be more complex to sort out and discuss—*quicksand, deadbeat, pigeonhole, roughneck,* for example—so these discussions are an important foundation.

Conclude the lesson by discussing the term *compound words* with your students and help them develop their own definition based on the words they see in the sort.

Deriving Words from a Common Base Word

Understanding Prefixes.   Because the meaning elements within most English words are spelled consistently, teachers should emphasize these meaning chunks in their work with students. As this chapter's opening vignette illustrated, English words and affixes share considerable similarities with Spanish and French—as well as with many other Western languages. Although there are significant structural similarities in the ways many languages signal relationships among concepts and ideas, there is not perfect overlap. For example, in the following lesson, Stacy Wainwright—who has a number of native Spanish speakers in her middle grade classroom—is going to teach about the prefix *in-* and how it combines with base words. This prefix and its most common meanings, "not" or "opposite," occur in most Western languages with considerable frequency. Because of this, Stacy is beginning with *in-* rather than with *un-*, which is usually addressed first in a scope and sequence for native English speakers (see Appendix A). Modifying the first sample lesson in Appendix A, Stacy begins with common base words and then adds to them.

1. Stacy writes the word *correct* on the overhead and asks the students, "If an answer is correct, what does that mean?" Students discuss; if necessary, they discuss in pairs first.
2. She adds the prefix *in-* to *correct* and asks, "If an answer is incorrect, what does that mean?" Students discuss.
3. She writes the word *complete* on the overhead, and students discuss its meaning.
4. She adds the prefix *in-* to *complete*, and asks, "If an answer is incomplete, what does that mean?" Students discuss. "So, what do you think *in-* means?"
5. Stacy tells the students that the meaningful word part *in-* is called a *prefix*. A prefix is added to a base word to create another word.
6. For her native-Spanish-speaking students—if they haven't pointed it out already—Stacy writes the words *incorrecto* and *incompleto* on the board, and they discuss how these cognates are similar to the English words.

In the first sample lesson in Appendix A, the spelling *im-* for the prefix *in-* is also discussed; in this modified lesson, Stacy may wait to discuss *im-* until the following day. In the meantime, she asks the students to be on the lookout for words that begin with *in-* and write at least five in their Vocabulary Notebooks with the meanings that they think the words have; some of these words will then be discussed on the following day as well. As resources for her lessons with Spanish words and word parts, Stacy uses Davies's *Frequency Dictionary of Spanish* (2006) and is becoming more knowledgeable about using the comprehensive online "Corpus del Español" (www.corpusdelespanol.org); see the "Resources" section at the end of this chapter.

A number of prefixes are easily recognized in some cognates and have similar meanings. In Spanish, for example, there is *intolerante* (intolerant) and *revisar* (revise). On the other hand, the prefix *un-* does not exist in Spanish, and the prefixes *dis-, mis-,* and *de-* seldom occur. Their meaning is usually captured by the prefix *des-* as in *desconocido* (unknown), *deshonesto* (dishonest), *descorazonar* (discourage), and *desinflar* (deflate).

Base Word + Prefix.   In this activity, Stacy adapts the "Day 1" portion of the first sample lesson in Appendix A. She reminds the students what a prefix means and tells them that today they will be working with two new prefixes.

Stacy begins by asking them how to spell the word *misspell* (a word that is often misspelled). She asks them to discuss why there are two *s*'s in the word. If she needs to, she divides the word between *mis* and *spell* and asks the students if one of those pieces looks like a whole word. Because this word is frequently misspelled, discussing the meaning of *mis-* and what it means when combined with *spell* is an important and valuable process for students.

Next, Stacy displays the following words:

disappear	misplace
disagree	misbehave
disrespect	misjudge
disobey	misread
dishonest	

She points to each word in the "dis" column as she reads it with the students, and then does the same with the "mis" column. She then asks the students, "What do you notice about these words?" They will probably mention that the words in each column begin the same. "If something *dis*appears, what does that mean? If you *dis*agree with someone, what does that mean? If you *dis*respect someone, what does that mean?" Continue the same type of question with the *mis-* words. If the word *misjudge* is unfamiliar, use the following sentence and discuss what the word might mean: "Sometimes we *mis*judge someone when we think they will behave in a certain way and then they behave very differently."

Stacy continues: "So, what might we say the prefix *dis-* means?" ("the opposite of") How about the meaning of *mis-*?" ("wrongly")

She then explains, "There are two things we're going to do in our Vocabulary Notebooks today. First, write down our *dis-* and our *mis-* words. Then, write down our definition for *dis-* and for *mis-*."

Base Word + Suffix. The English comparative suffixes *-er* and *-est* are not found in comparable forms in Spanish, French, and a number of other languages. Because of their widespread usage in English, however, these suffixes and the relationships they signal should be directly addressed for English learners. The following lesson (adapted from Bear et al., 2007) illustrates how Stacy Wainwright conducts this type of investigation with her students.

First, Stacy displays the following sentences on a transparency:

Julie is <u>cold</u>.
Ferraro is <u>colder</u>.
Daniel is the <u>coldest</u> of all.

She asks the students how the underlined words are alike. The discussion highlights similar meanings and similar spellings. She follows with questions such as "Who is colder: Julie or Ferraro?" "Is Daniel colder than Julie and Ferraro?" For some students, it may be necessary to use concrete manipulatives to illustrate these relationships—such as for short, shorter, shortest or tall, taller, tallest.

Stacy then has students add *-er* and *-est* orally to known words: *close, kind, weak.* They discuss the differences in meaning, and if necessary, act out the terms to illustrate the differences in meaning. She then tells the students that *-er* and *-est* are examples of a *suffix*, a meaningful word part that is added to the end of a word.

Stacy displays the following words:

finer hotter cleaner nicest longer finest fancier cleanest
biggest funniest nicer longest angriest luckier angrier
bigger earlier funnier hottest luckiest earliest fanciest

Students read and, if necessary, discuss the words. She then models a word sort on the overhead by setting up four columns: *-er, -est, -ier, -iest.* She asks the students to help her decide in which column each word should go. As they sort, Stacy has them discuss the meanings of the words and what the suffix does to the base word. She sorts all of the *-er* and *-est* words, and if the students do not notice the difference between *-er* and *-est,* Stacy tells them: When comparing two things *-er* is used; when comparing more than two things, *-est* is used.

Stacy then sorts the *-ier* and *-iest* words. She asks them what the base word is in each case, and leads them to the realization that words that end in -y will need to have their comparative forms spelled *-ier* and *-iest.* The completed sort should look something like the following:

-er	*-est*	*-ier*	*-iest*
nicer	nicest	luckier	luckiest
hotter	hottest	angrier	angriest
finer	finest	earlier	earliest
cleaner	cleanest	fancier	fanciest
bigger	biggest	funnier	funniest
longer	longest		

Emphasizing Spelling–Meaning Relationships.   The spelling–meaning relationships among words are quite evident if teachers group words in spelling–meaning families and discuss these relationships. For example, when words are grouped together and "stacked," their visual similarity is obvious:

elevate	create	equal
elevator	creator	equality
elevation	creation	inequality

For both English learners and native English speakers, it is important whenever possible to use these related words together in your teaching to illustrate the core meaning that the words share. For example, an *elevator* literally *elevates* people to higher *elevations* in a building, but *elevation* is not usually used to describe ascending to a higher floor; rather, the most frequent use of *elevation* is usually in the context of talking about mountains. Instruction that builds on spelling–meaning relationships, therefore, has two parts:

- Stacking words and presenting them in spelling–meaning families teaches the core meaning that each spelling–meaning family shares.
- Using the words in context through conversation and direct teaching facilitates learning how the words are used and the types of contexts in which they are used.

As pointed out in Chapter 2, most productive spelling–meaning relationships reflect processes of derivational morphology. *Inflectional* morphology in English is often challenging for English learners to understand because the relationships it reflects are difficult to describe; inflectional morphology is part of the intuitive glue within sentences that is learned by native speakers over several years of meaningfully embedded oral exchanges. The "stacking" technique of presenting words that are related inflectionally, therefore—together with using words in context—is helpful in supporting students' awareness and understanding. Consider the following example, building on the base word *elevate:*

elevate	I <u>elevate</u> my feet.
elevate*s*	Xuan <u>elevates</u> his feet, also.
eleva*ting*	Xuan and I are <u>elevating</u> our feet.
elevat*ed*	Yesterday Xuan and I <u>elevated</u> our feet.

If you have studied another language, you are well aware of the "ripple effect" from changing almost any noun or verb; these changes set off grammatical rules that affect the spelling and selection of other words within the sentence. In the case of English inflectional morphology, a network of subject/verb/helping verb/modifier relationships that is intuitively obvious to native speakers appears quite complex to English learners. This is why your best approach, over time, is to combine directed lessons in these relationships with pointing out examples in students' reading and writing. This instruction, embedded in lots of conversations in which these relationships are evident, will lead students to understanding and generative knowledge.

Cognates

The instructional vignette at the beginning of this chapter illustrates the importance of cognates in language instruction and how they may be addressed in instruction. *Cognates* are words that have the same or similar meanings in different languages and are spelled the same or similarly, as the following list demonstrates:

camouflage	(English, French, Danish, Dutch)
camuflaje	(Spanish)
kamouflage	(Swedish)
kamuflaż	(Polish)

Students who become aware of, explore, and understand cognates acquire an invaluable tool that helps to bridge their heritage language with the language they are acquiring (August & Shanahan, 2006; Bear et al., 2007; Bravo, Hiebert, & Pearson, 2007; Diamond & Gutlohn, 2007). Attention to cognates is appropriate not only for English learners, but for native English speakers as well. As students read, talk about, and explore cognates they are learning much more than the meanings of particular words in a new language—they are learning processes of thinking about language in general and the types of language and contexts that scaffold meaning systems in the new language (Corson, 1995; Gee, 2005).

Table 7.1 presents a number of common, frequently occurring words in English and their corresponding cognates in Spanish, French, Italian, and German. As you look over the Spanish, French, and Italian words, notice how many are definitely cognates

TABLE 7.1   Common English Words and Their Counterparts

Common English Words	Corresponding High-Frequency Words			
	German	*Spanish*	*French*	*Italian*
first	erster	primero	premier/première	primo
last	letzte	último	dernier	ultimo
moon	Mond	luna	lune	luna
sun	Sonne	sol	soleil	sole
day	Tag	día	jour	giorno
night	Nacht	noche	nuit	notte
stop	anhalten	detener	arrêter	cessare
go	gehen	ir	aller	andare
brother	Bruder	hermano	frère	fratello
sister	Schwester	hermana	soeur	sorella
father	Vater	padre	père	padre
mother	Mutter	madre	mère	madre
boy	Knabe	niño	garçon	ragazzo
girl	Mädchen	niña	fille	ragazza
baby	Baby	bebé	bébé	bambino
house	Haus	casa	maison	casa
table	Tisch	mesa	table	tavolo
window	Fenster	ventana	fenêtre	finestra
school	Schule	escuela	école	scuola
money	Geld	dinero	argent	denaro
morning	Morgen	mañana	matin	mattina

for one another; the English words, however, are not. Some of the English and German words appear to be related—*last/letzte, night/Nacht, father/Vater, house/Haus*—because the origins of English lie with the Germanic language (Chapter 3). Notice that the Spanish, French, and Italian words appear to be more "literary" or "academic" than the English words. This has very important implications for vocabulary instruction with both English learners and native speakers as well.

Because the majority of English learners in the United States speak Spanish as their first language, most examples in this chapter will involve Spanish. Table 7.2 compares English words with Spanish words, arranged according to spelling: those that are spelled the same, nearly the same, "close enough" that they are recognizable, or different. For the words that are clearly spelled differently, there is an English cognate for the Spanish word that is more literary or academic, and this is included in the last column.

English learners are often surprised to discover how many cognates exist between English and their primary languages. Significantly, a very large number of English core academic or content-specific academic vocabulary words are cognates of more common, everyday conversational words in several other languages. This may be an advantage for English learners acquiring core and content-specific academic vocabularies in English. Examples of this phenomenon are shown in the "English Cognate" column in Table 7.2. For example, most English-speaking students will use the phrase "*prevent* something from happening"; in Spanish, the word for *prevent* is *impedir*, a very common word. The English cognate of *impedir*—*impede*—is not a frequent, everyday word in English but is definitely a core academic term that all speakers of English should learn. The core vocabulary word *tenet* (a principle or belief that individuals or organizations may *have*) is a cognate of the Spanish verb *tener* (to *have*), one of the most frequent words in Spanish. *Tenet,* on the other hand—though an important word to learn—does not occur nearly as frequently in English. The Spanish word for *young* is *joven*, which is much closer in appearance to English *juvenile* than is *young*. Not just in Spanish, but in many other languages as well—French, Italian, Romanian to name but a few—common, everyday words have English cognates that are *not* common, everyday words. Significantly, however, these English cognates are in fact important academic vocabulary.

TABLE 7.2 *English and Spanish: Comparisons across Cognates*

Spelled the Same	Nearly the Same	Close Enough	Different	English Cognate
doctor	system/sistema	courage/coraje	tenth/décimo	decimal
hospital	ambitious/ ambicioso	hybrid/híbrido	flower/flor	floral/flora
admirable		gravity/gravedad	seed/grano	granular
tropical	export/exportar		wind/viento	vent
variable	complete/ completar		prevent/impedir	impede
	instruction/ instrucción		egg/óvulo	ovulate
	nutrient/nutriente		have/tener	tenet
	condensation/ condensación		bug/insecto	insect
			young/joven	juvenile
			library/biblioteca	bibliography
			time (n.)/tiempo	tempo
			tree/árbol	arbor/arboreal/ arboretum
			cleavage/fisura	fissure

Awareness of cognates is of particular value in the sciences and in mathematics, in which most cognates share exactly the same or very nearly the same meaning. Compare these English/Spanish cognates:

mitochondria	metamorphic
mitocondrias	metamórfico
ecosystem	bacteria
ecosistema	bacteria
bisect	congruent
bisector	congruente
volume	precision
volumen	precisión

In recent years, textbook publishers have increasingly included attention to cognates, primarily English/Spanish, in science and math, due largely in response to state-mandated content standards and curriculum frameworks (e.g., California Department of Education, 2008; Texas Education Agency, 2008). This increasingly common practice in textbooks for intermediate and secondary grades can be a valuable resource for you in your instruction.

Many languages share cognates because these languages have inherited words and word parts from Greek and Latin. While the meaning of these words and word parts may have changed in subtle and sometimes significant ways as they developed within a particular language, usually they retain the same core meaning across languages. That is why instruction in cognates is potentially so important and effective. Because most students, beginning in the intermediate grades, are conceptually ready to begin exploration of both roots and cognates at the same time, it is not necessary to teach a number of Latin and Greek roots before exploring cognates (Templeton, 2009). All of this study supports and reinforces students' understanding of the spelling–meaning relationships in English. If anything, including cognates in our Greek and Latin root instruction may help students appreciate to an even greater degree the generative potential of these word parts (Stahl & Nagy, 2006; Templeton, 2004a, 2004b).

Beginning Cognate Instruction.   Cognate instruction should proceed from the obvious or transparent to the more abstract (Templeton, 2009). The first vignette at the beginning of this chapter illustrates an effective introductory lesson. Focus is on words in different languages whose spelling is the same, nearly the same, or "close enough," and which represent the same concepts. The correspondence between the English and Spanish forms of these cognates is direct and straightforward—*creative/creativo, artistic/ artístico, elegant/elegante,* and so forth.

The following cognates also illustrate this type of transparent instruction. The first set compares some words from the top 100 most frequently occurring words in Spanish (Davies, 2006) with their English counterparts; the second set is drawn from the most frequently occurring words in academic English (Coxhead, 2000).

English:	moment	part	person	form
Spanish:	momento	parte	persona	forma

English:	analysis	indicate	similar	specific
Spanish:	análisis	indicar	similar	específico

Recall the vignette at the beginning of Chapter 1 in which Tamara Baren explored the meaning of the root *dec* in several words, culminating with the story about how the meaning of the root once gave a literal meaning to *decimate.* An effective follow-up to that lesson would be to point out the English/Spanish cognates for these words, and to do so by reminding the students that some cognates are spelled the same, some are spelled nearly the same, and some may appear different but are "close enough" because they still contain a few of the same letters:

	Same	Nearly the Same	Close Enough
English:	decimal	decade	decimate
Spanish:	decimal	década	diezmar

For many students, as well as for the first few lessons in which cognates are examined, a structured lesson is advisable. To illustrate, here's how Khaled Akkeh set up one of his first lessons addressing cognates.

Using as a guide the *Kernerman Multilingual English Dictionary* (http://dictionary .reference.com/languages), Khaled selected the following words:

television	*computer*	*telephone*
téléviseur (French)	ordinateur (French)	telephone (French)
televisión (Spanish)	ordenador (Spanish)	teléfono (Spanish)
televisietoestel (Dutch)	computer (Dutch)	telefoon (Dutch)
televizyon (Turkish)	bilgisayar (Turkish)	telefon (Turkish)
televisi (Indonesian)	komputer (Indonesian)	telepon (Indonesian)

He then set up his students' exploration. On the interactive whiteboard, Khaled displayed a picture of a telephone, a television, and a computer. The English name for each appeared beneath each picture. He asked his students if they knew the names for *telephone* in a language other than English. His Spanish-speaking students suggested *teléfono,* and a student from Indonesia suggested *telepon.*

"Thank you! Let's take *teléfono*—how is that spelled?" As students call out the spelling, Khaled writes it underneath *telephone.* If they do not mention the *diacrítico* or accent mark, he stops after spelling the word and wonders aloud about something missing. Students who are at intermediate-level Spanish literacy usually will mention the accent; if not, he adds it and asks what it tells us about pronouncing *teléfono.*

"Now, how about *telepon*?" He also writes it under *telephone.* "Now let's think about *television.* What are some other words for *television*?" And so it continues.

After students have suggested other words, Khaled displays the following words, telling the students that some are from Spanish, some from French, others from Indonesian, still others from Dutch or Turkish. The letter following each word stands for the language from which it comes (an option is to turn to a map to indicate the location of the major countries in which these languages are spoken):

téléviseur-F   ordenador-S   computer-D   televisi-I

telefon-T   telefoon-D   bilgisayar-T   televisietoestel-D

televisión-S   telepon-I   televizyon-T   komputer-I

teléfono-S   ordinateur-F   téléphone-F

"Let's see which of these you've already suggested." As students call the Spanish and Indonesian words out, Khaled draws a line through each:

téléviseur   ~~ordenador~~   computer   ~~televisi~~

telefon   telefoon   bilgisayar   televisietoestel

~~televisión~~   ~~telepon~~   televizyon   komputer

~~teléfono~~   ordinateur   téléphone

"Now turn to a partner and decide where the remaining words go. It will be interesting to see if we have any words left that we're unsure about!" After a couple of minutes, Khaled asks the students to volunteer the remaining words; on the whiteboard, the students see each word then move to the column underneath the pictures of the computer, telephone, or television. *Bilgisayar* is the one left over.

"As we look down the *telephone* column, what do you notice about these words?" Khaled then responds as appropriate to the students' observations, discussing with them the similar letters and different sounds. Pointing to *televisietoestel*, he asks them if they have a clue to its meaning even though they may be uncertain of its pronunciation, and why. They discuss how *computer* is the same in English and Dutch and Indonesian *komputer* is very nearly the same, but how Spanish and French have *ordenador* and *ordinateur*, very different-looking words from *computer*. The students agree, however, that *ordenador* and *ordinateur* look similar; Khaled wonders aloud if they might have something to do with "ordering" or "organizing data and information—maybe that's where the similar spellings came from." Two students volunteer to look into that on an online translation site.

"And what about the Turkish word for *computer*? You know, I was really fascinated by that. Just for fun, I typed in *bilgi* on a translation website [the *Kernerman Multilingual English Dictionary* referred to earlier], and it turns out to be a word by itself in Turkish, and it refers to knowledge, learning, information, and data. I typed in the rest of the word for *computer*—*sayar*—and a similar-looking word popped up that has to do with counting and numbering. Putting these meanings together, like a compound word in English, we get the meaning related to counting or numbering knowledge, learning, information, and data.

"We've agreed that most of our words for telephone, television, and computer look more alike than different. Words with similar spellings and similar meanings in different languages are called cognates. Turn to a partner and talk about how cognates may be helpful to you when you're learning another language."

What had Khaled tried to do in this beginning lesson on cognates? He knows that a number of his students, including those who are in the early intermediate stage of English proficiency, will not be picking up on everything that he and other students are discussing. He does have a wide range of language competence and background knowledge represented in this class, and he has structured his lesson to capitalize on that. He has used pictures, chosen enough cognates that are clearly similar, provided for student- and whole-class discussion, and included some examples—*ordenador/ordinateur* and *bilgisayar*—that are appropriate for his more advanced students as well as serving to pique the curiosity of the rest of his class.

Cognates are not limited to single words. In the following example, a math and an English teacher at the intermediate grade level who often plan together address concepts that are represented by two or more words in both English and Spanish:

bar graph	compatible numbers
gráfico de barras	números compatibles
place value	congruent figures
valor de posición	figuras congruentes
equivalent fractions	
fracciones equivalentes	

When the English teacher has the students explore this variation in word order, she asks questions that often lead to a discussion about parts of speech. For example, "Do Spanish adjectives show number? Do English adjectives?"

While not exhaustive, the remaining instructional examples do provide some sound, basic approaches to the exploration of different aspects of cognates while facilitating student engagement.

Cognates and Suffixes.   In comparing cognates, students can benefit from exploring the suffixes that are often a part of the words. English learners studying English suffixes often understand their own language in more depth, and the same goes for English speakers studying another language. At the beginning of this chapter, recall how Sara Jones directed her students' attention to the several different suffixes shared by the cognates. She pointed out several within the context of the lesson; other teachers might begin with just one or two, depending on the proficiency and competence levels of their students. For example, after matching the following cognates, students would discuss how the suffixes are alike and different and discuss the possible meaning of each:

abreviación	abbreviation	creación	creation
anticipación	anticipation	imitación	imitation
declaración	declaration	vegetación	vegetation
elevación	elevation	vocación	vocation

As with other examples throughout this book and as shown here, related cognates should be "stacked" so that the similar spelling is obvious. Students may also compare the base words and the suffixed forms within each language, so that they think about the cognate forms and their derivatives the same way they think about the bases and suffixed forms in their own language. This will reinforce the meaning relationship among all of the words in a spelling–meaning family:

abreviar	elevar
abreviación	elevación
imitar	declarar
imitación	declaración
anticipar	abbreviate
anticipación	abbreviation
elevate	imitate
elevation	imitation
anticipate	declare
anticipation	declaration

English and foreign language teachers can have their students explore online translation websites, some of which are dedicated to individual words and phrases (a few of the most comprehensive are listed in the resource section at the end of this chapter). They provide rich terrain for exploring cognates, but they do not answer all the questions a neophyte language learner may have. Nonetheless, they offer innumerable opportunities for thinking and learning about other languages. Consider the following example.

On an English/Spanish translation website, students typed in *courage* in order to find the Spanish cognate. *Coraje* was first in a list of several Spanish words that came up; although not an exact spelling match, the visual correspondence between *courage* and *coraje* was close enough for the students to appreciate. Other listed Spanish words carrying the sense of "courage" were *arrojo, bravura, brío, denuedo, envalentonamiento, intrepidez, osadía, valentía, valerosidad, valor.* The teacher, Jeanette Spence, asked the students which of the Spanish words reminded them of English words. The students noticed *bravura* and *valor.* Writing these two words on the board, Janette engaged the students in discussion.

"So, you found not only an obvious cognate for *courage,* but some additional cognates as well!" She writes *brave* under *bravura* and *valor* under *valor.* "Let's look to see if we can discover some other Spanish words that are similar to English words . . ." After a few seconds, a student mentions *Intrepid*—it was the name of a ship in a story he was reading. As the teacher writes *Intrepid* underneath *intrepidez* she asks, "I wonder why they named the ship *Intrepid*? Does that have something to do with *courage?*" Jeanette asks if the students see any others. There's no further response, so she writes *valentía* on the board, and underneath, *valiant.* "If someone behaves or acts in a valiant manner, how might you describe that?" She then comments, "You know, one of us has a last name that is related to *valiant* and *brave . . .*" After a few seconds, one of the students hollers "Tina?" "Yes!" Jeanette responds. "Tina's last name is . . ." She pauses for the students to call out "Valencia" and writes it on the board.

"You know, we have the word *brio* in English—we've run out of time, so you'll need to figure that one out on your own! I wonder if it'll have anything to do with courage? If not, I wonder why the website lists it as a Spanish word associated with *courage?*"

On another day, an excellent follow-up question is to ask "Why did so many Spanish words come up when you typed in *courage?*" Students usually understand the concept of synonyms in their own language and often the social context in which different synonyms may be used, but when they begin to explore a new language they often expect a one-for-one correspondence between an English word and a word in another language.

Teachers who have native Spanish speakers in their classrooms encourage these students to describe the differences between different synonyms for a particular word, just as they encourage native English speakers to do the same with English synonyms. Such discussions help students to differentiate and expand concepts.

Cognates: A Deeper Exploration.   After exploring a number of transparent relationships among cognates, teachers may help students apply their awareness of cognates in more breadth and depth, exploring words that represent the same concept but that are *not* cognates. These words, however, live in a conceptual network that *does* contain cognate forms.

In her science class, for example, Lucia Gutierrez is teaching a unit focusing on ecosystems. She has already introduced and explored a few cognates in science, and she wishes to extend her students' awareness and knowledge of cognates in science and how cognate knowledge in general may help them. Most of her students speak Spanish at home, and they are reading on or close to grade level in Spanish. Based on their science textbook (Badders et al., 2007, p. H25), Lucia provides the following explanation:

"The terms *decomposer* in English and *desintegrador* in Spanish represent the same concept. Please turn to the glossary in our science text and let's compare the definitions for these words, *decomposer* and *desintegrador*. We see the Spanish definition for *desintegrador* is '*Ser vivo que descompone los restos de los organismos muertos.*' Do you think that *descompone* [writes it on the board], the verb in this definition, is a cognate of the English word *decomposer* [writes it beneath *descompone*]? How about *desintegrador* [writes it on the board]? Is it similar to *disintegrate* [writes it beneath *desintegrador* on the board]?"

When Lucia's students explore these types of relationships, they are involved in thinking more precisely about the features of the concepts that underlie terms such as *decompose/descompone/disintegrate/desintegrador*. They will explore how these cognates are alike and how they are different. For example, having already learned that a decomposer is a living thing that breaks down or *decomposes* the remains of dead organisms, Lucia's students learn that the term for a decomposer in Spanish is *desintegrador*. Lucia will explain that, while Spanish also has the cognate *descomponedor,* the term *desintegrador* is more precise in Spanish. This is an excellent opportunity for her to point out the English word *disintegrate* and to talk about the same core meaning that underlies the English words *decompose* and *disintegrate* and the Spanish word *desintegrador*.

Lucia is also helping students understand that, even when cognates exist, the use of the cognate in each respective language may be somewhat different. When reading a science text in English, the native Spanish speaker who comes across the word *soil* and who tries to think of a similar Spanish word (*suelo*) will be "close enough" to the appropriate meaning (the more precise term in Spanish is *tierra*).

Following are some examples of word pairs that illustrate the types of possibilities for exploration and questioning when cognates don't have a precise or exact match between or across languages:

addition/suma   library/biblioteca   constipated/estreñido

- For *addition* and *suma*, teachers may point out how these terms both represent the same operation in math. The English cognate of *suma*—*sum*—refers more specifically to the result of that operation—but it is "close enough" for Spanish heritage speakers to learn this more specific meaning of *sum*. The Spanish cognate of *sum*—*suma*—is close enough for English heritage speakers to learn the more general meaning of *suma*.

- *Library* and *biblioteca* both have to do with books. In this case, however, there is an excellent opportunity to point out to students that roots with the same or similar meanings can come from Greek and Latin words with the same meaning. The Greek root meaning "book" is *bibli;* the Latin root is *libr.* What are some English words that have *bibli* in them? What are some Spanish words that have *libr* in them?

- Most ninth-graders are still interested in and amused by just about anything having to do with bodily functions and fluids. Taking advantage of this, Jamal Banks—who teaches four sections of freshman English—writes the word pair *constipated/estreñido* on the overhead. He likes to give his students a "brain teaser" to think about overnight and address at the beginning of the next day's class, and he knows that this one will definitely get his students' attention. This time, he tells his students "I really don't have much to say about these two words, except that they have the same meaning in English and Spanish. Those of you who speak Spanish know a word in Spanish that looks a lot like *constipated*, but it certainly doesn't have the same meaning . . . yes, Antonio?"

"Constipado! It means, like, a cold, having a cold."

"Thank you, Antonio! And therein, ladies and gentlemen, is our brain teaser for tomorrow: What do *constipated* and *constipado* have in common?"

Beyond engaging the interest of his students, of course, Jamal's more consequential objective is to get his students to think of the core meaning of the cognates. They both have to do with being "stuffed up." Depending on his students' responses the next day, Jamal may explore the relationships among *estreñido* and *strenuous* in English—the notion of strain. Jamal does not need to become graphic at all; he will simply mention that "strain" may be involved in these conditions.

The following example, again from Tamara Baren's classroom, illustrates a common situation in which students feel they have a pretty good handle on a root—and then think of some other words that appear to have the same root but the meaning of the root doesn't seem to apply in those words. We don't want this situation to become a disincentive to learning about roots in general; notice how Tamara turns this disequilibrium into an opportunity to learn an additional root as well as some new cognates. Along the way, she also models what to do when a learner encounters an apparent "exception."

After talking about *decade, decimal,* and *decimate,* a student remembered seeing an ice cream ad that included the words "purely decadent." "What about that?" he challenged Ms. Baren. Tamara comments, "That's interesting . . . let's see what that might be about." She wrote the word *decadent* under *decade,* and continued:

"These two words sure look alike, don't they? But unless *decadent* has something to do with how many calories might be in the ice cream, the meaning of 'ten' doesn't seem to work, does it? What *might* it mean?" After discussing the possible meanings, Tamara asked one of the students to look the word up in the dictionary. The student said that the dictionary says "see *decadence*," so she looked that up and found that there are two definitions. Tamara asked her to read the first definition, which is "a falling off in quality or strength, a sinking to a lower state or level." Tamara asked the students if that definition applies to ice cream, and they didn't seem to think so. She then asked the student to read the second definition, which is "the tendency to give in to one's desires for comfort and pleasure." Several of the students exclaimed that *that* definition seems to work. Tamara asked them if the two definitions were in any way related. If they didn't pick up on her cue, she asked them if "giving in to one's desires for comfort and pleasure" could be an example of "falling off in strength, sinking to a lower state." If necessary, she asked them if they'd ever known anyone who was on a diet and was trying hard not to eat as many sweets, including ice cream, but their strength gave way and they gave in to their desire.

Tamara had the students check the etymological entry for *decadence* in an unabridged dictionary. They saw that it comes from the Latin words *de cadere*—literally, "fall" (cadere) "away" (de). Tamara talked about how this original meaning in Latin lives on in the modern meanings of *decadence.* She concluded by emphasizing that, although *decade* and *decadence* look like cousins on the surface, they actually have different roots. "When the meaning of a root that you know does not seem to help explain the meaning of a word you do not know—just like *decade* didn't help with *decadence*—do some more sleuthing. You'll usually learn both a new word as well as a new root." (With younger students the term "word detective" is effective; it's a bit of an eye-roller for older students, so "sleuthing" is more intriguing.)

The following day, as a sponge activity to pull students in, Tamara wrote *decadence* and *decadencia* on the overhead and asked the students to write a brief description of their meaning in their Vocabulary Notebooks. She did not mention that they are cognates.

Over these two days, Tamara addressed her original objectives of expanding her students' awareness and understanding of how the meaning of a root can become extended to apply well beyond its literal meaning (the meaning of *dec*) as well as incorporating student feedback (confusion about *decadent*). She kept her students' interest engaged while negotiating between her "prepared" lesson and her students' response to that lesson.

These few examples illustrate some ways in which teachers engage their students' deeper exploration of cognates. Inevitably, these explorations involve discussing what are referred to as "false" cognates—*constipated* and *constipado*, for example—and as the latter word pair illustrates, "false" cognates are usually not *totally* false.

Because cognates are presented most often as the same parts of speech, their spellings fall into the "nearly the same" or "close enough" spelling categories. Frequently, however, a different part of speech reveals a closer spelling. Teachers should be on the lookout for these, and draw on their students who speak other languages as valuable resources. This may also open up broader word families across languages, helping students become aware of and understand relationships that extend beyond cognate pairs. For example, *difficult* and *difícil,* both adjectives, are "close enough" in their spelling. By pairing the English adjective with the Spanish noun, however, the relationship now falls into the "nearly the same" category: *difficult/dificultad.* Similarly, the verbs *possess/poseer* are "close enough," but presenting the noun form in Spanish reveals they are "nearly the same": *possess/posesión.*

Collocations, or words that occur around the target word, are critical supports for English learners getting a sense of how words are used. Teachers will find the online *Corpus of American English* a ready source of authentic sentences in which target words are used. Different text genres may be searched; a quick scan of the occurrences of *difficult* in the magazine genre yielded the following examples:

> . . . it's not *difficult* to wonder . . .
> Agents have made it *difficult* for the athletes . . .
> I have been amazed at how *difficult* it has been . . .
> . . . more *difficult* decisions must be made

Students may easily learn how to use this resource and become involved in selecting words and representative sentences to illustrate them.

"False" Cognates. A small percentage of cognates are often referred to as "false"—although they are spelled similarly, they do not have the same or similar meanings between or among languages. Snow and Kim (2007) and Templeton (2009) emphasize the importance, however, of the exploration of "false" cognates: "Ideally, such pairs would be studied and the similarities as well as the differences in their meaning probed, rather than, as often happens, simply being dismissed as false cognates" (Snow & Kim, p. 131). Because of their shared etymological roots, it is rarely the case that two "false" cognates are truly unrelated. Although false cognates may not stand for the same exact referent, they often *do* belong to the same conceptual network. For example, when students realize that the Spanish/English words such as *asistir* and *assist, embarazada* and *embarrass,* and *constipated* and *constipado* do not have obviously similar meanings, they can discuss *possible* relationships. They become aware of how the different meanings developed, learning along the way the current meanings more efficiently and deeply. Older students are quick to realize how Spanish *embarazada,* meaning "pregnant," and English *embarrass* might be related.

Online translation sites make this exploration much easier and more productive (see the "Resources" section at the end of this chapter). To illustrate, Jamal Banks assigned different "false" cognates to pairs of students to explore and discuss and then report on to the class:

assist/assistir   ancient/anciano   antique/antiguo   content/contento

Languages without English Cognates.   What about students whose home languages do not include a Greco-Latin component and so do not share cognates with English— for example, Hmong, Chinese, Vietnamese, and Korean? The key is first to help these students think about language in general and what it does. Almost all languages do the same sorts of things—for example, use words and phrases that once had quite literal meanings that, over time, became extended metaphorically. All languages evolve, all languages have etymologies or word histories, and the writing systems of most languages carry within them keys and insights into these legacies. So, in addition to the word-specific strategies and activities we have discussed, teachers may build on students' understanding of their *own* spoken and written language and then extend these understandings to English. This type of reflection on language and its relationship to meaning is the type of metacognitive activity that is essential for learning a new language—and it benefits native-English-speaking students as well.

Encourage students already literate in their home language to share information about how meanings and words function in their native language; for example, talking about word structure and how different idiomatic expressions in the students' native language and in English can refer to the same event or situation (p. 137). With respect to word structure, for example, students whose home language is Persian or Farsi may demonstrate how Persian or Farsi script, like English, is alphabetically based: Arabic letters are also matched to sounds; however, the script is read from right to left. This is similar to Hebrew, which uses similar letters to represent consonants. Arabic writing developed a system of dots to distinguish its consonants from other similar scripts, such as Hebrew. In contrast, Chinese characters are not alphabetical; in both written Mandarin and Cantonese the symbols reflect more directly the meaning or morphological basis of the spoken language. The meanings of morphemes are consistently represented by the written characters.

If students are unable or reluctant to share, however, invite to class a bilingual/biliterate speaker of English and a home language of students in the classroom. They may give a brief explanation of how words work, for example, and answer students' questions. This helps English learners and native speakers alike think explicitly about how language functions.

Helen Shen, a native speaker of Mandarin Chinese, visited Sara Jones's freshman English class and teamed with Sara to compare and contrast written words in Mandarin Chinese with written words in English (see Figure 7.1). Sara wanted her students, some of whom speak a dialect of Chinese at home, to see how very different writing systems

FIGURE 7.1   Visual Meaning Patterns in English and Chinese

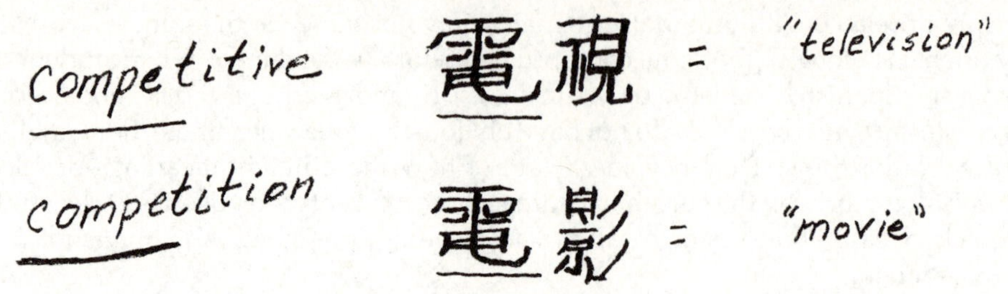

<u>competitive</u>

<u>competition</u>

電視 = "television"

電影 = "movie"

still are able to express meaning *visually* in the way they are written. First, using the English words in Figure 7.1, Sara reminded the students of the spelling–meaning connection in English—how words that are related in meaning are visually similar, despite differences in pronunciation. Then, Helen shared a few examples of Chinese words. She discussed how the character that means "electricity" appears in the words for television and movie and underlined in the character in each term (McBride-Chang, She, Ng, Meng, & Penney, 2007). This led to an interesting discussion about *how* different characters or morphemes combine and are understood by readers of Chinese.

Sara wrapped up the joint presentation by pointing out that both English and Chinese spelling have visual patterns that correspond to meaning, and that readers in both languages can learn to look for these visual patterns when they run into an unfamiliar word. They may recognize a pattern that is familiar, which may provide a clue to the new word.

RESOURCES

There are a number of online translation sites available. Those that are linked to major dictionary websites are most reliable, though it is important to bear in mind that translations for words and phrases are approximations—they will get you in the ballpark but it is always a good idea to check with a native speaker to determine correctness and appropriateness for use with your students. The *Kernerman English Multilingual Dictionary* (currently available at http://dictionary.reference.com/languages) is very good and is also accessible from one of the most respected dictionary websites (www.onelook.com). For Spanish, the *Corpus del Español* (www.corpusdelespanol.org), created by Michael Davies, is the best currently available. It provides information about the frequency and usage of words in different print and conversational domains: popular journalism, academic publications, conversational Spanish, and so forth. It also provides extensive information about collocations—those words and phrases in which a target word appears. Davies has also developed the *Corpus of American English* (www.americancorpus.org) which, in addition to being an excellent resource for English word study, may also be a helpful resource for planning lessons with English learners. Like the Spanish resource it, too, offers information about usage in different print and conversational domains, as well as collocations in different representative contexts.

Spanish Print Resources

Davies, M. (2006). *A frequency dictionary of Spanish: Core vocabulary for learners*. New York: Routledge.

Nash, R. (1997). *NTC's dictionary of Spanish cognates thematically organized*. Chicago: NTC Publishing Group.

Other Languages and Their Writing Systems

Bear, D. R., Helman, L., Templeton, S., Invernizzi, M., & Johnston, F. (2007). *Words their way with English learners.* Upper Saddle River, NJ: Pearson.

Birch, B. M. (2002). *English L2 reading: Getting to the bottom.* Mahwah, NJ: Lawrence Erlbaum.

Dictionaries for Students (excellent for defining words in accessible language and for using more familiar contextual examples)

Longman Dictionaries (Pearson). Longman publishes the most comprehensive group of dictionaries appropriate for English learners and bilingual students. Dictionaries for different beginning levels of English proficiency on up are available. Longman's *Dictionary of Contemporary English* is available online: www .ldoceonline.com

Collins COBUILD Dictionaries. Most of the Collins dictionaries have been specifically developed for older English learners and are appropriate for many *intermediate* and most *advanced proficiency* middle and secondary students. The English dictionary is available at the website, where reliable information about synonyms is also available, as well as links to bidirectional translation webpages for English and several other languages: http://dictionary.reverso.net/english-cobuild

LOOKING AHEAD

This chapter brings to a close our exploration of teaching generative and word-specific vocabulary strategies and knowledge across the various content areas, for both native-English-speaking students and English learners. As we explore the assessment of students' vocabulary knowledge in Chapter 8, it is important to note that effective assessment and effective instruction are really two sides of the same coin. For this reason, the discussion of assessment in Chapter 8 summarizes and extends much of the content of this book, emphasizing how we learn what our students know and are learning *during* our instruction. However, Chapter 8 also helps us plan for and think more directly about how we gather and make sense of our students' developing generative and word-specific understanding.

8
Vocabulary Assessment and Organization

Vocabulary assessment is an *ongoing* process that occurs before, during, and after instruction. Critical to the success of an ongoing assessment of vocabulary growth is involving students in the assessment process. Early in the year, introduce students to teacher-guided and student self-assessment activities, recognizing that many students may be unfamiliar with the assessment process. Help them realize that the informal ways you assess them or they assess themselves will give them a more complete picture of what they do and do not know about vocabulary. Explaining that assessment helps to bridge the known to the unknown can further engage students in their own assessment while learning from it. You might say to students, "With an assessment process in place, you will be able to be more accountable for your own learning and your own success in school." Then take time to explain some of the ways that you will test their growth in vocabulary knowledge.

Assessing vocabulary knowledge is a four-step process: observation, documentation, interpretation, and evaluation and planning. Table 8.1 provides an assessment model. In the first column, the four areas of vocabulary assessment are described. In the second column are questions that teachers can ask students about their vocabulary knowledge related to each of these four areas. Finally, in column three, activities related to the student questions from column two are listed. Many of these activities are found in Chapters 4, 5, and 6. This assessment model identifies how to involve students in each phase of the assessment process so they can understand the purpose of each kind of assessment and how it can inform their need for vocabulary study and thus affect their success in school.

This assessment process fits within the school schedule—the testing and grading periods—such as nine-week periods or typical school quarters. For example, Mrs. Nomura, a middle school teacher, provides time every week for her sixth grade students to document their vocabulary learning by placing materials in the vocabulary section of their three-ring notebooks. She also has them copy or take digital pictures of charts and large figures posted around the room that they have had a hand in making. Then each quarter, students review their notebooks to self-assess and grade themselves as part of the interpretation and evaluation of their vocabulary learning, using the questions listed in Table 8.1. Based on their self-assessments, students then set goals for the next quarter. Mrs. Nomura emphasizes how *value* is the basis of evaluation and that through the assessment process they will see how to value their own learning and, in turn, how she will value their learning.

TESTING AND GRADING

Testing and grading are part of the evaluation and planning parts of the assessment process. This is a time when teachers show students how value is placed on their vocabulary learning. Vocabulary learning for most students will improve when

- Grading and learning periods extend beyond the weekly cycle
- Instruction is at students' instructional and developmental levels
- Instruction is more intense and frequent (Bronfenbrenner & Morris, 1998)

TABLE 8.1   *Vocabulary Assessment Model*

Four Areas of Vocabulary Knowledge	Guiding Questions	Assessment Activities
Current Vocabulary Knowledge. What vocabulary students already know, and how deeply they know the meanings and concepts that underlie the vocabulary. Do they recognize and produce the vocabulary when needed?	What vocabulary do I already know? What relations do I see among words?	• Vocabulary self-assessment • Vocabulary brainstorming • Vocabulary Fist-to-Five • V-KWL • Concept sorts • Semantic maps • Ongoing review of Vocabulary Notebooks
Morphology. What students know about word structure: derivations, roots, and affixes.	Do I see word parts and relations within the vocabulary? What do I know of how words work? Do I know the meaning of prefixes, suffixes, and roots?	• Sorts for affixes • Producing words with affixes • Generating related words • Test of morphological structure • Homophone vocabulary and spelling assessment • Word study with words • Progressive Root Web • Study of inflected and derivational morphology • Study of etymologies
Learning Strategies. What types of vocabulary activities benefit students? Consider students' literacy development and instructional levels.	What are effective vocabulary learning strategies?	• Vocabulary cards • Self-study • List/group/label • Study groups • Vocabulary Notebook review • Oral support for materials that are at a frustration level • Partner sorts
Learning Goals. How students perceive their learning, what strategies they can develop, and what goals they establish and can achieve.	What have I learned? What do I value? What are my goals for learning new vocabulary? Where am I in my development as a reader?	• Goalsetting interviews • Self-assessments of what I know, what I can read, and what I can learn • Vocabulary self-assessment review • Content-specific spelling inventories • Academic vocabulary spelling inventory

The pace of the "weekly" vocabulary tests can be adjusted to create learning cycles that are paced to students' needs. Not everyone learns the same vocabulary in the same period of time. By extending testing periods, students study words more deeply and frequently because there is more time to schedule repeated practice and extension activities. Above all else, vocabulary learning and test scores advance when students read extensively and have opportunities to encounter new vocabulary words in their reading.

Testing vocabulary can take various forms, such as examining *production*, like assessing the vocabulary in students' writing or their ability to produce the vocabulary from the definition; or by examining *recognition* tasks, like matching vocabulary and definitions or choosing the best answer in a multiple-choice format. When correct spelling is attached to vocabulary testing, the amount of study time and the resulting performances vary by students' language and literacy development, the subject of the latter part of this chapter.

Rubrics, contracts, and schedules are often used to assist in grading, with points assigned to each aspect. Rubrics help to objectify the way grades are assigned. In the self-assessment process, students see where they started and where they can go. This process is motivating and leads to ownership. The teacher conferences with students about their grades require extra time to meet with students to review performance, contracts, and learning. This means that the rest of the class must be meaningfully engaged in individual, partner, or small-group activities.

Vocabulary Notebooks are integral to grading. Notebooks might be graded three times over a quarter grading period. Create a rubric by listing the required entries and vocabulary assignments and descriptions of how the quality of the entries relates to scores.

Before teachers complete their assessments and grading, students' views of their learning should be included in the grading process. Teachers and students use the same rubrics, and students compare their ratings with the teacher's. If the grade the teacher then assigns is a whole letter grade lower than what a student assessed for herself, the teacher should meet with the student to discuss the difference or discrepancy. These differences are infrequent when the criteria are clearly designed. Learning goals can also be crafted through this interactive process in which students' development and what they know are discussed. Goalsetting is an activity that can improve planning and motivation and will be described later in the chapter.

Not surprisingly, standardized testing is a central component in classrooms. Tests of vocabulary are included as subtests of comprehensive standardized reading tests; the Gates-MacGinitie Reading Tests (MacGinitie, MacGinitie, Maria, & Dreyer, 2000) and the Nelson-Denny Reading Test (Brown, Fishco, & Hanna, 1993) are good examples. In these tests, students most often choose the best definition of a term in a multiple-choice format and test-taking skills may improve performance. Because vocabulary subtest scores correlate highly with other reading scores, it is useful to check for discrepancies among the scores in reading, vocabulary, and spelling (see below), and uncover what may be contributing to these discrepancies. Vocabulary and spelling are the scores that most strongly indicate overall literacy proficiency.

CONTENT-SPECIFIC VOCABULARY ASSESSMENT AND LEARNING

Using guided assessments, teachers help students learn about themselves and assess their own learning needs. These ongoing assessment activities are conducted in several contexts, including individual, small-group, and whole-class settings.

Set the Stage for Students to Assess What They Know

The first area of vocabulary knowledge involves having students assess their content-specific knowledge when they approach a new topic. Showing students content vocabulary objectives and standards and asking them to determine the vocabulary and concepts they already know that are related to the next unit of study can help students link their knowledge to new content learning. You might begin this process in a discussion by asking open-ended questions. "What do you know about _____?" is an open-ended question frame that encourages elaborated student responses. Follow-up questions are also open-ended: "Tell us more about _____." Avoid questions that are answered simply with a yes or no. To be attentive and encourage student talking, teachers often chart students' responses on the whiteboard. Explain to students that exploring what they already know will guide you in knowing what to introduce to them, making you a better teacher. In this and similar "getting to know you" assessments, the students will be graded for their effort and cooperation and not by how many questions they answer correctly. Students are encouraged to answer even when they are not sure they know the answer. "Take a guess; you may have the right answer. Spell the words the best you can—you will not be graded for spelling. Write down your ideas the best you can."

The following assessments involve the students in monitoring their progress and learning. These assessments are ongoing and expand as knowledge is obtained. The first activity, Vocabulary Self-Assessment, is the most comprehensive and individualized. The other assessments are often conducted as small-group and whole-class activities in which the assessment process also teaches students learning strategies and study skills.

Vocabulary Self-Assessment

An interactive self-assessment that presents a scale for students to rate their knowledge of vocabulary (see Figure 8.1), vocabulary self-assessment is similar to scales used in research on vocabulary assessments (Pearson et al., 2007). The goal of this activity is for students to rate their knowledge of vocabulary periodically. Teachers want to see vocabulary words become like "old friends" to the students—familiar acquaintances accompanying them as they read, write, and speak. The vocabulary will guide students through the exploration of new ideas and worlds.

Begin by choosing important terms from an upcoming unit. A blank template can be found in Appendix G.12. Model how to rate one's knowledge of a word and then add related words. As can be seen in Figure 8.1, students signify when they are guessing with a question mark (?).

With a little practice, vocabulary self-assessments can become an ongoing activity. In the beginning, during, and at the close of a chapter or unit of study, students check through the vocabulary to see which words they are beginning to master. They can use different symbols each time, like those in Figure 8.1 (X, O, ✓), or a different color each time they work through the grid. Students continue to add vocabulary and related information throughout a unit. A column can be added for the source or page number for this word. These vocabulary self-assessments should be added to students' three-ring Vocabulary Notebooks or quarterly folders. Students can also use the blank template and select their own key vocabulary words in a section as they read and then complete the knowledge grid. This process creates a lifelong habit for identifying new vocabulary and monitoring a growing understanding of word meanings.

Vocabulary Brainstorming

Brainstorming is an important activity to conduct regularly in vocabulary instruction. The following assessment activity reveals how effective students are at brainstorming, both individually and in a small group. Students' vocabulary, ability to brainstorm, and spelling knowledge can all be assessed.

Directions
1. *Introduce the vocabulary brainstorming activity.* Tell students, "This activity creates a page in your Vocabulary Notebook that you may share with classmates later in small groups, or with me when we review your Vocabulary Notebook."
2. *Share an example or model briefly how to brainstorm and write down ideas.*
3. *Choose a topic.* Choose a word related to the content area that they know a lot about and are motivated to discuss.

FIGURE 8.1   **Vocabulary Self-Assessment for Weather**

Weather

Vocabulary Self-Assessment

Student _____   Dates _____*September 18*_____ (X)

_____ (O)

_____ (✓)

Vocabulary	Knowledge Rating			
	Never Heard of It	Heard It	Have Some Ideas	Know It Well
meteorologist				x *weatherman meteor ologist*
anemometer			x *measure, meter*	
doppler		x		
isobar	x			
hemisphere				x *half earth hemi sphere*
radiosonde	x		*radio*	
precipitation				x *rain, snow, etc.*
front			x *not back?*	

4. *Take two minutes to write down as many words about the topic as possible.* "See how many special words you can think of that are related to the topic. Even if you do not know how to spell a particular word, go ahead and write it down as best as you can."

5. *Have students work in groups.* Students divide into groups to discuss and combine the ideas they came up with individually. The "Classroom Organization" section at the end of this chapter presents a number of ways the students may be grouped. Have one person serve as scribe, another as timekeeper, a third as discussion facilitator, and a fourth as reporter. After 15 minutes of brainstorming, the reporters share their group's ideas.

Keep in mind the following considerations as this activity proceeds. Though there is no score for the number of items students brainstorm individually, teachers may consider differences among students. Students who are unable to brainstorm more than four or five words need to be observed further. Are they involved or motivated? Is their home language a different language than English? If so, what is their proficiency level in English? In addition to looking at individual brainstorming, reflect on the way students functioned in small groups and then how they reported their findings to the whole group:

- Are students able to generate items related to the topic? How many related vocabulary words do students generate? What is the range of words generated? Students who can think of related vocabulary words are in a position to understand a text on the subject. Students who cannot generate more than a few items related to a topic will benefit from prereading activities that build background knowledge.
- Analyze the types of vocabulary words that were generated. Do they include words that are found in the tests to be studied? How sophisticated or complex are the words that students generated?

There are other observations to make about the group dynamics, including the following:

- Do students move into groups easily?
- Are the dynamics of the small group productive?
- How are students' literacy proficiencies a factor in their interactions?
- Are students familiar with the various roles: scribe, timekeeper, discussion facilitator, whole-class reporter?
- What are the verbal interactions like in the small groups? Do students listen to each other?
- Do students pay attention during the time that the small groups are reporting?
- What grouping patterns would benefit interaction and learning?

Vocabulary KWL (V-KWL)

The KWL chart is a well-known way to record what students Know, what they Want to learn, and what they Learned (Ogle, 1986) about a topic. The Vocabulary KWL (V-KWL) is an adaptation of the KWL. Simply add a column for "Vocabulary" just before the "Learned" column. Introduce this first as a group activity and complete the chart together. Students can make their own copy to add to their Vocabulary Notebooks. As students read and add to the V-KWL chart, they can add page numbers to note where the vocabulary is discussed. The "Vocabulary" column also provides a list of key terms for review.

Variation.   A variation of the V-KWL focuses only on vocabulary. Students work with five or six key vocabulary words chosen from the content material. They record what they know about a term (for example, *chlorophyll*). The second column, under the W, is where students record what they want to learn about the vocabulary (for example, *What is chlorophyll? What does chlorophyll look like? What does chlorophyll have to do with leaves turning colors?*). In the final column, under L, students state what they learned (for example, *Part of photosynthesis. Why leaves change color. Chlorophyll is a "chlorin pigment," part of photosynthesis, liquid form*). Once students are familiar with the process they can be involved in choosing the vocabulary by finding five or six key words in what they are going to read and completing the KWL chart independently.

Vocabulary Fist-to-Five

Vocabulary Fist-to-Five is an adaptation of a consensus-building activity in which students vote with their fingers to indicate the strength of their opinions on a topic (Patterson, Patterson, & Collins, 2002). Students use their fist and five fingers to show what they know about each key term they are to study. There is a playfulness to this voting that students enjoy. Students see that other students are in the same or similar position as themselves. Create a listing like the following to explain the criteria:

What do you know about the vocabulary we are going to study?

5   I know a great deal. (I'm an expert. I think I made it up!)
4   I know a lot. (I understand the word. I can use it and explain it to others.)
3   I know a fair amount. (I know what it means when I read it.)
2   I know some. (I have just a little knowledge of the word.)
1   I know a little. (I have heard the word but I am not sure what it means.)
0   I do not know the word. (I have never heard the word and don't know what you're talking about. Am I in the right place?)

Just a few steps are involved in Vocabulary Fist-to-Five. Introduce the activity by practicing raising fingers on easy topics such as foods, music, and autos. "How much do you know about this type of music, food, auto, or clothing style?" or "I am serving you breakfast tomorrow (just kidding), and I want to know how many eggs to buy. Use your fingers and fist to let me know how much you like eggs."

The next step involves the five or six key words the teacher has selected: "When I say a word hold up your fingers to show me how much you know about the word." Teachers may explain that this activity helps them to be a better teacher: "How can we teach unless we know what you know?" Keep a good pace in voting—usually there is no real counting—though it is important that students hold their fingers up long enough for the teacher to see. Students will look around to see what others know about the topic, and teachers often respond, "Oh, it looks like we have a few experts here, but most of us know at least a little about oxygen."

Variation.   Vocabulary Fist-to-Five can also be a paper-and-pencil activity in which students write their responses on a piece of paper. This can be effective when students are a little shy and we wish to respect their privacy.

Concept Sorts to Assess Specialized Content-Specific Vocabulary

Concept sorting is an active and dynamic way to assess students' vocabulary and to see how they order and arrange concepts and then explain their thinking. In the process, concept sorts can reveal the depth and breadth of students' vocabulary knowledge. As with any sort, students read the words, sort the words into categories, and then share their reflections, explaining why they sorted the way they did.

Figure 8.2 presents a concept sort for intermediate or middle grade students studying basic chemistry in earth science (see Appendix G.6 for a copy of this sort and for the additional word cards). In their study of elements, compounds, and mixtures, students were given a closed sort that included the key words presented in bold. Students were instructed to read the sort and set aside words they did not know—words they could not read accurately and words for which they did not know the meaning. After sorting, students can be asked to record their sort and rationale in their Vocabulary Notebooks as a way to document their understanding.

Especially if sorting is new to students, teachers should begin with a closed sort like Figure 8.2 to teach them the process of sorting. Teachers talk to students about the key words used as headings for the sort. In the example in Figure 8.2, the teacher instructed the students by saying "Look at the key words, the words in bold print. Yesterday, we talked of ways to describe the chemical structure of the physical world: elements, compounds, and solutions or mixtures. In your sort, use these three words as the key words to head your columns for sorting."

At the end of a unit, students can be asked to complete the same sort again or they may be given a more complex sort that builds on the earlier sort to demonstrate what students have learned. See the additional uncut sorting pages added to Figure 8.2. When

FIGURE 8.2   **A Concept Science Sort on Elements, Compounds, and Mixtures**

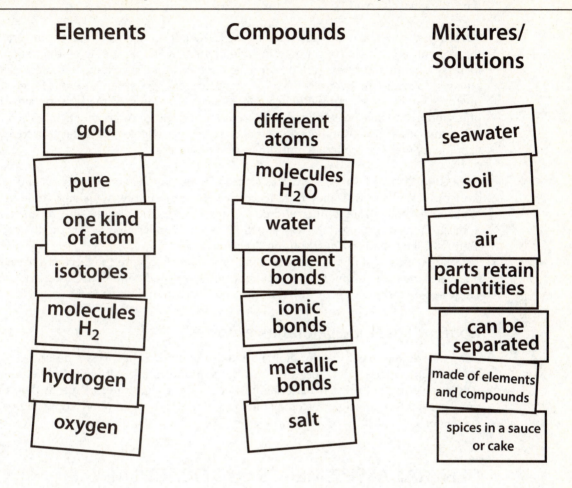

Elements

gold

pure

one kind of atom

isotopes

molecules H_2

hydrogen

oxygen

Compounds

different atoms

molecules H_2O

water

covalent bonds

ionic bonds

metallic bonds

salt

Mixtures/ Solutions

seawater

soil

air

parts retain identities

can be separated

made of elements and compounds

spices in a sauce or cake

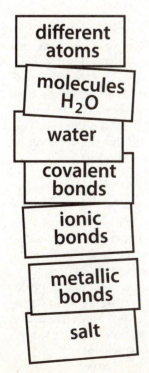

different atoms

molecules H_2O

water

covalent bonds

ionic bonds

metallic bonds

salt

unique properties	elements chemically joined	no reaction when joined	Oddball
molecules	atoms lose individual properties	homogeneous	particles
exist independently	composition	heterogeneous	chemistry
metals	chemical formulas	not chemically joined	gases
nonmetals	sugar	H_2	liquids
2 is a subscript for oxygen	solids	gases	

students can cut apart these cards and sort them conceptually, they have generalized what they have learned.

Variations.   To make this an ongoing activity, additional word cards are added throughout units of study and may include phrases, symbols, and even diagrams. To increase the difficulty of the sort, provide the words without supplying the categories in advance. Provide blank word cards for students to create their own headings for groups of words but be ready to provide headings if needed. Adding a timed component also offers more challenge by involving both accuracy and speed. Assessments that students can complete accurately and quickly reflect a strong knowledge of a subject, in contrast to students who sort accurately but slowly and hesitantly.

Assessing Concept Sorts.   Much is learned in discussions about the sorts and why students sorted the way they did. Teachers may start simply by asking students to explain how they grouped their words using open-ended questions and probes such as these. "Why did you sort the way you did?" "I was wondering why you put that word there." "Tell us about the next column."

The process of student self-assessment, in conjunction with the teacher's observations, sets the stage for more encompassing self-assessment and goalsetting activities. These self-assessments are included in students' Vocabulary Notebooks.

Content-Specific Spelling Inventories

Content spelling inventories for biology, geometry, and U.S. history are described later in this chapter. These inventories give teachers an indication as to how well students will be able to read printed materials related to the content areas, and, at the same time, provide some insight into the students' conceptual background knowledge and vocabulary.

GENERAL ASSESSMENTS OF VOCABULARY KNOWLEDGE AND DEVELOPMENT

Thus far, vocabulary assessment has been related to ongoing assessments with content-specific vocabulary. The informal assessments of vocabulary presented in the next section take a broader look at students' general vocabulary knowledge and development and include both *orthographic knowledge* or spelling and *generative* knowledge—students' knowledge of morphology, including inflectional and derivational morphology (see Chapter 2). A variety of measures reflect a developmental understanding of vocabulary in conjunction with literacy development more generally (Read, 2004). Students are quite different in their language and vocabulary proficiencies, and this presentation of assessments provides a developmental scope for teachers to choose from.

Listening to Oral Vocabulary and Language

Vocabulary is observed informally all the time in students' speech. Teachers can "earball" students' vocabulary—listen for the complexity of the language structures and ideas as students discuss with peers and small groups in class. Listen for the length of the oral sentences, the complexity of the grammatical relations, and the student's vocabulary. Does a student speak in short sentences or is there an elaborated character to the speaking? Language and dialectical differences among students may contribute to students not being ready to process some sounds like inflectional endings (*-ed, -ing*). There are many sounds that English learners may not know (Bear et al., 2007). In listening to oral language, teachers have a map for proceeding to written language measures.

Sentence Repetition to Understand Language Development.   Sentence repetition is a classic language assessment that provides a general indicator of which language structures students might understand. In formal sentence repetition assessments, sentences of increasing difficulty and length are read to the student and the student is to repeat the sentence back—for example, *He closed the front door* versus *It was improbable that from the seething whirlpool such a force could arise.* Standardized tests present norms to follow and identify students who may have language difficulties. Sentence repetition is a fairly low-level productive task that measures basic language skills and is highly related to levels of education. For some students, this task is a look into syntactic knowledge. This is an assessment that may indicate that further assessments are needed.

Secondary teachers can translate this activity into an assessment in the classroom. There are times students may be asked to repeat back sentences as if in a chant. Are students able to memorize key lines of text from plays and short stories? Can they repeat back a sentence just practiced? For example, "I am going to say a quote from the play, and you repeat it to a neighbor." Or "I am going to call out a few important phrases from the science book and you repeat them to a neighbor." In such circumstances, teachers have an opportunity to listen for the same features that are measured in sentence repetition measures: sentence length, vocabulary, and syntax.

Writing and Vocabulary

If listening to students speak is *earballing*, looking at students' vocabulary in writing is *eyeballing*. Advanced word choice and complicated sentence structures characterize students who have a facility with language learning. Students' writing is a treasure trove of information to assess their vocabulary and literacy development. Ten- or fifteen-minute freewrites are a common assessment activity, as are ten-minute freewrite assessments with prompts for students in an entire grade level. A prompt appropriate for secondary students, for example, is "Why is it a civic duty to vote?" After collecting these "writing on demand" papers, teachers make notes about the proficiencies evident for each paper. Guidelines are provided in Appendix G.7. When possible, for documentation, papers are scanned or copied. This checklist is also used to assess students' writing of multiple drafts at different times over the year.

ASSESSING MORPHOLOGY

It is important to assess morphology because it underlies students' learning and application of generative vocabulary strategies. There is a general progression in the level of difficulty of the morphology assessment tasks described in this section. Assessment progresses from examining students' knowledge of easy prefixes and base words to Greek and Latin word roots and then to more difficult prefixes and suffixes. The items in these assessments are arranged in a developmental sequence to suggest when the assessment might be discontinued. A sequential order makes it easier to analyze, interpret the results, and plan instruction.

Test of Morphological Structure

The Test of Morphological Structure (TMS) presented in Appendix G.2 was adapted from Joanne Carlisle and has been a widely used research tool (Carlisle, 2000). This assessment, based on research with intermediate students, provides insight into intermediate and middle school students' knowledge of English grammar and morphology. This assessment may be especially beneficial for assessing the morphological development of English learners at these levels.

The TMS was designed to be administered orally, and there are two presentation conditions. The first, "Derivation," assesses a student's ability to generate a derived form from a base word. The second, "Decomposition," assesses the ability to analyze a derived form in order to recognize the base word. The *major/majority* pair in the sample below would actually come in later developmentally than the *-er* of the *wash/washer* pair. This is because most learners acquire understanding of simpler and more concrete base words such as *wash* before developing understanding of the concepts underlying words such as *major* and *majority*. In addition, as was noted in Chapter 4, *-er* is a more frequently occurring suffix than *-ity*. Four examples from the TMS illustrate this type of assessment:

Derivation
major He won the vote by a _____. [majority]
wash Put the laundry in the _____. [washer]

Decomposition
variable The time of his arrival did not _____. [vary]
decision The boy found it hard to _____. [decide]

This assessment requires students to determine the correct suffix given the sentence context. To do this, they must understand the relationship between form and meaning, drawing upon both semantic and syntactic knowledge. Some of the changes are straightforward and require a basic vocabulary (*warm/warmth, four/fourth*). Other items require changes in pronunciation of polysyllabic words (*equal/equality, human/humanity, divide/division*). While the TMS was designed for an oral one-to-one administration, it is usually more practical in the school setting to administer this assessment with written responses in groups or as a class. The students write the words in order down the side of their papers. Teachers may choose to administer the two parts on separate days. The directions in Appendix G.2 are presented for both oral and written formats.

Teachers may compare a student's performance on the TMS with the appendix to Chapter 4, Sequence of Instruction for Core Affixes and Roots, and through an analysis of the errors and correct scores, be able to determine what level of morphological analysis would be beneficial for that student. Students' scores on this test are highly related to standardized measures of vocabulary (Smith, Ives, & Templeton, 2007). This assessment is ideal for examining the depth of students' knowledge of basic morphological structures and covers the range of development from late transitional and syllables and affixes spelling to middle advanced stage reading and derivational relations spelling.

Producing Words with the Same Suffixes and Prefixes

An assessment that examines students' productive knowledge of prefixes and suffixes provides insights into this upper-level area of word knowledge. Developmentally, this assessment is useful with intermediate and advanced readers. Students in the transitional stage of reading are not likely to provide many words, and this assessment is at the frustration level for usually older, remedial readers.

For this assessment, Appendix G.1 provides two lists; in the first, students produce as many words in a timed setting as they can with the given suffixes. In the second list they produce words with a given prefix. Students who generate more words with these prefixes and suffixes probably know more about their meanings, and they probably have relatively deeper vocabularies.

Matching Greek and Latin Roots with Their Meanings

Matching is a common format for vocabulary assessments. The testing form in Appendix G.9 is an example assessment for specific Greek and Latin roots. It comes from the supplement *Words Their Way—Word Sorts for Derivational Relations Spellers* (Templeton et al., 2009). The answer key is in Appendix G.9 as well. After students have made the matches, teachers can call out words with these roots that students spell and define. Students who score 90 percent or above are considered at a mastery level. Students who score less need more instruction with these roots. The *Derivational Relations* supplement contains additional assessments like this, including one for prefixes.

Generating Related Words

This assessment found in Appendix G.11 is an example of a task in which a broad range of bases and roots are given to students to build other words. It includes base words like *turn* and *give,* as well as Greek and Latin roots like *spec* and *tract* that occur in many disciplines. This helps students make meaning connections among words across different reading contexts. Content area teachers can choose content-related base words and roots to create their own assessments. In a biology class, for example, roots for building words might include *photo, bio,* or *eco.* Assessment scores are meant to suggest the difficulty level of the affixes and roots students are ready to study.

Variations.   Vary the word parts for building by again using the appendix to Chapter 4, Sequence of Instruction for Core Affixes and Roots. This assessment can be turned into a small-group activity to assess how students brainstorm together.

VOCABULARY AND LITERACY DEVELOPMENT AND INSTRUCTION

To determine learning trajectories and to plan vocabulary instruction, it is essential to have a complete picture of both students' vocabularies *and* their literacy development. In this section, literacy development is discussed in terms of how it affects students' vocabulary learning and how knowledge of development can guide differentiated vocabulary instruction.

The relationships among reading, vocabulary, and spelling have been well researched and clearly described (Cunningham, Perry, & Stanovich, 2001; Templeton, 2004a). In the middle and secondary grades the source of most new vocabulary students learn comes from reading. This is why the intermediate grade student who has an exceptional oral vocabulary has probably done a fair amount of reading. Reading, writing, and spelling development run in parallel and pull from the same knowledge base. Through the assessments presented here, patterns in students' spelling and vocabulary knowledge are discerned and a stage of spelling and an understanding of the depth of students' vocabulary can be determined for each student. Expectations for vocabulary learning are tempered by the reading materials students can read with adequate accuracy, fluency, and comprehension.

Stages of Literacy Development

The model of literacy development presented in Table 1.3 of Chapter 1 is elaborated here with more specific descriptions of reading, writing, and spelling behaviors that are observed at each stage. Chapter 2 described the what and how of the process by which students learn about the spelling system of English. Here, the discussion of development and spelling or word knowledge is refined and applied to instructional planning.

The first stage presented in the developmental model in Chapter 1 (Table 1.3) is the emergent stage where students know little, if anything, about how letters and sounds work together. Middle and high school students in the emergent stage are usually recent arrivals who do not yet know English and have little literacy in their first languages.

Beginning Reading and Letter Name–Alphabetic Spelling.   The second stage of reading is the beginning stage, accompanied by the letter name–alphabetic stage of spelling. The reading behaviors of beginning readers include word-by-word reading and reading aloud to themselves with early to mid first grade–level reading materials. The spelling stage is called the letter name–alphabetic stage because students use the names as well as the sounds of the letters to spell. During this stage students may misspell *float* as FLOT, where each letter represents a sound. Beginning readers have learned the alphabetic principle that there is a letter–sound correspondence between letters and sounds. At the middle and secondary levels, any students in this stage are usually taught by specialists.

Transitional Reading and Within-Word Pattern Spelling.   The middle and secondary grades count many students at this developmental stage, all needing additional support in and outside of the classroom. Reading achievement may vary depending on how well the students have learned coping strategies that help them to succeed in school, even though they may only read at a second, third, or fourth grade reading level. By the time they are identified in the middle school, transitional readers may have learned strategies that help them succeed in school even though they read their texts at a frustration reading level. They read silently to themselves if the reading is not too difficult; if they read aloud, they sound as if they are approaching fluency, and they begin to read with some expression.

Beginning with this stage, vocabulary study is slightly ahead of spelling instruction, with a focus on easy and common prefixes and suffixes. This is the beginning of students' explicit study of inflectional morphology. Grammar is folded into word study as the *-ed* of past tense endings, plural endings, contractions, and possessives are taught. Students in the transitional reading stage are in the *within-word pattern* stage of spelling. They now know how to spell most short vowel words and they are learning about the long vowel patterns within single-syllable words. For example, in trying to spell *float*, students experiment with different ways to spell long vowel words (e.g., FLOTE or FLOWT).

Intermediate Reading and Syllables and Affixes Spelling.   The last two stages comprise upper-level reading and word study. When reading at their independent level, students at the intermediate stage read mostly silently and should be reading well over 100 words per minute. Comprehension may suffer when students' silent reading rate is below 100 wpm—it is difficult to hold the syntax together and the basic gist of the writing is lost when moving so slowly through the text. Students reading this slowly may also lack sufficient word reading accuracy. Comprehension may be improved by reading orally for expression in poetry and drama or by supporting a point of view or answering a question during a discussion of what has just been read. Oral reading can assist comprehension because when students read aloud, they purchase processing time—while they are trying to read an unfamiliar polysyllabic word, they can hold the syntax together long enough to comprehend.

During this stage, students' primary source for new vocabulary comes from what they read. Students should continue to study affixes, particularly less common prefixes that may be confused in sound with other word structures (for example, *pur-, per-, pre-*). Intermediate readers often begin to study Greek and Latin roots (*erupt*ion).

Students' writing styles often mimic the styles of the authors they read, but their beginning sentence structures can be awkwardly long, with compound phrases held loosely together with conjunctions. By the end of this stage, students use prepositional and other embedded phrases easily in their writing, and they try out different genres if motivated by access to and support for these genres. They begin this stage writing two-syllable words with modest facility, and by the end are regularly using three- and four-syllable words. Their familiarity with the specialized vocabularies from the content areas increases when the internal structures of words are examined.

Students in the intermediate stage of spelling have mastered most single-syllable words. They begin the stage learning to spell complex consonant blends (e.g., *fudge*) and unusual vowel patterns (*weight*). With a solid knowledge of single-syllable words, these exceptional patterns are learned rapidly. Consonant doubling and the spelling of unaccented syllables are learned, and students learn to look at syllable structures of open and closed syllables (*pilot/capsule*). Students learn the spelling–meaning connection in the study of two-syllable homophones and homographs.

Advanced Readers and Derivational Relations Spelling.   Advanced readers build on what they learned in the intermediate stage. Reading and writing are fluent activities with silent reading rates in the 250 wpm range, with students able to adjust reading rates and styles according to the difficulty of the text and their purpose for reading. Students' interests in specific genres are developed at this time for a lifetime. Vocabularies grow with the volume of their reading and content area instruction.

Advanced readers explore content vocabulary and collect new vocabulary words based on their content studies. They may collect a series of key terms to remember in geometry and make notes about their meanings. Etymological studies are explored in greater depth and students learn the meaning of less straightforward prefixes and suffixes and Greek and Latin roots such as *mot* and *rupt*. Students should study how words are spelled to preserve meaning, despite changes in sound (Templeton, 1979, 1983, 2004a). Spelling becomes vocabulary study and the meaning connection is made when informed by plentiful examples of words. Students enjoy finding meaning patterns in words (for example, making a list of "phobias") and benefit from the study of affixes such as *-ion/-tion/-sion/-ian*. Assimilated prefixes open the meanings of thousands of words through spelling changes For example, *com-*, which means "with," is spelled variously *con-*, *cor-*, or *col-*, as in *construct*, *correlate*, and *colleague*.

Homophone Vocabulary and Spelling Assessment

The Homophone Vocabulary and Spelling Assessment for Pacing Vocabulary Instruction in Appendix G.4 is an informal assessment to understand students' vocabulary development that can be used to estimate where students are developmentally in terms of spelling (Bear, Invernizzi, Templeton, & Johnston, 2008). Students are told a word, listen to it in a sentence, and then spell the target word. Afterward, they are asked to produce and spell a homophone for the word. Because homophones are words that sound alike and have different spellings, students have to make the meaning connection with the spellings of both words. The homophones increase in difficulty level by orthographic (spelling) pattern (*penance/pennants*), by how frequently they occur (*depose/depots*) (Zeno et al., 1995), and by difficulty in knowing the differences in meaning (*affect/effect* or *ascent/assent*).

The order of difficulty of the homophone pairs makes it possible to learn about students' vocabulary and orthographic development. Students who know the differences in meaning and can spell 90 percent of the homophone pairs have both a broader and deeper knowledge of English vocabulary than someone who scores 50 percent or less. This is because students who score higher have most likely read more widely and perhaps deeply in particular genres, because it is only in print that the spellings of homophones are obvious. In the directions, there are a number of variations that make it possible to adjust the difficulty of the assessment.

The pacing table in the directions interprets the scores for vocabulary instruction and offers guidelines for pacing instruction. Students who know most of the differences in the meanings of the first 11 homophone pairs are probably intermediate-level readers from a developmental perspective. They will read most vocabulary in context with ease, but very long words with difficult structures may be challenging for reading and spelling. This means that vocabulary instruction needs to follow a slightly slower pace. These students may also read more slowly than the advanced readers who can read rapidly through a greater volume of material. Students who know most of the pairs will be ready to quickly learn difficult, polysyllabic, specialized vocabulary words.

SPELLING INVENTORIES TO ASSESS LITERACY AND CONTENT VOCABULARY

Several easy-to-administer spelling assessments are explained here. Some have feature guides that you can use to analyze and interpret the results. Directions for administering, feature guides, samples, and guides to plan instruction are found in Appendix G.3.

Why Spelling?

Spelling assessments are conservative measures of what students know about words. Students' spelling and writing are production tasks that are also windows to their reading. Through analyzing students' spelling and writing, a good deal is learned about how students' reading is progressing (Bear & Templeton, 2000; Henderson, 1981; Invernizzi & Hayes, 2004). Why is spelling so closely related to reading? It is because students' knowledge of how words are spelled draws on the same knowledge base they use when reading words. As a result, spelling indicates how easily students will read their texts.

In several studies of secondary students and adults, there is a strong relationship between what students can spell and what they can read (Bear, 1992; Bear, Templeton, & Warner, 1991; Bear, Truex, & Barone, 1986; Edwards, 2003; Viise & Austin, 2005). In one study of eighth- and tenth-graders (Edwards, 2003), the correlation between reading comprehension on a standardized measure and spelling accuracy on a qualitative spelling inventory was 0.8, indicating a very significant positive relationship. Students at different levels of spelling development will read their textbooks with different proficiencies in word accuracy, reading rate, and probably comprehension. They will also have different skills to bring to vocabulary learning. An obvious example is to compare how students spell words on a content-based spelling inventory. For example, a student who spells *oxygen* as AKOGEN and *hypothesis* as HIPAUTSE is likely not as good a reader as another student who spells these words accurately. This also means that students' language and literacy are going to be at different instructional levels.

Qualitative Spelling Checklist

Through a series of 20 questions, the qualitative spelling checklist is a progression through the orthographic features that students learn and an excellent first step in analyzing students' spelling. With the checklist presented in Appendix G.8, you can look at students' spelling and see which features are used correctly all of the time, often, or not at all. Through this checklist, a student's spelling stage from the letter name–alphabetic level through the derivational relations spelling level can be located.

The checklist is presented starting with question one and working through until No responses start to be checked. Because the checklist describes a progression, it is apparent when a student's knowledge fades or gives out. For example, a student should get all Yes responses to begin and then gradually collect some Often responses and then perhaps two or three No's in a row. The responses should not go from Yes to No and back to Yes more than perhaps once. When students start to miss items, they should continue to miss. For example, one does not usually learn to spell words like *fortunate* correctly before *bump,* nor do students stabilize on consonant doubling before mastering short vowel patterns.

Upper-Level Qualitative Spelling Inventory (ULSI)

The ULSI is used widely in middle school through postsecondary classrooms and for specific programs, including intervention programs (Appendix G.3). It has been used to help assess students at the university level who are having reading difficulties as well as to assess students for GED programs to obtain a high school diploma.

The words in this assessment were chosen because they identify what students in the syllables and affixes and derivational relations stages are doing in their spelling. The words are arranged in order of difficulty. If students miss seven or more of the first ten words, the test can be discontinued. Students who score at this level are usually in the within-word pattern stage.

Students' spelling on this upper-level list shows how they make the meaning connection with the orthography (Templeton, 1983, 2004a). Students in these final stages of spelling learn to preserve meaning in spite of changes in sound. For example, in pronunciation, the second vowel in *reside* changes from a long *i* to a schwa sound (/uh/) in *resident*—that is, it is reduced in the second syllable. In spite of this sound change, the spelling remains the same and is a cue to meaning.

Feature Guide to Analyze the Spelling.   The ULSI feature guide in Appendix G.3 should be completed for each student. In checking the features students know and those they spell incorrectly teachers can see how the planned vocabulary matches students' word knowledge and development. The feature guides also identify what stages of spelling students are in, which in turn suggests a reading stage. Look for where students first miss two or more on a feature and then look for the stage at the top. Information about stages is used for organization and planning instruction. Some teachers move directly from scoring the papers to the power score discussed next to determine a stage, then developing feature guides for the students for whom they need more ideas for instruction.

An example of a marked upper-level guide is presented in Figure 8.3. You can see that while Roberta's spelling errors cover the range of the last two spelling stages, she was determined to be in the later part of the syllables and affixes stage. She has learned many of the more difficult affixes and troublesome doubling principles. The Affixes column is the first place where she missed more than one feature. Word study should begin with a small step backward to orient Roberta to the study of polysyllabic words by studying syllables, accent, and unstressed syllables. She would then be ready to study the meanings of prefixes and suffixes. Her score of 75/99 is strong for a seventh-grader.

Power Score and Stages of Spelling.   The number of words spelled correctly on the ULSI is called a *power score*. In several research studies, the number of words spelled correctly on a spelling inventory and the stage assessment are highly related to standardized reading achievement measures at all levels, from kindergarten through postsecondary levels (Bear, 1992). The estimates of stages using power scores from the ULSI can be summarized as follows:

Number of Words Spelled Correctly	Stage of Development
2	early within-word pattern
6	middle within-word pattern
7	late within-word pattern
9	early syllables and affixes
11	middle syllables and affixes
18	late syllables and affixes
21	early derivational relations
23	middle derivational relations
27+	late derivational relations

FIGURE 8.3 Example of a Scored Feature Guide: Roberta

Student: Roberta Teacher: Kridel Grade: 7 Date: September 3
Words Spelled Correctly: 20/31 Feature Points: 55/68 Total: 75/99 Spelling Stage: Late Syllables & Affixes

Words	Within-Word Pattern — Early: Digraphs and Blends	Middle: Vowels	Late: Complex Consonants	Syllables and Affixes — Middle: Inflected Endings and Syllable Juncture	Early: Unaccented Final Syllables	Late: Affixes	Derivational Relations — Early: Reduced Vowels in Unaccented Syllables	Middle: Greek and Latin Elements	Late: Assimilated Prefixes	Feature Points	Word Spelled Correctly
1. switch	sw ✓	i ✓	tch ✓							3	1
2. smudge	sm ✓	u ✓	dge ✓							3	1
3. trapped	tr ✓			pp ✓						2	1
4. scraps		a-e ✓	scr ✓							2	1
5. knotted		o ✓	kn ✓	tt ✓						3	1
6. shaving	sh ✓			e-drop ✓						2	1
7. squirt		ir ✓	squ ✓							2	1
8. pounce		ou ✓	ce ✓							2	1
9. scratches		a ✓	tch ✓	es ✓						3	1
10. crater	cr ✓			t ✓	er ✓					3	1
11. sailor		ai ✓			or ✓					2	1
12. village				ll ✓	age ✓					2	1
13. disloyal		oy ✓			al ✓	dis ✓				3	1
14. tunnel				nn ✓	el ✓					2	1
15. humor				m ✓	or ✓					2	1
16. confidence						con ✓	fid ✓			2	1
17. fortunate					ate ✓			fortun ✓		2	1
18. visible						ible ✓		vis ✓		2	1
19. circumference						ence ✓		circum om		1	0
20. civilization							liz ✓	civil		2	1
21. monarchy								arch ark		0	0
22. dominance						ance e	min ✓			1	0
23. correspond							res ris		rr ✓	1	0
24. illiterate					ate ✓				ll l	1	0
25. emphasize						size ✓	pha f			1	0
26. opposition							pos ✓		pp ✓	2	1
27. chlorine						ine ene		chlor clor		0	0
28. commotion						tion s			mm ✓	1	0
29. medicinal					al le			medic ✓		1	0
30. irresponsible						ible a	res ✓		rr r	1	0
31. succession						sion ✓			cc c	1	0
Totals	5/5	9/9	7/7	8/8	8/9	6/10	5/7	4/7	3/6	55/68	20/31

These power scores are not exact but a guide to the general stage of development. The feature guide provides a qualitative and quantitative assessment that is more helpful in planning spelling and vocabulary activities.

Intermediate-Level Academic Vocabulary Spelling Inventory

The academic vocabulary spelling inventory assesses students' knowledge of academic vocabulary as well as their orthographic knowledge (Townsend, Bear, & Templeton, 2008). A pilot study using a very similar spelling inventory found a significant relationship between the number of words spelled correctly and standardized reading measures among seventh- and eighth-graders.

In the academic spelling inventory, students are asked to spell words, and in addition are asked to rate what they know about the words. An interesting part of the academic spelling inventory is that students are also asked to write additional words that preserve the form of the word's spelling or meaning. They can add or take away word parts to form other words; for example, for the word *procedure*, the words *procedurally*, *proceed*, and *process* contribute to their scores. This provides information about how well students can make morphological connections across related words.

Content-Specific Spelling Inventories

The words teachers select for content area inventories are often the key vocabulary words for biology, geometry, and U.S. history courses. The words in the content spelling inventories function as a prompt in the same way that maps, structured overviews, webs, or clusters help students to think about topics they are studying. Before calling out the words, explain that how students spell will help you know what to teach but will not be a part of their grades; instead, say "You will earn a grade by your efforts."

These inventories reveal which students will need additional support to learn new vocabulary. As examples, transitional readers will struggle to read grade-level textbooks and will need other sources of information, whereas advanced readers use print with ease to acquire new words.

Content-specific spelling inventories have been developed with secondary teachers who want to assess students' general orthographic knowledge as well as their knowledge of the content-specific vocabulary. Students who score well on these content-specific inventories tend to do better in these classes than students who are unable to spell many of these content words correctly. It may be that students who have a difficult time spelling the content vocabulary also have a difficult time reading the texts (Bear & Templeton, 2000; Bear et al., 1991). The premise underlying the content area spelling assessments is that when students' orthographic knowledge is strong, their reading is easier and more fluent.

Instructional-Level Spelling and Reading in Biology.　Consider for a moment a few of the spellings of three students who took the biology spelling inventory:

Word	Brian	Samantha	Teresa
allergy	alurjee	alergie	allergy
antigen	antijun	antigene	antigen
immunity	imunty	imunety	immunity
carcinogen	carsongen	carsinagen	carcinigen
vaccine	vackseen	vacine	vaccine

From this and other writing samples, it was clear that Brian was a student in the within-word pattern stage. He spelled words by sound and sometimes dropped syllables as in

IMUNTY for *immunity.* His spelling of *vaccine* as VACKSEEN is phonetically possible but suggests that he does not remember ever seeing this word before. He is very likely to find the text beyond his reading ability. Samantha's spellings, while still wrong, are more sophisticated and suggest that she is probably in the syllables and affixes stage. She will need support for reading the text. Teresa is in the derivational relations stage and will most likely find her text easy to read.

Instructional-Level Spelling and Reading in Social Studies. Susana and Fernando are two English learners in the ninth grade who in their social studies classroom took the U.S. History Spelling Inventory at the beginning of the year; their work is presented in the first part of Figure 8.4. After scoring the inventories for accuracy, the teacher passed on the results to the English language specialist. Given their development and a desire to see how they would spell single-syllable words, the teacher chose to administer the

FIGURE 8.4 Social Studies and Elementary Qualitative Spelling Inventory Assessments by Two Ninth-Graders

Social Studies Qualitative Spelling Inventories

	Susana (SSQSI 8/20, 40%)	Fernando (SSQSI 0/20, 0%)
1. abolition	1. Abolition	1. abelshon
2. political	2. Politicle	2. politicall
3. president	3. President	3. presedent
4. technology	4. technology	4. techolegy
5. alliance	5. Alience	5. aubnsg
6. progressive	6. Progressive	6. progesive
7. citizen	7. Citizen	7. sitesen
8. communism	8. communism	8. conyousafm
9. frontier	9. fronter	9. fronter
10. government	10. goverment	10. govermot
11. discrimination	11. discrimination	11. desgmenshon
12. occupation	12. ocupation	12. opashon
13. segregation	13. Segregation	13. segregshon
14. immigrant	14. imigrent	14. imigrant
15. business	15. Buisness	15. bissnes.
16. racism	16. racesim	16. raisemon
17. foreign	17. forin	17. foren
18. neutral	18. nutral	18. nutroll
19. community	19. commity	19. comety
20. bureau	20. buro	20. brall

Elementary Qualitative Spelling Inventories

Susana (PSI 22/25, 88%)   Fernando (PSI 10/25, 40%)

#	Word	Susana	Fernando
1.	bed	Bed	bed
2.	ship	Ship	ship
3.	when	When	when
4.	lump	lump	lump
5.	float	float	flote
6.	train	train	train
7.	place	Place	plaece
8.	drive	drive	drive
9.	bright	bright	brite
10.	shopping	Shopping	shopping
11.	spoil	Spoil	spole
12.	serving	Surving	serving
13.	chewed	Chewed	chewed
14.	carries	Carries	ckarreis
15.	marched	Marched	march
16.	shower	Shower	shower
17.	bottle	bottle	bottle
18.	favor	favor	fairvor
19.	ripen	ripen	rippen
20.	cellar	Celler	seller
21.	pleasure	Pleasure	plesher
22.	fortunate	fortunet	frochnot
23.	confident	confident	cofinot
24.	civilized	Civilized	seviled
25.	opposition	Opposition	operon

elementary spelling inventory from *Words Their Way* (Bear et al., 2008). The results of the inventory, presented in the second part of Figure 8.4, indicated that Susana was in the middle of the syllables and affixes stage, a level that related to a ninth grade instructional level, while Fernando was in the within-word pattern stage. These results suggest that Susana would probably be able to read the social studies text at an instructional level but that the text would be too difficult for Fernando. Reading with the students confirmed what the spelling indicated; Susana read slowly but with good accuracy while Fernando read at a third grade level. Fernando will need alternative reading material and access to the vocabulary through multiple modalities (oral, visual, experiential) to master new words and concepts.

Students Assess Their Content Vocabulary Knowledge after Spelling.   After spelling the words on these content lists, students can assess their knowledge of the meanings of the words. The form provides a way for students to reflect on their knowledge of the words they spelled in the content spelling inventory. Teachers should ask students to revisit the words they do not think they spelled correctly and to give them another try—without crossing through previous attempts. "If you think you misspelled a word, try to spell the word a different way." Together, these activities create powerful data to document and understand what students know about words. If students can take their learning seriously and also think they can be successful, they will be earnest in their self-assessments.

Without the form teachers can ask students to star the words on the list that are familiar: "Put a star beside the word if you know the meaning of a word, no matter how you spelled the word. Look at the words and think about what the words mean. Do you know the meanings of the words? If you do not know a word, write VS beside it; these are words for vocabulary study." Students who spell accurately tend to star more words than students who spell approximately half the words correctly. Teachers can also have students rate their knowledge of words on a five-point scale like the one introduced for Vocabulary Fist-to-Five. Records of familiarity with the subject can be a reference to track students' vocabulary growth in the particular content area. Before collecting papers, teachers can take a moment to ask students to think about how words are related to the content area following the brainstorming steps discussed previously in this chapter. Together, the teacher and students brainstorm a list of related words. For example, if *geology* were a word on an inventory, students could work together to find other words that have *geo* in them. Similarly, some teachers ask students to sort the words in the content inventory into related groups so that they can see the meaning relations among the vocabulary, a topic that is at the heart of vocabulary study in the content area.

INVOLVE STUDENTS IN INTERPRETATION AND PLANNING

Like the self-reflection activities discussed for spelling, teachers can involve students in the last two steps in the assessment process: analysis and interpretation and evaluation and planning. Teachers should not discuss students' learning in front of students as if they were not there; if we talk about students, we talk *with* them. The discussions of specifics regarding students are best left to individual meetings. Teachers can have two types of folders for students: the teacher's folder contains the assessment materials and the student folder is much like Mrs. Nomura's three-ring notebook discussed at the beginning of this chapter. Students are responsible for keeping them current.

Explain Vocabulary Learning and Development to Students

A reproducible that describes instructional levels for students and parents is found in Appendix G.5 and is titled Functional Reading Levels. Most of students' reading should be in between their independent and instructional levels. As a reference for teachers, a description of developmental reading rates is presented in the table at the bottom of the page. By taking a few measures of reading rate, teachers can see how long students will take to read their texts. The score is based on words per minute (wpm = words/minutes), and when they read orally, reading accuracy can also be determined (95 to 97 percent accuracy for instructional-level texts).

Some teachers talk to students about the state standards that match development and add these to the chart. For example, each state includes standards for students to understand common affixes and Greek and Latin roots. Other teachers show students the standards for that year and ask them for ideas about methods or activities they think could help them become proficient. The same is true for the textbook: "What are effective ways to learn the vocabulary and ideas that you see in the textbook?"

The "so what" of the assessments is summarized in the tables that describe implications for instruction at the last three stages of reading (Tables 8.2, 8.3, and 8.4). During individual meetings with students, these tables illustrate the types of vocabulary and reading activities organized by developmental stages. Notice in these tables that vocabulary instruction precedes students' abilities to spell and perhaps even read the vocabulary that is integral to their studies. The ideas for instruction depend on the students' literacy development.

These tables come in handy again in the discussion of the organization of vocabulary instruction in the classroom. At the beginning of a unit, introduce the vocabulary in relation to students' developmental levels. For example, students in the intermediate stage will find words like *igneous, metamorphosis, hypotenuse,* and *quadrilateral* a little difficult to read at first and more difficult to spell. For students in this stage, extra time to study the most important vocabulary is needed. The guides in Tables 8.2, 8.3, and 8.4 are also shared with parents to add specificity to the developmental chart presented in Table 1.3.

With students in the transitional reading stage, teachers plan activities and materials while mindful of students' developmental and conceptual needs, including oral support, multimedia materials, and partnering for tutoring. Advanced readers are on a good track and need the motivation and experiences that will make it possible for them to achieve on grade level. Owning one's learning is necessary at all developmental levels, as discussed further in the next section.

Goalsetting Interviews

Goalsetting interviews are a way to meet with students individually or in small groups to discuss goals for vocabulary learning. This is a time to bring the assessments together to share with students (1) what they know and have accomplished in their vocabulary learning and (2) which proficiencies are needed for success and how they think they might achieve them. Goalsetting can begin with a discussion of the types of vocabulary activities that are suggested by stage in Tables 8.2, 8.3, and 8.4.

Keep the tone positive when discussing students' learning. Have students describe what they know in *I can* statements; these *I can* statements are a way to encourage positive language about learning (Au & Raphael, 2007). After previewing their texts, students say things like the following about the vocabulary in their texts: *I have heard and seen these words before. We studied these a few years ago. I remember some of these names. I know about half the vocabulary. I can study this chapter to learn the material. I can learn from the textbook. I can find other materials on this subject. I can find some interest in some of the topics.* Brainstorming by the whole class is a good way to get started.

When students look through their texts and other materials that are relevant to vocabulary learning, they consider what vocabulary they know and how easily they can read the text. If some students and their teachers determine, for example, that the texts are too difficult, then it is particularly important to include additional materials at students' instructional levels (Guthrie, McRee, & Klauda, 2007). Students and teachers use the rubric for vocabulary learning in Appendix G.10 to assess vocabulary knowledge. This rubric is similar to the Fist-to-Five but is more explicit in the criteria for knowing.

Students' Strategies for Learning Vocabulary

Teachers can guide students in small groups or in a whole-class setting to discuss strategies they already have for learning vocabulary. As a precursor to meeting individually

TABLE 8.2   Guide to Vocabulary, Reading, and Word Analysis Instruction with Transitional Readers and Within-Word Pattern Spellers

Vocabulary	Reading	Word Analysis
Characteristics		
• Recognize, analyze, and with practice can understand most new vocabulary in grades 4–8	• Approach fluency, with reading rates from 60–100 words per minute	• Single-syllable word study
• Initially, may not read grade-level vocabulary correctly (e.g., *container, vacation, ocean, column*)	• Read one- to three-syllable words with ease in context	• Long vowel sound discrimination
• Types of spelling errors: FLOTE/*float* BRITE/*bright* CHOOED/*chewed* VILEG/*village* CORSPND/*correspond* EARSPNSABUL/*irresponsible*	• Begin to read faster silently than orally; in instructional-level materials, prefer to read silently	• Consonant blends and digraphs
	• Instructional reading level of grade 2	• CVCe pattern
• Write vocabulary slowly; provide models for syllabication; writing the vocabulary will be slow and inaccurate	• Grade-level texts (4–12) are at frustration level; disfluent and inaccurate reading	• Basic long vowel patterns (CVVC, CVV, CV)
• Vocabulary study requires oral and written support		• Complex vowel patterns
		• Single-syllable homophones
• Study base words and easy inflectional morphology; plurals; past tense endings; easy prefixes and suffixes		
• Guided practice; provide model of how to divide polysyllabic words into syllables and meaning parts; provide models and demonstrations and repeat in sorts; fewer words provided in brainstorming related words for vocabulary study (*declare/ declaration/declarative*)		
• Provide sets of reading materials at instructional levels		
Activities		
• Pair with partner for reading support	• Fluency activities for rate and expression; repeated reading rate charts; rubrics for dramatic reading	• Picture sorts for long and short vowels
• Diagrams, videos, and audio recordings provide support	• Book clubs with instructional-level materials	• Word sorts and games for pattern
• Word hunts for word parts (-*ed*, -*ing*, *re*-)	• Grade-level materials available for listening	• Word study notebook section to record sorts and word hunts for single-syllable word patterns
• Write words in Vocabulary Notebooks		
• Vocabulary cards are focused on most important key vocabulary		• Sorts for homonyms; Homophone Rummy
• Word sorts for endings; compare base to non-base words (*untrue/happily*); word creation matching inflections with base words		
• Understand meaning of roots and harder prefixes and suffixes; difficulty reading and recalling spelling of word parts (affixes and roots)		

TABLE 8.3 Guide to Vocabulary, Reading, and Word Analysis Instruction with Intermediate Readers and Syllables and Affixes Spellers

Vocabulary	Reading	Word Analysis
Characteristics		
• Recognize, analyze, and understand new vocabulary; some words in grades 6–12 require practice	• Read fluently with silent reading rates from 100–200 words per minute	• Inflectional morphology
• Initially, may not read grade level vocabulary words correctly (e.g., *constitution, supersaturate, convenient, metamorphosis*)	• Read ≤ six-syllable words with ease in context	• Study spelling of base words with inflected endings (e.g., *luckily*)
• Types of spelling errors: VILAGE/*village* VISABEL/*visible* CONFADANCE/*confidence* CORESPOND/*correspond* ENFASIZE/*emphasize* IRESPONSIBLE/*irresponsible*	• Instructional reading levels of grades 3–8	• Consonant doubling principle
	• Grade-level (9–12) texts are at a frustration level; disfluent and inaccurate reading	• Open and closed syllables
• In the early part of stage, cannot write vocabulary and content words with ease or accuracy; by the end of the stage, most words can be spelled with some practice		• Syllabication and accentuation
• Vocabulary study in grades 6–12 requires oral and written support		• Two-syllable homophones
• Provide sets of reading materials at instructional levels		• Study additional prefixes and suffixes (e.g., *pre-, dis-, -tion, -sion*)
• All vocabulary available to study, can generate some examples of roots, and can spell most words correctly		
Activities		
• Diagrams, videos, and audio recordings provide support	• Develop study skills like skimming and scanning	• Word sorts and games to study consonant doubling (Hopping, Jumping Frog game)
• Pair with partner for reading support	• Book clubs with instructional-level materials	• Word study notebook sections for prefixes and suffixes
• Word hunts for word parts (derivations)		• Sorts for two-syllable homonyms
• Collect related words in Vocabulary Notebooks		• Sorts for open and closed syllables
• Create semantic maps		• Begin to use etymological references
• Record concept sorts on group charts and in Vocabulary Notebooks		
• Semantic feature analysis		
• Word sorts for endings; compare base to non-base words (*untrue/happily*); word creation matching suffixes with base words		
• Understand meaning of roots and harder prefixes and suffixes; hard to remember the spelling of the roots		
• Provide support in syllabication of polysyllabic words and in finding meaning parts and related words; there will be fewer brainstorming related words for vocabulary study (*declare/declaration/declarative*)		

Vocabulary	Reading	Word Analysis
	Characteristics	
• Recognize, analyze, and understand vocabulary; some words in grades 11+ require practice • Read grade-level vocabulary words correctly; have strategies to read unfamiliar words that have difficult roots and changes in stress • Types of spelling errors: CONFIDANCE/*confidence* IRRESPONSABLE/*irresponsible* CAMOFLAGE/*camouflage* INDITEMENT/*indictment* • Use knowledge of roots to understand new, technical vocabulary • Learn to spell new words with a little practice • Vocabulary grows with experience reading • Try out new vocabulary with oral and written opportunities • Study harder prefixes, prefix assimilation, derivational morphology, Greek and Latin roots • Provide sets of reading materials at instructional levels that may be above grade-level materials • Study specialized vocabulary carefully • Generate examples of the roots that they study and spell nearly all words correctly	• Read fluently, with expression • Develop a variety of reading styles and cultivate favorite genres • Read fluently with silent reading rates from 150–250 words per minute • Read words in context accurately and can read most complicated words with ease • Grade-level (5–12) material is at instructional level • Unfamiliar topics and difficult vocabulary and concepts may be frustration level	• Derivational morphology • Study spelling of roots, less frequent affixes, vowel reduction, assimilated prefixes • Continue study of syllabication and accentuation • Enjoy etymology • Pursue specialized vocabulary
	Activities	
• Diagrams, videos, and audio recordings provide support • Pair with partners to provide support to others • Word hunts for word parts (derivational relations among words within and across content areas) • Collect related words in Vocabulary Notebook • Create Progressive Root Web • Facility in tracing etymologies with various references • Record Greek and Latin roots in Vocabulary Notebooks • Word sorts for roots, assimilated prefixes, content-based concept sorts for roots (*hydro, hypo, micro, bio*) • Understand meaning of roots and harder prefixes and suffixes and can generate examples from reading • Easily divide polysyllabic words into syllables and meaning parts; draw on store of related words for brainstorming vocabulary study (*equal/equation /equality/equanimity*)	• Study skills like notetaking and time management • Book clubs with instructional- and independent-level materials	• Word sorts and games to study Greek and Latin roots (Latin Root Jeopardy) • Word study notebook sections for lists of difficult affixes and pages devoted to different roots • Use etymological references for word study • Sorts and word hunts for assimilated prefixes

or in small groups, students can complete the worksheet My Strategies for Learning Vocabulary presented in Appendix G.13. As part of this survey, students reflect on the relative difficulty of the materials and how they may benefit from reading related materials at different levels.

In a group setting, the feature guide can be shared so that students see what features are learned at different stages. As they consider their own spelling, students see where they are developmentally in reading. They also see similar errors in their own first draft writing. To focus on how their reading and spelling levels are related to vocabulary activities, teachers can show them the vocabulary activities found in the relevant table of activities from Tables 8.2, 8.3, and 8.4. "These assessments help us to plan activities for reading, vocabulary, and spelling. Consider in these tables what activities would be beneficial." Most of these activities have been discussed in Chapters 4 through 6. Teachers can use these tables to involve students in planning instruction and to help monitor their progress. These topics are discussed in the final section of this chapter.

CLASSROOM ORGANIZATION

Classroom organization for vocabulary instruction begins with the very first activities that you conduct. Looking back, you can see how each of the opening assessment activities in this chapter, like brainstorming and vocabulary self-assessment, involved small-group or partner work. During these assessments, teachers learn how students study together by moving around the room to observe students' roles and performance in generating vocabulary related to the content under study. The organization and planning instruction is developed and refined when teachers have assessed students' vocabulary knowledge and progress. Once the teacher knows about students' literacy proficiency, then it is possible to organize study groups and plan and implement vocabulary instruction, as shown in this section. Additional discussions of classroom organization in the secondary grades can be found in other books on word study instruction (Bear et al., 2008, Chapter 3; Flanigan et al., in press).

The examples of classroom organization for vocabulary can be modified for different schedules and configurations. Some classrooms are organized homogeneously; in middle school grades there may be an entire class of intermediate readers, and in high school, a class of nearly all advanced readers. More commonly, perhaps, in secondary classes, student abilities will range over two or three developmental reading and writing stages. For example, in a ninth grade classroom, there may be seven or eight students in the middle intermediate stage of reading, eight to ten students who are late intermediate readers, with another ten advanced readers.

Schedules for Vocabulary Instruction

Classroom routines are established early on so that students can focus on learning. We begin with a suggested weekly schedule for vocabulary instruction and then present ways to integrate vocabulary instruction into the overall classroom schedule.

Schedule of Vocabulary Activities. Over the course of a week, it is possible for students to learn and study many words deeply. Figure 8.5 presents a five-day sequence for vocabulary study that begins with an introduction of the vocabulary and then follows a sequence of activities that takes students through the steps of vocabulary study by first finding the vocabulary words in context, then thinking of related words and recording them in their Vocabulary Notebooks, after which students consult etymologies, sort related words in a concept sort with a partner, and play vocabulary games, finally writing a reflection on what was learned and sharing with others.

FIGURE 8.5   Weekly Vocabulary Schedule

Days	Teaching Focus	Key Independent Activities
1. Monday	Introduce vocabulary Use words in context in discussion with class	• Complete Day 1 vocabulary self-assessment • Hunt for interesting words • Vocabulary brainstorming • Practice vocabulary sort
2. Tuesday	Use words in context in discussions Vocabulary hunt Enter vocabulary in Vocabulary Notebook Deep study of a few words (2–3 words)	• Share interesting words and locate several key vocabulary terms in text • Concept organization of vocabulary with concept sorts, maps, or charts • Group sort with student participation and teacher scaffolding • Add related words • Consult etymologies • Explore online resources
3. Wednesday	Continued deep study of a few words (2–3 words) Share deep studies	• Continue to study several vocabulary words deeply • Make Vocabulary Notebook entry of new information from shared vocabulary study • Buddy concept sort • Introduce vocabulary games • Play one or two rounds of vocabulary games
4. Thursday	Share deep studies Prepare vocabulary reflections	• Enter related words in Vocabulary Notebook • Word hunts for related vocabulary words • Prepare written reflections on vocabulary • Play vocabulary games
5. Friday	Share vocabulary reflections Assessment Planning	• Review reflections of vocabulary learning with a partner or in a small group • Update vocabulary self-assessment with a partner • Assess, including sorts and writing sorts • Consider pacing in planning for new sort or continuing the current sort

Integrated Schedules for Differentiated Instruction.   Two schedules to integrate and organize vocabulary study are presented in Figures 8.6 and 8.7. The keys at the bottoms of the tables elaborate the types of activities that can be included. The schedule for a 90-minute block in a ninth grade English class is presented in Figure 8.6. This schedule sets out three sessions a week, with each 90-minute session divided into three 30-minute activity periods that include reading, writing, and vocabulary work. Instruction takes place in whole class (WC), small groups (SG), or independent work (IW), and the small groups facilitate differentiation for varying ability groups if needed. Figure 8.7 presents a 50-minute daily schedule for a science class. In both configurations, the teacher is shown with the star (*) as moving across groups for individual and group meetings. The Individual English Contract is often used at the beginning of the school year to concen-

FIGURE 8.6   **Two-Week Schedule**

Schedule for Ninth Grade Extended 90-Minute Block

		9:15–9:45	Get Set	9:45–10:15	Evaluation & Break	10:15–10:45	Closing
Day 1	Group 1	WC (bibliographies)		WC VS (power map)		SG (contracts)	
	Group 2						
	Group 3						
Day 2	Group 1	SG* (literature discussions)		WW VS (vocabulary cards)		IS (bibliographies)	
	Group 2	IS (bibliographies)		SG* (literature discussions)		WW VS (vocabulary cards)	
	Group 3	WW VS (vocabulary cards)		IS (bibliographies)		SG* (literature discussions)	
Day 3	Group 1	WC		VS (list/group/label)		SG (literature discussions)	
	Group 2			VS (list/group/label)		SG (literature discussions)	
	Group 3			VS (list/group/label)		SG (literature discussions)	
Day 4	Group 1	WW VS (vocab-o-gram)		IS (written vocabulary reflection)		SG (literature discussions)	
	Group 2	SG				SG (literature discussions)	
	Group 3	WW VS (vocab-o-gram)				SG (literature discussions)	
Day 5	Group 1	WW		IS		WC (autobiographies)	
	Group 2	WW		SG (vocab-o-gram)			
	Group 3	WW*		IS			
Day 6	Group 1	WW*		VS (share word study notebooks, submit)		WC (4-square concept map)	
	Group 2	VS (share word study notebooks, submit)		WW*			
	Group 3	WW		VS (share word study notebooks, submit)			

Key

*	Student–Teacher Conference
VS	Vocabulary Study
SG	Small Group
WC	Whole Class
WW	Writers Workshop
IS	Independent Study (Independent study includes written responses, double-entry draft, vocabulary study, independent reading, project research, and writing process activities, like revising or editing.)

trate on individual understanding of class routines. Once students are familiar with the activities that comprise the routines, like how to conduct a small-group literature discussion or how to develop pages in their Vocabulary Notebooks, the individual contracts can be deleted with the schedules like those in Figures 8.6 and 8.7 remaining.

FIGURE 8.7 **Science Schedule Card and Individual English Contract**

Science Schedule Card

5th Period		1:40 – 1:55	2:00 – 2:15	2:20 – 2:35
Day 1	WC	Get set for week Brainstorm related vocabulary Introduce Vocabulary Semantic Feature Analysis		VS (partner vocabulary self-reflection) VS (partner vocabulary self-reflection) VS (partner vocabulary self-reflection)
Day 2	Group 1	JS (preparation*)	IS	VS (semantic feature analysis)
	Group 2	VS (semantic feature analysis)	JS (preparation*)	IS
	Group 3	IS	VS (semantic feature analysis)	JS (preparation*)
Day 3	Group 1	JS (preparation*)	IS	VS concept sort and related word hunt
	Group 2	VS (concept sort and related word hunt)	JS (preparation*)	IS
	Group 3	IS	VS (concept sort and related word hunt)	JS (preparation*)
Day 4	WC	Jigsaw		
Day 5	Group 1	WC prereading activities	VS*(self-reflection, Vocabulary Notebook)	IS
	Group 2		IS	VS*(self-reflection, Vocabulary Notebook)
	Group 3		IS	

Key

JS Jigsaw (small-group teaching)—with textbook and selections from book sets

* Student–Teacher Conference—students work in groups and teacher travels

VS Vocabulary Study—Vocabulary Notebook activities, vocabulary sorts, vocabulary self-reflection, concept charting, partner brainstorming, concept sorts, semantic maps

WC Whole Class—includes sharing, teacher lecture, activities

IS Independent Study, including reading related materials in book sets and in magazines, recording sorts and vocabulary study into Vocabulary Notebook, jigsaw preparation, concept sorts, deep study with reference materials, project work, preparation of presentations, practice for debates

Individual English Contract

Name _____   Date Due _____

Grade Desired _____   *Any work lost, left in locker, or chewed by dog will be done over again.

	Points Worth	Points Earned
1. Participation in reading and discussion of _____	20	
2. Writing assignment: Rough draft and final	20	
3. Vocabulary Notebook activities: suffix sort, suffix hunt, suffix grammar sort, vocabulary cards	20	
4. Journal writing: 4 paragraphs with title	20	
5. Reading discussion groups	10	
6. Reader response to independent reading	10	

Total Points   100   Points Earned: _____   Notes:

Expect a quiz on homework readings.   Grade: _____

At the beginning of each session and between activity periods, the teacher, perhaps with the help of a timekeeper, calls for the group to come together for two to five minutes for an evaluation and break to discuss the progress that has been made. With three questions, teachers can ask students by group to look at their individual performance: "How did it go?" is a good first question, followed by "Did you finish your work?" and "What is next?" The final question can serve as a transition between activities. The feedback from students during the evaluation is important for teachers to adjust assignments. The evaluation is also a time to offer students advice on proceeding.

There are two whole-class activity periods for vocabulary study. As can be seen in Figure 8.7, one session on the first day is to discuss the vocabulary, and another class session is for students to present what they learned about the vocabulary words that they studied deeply. Throughout, students study independently and with partners to complete assignments for small groups.

Grouping for Vocabulary Instruction

Activities require different group configurations; some groups and partners are established by common interests and others by development and instructional levels. Groups operate on the premise that all members are capable of making meaningful contributions and that growth and performance by the group as a whole is important.

Teaching Students to Work in Groups. Orient students by partners and groups and create norms for behavior when they work together. Guide the discussion by having students brainstorm the ingredients for positive learning experiences and the teacher's and students' responsibilities, such as getting to class on time and having their notebooks. If students are unaccustomed to studying with partners or in groups, the teacher may pause every 15 minutes to examine how they are progressing. Once students become familiar with the daily schedules, groups can study together for 30 minutes before pausing to reflect on their work.

Think of the ways you already group students, and begin to include vocabulary activities with successful configurations. Students are familiar with whole-class, small-group, partner, and individual configurations. Other options to consider might include online groups across class periods, schools, and districts.

Students' vocabulary learning improves with exposure; activities are designed to have students hear, say, read, and write the vocabulary in meaningful contexts as often as possible. Deep study of the vocabulary is important. Playing the vocabulary games together increases exposure, besides being a way for students to enjoy studying together.

Proximal Partners. Students who are close developmentally are called *proximal partners*. They assist each other as they learn, because the questions they have and the vocabulary and learning strategies they need to learn are nearly the same. Furthermore, errors, self-corrections, and other hurdles that one partner faces are proximal for the partner to learn from, and often these interactions lead to new understanding.

Mixed Groups and Pairs. Sometimes other factors determine the make-up of small groups, including background knowledge, interests, language skills of English learners, group participation skills, and study habits. There are also social dynamics that govern how groups might be formed.

In mixed ability groups and pairs stronger readers can help students who may have difficulty reading the texts to learn the concepts. Be specific about what it means to assist partners without doing the work for them and how to share responsibilities. Sometimes there is a group product and other times partners are asked to support each other without doing the actual work. Diplomacy and good manners, like "no put downs" rule, are needed for partnering. For example, it can be a delicate matter for a student to ask another, "Would you read this paragraph to me?"

Differentiated Materials, Media, and Activities.　There are three ways to differentiate instruction: differentiate materials for students' instructional reading levels, differentiate the media that students use, or differentiate activities so that all students have access to new knowledge and can demonstrate their understandings of what they have learned. Vocabulary words that are found primarily in the core texts are studied in class activities. Differentiated reading materials might be at an easier level but should still include the essential vocabulary for content area learning. For struggling readers, content dictations can be created by students. They listen to a section of the text and then dictate a summary that includes the key vocabulary. Copies are made for students to place in folders or what can be called Personal Readers for frequent rereading (Bear et al., 2008).

There are many ways to present vocabulary to students if there is access to multimedia. Images can be found online to demonstrate vocabulary visually. Vocabulary programs like Vocabulary Grapher (www.vocabgrapher.com) present relationships among words while displaying many related words and even reading the words aloud; they also present pictures, provide vocabulary questions, and show grammatical and root information. Other sites offer video-related materials. For example, in reading about floods, it is useful to see a short movie about floods. Learning stations or centers are places where students can view multimedia materials. Likewise, there are several ways to show competence in vocabulary knowledge. Students can illustrate vocabulary, graph related words, or even create movies about the vocabulary.

Roles in Small Groups.　Several roles for group members have been described, including recorder/notetaker/scribe, timekeeper, discussion facilitator, and reporters. Other roles can include posting student work, collecting activity folders, conducting Internet searches, checking library references, and compiling notes. Different tasks require different responsibilities, and students can be involved in thinking of these roles and opportunities for leadership. Roles should rotate among group members to avoid the tendency to turn repeatedly to students who have already acquired a skill. For example, ask someone who has yet to acquire a skill to be responsible for technology, like opening and closing a computer program or documenting student work with a digital camera. Assigning mentors can provide scaffolding for students.

Groups and members of groups should be asked to assess their participation with questions such as *Am I listening to and observing my partner(s)? How can I contribute to the success of my partner(s)? How am I contributing to the vocabulary learning of members of the group? What advice, ideas, and references can I share?* These questions help to develop a learning ethic of caring, which is a rich part of vocabulary learning: sharing our ideas for the benefit of society. See page 159 earlier in this chapter for more questions to guide group assessment.

In closing this chapter on vocabulary assessment, and as the last paragraph of the formal text, consider the derivation and meaning of the word *teach*. The word *teach* can be traced back from Middle English *techen* to Old English *tcan*, and derives from the Indo-European root *deik* (to show, pronounce solemnly). The oldest form is *dei*, which can mean "bright, to shine" and is related to the Latin *deities* (*American Heritage Dictionary*, 2000). It is true that teachers are bright stars who shine. This chapter has been about assessment, which means literally "to sit beside." In assessing vocabulary, teachers sit beside students and as their vocabulary instruction shines so do the students. When students learn new vocabulary, they become brighter and more comprehensive thinkers.

APPENDIXES

APPENDIX A

Sample Generative Lessons: Intermediate/Middle Grades

Teaching about Word Parts: Prefixes, Suffixes, and Word Roots

Appropriate for most intermediate and middle grade students, these sample lessons may also be used for secondary students who need the structure these lessons offer or students whose literacy levels require instruction at this level. They are also appropriate for older students who are learning English as a new language. Teachers will find that, for students who need more of a challenge at these grade levels, the sample secondary grade lessons in Appendix B may be more appropriate.

As emphasized throughout the book, the most important aspects of these types of lessons are (1) the students' *awareness* and *understanding* of the prefixes, suffixes, and bases, as well as the roots that form them, as they explore how these elements combine; and (2) the *discussions* about these word elements and the words that contain them. The lessons provide "templates" for how lessons may be structured and how teachers can talk about words and word parts with students.

Although these sample lessons illustrate how the exploration of words may be arrayed over a four-day cycle, each lesson may be extended or shortened to accommodate teachers' schedules and styles. Based on an understanding of their students, teachers should use their own judgment about how much or how little time they feel is necessary for a lesson. Day 1 lessons will usually require 10 to 15 minutes on the average, though discussions may on occasion extend beyond that. Days 2 and 3 are usually follow-ups to Day 1, with additional activities. Day 4 will usually involve a brief wrap-up discussion.

These lessons reflect aspects of both *direct* and *exploratory* approaches to learning the meanings of the target word parts; at times it is indeed suggested that teachers tell the students directly about the meaning of the target word parts. The number of words per lesson varies; the number of words is not as important as the element or elements that are taught and how they combine to create the meanings of words. Because these lessons are focused primarily on *generative* rather than *word-specific* knowledge, most of the words will be familiar to the students. Familiar words provide the best context for figuring out and understanding the targeted elements. A few words will be unfamiliar, and students will apply knowledge of the target elements to try to determine their meanings.

Three of these lessons include a Background Information for the Teacher feature, illustrating how information addressed in several chapters in this book about the history or interesting features of the word parts being studied may be incorporated within a lesson. Often, this information can become the "stories" teachers share with students about words and where words come from, why they are pronounced and spelled as they are, and how they have come to have the meanings they now have.

FIRST PREFIX LESSON

in- (not, without)   *im-* (not, without)

incorrect   immature
incomplete   imperfect
inexpensive   impatient
incapable   improper
ineffective
incompetent

Day 1

Before following the steps in presenting the lesson, give a short introduction:

"Most words in English are made by combining prefixes and suffixes with base words and word parts from Greek and Latin. Greek and Latin were languages spoken over 2,000 years ago. This year, we're going to be learning more about the most important prefixes, suffixes, and Greek and Latin roots in the language. If you know these word parts, you will be able to read thousands of words in English. You will also be able to figure out the meanings of thousands of words in English, too!"

1. Write the word *incorrect* on the board/overhead/lumens. Ask the students, "If an answer is incorrect, what does that mean? So, if it is wrong or *not correct*, what do you think the prefix *in-* means? Is it similar to or the same as *un-*, our prefix from last week?"

2. Write the word *incomplete* on the board/overhead/lumens. Ask the students, "If the prefix *in-* means *not*, what do you think the word *incomplete* means?"

3. Write the following words:

   capable
   effective
   competent

   Discuss each one, and while pointing to each word, use a sentence to provide an oral context. For example, "[Name of a student] is capable of winning the race this weekend. What do you think is the most effective way to keep yourself awake after lunch? [Name of a student] is very competent in solving equations in algebra." Then, write *in-* before each word, and discuss how the meaning has changed. If necessary, use the sample sentences but substitute the *in-* words: "Do you think [name of a student] is incapable of winning the race?"

4. "The prefix *in-* is also spelled *im-*, as in the word *immature*. Have you ever heard someone referred to as immature? If *im-* also means *not*, what do you think the word *immature* means?"

5. "Now let's say we ran into this sentence when we were reading about a new outlet mall that is opening." Write the following sentence on the board/overhead/lumens:

   The stores in the outlet mall will sell <u>inexpensive</u> items such as clothes and electronics.

   "How can we figure out what the word *inexpensive* means?" Discuss with the students how they can combine the meaning of *in-* with the word *expensive* and, together with the rest of the sentence, figure out the meaning. A key idea here is the "outlet mall." Some students should know that stores in outlet malls usually have lower prices than other stores.

6. "There are two things you'll be doing in your Vocabulary Notebooks today: First, write down your *in-* and *im-* words. Then, write down our definition for *in-* and *im-*."

Day 2

1. Display the words from Day 1. Ask students, "What is our definition of the prefix *in-* and its other spelling, *im-*?"
2. Write the following words on the board/overhead/lumens:

   impatient
   improper

   Point to and read each word and then say, "With a partner, determine the meaning of each word, write a sentence for each word, and then write your sentences in your Vocabulary Notebooks."
3. "Today and tomorrow, keep your eye out for words that contain the *in-* prefix and its other spelling, *im-*. Record or write them down in your Vocabulary Notebooks. If you find any oddballs, write those down in a separate column. We'll share what you find over the next two days."

   (Optional, though highly recommended):
4. "I'll put up an *in-/im-* chart on the wall, and any *in-* or *im-* words you find that are really interesting, write them on our chart. I'll do that as well!"

Day 3

"What are some *in-* and *im-* words that you have found? Were you able to figure out the meanings?" (If a chart has been posted, check that as well.)

Day 4

Check any additional *in-* and *im-* words the students may have recorded. Review the meaning of *in-/im-*: "not, without." Share a few sentences that the students have written. If a student is not certain about the meaning of a word they found, this is a good opportunity to talk about the word with the class and try to tease out its meaning. If students can share the source of the word, that provides an excellent context for the discussion of the meaning.

Background Information for the Teacher

"Why do some words have the prefix *un-* and others have the prefix *in-*? Actually, both prefixes started out the same because they came from the same language, Indo-European, spoken about 5,000 B.C.E. As the years went by, some sounds changed, and eventually people who lived in Northern Europe said *un-*, while people in Southern and Western Europe said *in-*.

"Why do we say *immature* instead of *inmature*? Because it's easier to say *immature* instead of *inmature*. Try it out. Say both '*in*mature' and '*im*mature.' Back in Roman times, when they spoke Latin, they started out saying something like *in*mature but over time the /n/ sound disappeared because it was easier to say just the /m/ sound instead of *both* the /n/ and /m/ sounds. Then they changed the spelling of *in-* to *im-* to reflect this change in pronunciation."

SECOND PREFIX LESSON

pre- (before)	*post-* (after)	*re-* (again, back)
pregame	postgame	rebuild
preteen	postfix	recopy
preview	posterity	rewrite
prefix	postdate	relocation
prejudice		readjust
prejudge		recycle

Day 1

1. Write the following words on the board/overhead/lumens:

   pregame
   postgame

   Point to *pregame* and *postgame*, and ask the students to read each word. "Several of you are involved in different sports. Do any of you do pregame warm-ups or drills? What kind?" Have a short discussion. "Do any of you ever have postgame activities? Like going to have pizza? What's the difference between *pre*game and *post*game, then?"

2. "We've all heard the term *preteen*. What does it mean? What do you think: Is there such a word as *postteen?*" Students can check this in dictionaries; Merriam-Webster's online dictionary has it; other dictionaries list it as *post teen*. You can tell the students that this is one word they may want to track down on their own. One of them will probably find it over the next few days; if not, you can share with them at the end of the week.

3. "Turn to your partner and, in no more than ten seconds, come up with the definition of *pre-* and *post-*." When the time is up, let students share their words.

4. "Now, with our partner, let's figure out what these words mean."

   preview
   prefix

   "So when you see a preview of a movie, do you view the whole movie or just see a part of it? Why do the theaters do that? Why is that called a *preview?* And did you figure out why a prefix is called a *prefix?*" Have a brief discussion. "If a prefix is a word part that is 'fixed before' a word, do you think there is a word *postfix?*" Write *postfix* on the overhead. If students say no, encourage them: "Well, if there *were* such a word, what might it mean if it applied to words? What do we call word parts that come at the end of words?" (Suffixes.) "Actually, linguists—people who study languages—*do* have the word *postfix*, and it is another word for suffix. Even though you didn't think that this word really existed, you were able to figure out what it meant!"

5. Write the word *prejudice,* and read it for the students if none of them is able to. "Have you heard the word *prejudice* before? What does it mean to say that someone is prejudiced? What word does *prejudice* come from?" If no one mentions it, write *prejudge,* and ask the students to read it. "So, if someone is prejudiced, does that mean they have already prejudged someone?"

6. Write the following words:

   rebuild
   recopy
   rewrite

   "I think we've seen this prefix before. Turn to your partner and talk about what it means to *re*build something, to *re*copy something, to *re*write something."

7. "There are two things we're going to do in our Vocabulary Notebooks today: First, write down our *pre-, post-,* and our *re-* words. Then, write down your definitions for *pre-, post-,* and *re-.*"

Day 2

1. Display the words from Day 1. Ask students, "What is our definition of the prefixes *pre-* and *post-?* What is our definition of the prefix *re-?*"

2. Write the following words on the board/overhead/lumens:

   relocation
   readjust
   recycle

"With a partner, figure out the meaning of each word. The two of you will then choose two of the words, compose together a sentence for each of your words, and then write your sentences in your Vocabulary Notebooks."

3. "Today and tomorrow, keep your eye out for words that contain *pre-*, *post-*, and *re-*."

4. "You may also create your own words with these prefixes—as long as you can tell us a meaning for them! If you find any oddballs, write those down in a separate column. We'll share what you find over the next two days."

(Optional, though highly recommended):

5. "I'll put up a *pre-/post-* and *re-* chart on the wall, and any words you find that contain these prefixes and are really interesting—including any you create yourself—write them on our chart. I'll do that as well!"

Day 3

"What are some *pre-/post-* and *re-* words that you have found or created?" This is a good opportunity for students to share and explain any words they have created. (If a chart has been posted, check that as well.)

Day 4

Check any additional *pre-/post-* and *re-* words the students may have recorded. Ask, "Did one of the prefixes have more examples than the other? Which one?" Review the meanings of *pre-/post-* and *re-*. Share a few sentences that the students have written. If a student is not certain about the meaning of a word they found, this is a good opportunity to talk about the word with the class and try to tease out its meaning. If students can share the source of the word, that provides an excellent context for the discussion of the meaning.

If no one has found *postteen* during the week, share with them that it *is* a word, and that it is sometimes written *post teen*.

FIRST SUFFIX LESSON

-y, *-ly* (like, having the characteristics of)

squeaky	silently
scratchy	eagerly
wealthy	politely
guilty	unfairly
	clumsily
	hastily
	easily

Day 1

1. Write the following words on the board/overhead/lumens:

   scratch
   squeak
   wealth
   guilt

   Say, "Turn to a partner and discuss what each of these words means."

2. Add a *-y* to each word:

   squeaky
   scratchy
   wealthy
   guilty

Say, "Turn to your partner again, and talk about what adding the suffix *-y* does to each of these words. It will probably be pretty obvious if you think of a sentence with *squeaky* in it, another sentence with *scratchy* in it, and another sentence with *wealthy* in it—that will give you a clue about what *-y* does!"

Note. Getting the students to approach an understanding of how *-y* "works" through this type of discussion, using the words in sentences, is usually more effective than simply telling them the meaning of the suffix.

3. Write the following words on the board/overhead/lumens:

   silently
   eagerly
   politely
   unfairly

   Say, "Turn to your partner again, and talk about what adding the suffix *-ly* does to the base words. Just as with the suffix *-y*, you may find that thinking of one sentence with *silent* and another with *silently* helps you think of the meaning of *-ly*."

4. After students have discussed the *-ly* words, ask, "In our own words, what would be a good definition for *-y* and *-ly*? In your Vocabulary Notebooks, write down our definition."

Day 2

1. Write the following words from Day 1 on the board/overhead/lumens:

squeaky	silently
scratchy	eagerly
wealthy	politely
guilty	unfairly

   Then, write the following new words:

   clumsily
   hastily
   easily

   "What is the base of *clumsily*? Right, *clumsy*. Does *clumsy* have a base? Probably not." (If someone suggests "clum" might in fact be a word, ask a student to check a dictionary). "Turn to a partner, and decide what the base word is in *hastily* and in *easily*." It is possible that this discussion will turn up both *haste* and *hasty*, as well as *easy* and *ease*. If not, ask students afterwards if they have ever heard of the word *haste* or *ease*. Chances are, of course, that they have—so you are providing a gentle reminder.

2. After asking the students what they decided, write the following:

haste	ease
hasty	easy
hastily	easily

   "This is interesting, isn't it? A lot of words work like *hastily* and *easily*. We start taking off suffixes and we discover more words underneath! What about the *spellings* of these words? In *hasty* and *easy*, we have to change that *y* to an *i* before adding *-ly*, don't we?"

3. "In our Vocabulary Notebooks today, this is what we're going to be doing: You'll make three columns like this." Write on the board/overhead/lumens:

   <u>Base</u>   *-y*   *-ly* and *-ily*

   "For every word we've looked at today and yesterday, write the base *-y* words in the middle column and *-ly* and *-ily* words in the right-hand column. You might think of some more words that you could add in the *-ly* and *-ily* column. For example, we talked about *scratch* and *scratchy*, but might there also be a *scratchily*?"

Optional Day 2 Alternative. If parts of speech have already been addressed and you feel that most students could benefit from talking about them, the following type of discussion might be shared at some point during the week:

"Words such as *haste*, *hasty*, and *hastily* have a similar meaning, of course, but they are also slightly different. Their difference has to do with how they are used in sentences. For example, in the sentence 'I was hasty,' *hasty* describes *me*—I am the noun in this sentence, and words that describe nouns are called *adjectives*, so *hasty* is an adjective. In the sentence 'I acted hastily,' *hastily* describes how I acted—it tells something about the verb *acted*. Words that describe verbs are called *adverbs*. So, it tells us about the verb *acted*. *Hastily* is an adverb."

Following this type of discussion, students could sort words as follows:

"Write ADJECTIVE on the left side of the page, ADVERB in the middle, and ODD-BALL on the right. Go on a 'word hunt' with your partner. Look back through something you have already read, and when you find a word that ends in *-y* decide if it goes in the adjective column: Is it describing a noun? If a word ends in *-ly* or *-ily*, decide if it goes in the adverb column: Is it describing a verb? If you're not sure, write the word in the oddball column."

On another day, students can share the words they found and the class can talk about whether they are indeed adjectives or adverbs. This is usually a very helpful discussion.

Day 3

Have students go on a word hunt, looking for *-y* and *-ly* words. Add those words to the columns they began on Day 2. Add an "Oddball" column for words that end in these letters but which the students think do not come from a base word—for example, *lily* and *Emily*.

Day 4

Ask students to share some of the words they found on their word hunts, including oddballs. *Were* there many oddballs? (Probably not!) What does that tell them about words that end in *-y* and *-ly*/*-ily*? "So, turn to a partner and define *-y* and *-ly* again!"

SECOND SUFFIX LESSON

-ion (act, process)

suggest	illustrate	explode
suggestion	illustration	explosion
invent	imitate	divide
invention	imitation	division
instruct	erupt	intrude
instruction	eruption	intrusion
interrupt		
interruption		

The reason for an emphasis on *spelling* in this lesson is primarily to facilitate students' discussion about words, their meanings, and the relationships among them. Students should also begin to understand that spellings are not random but rather follow predictable *patterns*.

Day 1

1. Write the following word pairs on the board:

   suggest   invent
   suggestion   invention

   "We're going to examine the suffix *-ion* and see how it affects the base words it attaches to." Pointing to the *suggest/suggestion* word pair, ask the students, "What do you notice about these words?" Do the same with the *invent/invention* pair. If necessary, ask more specific questions, such as:

   - "What happens to the base words when the *-ion* suffix is added?"
   - "How are the base word and its suffixed form alike? How are they different?"

2. These questions should help move the students toward thinking about *meaning* and about the role each word plays in a sentence—the *act* (for example, *suggesting*) in comparison to the *result* of the act (for example, the *suggestion*). Have the students turn to partners and talk about which word in each pair is the noun and which is the verb. Encourage students to cast the words into sentences; this will also highlight the similarities and differences.

3. Write the following words on the board:

   instruction   interruption   eruption

   "What is the base word of *instruction*? Right, *instruct*." Write *instruct* underneath *instruction*. "What is the base word of *interruption*? Right, *interrupt*." Write *interrupt* underneath *interruption*. "What is the base word of *eruption*? Right, *erupt*." Write *erupt* underneath *eruption*. "What do you notice about these words?" If necessary, ask more specific questions such as "What happens to the base words when the *-ion* suffix is added? How are the base word and its suffixed form alike? How are they different?"

4. "In your Vocabulary Notebooks today, label one column *Verb* and one column *Noun*, and write today's words in the appropriate column. Check with your partner to compare."

Day 2

1. Write the following words on the board:

   illustrate   explode
   division   imitation
   explosion   intrude
   intrusion   illustration
   imitate   divide

2. "Any ideas about the meaning of *intrude* or *intrusion*? If you know the meaning of one, does that give you clues to the meaning of the other?" Check their ideas with a dictionary.

3. "In your Vocabulary Notebooks, match up a base word with its suffixed form. For example, *illustrate* would be matched with which word? Right, *illustration*. After you finish, talk with your partner about any clues to spelling that you see. For example, what happens to the spelling of the base word when the *-ion* suffix is added?" This is a fairly advanced spelling skill, but there may be some students who figure it out. The "*e* drop" in words such as *illustrate* and *imitate* is pretty straightforward, but the *explode*, *divide*, and *intrude* examples are a little more advanced: "When adding *-ion* to words that end in *de*, change *de* to *s*."

Day 3

Have students go on a word hunt, looking for words that end in *-ion*. Have them write the words in columns labeled "No Spelling Change" (just adding *-ion*), "*e* Drop," and "Big Spelling Change" (two or more letters at the end of the base word change when *-ion* is added).

Day 4

Share some of the words students found on their word hunt, and discuss which column they placed them in.

FIRST ROOT LESSON (LATIN)

vis (see)	*dict* (say, speak)
invisible	predict
vision	predictable
revision	dictate
visit	contradict
visibility	dictionary
visor	
supervise	

Your walk-through of how these roots combine with affixes to create the meaning of each word is *very* important. For your students, you provide a model for thinking about more complex word structure. It will help them decode unfamiliar words, but more importantly, *learn* and *remember* the meanings of new words.

Day 1

1. "We've said that so many words in English come from Latin and Greek, two languages that were spoken over 2,000 years ago. The prefix *in-* and its different spellings and also the prefix *pre-* both come from Latin. This week, we'll begin looking at *roots* that come from Latin. A root usually cannot stand by itself as a word, but is a very important part of a word.

   "We know we've probably found a root in a word when we take off all of the prefixes and suffixes we can and are left with something that doesn't look like a word. For instance, let's look at these two words."

   unbreakable   invisible

   "With *unbreakable*, we can take off the prefix *un-* and the suffix *-able*, and we have the word *break*." Cover the affixes as this is explained, or draw a line through them. "With *invisible*, we can take off the prefix *in-* and the suffix *-ible* and what do we have left? Right! Just *vis*. Is *vis* a word? No, it isn't, so we've found the *root*."

2. "Roots usually have the same meanings they had back when people spoke Latin and Greek. In ancient Rome, where they spoke Latin, *vis* meant 'to see.' Let's look at *invisible* again. We know what the prefix *in-* means, don't we? Right! 'Not.' So, if something is 'not visible,' what does that mean?" (It cannot be seen.)

3. "Now let's look at this word."

   predictable

   "If something is predictable, what does that mean? If we take the suffix *-able* off, what's left? Right, *predict*. Do you see a prefix in *predict*? Yes, there's *pre-*. What does *pre-* mean? Right, 'before.' If we take *pre-* off, we're left with *dict*, which is not a word. So, *dict* is the root of *predictable*. It comes from a Latin word meaning 'to say or speak.' To predict that something will happen literally means that you *say* it will happen *before* it happens."

If the students seem to be picking up on the concept of *root* easily, ask them, "What do you think the root *dict* meant in Latin? If you predict that something will happen, what does that mean? How does combining the root and the prefix lead to the meaning of *predict?*"

4. Write the words *vision* and *revision* on the board. "*Vision* has to do with seeing, right? What about *revision?* We use this word when talking about writing, don't we? Turn to a partner and talk about what you think *revision* has to do with 'seeing' as it applies to writing. When you 'revise' something that you've written, what does that mean?" This discussion should help students understand that *revision* literally means "to see their writing again."

Note. Because *invisible* is discussed this first day, the additional information about why we have both of the prefixes *in-* and *un-* in English may also be shared; see "Background Information for the Teacher" below.

Day 2

Display the words from Day 1. Ask students, "What is our definition of the root *vis?* Of the root *dict?*" Write the following words on the board/overhead/lumens:

visit	dictate
visor	dictionary
visibility	contradict
supervise	dictionary

"With a partner, talk about how the meaning of each root works in each of these words. For example, how does the meaning of "say" or "speak" work in *dictionary?* When you contradict someone, what does that mean? Then, with your partner, compose a sentence for *visor* or *supervise* and for *dictate* or *contradict*." Underline these words on the overhead. "Write your sentences in your Vocabulary Notebook." Students may be surprised to realize that *visit* literally means to "go see" someone. You may have them look up *visit* in an unabridged dictionary or online; *it* actually is a root that means "go."

Day 3

Have students volunteer to share their sentences. You may wish to post a "golden sentences" chart or charts on which students may write their favorite sentences with the word containing the root underlined.

Day 4

"Using any of the prefixes we have explored so far together with either *vis* or *dict*, create a word. It may be a real word, or it may be a word that does not yet exist in English. In your Vocabulary Notebook write the word, a definition for it, and—if it can be illustrated—include the illustration, too." (The students' new words can be shared later or on the next day.)

Background Information for the Teacher

Why do we have the word *invisible* and not *unvisible*? The first "Background Information" section explained why both *un-* and *in-* are in the language. You may wish to share the following more specific information with your students:

"Most of our simpler words such as *happy*, *want*, or *bent* come from Old English, which was spoken over a thousand years ago in England. *Un-* was the prefix used then and it had the same meaning as it does today. About a thousand years ago the French invaded England and brought with them their prefix *in-*, which had come into their language from Latin, and we've been attaching it ever since to words that came from the French and most words that came from Latin and Greek.

If Students Ask

"What about *division?* This is an example of a *different* root being spelled the same—much like our 'multiple-meaning' words in English. Another meaning for *vis* is 'to separate'—and this is where we get our word *division.*"

"What about *video?* Yes, it also comes from the same Latin root meaning 'to see.' In a number of roots, the spelling changes slightly (usually one letter at most), because in Latin the spelling changed depending on the role a word played in a sentence (subject, object, verb)."

SECOND ROOT LESSON (GREEK)

micro (small), *peri* (around), *tele* (distant)
phon (sound), *scop* (to look at), *photo* (light)

microscope	periscope	telecommunication
microscopic	periphery	telemetry
microphone	perimeter	telephoto
		television
		telephone
		telescope
		telescopic

Day 1

1. "Recently we began looking at roots that come from Latin. This week, we're going to be looking at a handful of roots that come from Greek. A large number of words contain Greek roots. These roots usually have a pretty consistent or constant meaning. Most often they do not occur by themselves as words, though on occasion some of them may do so. Learning the meaning of a number of these roots and understanding how they combine to create words will be extremely helpful to you in figuring out and learning new vocabulary."

   Write the following two words on the board/overhead/lumens:

   microscope
   microscopic

   "What's our first word? Right! And how about our second word? How are these two words related, or alike?" After students discuss this, point to *microscope* and say, "We know these words, but let's look at the Greek roots that make them up. *Scope* comes from a Greek word that means 'to look at,' and *micro* means 'small,' so when we put them together we *literally* get the meaning 'to look at something small.' A microscope is an instrument for looking at very small or tiny things, so if we say that something is *microscopic* what does that mean?"

2. Now write the following two words:

   telescope
   periscope

   "We know these words, but let's look at their Greek parts: We already know that *scope* means what? Right, 'to look at.' What do you suppose *tele* means?" The students will probably get close to the meaning of "far off" or "distant"; if not, however, tell them explicitly that *tele* comes from Greek and means "distant." A telescope is an instrument for looking at distant objects.

   If students are not certain about *periscope*, write *perimeter*, and remind them how it means "to measure *around.*" So, a periscope is an instrument on a submarine used to "look around"—quite literally, *all* the way around!

3. "How about these words? Turn to a partner and talk about how the Greek roots combine to create the meaning of each word."

   television
   telephone

"Did you talk about how television delivers vision from a distance? What do you think *phone* means?" If no students have an idea after their partner talk, tell them, "*Phone* comes from a Greek word that means 'sound.' So, *telephone* is sound that comes from a distance."

4. "How about this word?"

microphone

"When we put the roots together, we have the literal meaning 'small sound.' Of course, a microphone is not literally a small sound but it picks up sounds that would otherwise not be heard very well."

5. "In your Vocabulary Notebooks, write our words just as I have done, one underneath the other. That helps us remember how they are alike in meaning and what their roots mean."

Day 2

Write the following words on the board/overhead/lumens:

> telecommunications
> telemetry
> telephoto

"What type of communication might be involved in telecommunications? With a partner, talk about what telemetry and telephoto might mean. We know what *tele* means; how does it combine with the rest of each word? We haven't talked about their meanings, but you may recognize them!"

It may be necessary to discuss *telephoto* with the students—they may have heard the word in the context of a telephoto *lens* but not thought about the meaning. Tell them that *photo* means "light." This may lead to a productive discussion about the literal meaning of *telephoto*—"light from a distance." Does that make sense when they think of a "telephoto lens"?

Day 3

1. "In your Vocabulary Notebooks, write each Greek root that we've been learning about, and then write its meaning next to it. If you need to refresh your memory, check with a partner." Provide the example:

micro = small

2. "Using any of these Greek roots, create a word. It may be a real word, or it may be a word that does not yet exist in English. In your Vocabulary Notebook write the word, a definition for it, and—if it can be illustrated—include the illustration, too."

Day 4

New words that the students generated on Day 3 may be shared. This is a good point at which to post a chart labeled "Words That Don't Exist But Could," on which students can record their made-up words.

THIRD ROOT LESSON (LATIN)

rupt (break)	*port* (carry)	*struct* (build)
interrupt	import	structure
erupt	transport	construct
disrupt	export	instruct
rupture	report	infrastructure
	deport	

Day 1

1. "We've looked at a few Latin and Greek roots over the last few weeks. We're going to examine three more Latin roots this week. Remember, a root usually doesn't stand by itself as a word, but is a very important part of a word."

   Write the words *erupt* and *interrupt* on the board and underline *rupt*.

   "This root [point to *rupt*] means 'break.' When a volcano erupts it literally *breaks* [point to the root *rupt*] out [point to the prefix *e-*]. Yes, the letter *e* can be a prefix, as you'll discover in a lot of words.

   "Now think about the word *interrupt*. How does the meaning of 'break' work when you think about interrupting a conversation?" If they don't realize it themselves, help students understand that when they interrupt a conversation they literally *break* (point to *rupt*) *in between* (point to the prefix *inter-*) the words another is speaking. "Yes, whenever you see the prefix *inter-* it will mean 'in between.'"

   Write the following sentences on the board:

   We tried to <u>disrupt</u> the fight.

   There was a <u>rupture</u> in the main water pipe.

   "Now turn to a partner and discuss how the root *rupt* contributes to the meaning of each underlined word." Follow up with the students.

2. Write the following words on the board:

   import   report
   transport   deport
   export

   Next, write the following sentence:

   The nation needs to <u>import</u> many goods from other countries.

   "What does the word *import* mean in this sentence?" After some discussion, tell the students, "The root *port* comes from a Latin word meaning 'carry.' And in the word *import*, the prefix *im-* means 'into.' So, goods that are *imported* are 'carried into' the country. When we export goods, what does that mean? Are goods coming *into* or going *out of* the country? So, what do you think the prefix *ex-* means?" (Out of) "And how about *transport*? *Trans-* is a prefix meaning 'across.' So, when someone or something is transported, what is happening?" (They are being "carried across" something—for example, land or sea.)

3. "In your Vocabulary Notebooks today, write our *rupt* and *port* words. Then, write the meaning of the *rupt* and *port* roots. Finally, discuss with your partner how the meaning of the underlined words in the following sentences comes from combining the meaning of the root with the meaning of the prefix."

   After scouting the enemy's position, the soldier had to <u>report</u> to his commanding officer.

   There is a debate in our community about whether to <u>deport</u> some people who are working here.

Day 2

1. Briefly discuss yesterday's sentence activity with the words *report* and *deport*.
2. Then, write the following two words on the overhead and tell the students that today they're going to look at the third root for the week, *struct*:

   construct
   structure

   Ask them what they think the meaning of *struct* might be. If necessary, use each word in a sentence. If they are still uncertain, tell them that the root *struct* means "build." Talk briefly with the class about how the meaning of structure might come from the meaning of this root. Explain that in the word *construct*, the prefix *con-*

means "with, together," so to construct something literally means "to build *with* or to build *together.*"

3. Write the following words on the board:

   instruct
   infrastructure

   "Look at the word *instruct*. Using the meaning of the prefix *in-* that we learned yesterday, talk with your partner about how you think the meaning of *instruct* comes from the combination of the root and the prefix." (Literally, to "build" information or knowledge "into" someone.)

4. Pointing to *infrastructure,* tell the students that *infra* is a prefix that means "below." "So, *infrastructure* literally means what? Right, 'the structure below.' This is a term used to refer to the basic foundation for a community—its transportation system, communication, schools, and so forth. For example, we sometimes hear that, when a bridge collapses, it is an example of the aging of the nation's infrastructure."

5. "In your Vocabulary Notebooks today, write our *struct* words and the meaning for the root *struct.* The rest of the week, be on the lookout for words that contain any of our three roots, and add them to your Vocabulary Notebook."

Day 3

"Using any of the prefixes we have explored so far, together with any of our three roots for this week, create three words that do not yet exist in English. In your Vocabulary Notebook write the words, a definition for them, and—if your words can be illustrated—include the illustrations, too."

Day 4

Take a few minutes to share students' created words from Day 3, and add them to the "Words That Don't Exist But Could" chart.

Background Information for the Teacher

Discussing how roots and affixes combine also often helps with spelling. Many students misspell words such as *interrupt* as INTERUPT because there is only one /r/ sound in the word. When you walk through a word, attending to its meaningful parts, the spelling makes more sense: "Even though we hear only one 'r' sound, there are two r's. Why do you think this is?" If students do not come to the realization on their own, point out that the spelling of the prefix *inter-* ends with an r, and the spelling of the root *rupt* begins with an r. When these two word parts are put together, the r's must be kept. Remember, *word parts with consistent meanings are usually spelled consistently.*

If appropriate, share the following with students: While the meaning of the prefix *in-* and its other spellings is most often "not," "opposite," or "reverse," the *next* most often occurring meaning is "into." This will be helpful to think about when they are trying to analyze an unknown word in their reading that begins with this prefix. First, try the meaning of "not," but if that doesn't seem to help, then try the meaning of "into."

If students do not ask, then at some point during the week tell them that, although most of the time word roots cannot stand by themselves as words, occasionally they do. *Port* is a good example of this. It is used today not only as a root but as a word, as in the case of a *port* into which ships sail. The meanings of words so often become extended to other things; it may be helpful to have the students discuss the following question:

> How is a <u>port</u> on a computer like a <u>port</u> in a big city, like San Francisco, Philadelphia, or Houston?

199

APPENDIX B

Sample Generative Lessons: High School

Teaching about Word Parts: Prefixes, Suffixes, and Word Roots

In contrast to the sample lessons in Appendix A, these lessons are not presented in daily formats. Most of the content of each lesson may be addressed during one class period, with follow-up activities done by the students independently or in pairs throughout a one- or two-week period. The words for each lesson will be sorted into different categories, either before or after the teacher demonstration. The teacher then guides students' reflections on what they notice and think about the target elements—affixes, bases, and roots. Although intended for secondary students, these lessons will also work for those middle grade students who are farther along in their literacy development.

As emphasized throughout the book, the most important aspects of these lessons are (1) the students' *awareness* and *understanding* of the prefixes, suffixes, and roots they will explore and how these elements combine, and (2) the *discussions* about these word elements and the words that contain them. The lessons provide "templates" for how lessons may be structured and how teachers can talk about words and word parts with students.

The number of the words per lesson varies; the number of words is not as important as the element or elements that are taught and how they combine to create the meanings of words. Because these lessons are focused primarily on *generative* rather than *word-specific* knowledge, students will already be familiar with most of the words in each lesson. A few words will be unfamiliar, and knowledge of the target elements will be applied to try to determine their meanings. At the end of each lesson, additional words that contain the target elements are provided. These words offer further opportunities for analysis, sorting, dictionary exploration/etymology, constructing root webs (see Chapter 4), and recording in Vocabulary Notebooks.

GREEK NUMBER PREFIXES

mono- (one)	*bi-* (two)	*tri-* (three)
monolingual	bilingual	triangle
monologue	biennial	tricolor
monopod	bisect	triennial
monopoly	binary	trilogy
monorail	bimonthly	trigonometry
monotone	biweekly	tripod
monotony	bicameral	triathlon

Prepare a set of words to use for teacher-directed modeling. Save the discussion of word meanings until after sorting. Display a transparency of the words on the overhead or hand out the sheet of words to the students. Ask them what they notice about the words and get ideas about how the words can be sorted. Students usually notice that all the words contain prefixes. Remind them of the term *prefixes* (units added to the beginning of a word). Have them sort the words by their prefixes.

Begin students' refection on the words by discussing the meanings of the words they recognize and arrive at some conclusions about what each prefix means. Ask them to discuss the difference between *monolingual* and *bilingual*, explicitly referring to the meaning of *lingual* (language). This discussion will help establish how these words may be analyzed according to prefix and the remaining meaning element. Students will then have activated their prior knowledge about these prefixes enough to support analyzing the less familiar words. Printed or online dictionaries should be used to look up the meaning of words that are less transparent, such as *biennial*.

You may mention a number of roots and their meanings in the context of this sort. For example, have students heard the word *triathlon? Triathlete?* Do they see a similarity between *triathlon* and *athletic?* Where have they heard *trilogy?* (Most students will probably mention the *Lord of the Rings;* others may mention *Star Wars* or particular science fiction trilogies—John Christopher's Tripods Trilogy is popular reading at the middle and secondary levels.) What is a *tripod?* While some students may have read the Tripods Trilogy, most will probably recall the movie *War of the Worlds.* Mention that *pod* is a Greek root that means "foot." In that context, *tripod* makes even more sense: "How does this now give you a clue to what a *monopod* might be?" If someone speaks in a *monotone,* would it be interesting and exciting to listen to them? Similarly, if you speak about the *monotony* of a situation or experience, would that situation or experience be exciting? Since *bi-* means "two" and *sect* comes from *section,* what does it mean to say that an interstate highway *bisects* a city?

As a point of interest, tell students that in English we also have, of course, the word *two.* Have they thought about the relationship between *two, twin,* and *twice?* How about *three* and *thrice?*

What other *bi* and *tri* words can the students think of? Suggest additional ones not mentioned—for example, *triad, triceratops.* The number three is significant in mythology and religion. Have students be on the lookout for significant occurrences of "three."

Additional Words That May Be Explored

monarch, monochrome, monocle, monogamist, monolith, monopolize, bicentennial, bicuspid, bifurcate, bigamist, bilateral, binoculars, bipartisan, bipolar, bisexual, biped, biplane, trident, trilobite, trimester, triple, triplicate, trivet, triptych, trisect, trinity, triumvirate

LATIN ROOTS 1

man (hand)	*scrib/script* (to write)	*cred* (to believe)	*fac* (to make)
manual	circumscribe	incredible	factory
manuscript	inscribe	credible	manufacture
manicure	inscription	credence	facsimile
manure	postscript	discredit	facilitate
	ascribe	incredulous	artifact

Students may sort these words without teacher introduction. Have them sort individually, then compare with a partner. Students will notice that *manufacture* and *manuscript* may be sorted in more than one category. Ask them to discuss with their partners what they think each root might mean. After partner discussions, discuss the meanings the students have generated. Address those about which the students are uncertain.

Man and *scrib/script* are usually straightforward. *Manual* labor is working by hand; *manuscript* is writing by hand. Students will probably be quite curious about *manure*, however! Share with them that, etymologically, *manure* is actually closely related to *manual*: *manure* evolved from a Middle English word that meant "to cultivate land," which in turn evolved from a Latin word that meant "to work with the hands." Mention to the students that, knowing what they know about the present-day meaning of *manure*, how do they think people hundreds of years ago actually cultivated their land?

Contrast *credible* and *incredible*; *incredible* is the more common word. Discuss its meaning; then ask students what they think *credible* means? Scaffold their understanding that if something is *incredible* it is literally "not believable." *Credence* may also be unfamiliar. "Because she is so knowledgeable about setting up your own website, I put a lot of *credence* in her advice."

The way the root *fac* works in *factory* and *manufacture* is straightforward. Ask students if they see a familiar pattern in *facsimile*; after the root *fac* is removed, *simile* remains. What do they think *simile* might mean? For most students, this is the first time they become aware that *similar* is in *facsimile*—literally, "make similar." Isn't that what a *fax* machine does? (This may also be the first time students realize *fax* is short for *facsimile*.) *Artifact* is a good example of a word whose literal sum of its meaning parts—"something made from art"—no longer exactly fits, but allows you to discuss how a more connotative meaning has evolved, the most common of which is something made by humans at a different time and in a different culture.

Ascribe means, literally, "to write to"—and by extension, "attributed to." This word can be introduced with the sentence "I *ascribe* Devon's constantly falling asleep in class to his staying up late every night watching movies." After discussing some of the *scrib/script* words, ask students if they think the word *scribble* is related and why—again, most will not have consciously made this connection.

On another day, you may elect to discuss why the spelling of some roots changes across related words, as in *scrib/script*; *fac/fic/fect*. These forms come from the original Latin verbs, in which the sound changed in different forms or declensions, so the spelling changed as well. This is similar to what happens in many English verbs: We *come* to visit today/we *came* to visit yesterday; I will *run* quickly; I *ran* quickly (see Chapter 3).

Following are possible extensions of this lesson:

- Ask students to generate other *scrib/script* words ending in *-ion* (e.g., *subscribe/subscription*; *transcribe/transcription*).
- By this point, students have explored a sufficient number of Latin and Greek elements to play Latin Root Jeopardy and Double Latin Root Jeopardy (Appendix E). This is an extremely popular game format with students that will continue to be useful as students advance in word knowledge. Eventually they can prepare their own Jeopardy games, exploring new roots as well as using the format to develop and reinforce content area vocabulary in science, math, and social studies, for example. Other games may also be explored here and as the students move through subsequent units.

Additional Words That May Be Explored

emancipate, manacle, manipulate, manage, conscription, describe, scribe, script, scriptwriter, subscribe, credit, credentials, accredited, credulous, faculty, benefactor, facile

LATIN ROOTS 2

leg (law)	*leg* (read)	*biblio* (book)	*mod* (manner, measure)
legalistic	legible	bibliography	moderate
legislate	legend	bibliophile	mode
allegiance	legion	biblically	modern
privilege		bibliomania	modality
		bibliotheca	accommodate

Have students sort the words according to roots and then discuss with a partner. Afterward they share any uncertainties they have about where particular words should be categorized. For example, the *leg* root may not be obvious in *privilege* and *allegiance*. Because of the nature of these roots and their combinations, a substantial amount of background information is included in the steps below.

Discuss the *biblio* words. Students may have a good idea about the meaning of this root. Begin with *bibliography*, a written list of books. Students may note that *biblically* is related to *Bible*—perhaps the first time they may have thought about the word *Bible* meaning "book." *Bibliophile* offers an opportunity to mention the Greek combining form *phile*, which means "having a strong preference for, loving," such as in *Philadelphia*, "city of love" or *anglophile*, someone who loves England and things English. *Bibliotheca* is "a collection of books." Students who are studying Spanish or whose first language is Spanish will notice relationship to the word for "library" in Spanish—*biblioteca*.

Have the students work in pairs to sort words that have the *leg* root into two categories: words that have to do with law and words that have to do with reading or literacy. This process will not be entirely straightforward, so after they have sorted and discussed bring them back together and do a group sort. Discuss those words about which they are uncertain, and if necessary share with them the following information: *legend*, *legible*, and *legion* all come from an Indo-European root that meant "to gather or collect." If something is *legible* one can read it, "gathering or collecting" information; *legend* comes from a Latin word that referred to something that was "to be read," referring to written stories. The word *legion* more directly refers to a "gathering" of individuals, as in the original meaning in Roman times. In the military, the Roman *legion* was the basic unit of organization in the army. *Privilege* actually contains two roots: *priv* ("single, alone" as in *private*) and *leg*—literally, "law for an individual."

Moderate relates to "measure" in that it refers to keeping within reasonable limits, as when one is a moderate eater or eats moderately. Note that *moderate* can be both a verb and a noun and the pronunciation will change accordingly: "Mr. Williams has *moderate* views on remodeling the legal system and will *moderate* a panel discussion next week."

You may wish to tell the students that *accommodate* is one of the most frequently misspelled words by highly literate adults. They usually leave out one *m*. Walking through its etymology may help this confusion. At the very least, it provides students with more information to associate with the spelling. *Accommodate* is related to *commodious* (literally, "to measure with"), which means "spacious, roomy"; *accommodate* has come to mean "to make room for." When you accommodate someone you "make room for" them or for their wishes, ideas, point of view. The most common meaning for *mode* is the "manner" of doing something, and this in fact goes back to the Latin meaning for *mode*—"manner" or "style." If you prefer a particular manner or style of learning something, for example, this is often referred to as a preference for a particular *modality*. Interestingly, this meaning applied to *modern* as well: "in a certain manner, just now."

The Latin Root Jeopardy and Double Latin Root Jeopardy games will be very appropriate for these and for subsequent root-focused sorts. Students may apply this format to creating their own Jeopardy games.

Additional Words That May Be Explored

allege, allegedly, allegation, illegal, legally, legacy, legation, legislature, legislation, legislator, legitimate, paralegal, bibliotherapy, bibliographic, bibliophobia, relegate, immoderate, modest, immodest, model, modernity, moderator, modicum, modify, modulate, outmoded, a la mode

LATIN ROOTS AND PREFIXES

bene (good, well)	*mal* (bad)	*ante-* (before)	*post-* (after)
benefit	malfunction	antebellum	postdate
beneficial	malaria	ante meridiem	post meridiem
benefactor	malefactor	antedate	postbellum
benevolent	malice	ante mortem	post mortem
	malfeasance	anterior	posterior

These roots and prefixes may be presented all on one day or divided into two days, with day 1 for roots and day 2 for prefixes. When addressing the roots, give attention to the ways in which they function within the words. Note that some Latin phrases are included (see Chapter 5).

A handful of the *bene* and *mal* words may be sorted into different categories. Begin your discussion by asking the students which words they think they know the meaning of, and discuss these. Be sure to elicit that *benefit* it has to do with "good." Discuss *malfunction*. If something *malfunctions* does it function well or poorly? Then discuss *benefactor*; do the students recognize another root they've recently explored? (*fac*, "to make.") A benefactor, then, is literally someone who "makes good," who is *beneficial* and *benevolent*—which literally means "good will" (*vol* = "will"). Contrast *benefactor* with *malefactor*.

Introduce the prefixes *ante-* and *post-* with the words *antedate* and *postdate*. Discuss what *postdate* means, as in "postdate a check," and then explain that *antedate* literally means "to date before." More specifically, it refers to something that has occurred earlier in time or history: "Bebop *antedates* hip-hop by almost half a century." Tell the students that they are likely to run into several of the *ante-* and *post-* words and phrases in history texts; *antebellum* and *postbellum* literally mean "before the war" and "after the war." In America, *antebellum* is most often used to refer to before the Civil War, as in antebellum architecture or antebellum attitudes and beliefs. Students have probably heard the term *post mortem*; discuss this and then ask them what *ante mortem* probably means. They may also have heard of *ante meridiem* and *post meridiem*. If not, ask them what they think AM and PM refer to? Share that *meridiem* comes from a Latin word meaning "midday." *Anterior* and *posterior* refer to "before, in front" versus "behind, in back." (Students may be familiar with the euphemistic use of *posterior* to refer to one's rear end!)

Additional Information to Share with Students

- *malfeasance* is closely related to *malefactor*; someone who is accused of *malfeasance* is someone who "does bad"—more specifically, usually a public official who engages in wrongdoing or inappropriate conduct.
- *dis* in *dismal* is not a prefix but rather comes from the Latin *dies*, meaning "day." So, *dismal* literally means "day that is bad."
- *malaria* = "bad air." Originally the cause of malaria was literally thought to be "bad air."
- *malice* = "state of being bad." In this word, *-ice* is a suffix (which usually occurs with nouns, as in *cowardice*) that means "state or condition of."
- *maladroit* = "not adroit." Ask the students what the base word of *maladroit* is—have they heard of it? If someone is *adroit* at something what does that mean? So, if someone is *maladroit*, what does that mean?

As an extension, remind students of the name of one of Harry Potter's classmates, Malfoy. J. K. Rowling created many of the characters' names using Greek and Latin elements. Challenge students to brainstorm other names from the series that give a clue to the personality of the character.

Additional Words That May Be Explored

benefactress, beneficiary, benevolence, malady, malaise, malapropism, malediction, malformation, malformed, malign, malignant, malinger, malnourished, malpractice, maltreated, antecedent, antechamber, antepenult, anteroom, postgraduate, posthumous, postnasal, postpaid

GREEK AND LATIN ROOTS RELATED TO THE BODY

cap (head, to take)	corp (body)	dent/dont (teeth)	ped/pod (foot)
decapitate	corpse	dentist	pedal
capitol	corps	orthodontist	pedicure
capital	corpulent	periodontal	podiatrist
captain	corporal	dentures	podium
recapitulate	corporation	indent	pedestrian

Tell students that these roots all have to do with the body. Have them sort the words according to word root. For each root, ask the students if they have a sense of its meaning. The following information will help support students' discussion; share specific information with students as necessary.

Ask what *decapitate* means; students' mentioning of "head" allows you to discuss *capital* and *capitol*—they both have to do with "head" of government, but why the difference in spelling? *Capital* refers to the city where the government is located, and *capitol* refers to the actual building in which the legislative body of the government meets. *Recapitulate* refers to stating again (*re-*) the main point, the "heading."

Address the root *corp* by first discussing *corpse,* quite literally a body; move then to *corps,* which is a military unit or body or a group such as a *press corps.* Then discuss how *corporal* and *corporation* reflect the concept of "body." The primary meaning of *corporal* is "having to do with the body"; the more familiar meaning, of course, is the designation of a particular rank in the military.

Most students should readily identify with *dentist* and *orthodontist.* Ask students what *orthodontists* do and explain that *ortho* means "straight or right." Establish that *dent* and *dont* are two versions of the same root. *Peri,* if you recall, means "around," as in *periscope,* so "around the teeth" refers to the gums where *periodontal* disease may occur. *Indent* is interesting. If you bite something you might leave a dent. The word *dent* means "to notch or bend inward." When you indent a paragraph you might, in a sense, take a bite into it.

Explain that *pod* and *ped* mean the same thing and thus they are combined into one column. Have students read through the words to see if they can get a sense of what the root might mean. Ask how *pedal* and *pedicure* might be related. *Pedicure* has two roots; *cure* means "care of." *Expedite* means "to speed up, execute more quickly"—literally, in Latin the root meant "to free from entanglements," and going back further to Indo-European, literally "to free one's foot from a snare." *Expedition* (literally, "going out by foot") is derived from *expedite.* Similarly, *impede* has evolved to mean "obstruct the progress of" something. *Podiatry* is literally "the healing of" (*iatry*) the foot; a *podiatrist* practices *podiatry* (*iatry* occurs in a number of words, and always refers to healing). The meaning of *podium*—"base"—evolved from "foot." Now that they know what *ortho* means, ask them to speculate about the meaning of the word *orthopedic.* Based on what they know about dentists and orthodontists, what might a orthopedist do?

It is important to note that *cap* can also mean "to take" or "seize" as in *captive,* and *ped* can also refer to a "child" as in *pediatrician. Pedagogy* comes from *pedagogue,* which literally means "one who leads children." This meaning derived from classical Greece, when a slave took children to and from school. It is a short step from one who leads children to and from school to one who teaches children. *Pediatric* refers to medical practice specializing in the treatment of children. A *pedant* is one who makes a conscious effort to display or show off his learning, so *pedantic* behavior is characterized by that type of showing off.

Additional Words That May Be Explored

per capita, corpus, incorporate, corpuscle, dental, dentin, dentifrice, pedometer, quadruped, pedigree, biped, millipede, moped, arthropod, tripod, chiropodist

GREEK AND LATIN ELEMENTS RELATING TO AMOUNTS

magni (great)	*macro* (large)	*poly* (much, many)	*equ* (equal)	*omni* (all)
magnificent	macroscopic	polysyllabic	equator	omnipotent
magnification	macroeconomics	polygon	equation	omnivore
magnitude		polysemous	equanimity	omniscient
		polyglot	equivalent	omnidirectional

These Greek and Latin elements have to do with the concept of "amount." Although the meanings of these elements are fairly straightforward, their combination with other elements to form a number of the words in this sort are more abstract. If you wish, you may walk the students through this sort sharing some or as much of the following background information as you believe may be helpful.

The Greek elements *magni, macro,* and *poly,* and the Latin elements *equ* and *omni* usually occur as prefixes and appear in a very large number of words. For example, *magnificent* includes the Latin root *fic,* which is another form of the Latin root *fac* (to make). So, *magnificent* literally means something or someone that has been "made great."

You may wish to ask students if *macroscopic* reminds them of another word they know; usually they will suggest *microscopic.* So, what do they think *macroscopic* means? Begin the *poly* discussion with the word *polysyllabic*—which may be said of a word that has three or more syllables. They will probably be familiar with *polygon* (*gon* meaning "angle"); the other *poly* words are probably less familiar. *Polymath* is interesting because *math* is a Greek combining form that means "to learn," so literally the word *polymath* means "to learn much"—it is usually used to refer to a person. *Polyglot* also refers to a person—one who knows many languages (*glot* comes from a Greek word meaning "tongue, language"—*glossary* is a related word). The other root in *polysemous* is *sem,* which comes from a Greek word meaning "to signify, a sign." A related word is *semantics,* which refers to "meaning," usually in the context of language. So, a *polysemous* word is one that has many meanings—for example, *dog* and *table.*

Equ is fairly straightforward: Begin your discussion with *equator,* discussing its meanings, and then discuss *equatorial*—having to do with or characterizing the equator. An *equation* has to do with things being equal. Discuss what an *equitable* solution refers to. *Equanimity* may be a new term: literally, "even (equal)-tempered"; if someone possesses equanimity they are calm and even-tempered. *Equanimity* comes from the Latin *animus,* meaning "mind," which in turn is related to Latin *anima* ("soul"). Yes, the root also occurs in *animal* and *animated* ("living, soul"). Students will probably know the meaning of *equivalent,* but point out that it is made up of *equ + valent,* which comes from the Latin root for "force, strength"—literally, "equal force or strength."

In introducing *omnivore,* ask students to define the word *voracious.* The sense of rabid eating will usually emerge; then, ask them what an *omnivore* might be. Next, write *science* on the board and ask the students if it gives any clue to *omniscient.* Then tell them that *science* comes from a Latin word meaning "to know." So, *omniscient* means "all knowing." You may wish to introduce the word *prescient* (*presh*-unt), as in "She was uncannily *prescient* in her observations about how the election results would turn out." Someone who is *prescient* displays the quality of *prescience* (*presh*-uns).

Have the students sort the words by prefixes, discussing the meaning of the words they know and working to infer the meaning of the remainder. They may check their hypotheses in their dictionaries.

Additional Words That May Be Explored

magnify, magnanimity, magnum, macrocosm, macrostructure, macroeconomics, polychrome, polyester, polyhedron, polymer, polysaccharide, polytheism, polyunsaturated, equal, equality, equity, equilibrium, equivocate, equidistant, equinox, inequity, omnipresent, omnibus

APPENDIX C
Greek/Latin Paired Roots

The purpose of this table is primarily for quick reference. Both teachers and students are encouraged, however, to take a few minutes to look over it. While there will be unfamiliar meaning elements and words, there will also be some familiar ones. There may be some relationships that were previously unnoticed, as well as some surprises. If you teach a specific subject matter area you will see some elements from your area of expertise, as there are some affixes and roots that also appear in the Generative Roots and Affixes table for your content area in Chapter 6.

As described in Chapter 3, many words and word elements passed from Greek into Latin, and the Latin forms are more common in present-day English. A number of words and elements from Greek, however, have passed directly into English—and this is why two or more roots or two or more prefixes exist for the same core meaning. Often the meaning is straightforward. Even though the prefixes *mono-* and *uni-* look quite different, the meanings of words that contain them are also obvious and students can learn that both prefixes mean "one." Other times, while the core meaning of a Greek or Latin root still exists, it will have taken on a different connotation in the words that derive from it. For example, you will see in the table that the concept of "old" is represented by the Greek root *paleo* and the Latin roots *sen* and *veter.* Words in which *paleo* occurs usually have to do with science, while words in which *sen* occurs have to do more with describing people. The Latin root for "mother" is *matr/mater* (matricide, maternal) and *metr* in Greek (metropolis). The Latin root literally refers to "mother" while the Greek usage is more metaphorical, conveying the idea of a city as "mother."

English/language arts teachers may from time to time engage students in discussing these differences as well. Students may also compare and contrast the uses and meanings of a root that appears in this table across different content areas—for example, *eu*phemism in English and *eu*bacteria in biology; *morph*ology in biology and *morph*eme in English; *fract*ious in history and *fract*ion in math; *rect*angle in math and *rect*ify in English.

Teachers may also look for roots in this table that do not appear in the Generative Roots and Affixes table for their content area in Chapter 6 but which may apply to their subject area. For example, *pugn* (fight) in *pugn*acious may be used by the science teacher to describe the behavior of a virus; *rad* (root) in *erad*icate may be used to refer to efforts to "pull out by the roots" the cause of that virus. A political movement in history may re*cede* ("go back" or decline in popularity and influence) just as the ocean tides re*cede* on a predictable basis.

Concept	Greek	Latin
Number		
one	**mono** *mono*chrome *mono*gamy *mono*graph *mono*lith *mono*mial	**uni** *uni*verse *uni*fy *uni*te *uni*que
alone	**mono** *mon*k *mon*astery	**sol** *sol*itary *sol*itude *sol*iloquy *sol*o
two *twice* *twe*lve (ten plus two) *twenty* (twice ten) *twi*light ("two lights")	**di** carbon *di*oxide *di*ploid *di*chotomy **dy** *dy*ad	**bi** *bi*sect *bi*centennial *bi*nary *bi*lingual **duo** *dua*l *du*plicate *duo*decimal
three *third* *thr*ice	**tri** *tri*logy *tri*gonometry *tri*chotomy	**tri** *tri*angle *tri*o *tri*umvirate
four	**tetra** *tetra*d **tra** *tra*pezoid	**quadr** *quadr*angle *quadr*ant *quadr*ilateral *quat*rain **quart** *quart* *quart*er
five	**penta** *penta*gon *penta*thlon	**quint** *quint*ile *quint*et *quint*essential
six	**hex** *hex*agon *hex*apod	**sex** *sex*tant *sex*tet *sem*ester (six months) *sex*tuplets
seven	**hepta** *hepta*d	**sept** *Sept*ember *sept*uagenarian
eight	**oct** *oct*opus *oct*agon	**oct** *Oct*ober *oct*ave *oct*opus *oct*ane
nine	**ennea** *ennea*hedron	**nov** *Nov*ember **non** *non*agon
ten	**deca** *deca*de *deca*thlon	**decem/decim** *Decem*ber *decim*eter
hundred	**hect** *hect*are *hect*ometer *hect*ogram	**cent** *cent* *cent*ury *cent*imeter *cent*ennial *cent*enary *cent*igrade *cent*igram *cent*ipede per*cent* per*cent*ile
thousand	**kilo** *kilo*meter *kilo*gram *kilo*watt *kilo*hertz	**milli** *mile* *milli*on
ten thousand	**myriados** *myriad*	
tiny	**nano (as billion)** *nano*second	
monster	**tera (as trillion)** *tera*byte *tera*meter	
large	**mega/megalo** *mega*phone *megalo*mania *megalo*polis **(as million)** *mega*byte *mega*watt	**magn** *magn*ify *magn*ificent *magn*animous
half	**hemi** *hemi*sphere	**semi** *semi*circle
one-and-a-half		**sesqui** *sesqui*centennial
many	**poly** *poly*gamist *poly*nomial	**multi** *multi*ply *multi*lingual *multi*tude
pile up		**cumul** *cumul*ative
equal	**iso** *iso*metric *iso*morphic	**equ** *equ*al *equ*ator *equ*ation *equ*ivalent *equi*distant *equ*ality *equi*librium *equi*lateral *equi*nox
few	**olig** *olig*archy *olig*opology	**pauc** *pauc*ity
all	**pan** *pan*orama *pan*acea *pan*opoly	**omni** *omni*scient *omni*vore
both	**ambi/amphi** *ambi*dextrous *amphi*bian *ambi*valent *amphi*theater	**bi** *bi*directional

Concept	Greek	Latin
	The Body	
body	**soma** *soma*tic chromo*some* psycho*soma*tic	**corp** *corp*uscle *corp*s
blood	**hemo/hema/em** *hema*tocyst hypogly*cemia* an*emia* leuk*emia*	**sang** *sang*ria *sang*uine
ear/hear	**oto** *oto*logy par*otid*	**aur** *aur*al *aur*icle
eat	**phag** *phag*ocyte sarco*phag*us	**vor** *vor*acious carni*vor*ous herbi*vor*ous omni*vor*ous de*vour*
teeth	**dont** ortho*dont*ist	**dent** *dent*ist
hand, hands	**chiro** *chiro*practor *chiro*ptera	**man** *man*ufacture *man*ual *man*ipulate *man*ure
healing	**iatr** psych*iatr*y ped*iatr*ic ger*iatr*ic *iatr*ogenic	
heart heart/breast	**card** *card*iac *card*iovascular	**pect** *pect*oral
foot	**pod** *pod*ium *pod*iatry	**ped** *ped*al bi*ped* quadru*ped* *ped*estrian *ped*estal
flesh	**sarc** *sarc*ophagus *sarc*asm (literally, "to tear flesh")	**carn** *carn*al rein*carn*ation *carn*ation *carn*age in*carn*adine
life	**bio** *bio*logy *bio*graphy	**viv/vit** *viv*acious re*viv*e *vit*al **anima** *anima*l *anima*ted
death kill	**necro** *necro*polis *necro*mancy	**mort** *mort*uary im*mort*al **cide** sui*cide* geno*cide*
man	**andr** *andr*oid *andr*ogynous **anthropo** *anthropo*logy *anthropo*morphism *anthropo*centric mis*anthrope* mis*anthrop*ic	**masc** *masc*uline **vir** *vir*ile **homo** *homo* sapiens
woman	**gyn** *gyn*ecology andro*gyn*ous miso*gyn*ist *gyn*ecocracy	**fem** *fem*inine *fem*ale
mother	**metr** *metr*opolis	**matr/mater** *matr*imony *mater*nal
father		**patr/pater** *patr*imony *pater*nal
air, breath/breathe, lung	**pneum** *pneum*onic *pneum*onia *pneum*atic	**spir** *spir*it in*spir*e tran*spir*e ex*pir*e re*spir*ation
see	**scop/scept** *scop*e Epi*scop*al horo*scop*e *scept*ic	**vis/vid** *vis*ion tele*vis*e *vis*age pro*vid*e e*vid*ent *vis*ible in*vis*ible **spec** *spec*ious *spec*ulate a*spec*t per*spec*tive pro*spec*t
skin	**derm** epi*derm*is	**cut** *cut*icle sub*cut*aneous
nude	**gymn** *gymn*asium *gymn*ast *gymn*oplast *gymn*osperm	**nud** de*nud*e *nud*ism
call, voice	**vox** "*vox* populi"	**voc/vok** *voc*ation e*vok*e pro*vok*e *voc*alic
speak, talk	**pha/phe** a*pha*sia pro*phe*t	**loc/loq** e*loc*ution *loq*uacious soli*loq*uy

Concept	Greek	Latin
tongue/language	**glos/glot** *glos*sary *glot*tis poly*glot*	**lingu** *lingu*istics bi*lingu*al *lingu*ini *lingu*aphile
sleep	**hypno** *hypno*tize *hypno*therapy	**dorm** *dorm*itory *dorm*ant *dorm*er

The Mind

Concept	Greek	Latin
feeling, emotion	**path** sym*path*y em*path*y	
good, well	**eu** *eu*logy *eu*phemism *eu*phony *eu*phoria *Eu*charist *eu*genics *eu*bacteria	**bene** *bene*fit *bene*factor *bene*volent
god	**theo** *theo*cracy a*theo*ist	**deus** *de*ity *de*ify
frighten		**terr** *terr*ified *terr*or *terr*orize
to know	**gn(o)** dia*gno*se pro*gno*sis a*gno*stic *Gno*stic i*gno*re co*gni*tion reco*gni*ze	**sci** *sci*ence con*sci*ence pre*sci*ent
word, speech, reason	**log** *log*ic *log*arithm	**rat** *rat*ional ir*rat*ional
love	**phil/phile** *phil*osophy *phil*harmonic biblio*phile*	**amor** *amor*ous en*amor*ed
fear	**phob/phobe** *phob*ia biblio*phobe* arachno*phob*ia	**tim** *tim*id in*tim*idate *tim*idity
memory, mindful	**mne** *mne*monic a*mne*sia a*mne*sty	**memo** *memo*ry com*memo*rate re*mem*ber
truth		**ver** *ver*ify *ver*acity
false	**pseudo** *pseudo*nym *pseudo*word	**fals** *fals*ify *fals*etto
to think	**dox/dog** para*dox* ortho*dox* hetero*dox* *dog*ma *dog*matic	**cog** *cog*itate
trust		**fid** con*fid*e *fid*uciary
write	**graph** para*graph* auto*graph* photo*graph* bio*graph*y tele*graph*	**scrib/script** in*scrib*e manu*script*

Physical and Natural World

Concept	Greek	Latin
animal	**zo** *zo*ology *zo*diac proto*zo*a Meso*zo*ic cyto*zo*ic	
bird	**orni** *orni*thology	**avi** *avi*ation *avi*ator *avi*ary
circle	**cycl** *cycl*e *cycl*one en*cycl*opedia	**circ** *circ*uit *circ*us *circ*ulate *circ*ulatory
day	**hemera** ep*hemera*l	**dies** *di*urnal circa*di*an **jour** *jour*nal ad*jour*n
night		**nox/noct** equi*nox* *noct*ural
earth	**geo** *geo*logy *geo*graphic *geo*metry *geo*politics	**terra** *terra*rium *terr*itory
deep	**bathy** *bath* *bath*os *bathy*scaph	
wing, feather	**pter** *pter*odactyl helico*pter* di*pter*ous ortho*pter*ous	**pen** *pen* (origin in a feather or quill)
hard	**sclera** *sclera*otic arterio*sclera*osis	**dur** *dur*able *dur*ation
color	**chrom** *chrom*ium *chrom*osome *chrom*atic *chrom*e	**color** *color*ize *color*ation
white	**leuko/leuco** *leuco*cyte	**alb** *alb*atross *alb*ino

Concept	Greek	Latin
green	**chloro** *chloro*phyll *chloro*form *chlor*ine *chloro*plast *chlor*ide	**verd** *verd*ant *verd*ure
leaf	**phyll** chloro*phyll* hetero*phyll*ous	**foli** *foli*age port*folio* ex*foli*ate
light	**photo** *photo*graphy	**luc/lum/lustr** *luc*id *lum*inate trans*luc*ent *lum*inous e*luc*idate *lum*inescence il*lum*inate *lustr*ous il*lustr*ate *lust*er
lizard	**saur** dino*saur* *saur*opod ichthyo*saur*	
producing, giving birth to, beginning	**gen** *gen*esis *gen*us	**gen** *gen*erate
rock	**petro** *petr*ify *petro*leum *petro*glyph **lith** *lith*ograph mono*lith* Paleo*lith*ic Meso*lith*ic Neo*lith*ic	**lapid** *lapid*ary
sea		**mar** *mar*ine *mar*iner *mar*itime sub*mar*ine
ship/sailor	**nau** *nau*tical *nau*sea	**nav** *nav*y *nav*al *nav*igate
shape, form	**morph** meta*morph*osis anthropo*morph*ic iso*morph*ic meso*morph*	**form** *form*ation in*form*
sharp, pointed, acid	**oxy** *ox*ide per*ox*ide *oxy*gen	**ac** *ac*id *ac*umen
sound	**phon** *phon*eme *phon*ics anti*phon*y eu*phon*y tele*phon*e sym*phon*y micro*phon*e	**son** super*son*ic *son*ic *son*ar *son*orous *son*net *son*orant con*son*ant re*son*ant *son*ata
star	**aster/astr** *aster*oid *astr*onomer *astr*onomy *astr*ology *aster*isk dis*aster*	**stel** *stel*lar constel*lation
water, fluid	**hydr** *hydr*aulic	**aqu** *aqu*arium
wood	**xylo** *xylo*phone *xyl*um	
worm		**verm** *verm*in *verm*icular *verm*iform *verm*icelli *verm*illion (color of red worms)
Orientation and Movement		
back	**ana** *ana*chronism	**re** *re*trace
apart, away	**se** *se*cede *se*gregate *se*clude	**ab** *ab*stract
bear, carry	**phor** meta*phor* electro*phor*esis	**fer** trans*fer* pre*fer* **port** trans*port* *port*able im*port* s*port*
beside	**para** *para*graph *para*dox *para*gon *para*llel *para*lysis *para*meter	**juxta** *juxta*pose
bind, connect		**nect/nex** con*nect* an*nex*
joint/join	**arthr** *arthr*itis *arthr*opod	**junct** *junct*ion con*junct*ion in*junct*ion
build	**tech** *tech*nology archi*tec*ture poly*tech*nic	**struct** in*struct*ive *struct*ure inde*struct*ible ob*struct* de*struct*ive in*struct*or con*struct*ive recon*struct*
choose		**lect** col*lect* se*lect* e*lect*
fold		**pl(ic)/pl(y)** multi*ply* multi*plic*ation tri*ple*

APPENDIX C

Concept	Greek	Latin
go		**ced/ceed/cess** sece*de* proce*ed* exce*ss* inter*cede* in*cess*ant con*cede* proce*ss*ion suc*cess*or
		it trans*it* trans*it*ion ex*it* circu*it* co*it*us
hang, weigh		**pend** *pend*ulum ap*pend* per*pend*icular com*pend*ium
fight		**pug(n)** *pug*ilist *pug*nacious im*pugn*
battle		**bat** com*bat* *bat*tle *bat*talion *bat*tery
gather		**greg** con*greg*ate *greg*arious se*greg*ate ag*greg*ate e*greg*ious
gather, pile up		**cumul** ac*cumul*ate *cumul*us
gnaw/scrape		**rod** *rod*ent e*rod*e cor*rod*e
make, do		**fac/fec/fic/fy** *fac*ile manu*fac*ture *fac*tory ef*fec*t *fic*tion terri*fy* petri*fy*
middle	**meso** *Meso*potamia *meso*derm	**med** *med*ian *med*ium inter*med*iate *Med*iterranean
outside	**ecto** *ecto*derm *ecto*plasm *ecto*morph	
right		**dextr** *dextr*ous *dextr*ity ambi*dextr*ous
left		**sinister** *sinistr*al *sinister*
touch		**tang** *tang*ible in*tang*ible *tang*ent *tang*ential
up	**ana** *ana*bolic *ana*lyze (loosen *up*)	
climb		**scend** a*scend* de*scend* cre*scent*
grasp		**prehen** com*prehen*d ap*pren*tice *prehen*sile
seize		**rapt** *rapt*ure *rapt*
stretch, strive		**tend/tens** *tens*ion *tend*ency *tend*on ex*tend* *tens*e con*tend*er *tent*
turn	**stroph** apo*stroph*e cata*stroph*e	**vert/vers** a*vert* re*vert* *vers*e *vert*ebra ad*vers*ary contro*vers*y di*vert* di*vers*e anni*vers*ary *vers*atile
under	**hypo** *hypo*dermic *hypo*thesis	**sub** *sub*marine *sub*-Saharan
		infra *infra*red *infra*structure
over	**hyper** *hyper*kinetic	**super** *super*structure *super*impose
work	**erg** *erg*y *erg*onomics	**oper** *oper*ate *op*us *oper*a

Other

Concept	Greek	Latin
correct	**ortho** *ortho*dontist *ortho*dox *ortho*graphy	**rect** cor*rect* *rect*angle *rect*ify
dry	**xer** *Xer*iscape *Xer*ox	**sicc** de*sicc*ate
large	**macro** *macro*cosm *macro*biotics *macro*instruction	
long		**long** *long*itude *long*eur
root	**rhiz** *rhiz*ome	**rad** *rad*ical e*rad*icate *rad*ish

212

Concept	Greek	Latin
secret	**crypt** *crypt cryptic* en*crypt* en*cryp*tion	
book	**bibli** *bibli*ography *bible bibli*otherapy *bibli*ophile	**libr** *library librarian libretto*
burn	**caust/caut** *caustic cauterize* holo*caust*	**calor** *calorie caldron caldera*
fire	**pyr** *pyre pyrite pyrotechnics*	**flam** *flame* in*flam*mable
old	**paleo** *paleo*ntologist *Paleo*lithic	**sen/veter** *senior senile senescent senator veteran*
ancient	**archa** *archa*eology *archa*ic	
young		**jun/juven** *jun*ior *June* (*Juno*) re*juven*ate *juven*ile
other, different	**hetero** *heterodox heterosexual*	**alt** *alt*ernate *alter*
same	**homo** *homo*genous *homo*sexual *homo*logous *homo*nym	**simul/simil** *simil*ar *simile* fac*simile simul*taneous
people	**demo** *demo*graphy epi*demic* pan*demic demo*gogue	**popul/pub** *popul*ation *popul*ar *popul*ace *pub*lic
	ethn *ethn*ic *ethn*ography	
rule	**crat/crac** auto*crat* auto*cracy* demo*crat* demo*cracy* theo*crat* theo*cracy*	**regula** *regula*te *regula*tion inter*regn*um
war		**bell** re*bell*ion re*bel bell*icose ante*bell*um
sing/song	**psalm** *psalm psal*ter	**cant** *cant*o *chant cant*icle re*cant*
sweet	**gluc/glyc** *gluc*ose hypo*glyc*emia	**dulc** *dulc*et *dulc*imer
tree	**dendr** *dendr*ology *dendr*ite philo*dendr*on	**arbor** *arbor arbor*eal *arbor*etum
empty		**vac** *vac*ant e*vac*uation *vac*ancy e*vac*uate *vac*ate *vac*ation *vac*uous
image	**icon** *icon icon*ic *icon*oclasm	
new	**neo** *Neo*lithic *neo*classicism *neo*logism *neo*phyte	**nov** *nov*elty re*nov*ate *nov*el
vessel	**angi** *angi*ogram *angi*na	**vas** *vas*cular cardio*vas*cular *vas*ectomy
world, order	**cosm** *cosm*os *cosm*ic *cosm*opolitan micro*cosm cosm*etic	**mund** inter*mund*ane *mund*ane
year		**enn/annu** cent*enn*ial bi*annu*al per*enn*ial
season	**horo** *horo*scope	

APPENDIX D
Spelling–Meaning Connections

Students first explore these spelling–meaning connections in familiar words, and then are guided through their application to the meanings and spellings of more unfamiliar words. The sample spelling–meaning word sorts offered here follow a concrete-to-more-abstract continuum:

1. Make students aware of the connection between the spelling of words and their meanings.
2. Help students understand how to use the spelling–meaning connection as a *strategy* for remembering problematic spellings.
3. Extend students' understanding and appreciation of how the spelling–meaning connection can expand their vocabulary by establishing links between known and new words.
4. Help students understand why spelling sometimes *does* change in related words.
5. Take time to clarify often-confused suffixes.
6. Examine absorbed or "assimilated" prefixes.

Additional spelling–meaning word sorts are provided in the following resource:

Templeton, S., Johnston, F., Bear, D. R., & Invernizzi, M. (2009). *Word Sorts for Derivational Relations Spellers* (2nd ed.). Boston: Allyn & Bacon.

THE CONNECTION BETWEEN THE SPELLINGS OF WORDS AND THEIR MEANINGS

The following words represent the straightforward, transparent sound changes that occur when a suffix is added to the base word:

Base Word	Derived Word	Base Word	Derived Word
type	typical	athlete	athletic
mine	mineral	grateful	gratitude
breath	breathe	crime	criminal
revise	revision	humane	humanity
nature	natural	ignite	ignition
nation	national	precise	precision

The words are presented to students as an unorganized jumble. Before having students sort these words, ask them what they notice about the words—how might *they* sort the words? They will probably notice that some of the words are base words. Have students work in pairs or individually to sort the words; suggest that they sort the words into base words and related suffixed or *derived* words. Once the related words have been matched up, ask the students if the vowel sounds in the accented syllables of the word pairs change. (Yes, they do.) Does the spelling of the vowel change? (No.) The spelling remains the same, despite the change in sound, because the words are related in meaning. We call this the *spelling–meaning connection*.

Some students might benefit from a brief discussion of how the suffix functions in the derived word. For example, point out how -al affects the base words *nature, nation, crime*—"like" or "characterized by" the meaning of the base word. As an extension activity, *grateful/gratitude* and *breath/breathe* also present opportunities for discussion. For example, is *grate* a word? Students usually say it is not; have one of them look it up in an unabridged dictionary and they will find that *grate* actually *was* a word in Middle English. As for *breath* and *breathe*, they both look like a base (is *breathe* a "suffixed" word?).

THE SPELLING–MEANING CONNECTION AS A STRATEGY FOR REMEMBERING PROBLEMATIC SPELLINGS

Many spelling errors occur when students are trying to spell the *schwa* sound, represented by the symbol /ə/ in the dictionary, the least-stressed vowel sound that occurs in the unaccented syllables of words with two or more syllables. Sound is not a clue to the spelling of the schwa; that is why it is helpful to study these spelling–meaning patterns. These sorts will also help students attend to accent within words.

Introduce the following sort by asking the students if they've ever had to stop and think about how to spell a particular word, such as *competition* or *admiration*. Tell them that thinking of a word related in spelling and meaning may provide a clue. For example, thinking of the base word *compete* will help with *competition*; thinking of the base word *admire* may help with *admiration*:

Base Word	Derived Word	Base Word	Derived Word
compose	composition	custody	custodian
compete	competition	define	definition
admire	admiration		

Have the students match up each base word with its derivative. In *composition*, is the second syllable clearly accented? Not really. Because of this fact—it is not accented—the vowel sound in the second syllable of *composition* sounds like an unaccented "short u" sound; there's no "oomph" behind it. How might they remember how it is spelled? (By thinking of *compose*.)

Students often notice and comment on relationships that do not appear to make sense in terms of spelling and meaning. Such observations usually offer opportunities for vocabulary expansion or clarification. For example, students may not realize how *custody* and *custodian* may be related, so discuss with them how *custodian* refers not just to the individuals who maintain the condition of a school; it has a broader application, referring to anyone who holds custody of something, including an idea—as, for example, when a people are referred to as "custodians of democracy." On occasion, words that are similar in spelling are not related in meaning, for example, *admiral* and *admire*. In such instances, the words usually come from different languages. *Admire* comes from French, in which it meant "to wonder" (and is related to *miracle* and *miraculous*, which also have to do with "wonder"); *admiral* comes from an Arabic word for "commander." Occasionally, these exceptions do occur. Exploring the history or etymology of the terms usually reveals the disconnect.

The following sort provides additional opportunities for using the spelling–meaning connection as a strategy for understanding and remembering problematic spellings. It is an excellent follow-up because it includes some *base words* with a potentially problematic schwa; the derived word in the spelling–meaning pair reveals the spelling:

Base Word	Derived Word	Base Word	Derived Word
similar	similarity	metal	metallic
familiar	familiarity	mobile	mobility
fragile	fragility	oppose	opposition
combine	combination	perspire	perspiration
invite	invitation	preside	president
legal	legality	prohibit	prohibition

Using *similar* and *similarity* as examples, discuss how accent affects each word. In *similar*, is the last syllable accented? (No.) What happens to that syllable when the suffix *-ity* is added? (It becomes accented or stressed.) Point out that, if they were uncertain about the spelling of the /er/ syllable at the end of *similar*, thinking of the word *similarity* might help them because they can clearly hear the vowel sound in the third syllable of *similarity* and they know how to spell that sound. Because words that are related in spelling are often related in meaning as well, the stressed syllable in *similarity* provides a clue to the spelling of the schwa sound in *similar*. Discuss one or two other word pairs in this same manner. You may also present a misspelling such as *oppisition*, for example, and ask students what word would clear up the spelling of the schwa sound, and why. Conclude your discussion by reminding students of the spelling–meaning strategy: *If you are uncertain about the spelling of a particular word, thinking of a related word may provide a clue.*

When added to a base word, the derivational suffix *-ity* results in a word meaning "having the quality or condition" of the base word. Because *-ity* is a very productive suffix, its effect on words may be examined further in words such as *individual/individuality, personal/personality, mental/mentality, eventual/eventuality, original/originality,* and *central/centrality.* Students realize that the unaccented final syllable in each base word will always become accented when *-ity* is added. In addition, they are expanding their vocabulary by relating unknown words such as *fragility, centrality,* and *eventuality* to the known words *fragile, central,* and *eventual.* This last point is critical: A spelling problem in a *known* word can be fixed by pointing out a related but *unknown* word. When we help students with this we do two things. First, we clear up their spelling error; second, we've just expanded their vocabulary.

SPELLING–MEANING LINKS BETWEEN KNOWN AND NEW WORDS

As emphasized in the previous sort, students learn that an unfamiliar word often explains the spelling of a known word. In addition to providing a clue to spelling, the related word is either not known or its relation to the misspelled word is more abstract. For example, the misspelling *presadent* may be related to *preside*—although the relationship between these words may not be immediately clear to students. Prompts can help to establish this relationship: What does it mean to "preside" over something? One can preside over a meeting or over a nation, as is the case with *president.* The familiar word *mandatory* may be misspelled *manditory.* Show students the unfamiliar word *mandate.* If something is mandatory, it must be done—it has been mandated. How can the spelling of the word *mandate* help with the spelling of *mandatory*?

In the following sort, students match up each base word with its derived word. Then have them sort these word pairs into the following two categories: those in which the accent within a pair changes when the suffix is added and those in which the accent does not change. For those words that provide opportunities for expanding vocabulary, be sure to engage the students in discussion about them, encouraging them to think of the meaning of the known word in the word pair as a clue to the meaning of the unfamiliar term. Note that students may only be familiar with *harmony* in terms of music, for example, and not in terms of relationships among people.

Change in Accent		*No Change in Accent*	
comedy	comedian	narrate	narrative
harmony	harmonious	mandate	mandatory
emphasis	emphatic		
labor	laborious		
janitor	janitorial		

For the following sort, rather than sorting the words into columns, have students sort the words according to spelling–meaning families, putting those words that they believe go together in groups. You may need to help out with some of the words; for example, students may not readily notice that *impunity* goes with *punish* and *punitive* or *impugn* with *pugnacious* and *pugnacity* (many quite literate adults, for that matter, are not aware of this connection).

syllable	defame	trivial	allege	academy
syllabic	defamatory	triviality	allegation	academic
diplomat	divert	pugnacious	punish	copy
diplomacy	diversion	pugnacity	punitive	copious
diplomatic	diverse	impugn	impunity	

Have the students discuss how the words within each group might be related in meaning. As a follow-up to discussing the meaning relationships, students may discuss the different ways in which the vowel and consonant spellings within related words are pronounced. For example, note the pronunciation of the letters *a* and *c* in *pugnacious* and *pugnacity*.

In the following sort, most students will know one of the words in each word pair and may therefore determine the meaning of the unfamiliar word.

Familiar	Unfamiliar	Familiar	Unfamiliar
reciprocate	reciprocity/reciprocal	polar	polarity
rhapsody	rhapsodic	immune	immunization/immunity
notorious	notoriety	paradigm	paradigmatic
obsolete	obsolescent	frugal	frugality
senator	senatorial	perspicacity	perspicacious

Have students sort words into spelling–meaning families. Two of these families will have three members. Have students discuss possible meanings for unfamiliar words and check their best guesses with one another and the dictionary.

SPELLING CHANGES IN RELATED WORDS

It is interesting to note that, although patterns such as *exclaim/exclamation* and *resume/resumption* appear to be "exceptions" to the spelling–meaning connection, they are exceptions that nonetheless follow a pattern: When spelling *does* change within a spelling–meaning family of words, it does so *predictably*. There is a *pattern*, in other words, that occurs across words of a certain type, and a number of words usually follow this pattern.

Base Word	Derived Word	Base Word	Derived Word
exclaim	exclamation	assume	assumption
proclaim	proclamation	presume	presumption/presumptive
acclaim	acclamation	consume	consumption
explain	explanation	resume	resumption
reclaim	reclamation	receive	reception/receptive
		conceive	conception

Have students sort the words by matching up base words with derived words. After discussing what any unfamiliar words might mean, students can check the definitions in the dictionary. You may also wish to comment to the students that, although there may be few instances of a particular pattern, you are addressing it in order to point out that even when we encounter words that appear odd, there are almost always other words that follow that same pattern.

In discussing *conceive* and *conception*, students may not realize that they are related to *concept*. Point this out to them and encourage discussion of how these three words or ideas are related to one another. This may also be a good place to remind students who struggle with the spelling of *conceive* and *receive*—because of the unusual *ei* pattern—

about the *i* before *e* except after *c* jingle. This is also a good opportunity to explain *why* the spelling in the base changes in some words. The short explanation is that, in Latin, when certain endings were added to a base the pronunciation of the base would change, and the spelling usually changed as well to represent this change in pronunciation. Chapter 3 provides a more in-depth explanation, and the second lesson in Appendix B also addresses this phenomenon for students.

For your more advanced English students, you may wish to share that another process also affected the spellings of other roots—roots such as *fac*, which means "make," but which may also be spelled *fec* and *fic*. Walking through the following roots with students reinforces their understanding that, when spelling *does* change, it is rarely haphazard but usually follows a pattern.

Write the following on the board or overhead, underlining the letters that represent the appropriate roots:

<u>sac</u>red	<u>fac</u>tory	a<u>pt</u>itude	<u>sed</u>entary
<u>sac</u>rament	af<u>fec</u>t	ada<u>pt</u>	pre<u>sid</u>e
con<u>sec</u>rate	suf<u>fic</u>e	in<u>ept</u>	

Four different roots are illustrated here, and in each, the spelling of the vowel changes.

- Remind students that, up to this point, they have learned how *suffixes* can affect the pronunciation and sometimes the spelling of a base or root in spelling–meaning families. In these words, however, the *prefixes* affected the pronunciation in Latin when they were added to a root or base, and the spelling changed to reflect this.
- Next, talk about each "root group" and how the meaning of the root contributes to the meaning of each word: *sac/sec* means "holy"; *fac/fec/fic* means "make"; *apt/ept* means "fit"; and *sed/sid* means "sit."
- Then share with the students that, depending on the root and the prefix that was added in Latin, the following "rule" applied: An *a* became an *e*, and an *e* became an *i*.
- Remind the students that the purpose in looking at these words and their roots is to illustrate that, even when the spelling *does* change among related words and roots, the changes are usually not haphazard—there is an explanation. This should also help the students remember that, when they run into an unfamiliar word, this is an additional skill that will help them figure out its meaning and remember the meaning more efficiently.
- Model how to do this for students. For example, in a news article about the visit of the Pope, the sentence "A new group of priests will be consecrated tomorrow" provides both context- and word-specific clues to the meaning of *consecrated*. The topic, the word *priests,* and the word itself—*consecrated*—all provide clues. Because we are aware that roots may be spelled differently, it is easier to understand that *consecrated* may have something to do with a sacred act—and once we've confirmed this suggested meaning in the dictionary, it will also be easier to remember the meaning of *con<u>sec</u>rated*.

This is a fairly high level of word consciousness—one that, quite frankly, most literate adults have not attained. Most important, however, we earnestly hope that more students—not just honors English students—will be brought to the level where they, too, can benefit from this level of insight. This is more likely to happen as we become aware of and more comfortable ourselves with examining and thinking about words this way.

OFTEN-CONFUSED SUFFIXES

When Is It -*able* and When Is It -*ible*?

The following sort develops the core understanding that, when adding this suffix to a base word, it usually is spelled -*able;* when adding to a word root, it is usually spelled -*ible*. Have the students sort the -*able* words together and the -*ible* words together. Then, ask them to examine each category to see if they notice a pattern. When is this suffix spelled *-able* and when is it spelled *-ible*? (*-able* for base words; *-ible* for word roots.) Talk about what the addition of the suffix does to the base word. (It changes verbs to adjectives.) This is a good opportunity to review any word roots covered in earlier lessons (see Appendix C).

-able		*-ible*	
dependable	adaptable	credible	irascible
profitable	attainable	audible	indelible
predictable	cherishable	legible	feasible
perishable	decipherable	plausible	compatible
laughable	sustainable	intangible	
punishable			

When Is It *-ent*/*-ence* and When Is It *-ant*/*-ance*?

The relationship between *-ent/-ence* and *-ant/-ance* is powerful and straightforward; however, students' understanding of this relationship depends on considerable experience with these patterns and the words that represent them.

-ent	*-ence*	*-ant*	*-ance*
confident	confidence	brilliant	brilliance
dependent	dependence	abundant	abundance
resident	residence	fragrant	fragrance
obedient	obedience	dominant	dominance
prominent	prominence		

Have students sort the words by pairs: align *confidence* under *confident* and *brilliance* under *brilliant*. Tell the students that by arranging the words this way they will find a clue to the *-ent/-ence* and *-ant/-ance* puzzle. The key understanding with these suffixes is that if you know how to spell one word that ends in *-ent* and *-ence* or *-ant* and *-ance*, then you can figure out how to spell the word about which you're uncertain. For example, if you are uncertain whether a spelling is *dependant* or *dependent* but you know how to spell the word *independence*, then *independence* is your clue to the spelling of *dependent*: *-ent* and *-ence* words go together, and *-ant* and *-ance* words go together. To extend this lesson, have students be on the lookout for which pattern, *-ent/-ence* or *-ant/-ance*, appears to be the most frequent. (It's *-ent/-ence*.) The "Defiance or Patience" Game and its variations (see Appendix E) is very appropriate at this point.

ABSORBED OR "ASSIMILATED" PREFIXES

Absorbed or assimilated prefixes are often misspelled, but in exploring them closely students will not only eliminate most prefix spelling errors but extend their vocabularies—as well as picking up a bit of understanding about language history and language change. The first sort explores prefixes that are attached to base words:

in-	*im-*	*il-*	*ir-*
incorrect	immobile	illegible	irreplaceable
inactive	immoral	illegal	irrational
inescapable	immeasurable	illiterate	irresponsible
incapable	immature	illogical	irreducible
innumerable	immortal	illegitimate	irregular

Have students sort words according to the spelling of the prefix: *in-*, *im-*, *il-*, and *ir-*. Discuss the meanings of a few of the words: *Incorrect* means "not correct," *immobile* means "not mobile," and so forth (in the words *inform* and *indent* the prefix does not, of course, mean "not"; instead, it has the meaning of "into"). Discuss how they have known about the meaning and function of the prefix *in-* for quite a long time. Now they are going to explore *why* the spelling of the prefix *in-* changes, even though the prefix keeps the same meaning.

Ask the students to look at the words in the *im-*, *il-*, and *ir-* columns. Do they see any clues as to why the spelling changes? Students usually notice the spelling of the first letter in the base words. In the *in-* column, however, why *doesn't* the spelling change? Have the students discuss this for a few moments (occasionally a student *will* in fact come up with the explanation). If they remain stumped, however, then proceed as follows (see also the explanation in Chapter 3): Ask students to try pronouncing several of the words in the *im-*, *il-*, and *ir-* columns *without* the spelling change in *in-*: *inmobile, inlegal, inregular.* Discuss how that feels odd or awkward—the tongue has to make a rapid change from the /n/ sound to the sound at the beginning of each word. Tell the students that this same awkwardness in pronunciation occurred in Latin two thousand years ago, so over time, the sound of /n/ became assimilated or "absorbed" into the sound at the beginning of the word to which *in-* was attached, and eventually the spelling changed to reflect this change. Most words in the *in-* column do not have such awkward combinations. A student may note that *incorrect* is a bit awkward: Why isn't it *iccorect*? Someday it may be—though you may wish to point out that the spelling system has changed far less since the printing press was invented, because a printed standard has tended to conserve existing spellings and spelling patterns. (Because several of these words include *-able/-ible*, you may wish to review these suffixes with these words.)

This second sort explores prefixes that are attached to word roots. For comparison, a few base words, such as *immaterial* and *immigrant*, are included. The same historical process applied to these words as to the words in the first sort. Students continue to develop their understanding of this process when they try to pronounce, for example, the following: *comlide, adtractive, subpression.*

com-	in-	ad-	sub-
collide	immaterial	attractive	suppression
corrode	immigrant	accountant	supportable
colleague	immense	arrange	suffix
correlate	imminent	aggressive	
	immune	affix	

APPENDIX E

Word and Word Part Games

LATIN ROOT JEOPARDY

At least three students are needed for this game—a host/scorekeeper as well as two players—but more students may play as well.

Materials

Create a grid with five columns and six rows. Make headers to indicate the categories. Clue cards are prepared by writing the number of points on one side and the answer on the other. During the game, turn over the square that is requested so the answer can be read. For a large group, make an overhead transparency of the Latin Root Jeopardy and Latin Root Double Jeopardy boards, and cover the clues with sticky notes. On a chalkboard, use tape to fix squares of paper in the correct order. If available, a lumens, VGA projector, or interactive whiteboard work particularly well: You or your students can construct a game board in a PowerPoint format. There are a number of very good free sites online with directions; simply type in "jeopardy game board" in your browser.

Procedures

The game consists of two rounds: Jeopardy and Double Jeopardy.

1. The game is modeled after the "Jeopardy!" television game. The clue is in the form of an answer and players must phrase their response in the form of a question:
   Answer clue: Coming from the Latin root *port*, it means "to remove from one place to another."
   Question response: What is *transport*?
2. Determine who will go first. The player will select the first "root" category and point value. The host uncovers the clue and reads it aloud.
3. The first player responding correctly adds the point amount of the question to his or her total or gets to keep the card that was turned over. That player then chooses the next root category and point amount. An incorrect answer means that the corresponding points are subtracted.
4. The winner is the one with the most points.

Variations

1. A round of Final Jeopardy can be added. When it is time for the Final Jeopardy question, players see the category, but not the answer. They then decide how many of their points to risk. When they see the answer, they have 30 seconds to write the question. If correct, they add the number of points they risked to their total; if incorrect, that number of points is subtracted from their total.

2. Play can alternate from one player to the next or from one team to the next rather than be based on who shouts out the response first. If one player misses, the other team gets a chance to respond. If they are correct, however, they get another turn.

3. Daily Doubles may be included if desired (the number of points for an answer is doubled, and if correct, added to the player's score; if incorrect, the doubled number of points is subtracted from the player's score).

4. Develop a Vocabulary Jeopardy game to accompany a unit of study:

- Generate vocabulary cards from a unit of study that fit into four or five categories—for example, *atmosphere, hydrosphere, biosphere,* and *lithosphere.*
- Write questions on cards that relate to the facts and concepts studied.
- Teams of students play the game as a whole-class vocabulary review of unit.

Word Lists for constructing additional Latin Root Jeopardy games are found in Appendix F.

LATIN ROOT JEOPARDY				
spect (to look)	*form* (shape)	*port* (to carry)	*tract* (draw or pull)	*dict* (to say, speak)
100 One who watches; an onlooker	100 One "form" or style of clothing such as is worn by nurses	100 Goods brought into a country from another country to be sold	100 Adjective: having power to attract; alluring; inviting	100 A book containing the words of a language explained
200 The prospect of good to come; anticipation	200 One who does not conform	200 One who carries burdens for hire	200 A powerful motor vehicle for pulling farm machinery, heavy loads, etc.	200 A speaking against; a denial
300 To regard with suspicion and mistrust	300 To form or make anew; to reclaim	300 To remove from one place to another	300 The power to grip or hold to a surface while moving, without slipping	300 A blessing often at the end of a worship service
400 Verb: to esteem Noun: regard, deference Literally: to look again	400 To change into another substance; change of form	400 To give an account of	400 An agreement: literally, to draw together	400 An order proclaimed by an authority
500 Looking around; watchful; prudent	500 Disfigurement; spoiling the shape	500 A case for carrying loose papers	500 To take apart from the rest; to deduct	500 To charge with a crime

"Questions" for Latin Root Jeopardy

	100	200	300	400	500
spect	spectator	expectation	suspect	respect	circumspect
form	uniform	nonconformist	reform	transform	deformity
port	import	porter	transport	report	portfolio
tract	attractive	tractor	traction	contract	subtract
dict	dictionary	contradiction	benediction	edict	indict

DOUBLE LATIN ROOT JEOPARDY

cred (to believe)	duct (to lead)	fer (to bear, carry)	press (to press)	spir (to breathe)
200 A system of doing business by trusting that a person will pay at a later date for goods or services	200 A person who directs the performance of a choir or an orchestra	200 (Plants) able to bear fruit; (Animals) able or likely to conceive young	200 A printing machine	200 An immaterial intelligent being
400 A set of beliefs or principles	400 To train the mind and abilities of	400 To carry again; to submit to another for opinion	400 Verb: to utter Noun: any fast conveyance	400 To breathe out; to die
600 Unbelievable	600 To enroll as a member of a military service	600 To convey to another place; passed from one place to another	600 To press against; to burden; to overpower	600 To breathe through; to emit through the pores of the skin
800 Verb, prefix meaning "not"; word means to damage the good reputation of	800 The formal presentation of one person to another	800 Endurance of pain; distress	800 State of being "pressed down" or saddened	800 To breathe into; to instruct by divine influence
1000 Adjective, prefix ac, word means officially recognized	1000 An artificial channel carrying water across country	1000 Cone bearing, as the fir tree	1000 To put down; to prevent circulation	1000 To plot; to band together for an evil purpose

"Questions" for Double Latin Root Jeopardy

	200	400	600	800	1000
cred	credit	creed	incredible	discredit	accredited
duct	conductor	educate	induct	introduction	aqueduct
fer	fertile	refer	transfer	suffering	coniferous
press	press	express	oppress	depression	suppress
spir	spirit	expire	perspire	inspire	conspire

IT'S ALL GREEK TO US

In this card game, the deck is composed of words derived from Greek roots. Three to five players may participate, one of whom will serve as game master and hold and read definition cards.

Materials

Using the list of Greek roots and derived words in Appendixes C and F, prepare 10 definition cards that consist of a root and definition such as *geo* ("earth"). For each root, create four or more words cards such as *geology, geographic, geometry,* and *geopolitics.* Write these words at the top of the card so they can be seen when held in the hand.

Procedures

1. The game master shuffles the word cards, deals 10 cards per player, and places the remaining word cards face-down.

2. The game master reads a definition card and lays it down face-up. All players who are holding a card that matches the definition read it and place it below the corresponding Greek root. If no player can respond to the definition, the game master places the definition card on the bottom of his or her cards for rereading later in the game.
3. To begin the next round a new definition card is laid down.
4. The player who discards all 10 word cards first is the winner and becomes the next game master.

JOINED AT THE ROOTS

A concept sort based on the exploration of Greek and Latin word roots, this game may be used with individuals, partners, and small groups.

Procedures

1. The teacher begins by modeling how to do the sort: Placing words with roots whose meanings fit within a particular category—for example, "Speaking and Writing," "Building/Construction," "Thinking and Feeling," and "Movement."
2. Students then work in small groups or in pairs. Each group or pair will take a particular category and sort the words whose roots justify their belonging in that category.
3. Students may record their sorts and share out later with the other students.

Sample Categories

Building/Construction	*Thinking and Feeling*	*Movement*
technology	philanthropy	synchrony
construct	philosophy	fracture
tractor	attraction	

Government	*Speaking and Writing*	*Travel*
economy	autobiography	astronaut
demagogue	photograph	exodus
politics	catalogue	
	emphasis	

DEFIANCE OR PATIENCE?

The game Defiance (if using the -*ant*/-*ance*/-*ancy* family) or Patience (if using the -*ent*/-*ence*/-*ency* family) is for three to five players. The object of the game is to make as many groups of two, three, or four cards of the same derivation and to be the first to run out of cards.

Materials

You will need to create a deck of 52 cards with suits of two, three, or four words (e.g., *attend, attendance,* and *attendant* is a set of three while *radiate, radiant, radiance,* and *radiancy* is a set of four). Use words from the lists in Appendix F. Write each word across the top of a card, and your deck is prepared.

Procedures

1. Each player is dealt five cards from the deck. The player to the left of the dealer begins the game. The player may first lay down any existing groups of two,

three, or four cards held in hand. This player then may ask any other player for a card of a certain derivation in his or her own hand: "Matthew, give me all of your *resistance*." (This could result in gaining *resistance*, *resistant*, *resistancy*, or *resist*.)

2. If a player does not have cards with the feature being sought, he or she responds, "Be Defiant" or "Be Patient" depending on which game is being played.

3. At this, the asking player must draw another card from the deck. If the card is of the same family being sought, the player may lay down the match and continue asking other players for cards. If the card is not of the correct derivational group, play passes to the person on the left and continues around the circle in the same manner. If the drawn card makes a match in the asking player's hand, but was not that which was being sought, he or she must hold the pair in hand until his turn comes up again. Of course this means there is a risk of another player taking the pair before the next turn.

4. Play ends when one of the students runs out of cards. The player with the most points wins.

5. Players may play on other people's card groups, laying related cards down in front of themselves, not in front of the player who made the original match.

6. Scoring is as follows:

   • Singles played on other people's matches: 1 point
   • Pairs: 2 points
   • Triples: 6 points
   • Groups of four: 10 points
   • First player to run out of cards: 10 points

Variations

1. The game Defy My Patience is a version that mixes sets of words from both lists to create an *-ent/-ant* deck.

2. Challenge My Patience or Defy My Challenge: In this version, during scoring before everyone throws down their hand, students should secretly write additional words for groups they have laid down, which have not been played. Before hands are revealed, these lists should be shared, and an additional point added to every player's score for each related word they wrote. If other players doubt the authenticity of a word claimed by an opponent, someone may challenge the word. The challenger loses a point if the word is valid, or gains a point if it is not. The player, likewise, counts the word if it is valid, or loses a point if the challenger proves him or her wrong.

3. Students should be encouraged to develop their own derivational families to be added to this game or another feature to be substituted for the *-ant/-ent* contrast.

ASSIMILE

This game can be played by two to six players.

Materials

Use a game board modeled after Monopoly; dice; game playing pieces; a deck of prefixes that can be assimilated (*ad-*, *sub-*, *in-*, *ex-*, *com-*, *ob-*); a deck of base words that can take assimilated prefixes (e.g., base words such as *company* [*accompany*] or *mortal* [*immortal*]); and a set of chance cards. The chance cards are similar to the base word cards but should be written on cards of a different color. Players will need a sheet of paper and pencil or pen to use in spelling words.

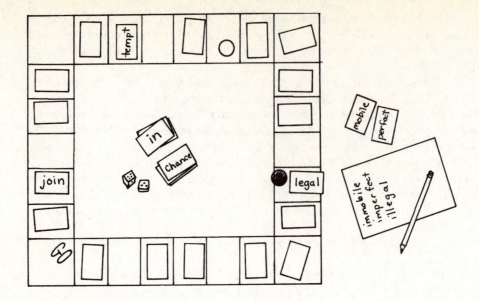

Procedures

This game is modeled after Monopoly.

1. Place base words face-down around the board, one in each space. A particular prefix is chosen as the focus and placed face-up in the center of the board. Chance cards are also placed in the middle.
2. Players roll the dice to see who goes first. The player with the highest number rolls again and moves the number of spaces on the board.
3. Upon landing on a particular space, the player turns up a word card and must determine whether this word can be assimilated to the prefix in the center of the board. If the card can be made into a word, the player attempts to both say the word and correctly spell it. A player who is able to correctly spell the word gets to keep the card. If the word cannot be assimilated, it is kept on the board face-up (this word will not be played again). However, if the word can be assimilated, but the player misspells the word, the card is turned back over to be played later in the game.
4. A player who is unable to come up with a word (for whatever reason) forfeits a turn, and play moves to the next player.
5. When a player passes "Go" or lands on a card that is face-up they can draw from the chance pile. Chance cards provide players a chance to think of one's own assimilated prefix word using the base word on the card and any assimilated prefix.
6. The game is over when all cards that can be played are played, and the winner is the one with the most correctly spelled words.

Variations

A separate set of Community Chest cards using all of the original assimilated prefixes can be placed in the middle of the board, from which players can draw after each round of turns. This ensures that all prefixes are studied. (Community Chest cards will have the prefixes *ad-*, *in-*, *com-*, *ob-*, *sub-*, *ex-*, *per-*, and *dis-*.) With this method, the word cards that cannot be played with one particular prefix are turned back over until they are able to be played.

WORD PART SHUFFLE

Any activity that engages students in combining prefixes, suffixes, bases, and roots is very beneficial and appropriate. There are a number of commercially available resources such as Reading Rods (Learning Resources, Inc.) in which students snap cubes or rods together that have prefixes, suffixes, bases, or roots printed on them. Both real words and words that *could* exist may be constructed. Older students, however, may be put off by a format that they perceive is somewhat "childish"—although we have found that older students will also buy into fitting rods and cubes together if you have presented the activity in a straightforward, adult, and respectful manner.

Word Part Shuffle avoids this issue altogether, however (Moloney, 2008). In this non-competitive activity, a group of students receives a stack of multicolored cards. Each color card represents a different word part (prefixes, bases/roots, and suffixes). Each group builds a number of words—20 is usually appropriate—that one might find in a standard dictionary. After that, each group coins one word, using as many of the cards as possible. They should develop a definition for the word. Each group then shares their coined word. A template for the word cards is provided on the following pages. The word parts and meanings can be cut apart and affixed to colored cards.

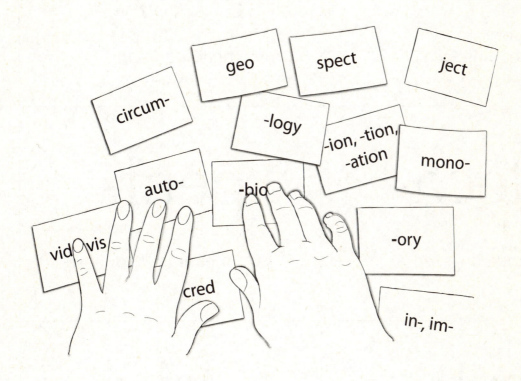

peri-

meaning: *around*

super-

meaning: *over, above*

trans-

meaning: *across*

poly-

meaning: *many*

deca-

meaning: *ten*

pent-

meaning: *five*

sub-

meaning: *under*

tri-

meaning: *three*

-er, -or meaning: *agent*	**-ion, -tion, -ation** meaning: *act or process of*
-ic meaning: *like, having the nature*	**-ory** meaning: *place for*
-ment meaning: *product, state*	**-ist** meaning: *one who*
-ism meaning: *act, condition*	**-ous** meaning: *characterized by*

APPENDIX E

un-

meaning: *not*

re-

meaning: *again*

in-, im-, il-, ir-

meaning: *not*

dis-

meaning: *not*

non-

meaning: *not*

en-, em-

meaning: *to cause something*

sub-

meaning: *under*

in-, im-

meaning: *in*

aud

Latin; meaning: *hear*

spect

Latin; meaning: *see, look at*

bio

Greek; meaning: *life*

dict

Latin; meaning: *speak, tell*

port

Latin; meaning: *carry*

form

Latin; meaning: *shape*

tract

Latin; meaning: *pull*

fer

Latin; meaning: *carry*

duc, duct	scrib, script
Latin; meaning: *lead*	Latin; meaning: *write*
gress	**ject**
Latin; meaning: *move*	Latin; meaning: *throw*
jud	**vid, vis**
Latin; meaning: *judge*	Latin; meaning: *see*
fid	**cred**
Latin; meaning: *trust*	Latin; meaning: *trust, believe*

chron	derm
Greek; meaning: *time*	Greek; meaning: *skin*
geo	graph
Greek; meaning: *earth*	Greek; meaning: *write*
logy	meter, metr
Greek; meaning: *study*	Greek; meaning: *measure*
micro	phobia
Greek; meaning: *small*	Greek; meaning: *fear*

APPENDIX E

path

Greek; meaning: *suffer*

hydra

Greek; meaning: *water*

phon

Greek; meaning: *sound*

photo

Greek; meaning: *light*

tele

Greek; meaning: *far*

scope

Greek; meaning: *see*

psych

Greek; meaning: *spirit, soul*

rupt

Latin; meaning: *break*

pre-	post-
meaning: *before*	meaning: *after*
mono-	uni-
meaning: *one*	meaning: *one*
anti-	auto-
meaning: *against*	meaning: *self*
circum-	inter-
meaning: *around*	meaning: *between*

APPENDIX F
Word and Root Lists for Games and Word Sorts

The sorts and lists in this appendix complement and extend the lessons in Appendixes A and B. They are particularly useful for English/language arts teachers (Templeton, Johnston, Bear, & Invernizzi, 2009).

Prepare word sorts to use with your students by writing the selected words on a template such as the one in Appendix H. We recommend that you enlarge it about 5 to 8 percent before writing in the words neatly. Be sure to write the words randomly so students can make their own discoveries as they sort. Many people find it easy to create computer-generated word sort sheets using the "table" function in a word processing program. First set the margins all around at 0.5, and then insert a table that is three columns by six to eight rows. Type in the words, leaving a blank line before and after each word. After typing in all your words, "select" the entire table and click on the "center" button. Select a simple font (Arial or Geneva works well) and a large font size (26-point font works well). After creating the sort, save it using a name that defines the features such as "Spelling-Meaning_Silent to Sounded Consonants." You can contrast spelling patterns, suffixes, prefixes, and word roots—for example, contrasting words with the prefixes *sub-*, *un-*, and *trans-*, or contrasting words derived from the roots *vis* and *aud*. Create a template that you use each time and you can turn out a professional looking word sort sheet in minutes.

Here are some reminders and tips about creating your own word sorts:

1. Create sorts which will help your students form their own generalizations about how words work. Use a collection of 15 to 25 words so that there are plenty of examples to consider.
2. Contrast at least two and up to four features in a sort. There are many sample sorts in this appendix to give you ideas.

Prefixes and Suffixes

uni-	*bi-*	*tri-*	*fore-*	*sub-*	*ex-*	*en-*
unicorn	biceps	triangle	forearm	subset	expel	enable
unicycle	bicycle	triple	forecast	subtract	express	endanger
uniform	bifocals	triceps	foretell	subdivide	explore	enact
unify	bilingual	triceratops	foresee	subgroup	exceed	enclose
union	binoculars	tricycle	foresight	submerge	excerpt	encourage
unique	bisect	trilogy	forehand	submarine	exclaim	enforce
unison	biweekly	trio	forehead	submerse	exclude	enjoy
universal		trivet	foreman	subway	excrete	enslave
universe		triplets	forethought	subtotal	exhale	enlarge
		tripod	foreshadow	subtitle	exile	enlist
		triad	forepaw	sublet	expand	enrage
		trinity	foremost	subsoil	explode	enrich
		triathlon		subject	exit	entrust

mis-	pre-	re-	un-	dis-	in- = "not"	non-
misbehave	precook	rebound	unable	disable	incomplete	nonsense
misconduct	predate	recall	unafraid	disagreeable	incorrect	nonstop
miscount	prefix	recapture	unarmed	disappear	indecent	nonfiction
misdeed	pregame	recharge	unbeaten	disarm	indirect	nonfat
misfit	preheat	reclaim	unbroken	discharge	inexpensive	nonprofit
misgivings	prejudge	recopy	uncertain	disclose	inflexible	nondairy
misguide	premature	recount	unclean	discolor	informal	nonstick
misjudge	prepay	recycle	unclear	discomfort	inhuman	nonviolent
mislay	preschool	reelect	uncommon	discontent	injustice	nonskid
mislead	preset	refill	uncover	discover	insane	nonstandard
mismatch	preteen	refinish	undone	dishonest	invalid	
misplace	pretest	reform	unequal	disinfect	invisible	
misprint	preview	refresh	unfair	dislike		
misspell	prewash	relearn	unkind	disloyal	in- = "in" or "into"	
mistake	predict	remind	unlike	disobey	income	
mistreat	precede	remodel	unlock	disorder	indent	
mistrust	prehistoric	renew	unpack	displace	indoor	
misuse	prepare	reorder	unreal	disregard	inset	
	prevent	repay	unripe	disrespect	insight	
	precaution	reprint	unselfish	distaste	inside	
	preschool	research	unstable	distrust	inlaid	
		restore	unsteady	different	inmate	
		retrace	untangle	diffuse	ingrown	
		return	untie	diffident	inboard	
		review	unwrap		inland	
		rewrite			infield	

Spelling–Meaning Alternations

Silent to sounded consonant		Long to short		Long to schwa		Short to schwa	
bomb	bombard	cave	cavity	able	ability	metallic	metal
column	columnist	flame	flammable	famous	infamous	academy	academic
soften	soft	grave	gravity	major	majority	malice	malicious
crumb	crumble	nature	natural	native	nativity	periodic	period
debt	debit	athlete	athletic	prepare	preparation	emphatic	emphasis
damn	damnation	please	pleasant	relate	relative	celebrate	celebrity
design	designate	crime	criminal	stable	stability	democratic	democracy
fasten	fast	decide	decision	compete	competition	excel	excellent
haste	hasten	revise	revision	combine	combination	perfection	perfect
hymn	hymnal	wise	wisdom	define	definition	critic	criticize
malign	malignant	know	knowledge	divide	division	habit	habitat
moisten	moist	episode	episodic	invite	invitation	mobility	mobile
muscle	muscular	assume	assumption	recite	recitation	prohibit	prohibition
resign	resignation	produce	production	reside	resident	geometry	geometric
sign	signal	convene	convention	compose	composition		
condemn	condemnation	volcano	volcanic	expose	exposition		
		serene	serenity	custodian	custody		
		ignite	ignition	pose	position		
		humane	humanity	social	society		

		Long to short with			
Schwa to short		**-y to -i change**		**Long to schwa**	
mental	mentality	apply	application	declare	declaration
general	generality	certify	certification	degrade	degradation
moral	morality	clarify	clarification	prepare	preparation
brutal	brutality	classify	classification	admire	admiration
central	centrality	gratify	gratification	combine	combination
eventual	eventuality	imply	implication	define	definition
personal	personality	notify	notification	deprive	deprivation
neutral	neutrality	purify	purification	derive	derivation
original	originality	modify	modification	incline	inclination
normal	normality	unify	unification	invite	invitation
mental	mentality	simplify	simplification	recite	recitation
formal	formality	multiply	multiplication	compile	compilation
equal	equality	magnify	magnification	perspire	perspiration
vital	vitality	specify	specification	explore	exploration
legal	legality	verify	verification		
local	locality	qualify	qualification		
hospital	hospitality	identify	identification		
personal	personality				

Adding the suffix -able/-ible

Root word + *-ible*	Base word + *-able*	e-drop + *-able*	-y to -i + *-able*	Drop *-ate* in base	Oddballs (*ce/ge*)
audible	affordable	achievable	variable	tolerable	manageable
credible	agreeable	admirable	reliable	vegetable	enforceable
edible	allowable	adorable	pliable	operable	noticeable
eligible	avoidable	advisable	pitiable	navigable	changeable
feasible	breakable	believable	justifiable	abominable	
gullible	comfortable	comparable	identifiable	negotiable	
horrible	dependable	conceivable	deniable	educable	
invincible	expandable	consumable	enviable	estimable	
legible	favorable	debatable	remediable	irritable	
plausible	laughable	deplorable		appreciable	
possible	payable	desirable			
terrible	preferable	disposable			
visible	predictable	excitable			
indelible	profitable	lovable			
intangible	punishable	notable			
compatible	reasonable	pleasurable			
combustible	refillable	recyclable			
	remarkable	valuable			
	respectable				
	transferable				

Adding -ant/-ance/-ancy and -ent/-ence/-ency

-ant	*-ance*	*-ancy*	*-ent*	*-ence*	*-ency*
abundant	abundance	abundancy	competent	competence	competency
relevant	relevance	relevancy	dependent	dependence	dependency
hesitant	hesitance	hesitancy	emergent	emergence	emergency
extravagant	extravagance	extravagancy	equivalent	equivalence	equivalency
malignant	malignance	malignancy	excellent	excellence	excellency
petulant	petulance	petulancy	expedient	expedience	expediency
radiant	radiance	radiancy	lenient	lenience	leniency
brilliant	brilliance	brilliancy	resident	residence	residency
relevant	relevance	relevancy	resilient	resilience	resiliency
defiant	defiance		violent	violence	
			convenient	convenience	

-ant	-ance		-ent	-ence
reluctant	reluctance		different	difference
exuberant	exuberance		diligent	diligence
fragrant	fragrance		evident	evidence
instant	instance		impatient	impatience
elegant	elegance		independent	independence
vigilant	vigilance		patient	patience
resistant	resistance		innocent	innocence
significant	significance		intelligent	intelligence
tolerant	tolerance		obedient	obedience
observant	observance		indulgent	indulgence

Prefixes

anti- (against)	auto- (self)	circum- (around)	inter- (between)	intra- (within)	mal- (bad)
antifreeze	autograph	circumference	interact	intramural	malice
antidote	automation	circumvent	international	intravenous	malignant
antitoxin	autobiography	circumstance	interfere	intrastate	maltreated
antibiotic	automobile	circumspect	interloper	intracellular	malpractice
anticlimactic	autocrat	circumscribe	interchange	intranational	maladjusted
antisocial	autonomy	circumlocution	interject		malnutrition
antigen	autopsy	circumnavigate	interrupt		malcontent
antipathy			intercede		malfunction
antiseptic			intermission		malady

peri- (around)	post- (after)	pro- (in front of, forward)		super- (over, greater)	trans- (across)
perimeter	posterior	proceed	profile	superpower	transfer
period	posterity	propel	promotion	supervision	transport
periphery	posthumous	produce	prohibit	supermarket	transmit
periscope	postpone	progress	procreate	supernatural	transplant
peripatetic	postscript	provide	propitious	superman	translate
periodontal	postmortem	program	pronounce	supersede	translucent
	postgraduate	projector	promulgate	supersonic	transparent
		protective	propensity	superstition	transform
		proclaim	proficient	superficial	transient
		profess	protracted	supercilious	transcend

Number-Related Prefixes (see uni-, bi-, and tri- under Prefixes and Suffixes)

mon-, mono-	cent-	mil-	oct-	poly-	semi-	multi-
monarchy	centigrade	million	octagon	polygon	semiannual	multitude
monastery	centimeter	millimeter	octopus	polygamy	semicolon	multiply
monogram	centipede	milligram	October	polychrome	semicircle	multicolored
monologue	centennial	millennium	octave	polyhedron	semisolid	multipurpose
monorail	century	millionaire	octahedron	polyglot	semiconscious	multicultural
monotone			octogenarian	polyester	semifinal	multimedia
monotonous		deca-		polygraph	semiweekly	multiplex
monolith		decade	pent-	polymath	semiprecious	multifaceted
monopoly		December	pentagon	polymers		multivitamin
monochrome		decahedron	pentameter	polyp		multifarious
monogamy		decagon	pentacle	polytechnic		multiplication

Assimilated or Absorbed Prefixes
in- meaning "not"

in-	*il-*	*im-*	*ir-*	*im-*
inaccurate	illogical	immature	irrational	impure
inefficient	illegal	immaterial	irreconcilable	impaired
inoperable	illiterate	immobile	irreparable	impartial
insecure	illegible	immodest	irregular	impossible
innumerable	illicit	immoderate	irrelevant	impediment
inactive	illustrious	immoral	irreplaceable	imperfect
inappropriate	illegitimate	immortal	irresistible	impersonal
incompetent		immovable	irresponsible	improper
indecent			irreversible	impractical

sub- meaning "under" or "lower"

sub-		*suf-*	*sup-*	*sur-*	*suc-*
subversion	subatomic	suffix	supplant	surreal	succumb
subterranean	subcommittee	suffuse	suppliant	surrender	succeed
suburban	subdivision	suffer	support	surrogate	success
substitute	submarine	suffice	supposition	surreptitious	succinct
substandard	subconscious	sufficient	suppress		
subsidize	subcontractor	suffocate	supplicant		
subclass	subjugate		supplement		
sublease	subscribe				
subscript	subscription				

com- meaning "with" or "together"

com-	*col-*	*con-*	*cor-*	*co-*
common	collection	conspire	correlate	coagulate
community	collide	concert	corroborate	coexist
combination	collision	connect	correct	coalition
committee	collage	congress	correspond	coauthor
company	collaborate	congestion	corrupted	coeducational
comply	colleague	congregation		cohabit
compress	collapse	conclude		cohesion
compound	collusion	condense		cohort
companion	collate	construct		coincide
compact	collateral	constellation		cooperate
complete	colloquial	connote		coordinate

ad- meaning "to" or "toward"

ad-	*at-*	*ac-*	*af-*	*al-*	*ap-*	*as-*
adjacent	attend	accompany	affinity	alliance	approach	assemble
adjoining	attune	acceptable	affable	alliteration	approximate	associate
addicted	attract	access	affection	allowance	appropriate	assimilate
adhesive	attach	accident	affluence	allusion	apprentice	assent
adaptation	attack	accommodate	affricative	alleviate	apprehend	assault
additional	attain	accomplish	affirmation	allotment	appreciate	assertion
adjective	attention	accumulate	*ag-*	*an-*	application	assessment
adjust	attempt	accomplish	aggregate	annex	applause	asset
admire	attitude	accrue	aggravate	annihilate	appetite	assiduous
admission	attribute	acquisition	aggression	announce	appendix	assistance
advocate	attrition	acquire	aggrieved	annul	appear	assuage
		acquisitive		annotate	appeal	assumption

dis- meaning "not," "opposite of," or "apart"

dis-

disadvantage	disarray
dissatisfied	disconcerted
disillusioned	discharged
disaster	disclaimer
disability	disconsolate
disagreeable	discouraged
disseminate	disregard
disappoint	disenchanted
discern	disoriented
disdain	

dif-

difficult
diffusion
different
diffidence

ex- meaning "out" or "from"

ex-

extract
excavate
exceed
exception
excerpt
excursion
exhale
exile
expansion
expenditure

ef-

efface
effect
efferent
efficiency
effrontery
effusive

ec-

ecstasy
eccentric
ecclesiastical

ob- meaning "to," "toward," or "against"

ob-

oblong	obscure	obscure
objection	observant	oblique
obligation	obstruction	obstacle
obliterate	obstreperous	obsolete
oblivious	obstinate	

op-

opponent
opposite
opportunity
opposition
oppress

of-

offend
offensive
offering
offense
officious

oc-

occurrence
occasion
occupation
occupy
occlude

Greek Roots

aer ("air")	aerate, aerial, aerobics, aerodynamic, aeronautics, aerosol, aerospace
arch ("rule, chief")	monarchy, anarchy, archangel, archbishop, archetype, architect, hierarchy, matriarch, patriarch
aster, astr ("star")	aster, asterisk, asteroid, astrology, astronomy, astronaut, astronomical, astrophysics, disaster
bi, bio ("life")	biology, biography, autobiography, biopsy, symbiotic, biodegradable, antibiotic, amphibious, biochemistry
centr ("center")	center, central, egocentric, ethnocentric, centrifugal, concentric, concentrate, eccentric
chron ("time")	chronic, chronicle, chronological, synchronize, anachronism
cosm ("world")	cosmic, cosmology, cosmonaut, cosmopolitan, cosmos, microcosm
crat ("rule")	democrat, plutocrat, bureaucrat, idiosyncratic, plutocrat, technocrat
crit ("judge")	critic, criticize, critique, criterion, diacritical, hypocrite
cycl ("circle")	cycle, bicycle, cyclone, tricycle, unicycle, recycle, motorcycle, cyclical, encyclopedia
dem ("people")	demagogue, democracy, demographics, endemic, epidemic, epidemiology
derm ("skin")	dermatologist, epidermis, hypodermic, pachyderm, taxidermist, dermatitis
dont ("tooth")	orthodontist
geo ("earth")	geology, geophysics, geography, geothermal, geocentric, geode
gn(o) ("know")	cognition, recognize, incognito, cognizant, recognizance
gram ("thing written")	diagram, program, telegram, anagram, cryptogram, epigram, grammar, monogram
graph ("to write")	graph, paragraph, autograph, digraph, graphics, topography, biography, bibliography, calligraphy, choreographer, videographer, ethnography, phonograph, seismograph, lexicographer
homo ("same")	homophone, homograph, homosexual, homogeneous
hydr ("water, fluid")	hydra, hydrant, hydrate, hydrogen, hydraulic, hydroelectric, hydrology, hydroplane, hydroponics, anhydrous, hydrangea, hydrophobia
logo ("word, reason")	logic, catalogue, dialogue, prologue, epilogue, monologue
logy ("study")	biology, geology, ecology, mythology, pathology, psychology, sociology, theology, genealogy, etymology, technology, zoology

meter ("measure")	centimeter, millimeter, diameter, speedometer, thermometer, tachometer, altimeter, barometer, kilometer
micro ("small")	microscope, microphone, microwave, micrometer, microbiology, microcomputer, microcosm
ortho ("correct, straight")	orthodox, orthodontics, orthography, orthodontists, orthopedic
pan ("all")	pandemic, panorama, pandemonium, pantheon, Pan-American
path ("feeling, emotion, suffer/disease")	sympathy, antipathy, apathetic, empathize, pathogen, pathologist, pathetic, pathos, osteopath
ped ("child"; see Latin ped for foot)	pedagogy, pediatrician, pedophile, encyclopedia
phil ("love")	philosophy, philharmonic, bibliophile, Philadelphia, philanderer, philanthropy, philatetic, philter
phobia ("fear")	phobia, acrophobia, claustrophobia, xenophobia, arachnophobia
phon ("sound")	phonics, phonograph, cacophony, earphone, euphony, homophone, microphone, telephone, xylophone, saxophone, phoneme, symphony
photo ("light")	photograph, telephoto, photocopier, photographer, photosynthesis, photocell
phys ("nature, natural")	physics, physical, physician, physiology, physique, astrophysics, physiognomy, physiotherapy
poli ("city")	politics, police, policy, metropolis, acropolis, cosmopolitan, megalopolis, Minneapolis
psych ("spirit, soul")	psyche, psychology, psychoanalyst, psychiatry, psychedelic, psychosis, psychosomatic, psychic
scope ("see")	microscope, periscope, scope, telescope, stethoscope, gyroscope, horoscope, kaleidoscope, stereoscope
sphere ("ball")	sphere, atmosphere, biosphere, hemisphere, ionosphere, stratosphere, troposphere
tech ("art, skill, build")	technical, technician, technology, polytechnic, architect
tele ("far")	telecast, telegraph, telegram, telescope, television, telethon, teleconference, telepathy
therm ("heat")	thermal, geothermal, thermometer, thermonuclear, thermos, thermostat, thermodynamic, exothermic
typ ("to beat, to strike; impression")	typewriter, typist, typographical, archetype, daguerreotype, prototype, stereotype, typecast
zo ("animal")	zoo, zoology, protozoan, zodiac, zoologist

Latin Roots

aud ("hear")	audio, auditorium, audience, audible, audition, inaudible, audiovisual
bene ("good, well")	benefactor, benevolent, beneficial, benefit, benign, benefactress, benediction
cand, chand ("shine")	candle, chandelier, incandescent, candelabra, candid, candidate
cap ("head")	captain, capital, capitol, capitalize, capitulate, decapitate, per capita
cide ("kill, cut")	fungicide, herbicide, pesticide, insecticide, suicide, homicide, genocide, incise, incision, concise, circumcise, excise
clud/clus, clos ("close, shut")	conclude, exclude, exclusive, preclude, occlude, seclude, seclusion, recluse, closet, disclose, enclose, foreclose
corp ("body")	corpse, corporal, corporation, corpus, corpulent, incorporate, corpuscle
cred ("believe")	credible, incredible, credit, credentials, accredited, credulous
dent ("tooth")	dentist, dentures, indent
dic, dict ("speak")	dictate, diction, dictionary, predict, verdict, benediction, contradict, dedicate, edict, indict, jurisdiction, valedictorian, dictation
doc ("teach")	documentary, indoctrinate, doctorate, doctor, docent, docile, doctrine
duc, duct ("lead")	conduct, conductor, deduct, aqueduct, duct, educate, educe, induct, introduction, reduce, reproduce, viaduct, abduct
equ ("equal")	equal, equality, equation, equator, equity, equivalent, equilibrium, equivocate, equidistant, equinox
fac, fec ("do")	factory, manufacture, faculty, artifact, benefactor, confection, defect, effect, facile, facilitate, facsimile, affect, affection

fer ("carry")	ferry, transfer, prefer, reference, suffer, vociferous, inference, fertile, differ, conifer, conference, circumference
fid ("trust")	fidelity, confident, confidence, diffident, infidelity, perfidy, affidavit, bona fide, confidential
fin ("end")	final, finale, finish, infinite, definitive, finite
flex, flect ("bend, curve")	flex, flexible, inflexible, deflect, reflection, inflection, circumflex, genuflect
flu ("flow")	fluid, fluent, influx, superfluous, affluence, confluence, fluctuate, influence
form ("shape")	conform, deform, formal, formality, format, formation, formula, informal, information, malformed, platform, reform, transform, uniform
grac, grat ("pleasing, thankful")	grace, gratuity, gracious, ingrate, congratulate, grateful, gratitude, ingratiate, persona non grata, gratify
grad ("step")	graduate, gradual, gradient, grade, retrograde, centigrade, degraded, downgrade
gress ("go")	digress, aggressive, congress, egress, ingress, progress, regress, transgression
ject ("throw")	eject, injection, interject, object, objection, conjecture, abject, dejected, projection, projectile, projector, reject, subjective, trajectory
jud ("judge")	judge, judgment, prejudice, judiciary, judicial, adjudge, adjudicate, injudicious
junct ("join")	junction, juncture, injunction, conjunction, adjunct, disjunction
langu, lingu ("tongue")	language, bilingual, linguistics, linguist, linguine, lingo
lit ("letter")	literature, illiterate, literal, literacy, obliterate, alliteration, literary
loc, loq ("speak")	elocution, eloquent, loquacious, obloquy, soliloquy, ventriloquist, colloquial, interlocutor
man ("hand")	manual, manufacture, manicure, manuscript, emancipate, manacle, mandate, manipulate, manage, maneuver
mem ("memory, mindful")	remember, memory, memorize, memorial, memorandum, memento, memorabilia, commemorate
min ("small")	diminish, mince, minimize, minute, minuscule, minus, minor, minnow, minimum
miss, mit ("send")	transmission, remission, submission, admit, transmit, remit, submit, omit, mission, missile, demise, emission, admission, commission, emissary, intermission, intermittent, missionary, permission, promise
mob, mot ("move")	mobile, motion, motor, remote, automobile, promote, motivate, motel, locomotion, immobile, emotion, demote, commotion
pat ("father")	paternal, patrimony, expatriate, patron, patronize
ped ("foot")	pedal, pedestal, pedicure, pedigree, biped, centipede, millipede, moped, impede, expedite, orthopedic, pedestrian, quadruped
pens, pend ("hang")	appendage, appendix, pending, pendulum, pension, suspended, suspense, compensate, depend, dispense, expend, expensive, pensive, stipend, impending, pendant
port ("carry")	porter, portfolio, portage, portable, export, import, rapport, report, support, transport, comportment, deport, important, portmanteau
pos, pon ("put, place")	pose, position, positive, a propos, compose, composite, compost, composure, disposable, expose, impose, imposter, opposite, postpone, preposition, proponent, proposition, superimpose, suppose
prim, princ ("first")	prime, primate, primer, primeval, primitive, prima donna, primal, primary, primogeniture, primordial, primrose, prince, principal, principality, principle
quir, ques ("ask")	inquire, require, acquire, conquer, inquisition, quest, question, questionnaire, request, requisite, requisition
rupt ("break")	rupture, abrupt, bankrupt, corrupt, erupt, disrupt, interrupt, irruption
sal ("salt")	salt, saline, salary, salami, salsa, salad, desalinate
sci ("know")	science, conscience, conscious, omniscience, subconscious, conscientious
scrib, script ("write")	scribble, script, scripture, subscribe, transcription, ascribe, describe, inscribe, proscribe, postscript, prescription, circumscribe, nondescript, conscription
sect, seg ("cut")	bisect, dissect, insect, intersect, section, sector, segment
sent, sens ("feel")	sense, sensitive, sensory, sensuous, sentiment, sentimental, assent, consent, consensus, dissent, resent, sensation
sequ, sec ("follow")	sequence, sequel, sequential, consequence, consecutive, non sequitur, persecute, second, sect, subsequent

sta, sist ("stand")	stable, state, station, stationary, statistic, statue, stature, status, subsist, assist, consistent, desist, insistent, persistent, resist
son ("sound")	sonic, sonnet, sonorous, unison, ultrasonic, assonance, consonant, dissonant, resonate
spec, spic ("look")	spectacle, spectacular, specimen, prospect, respect, retrospective, speculate, suspect, suspicion, aspect, auspicious, circumspect, inspector, introspection
spir ("breathe")	spirit, respiration, perspire, transpire, inspire, conspire, aspirate, dispirited, antiperspirant
stru ("build")	construct, instruct, destruction, reconstruction, obstruct
tain, ten ("hold")	detain, obtain, pertain, retain, sustain, abstain, appertain, contain, entertain, maintain, tenacious
tang, tact ("touch")	tangible, intangible, tangent, contact, tactile
ten ("stretch")	distend, tendon, tendril, extend, intend, intensify, attend, contend, portend, superintendent
term ("end")	term, terminal, terminate, determine, exterminate, predetermine
terra ("earth")	terrain, terrarium, terrace, subterranean, terrestrial, extraterrestrial, Mediterranean, terra cotta, terra firma
tort, torq ("twist")	contort, distort, extort, torture, tortuous, torque
tract ("pull")	tractor, traction, contract, distract, subtract, retract, attract, protracted, intractable, abstract, detract
vac ("empty")	vacant, vacuum, evacuate, vacation, vacuous, vacate
val ("strong, worth")	valid, valiant, validate, evaluate, devalue, convalescent, valedictorian, invalid
ven, vent ("come")	vent, venture, venue, adventure, avenue, circumvent, convention, event, intervene, invent, prevent, revenue, souvenir, convenient
vers, vert ("turn")	revert, vertex, vertigo, convert, divert, vertical, adverse, advertise, anniversary, avert, controversy, conversation, extrovert, introvert, inverse, inverted, perverted, reverse, subvert, traverse, transverse, universe, versatile, versus, vertebra
vid, vis ("see")	video, vista, visage, visit, visual, visa, advise, audiovisual, envision, invisible, television, supervise, provision, revision, improvise
voc ("call")	vocal, vociferous, evoke, invoke, advocate, avocation, convocation, equivocal, invocation, provoke, revoke, vocabulary, vocation
vol, volv ("roll, turn")	revolve, evolve, involve, volume, convoluted, devolve

APPENDIX G
Assessment Materials

G.1 PRODUCING WORDS WITH THE SAME SUFFIX AND PREFIX

Teacher Notes

This assessment examines students' productive knowledge of prefixes and suffixes. The ability to think of related words indicates the depth of students' vocabulary knowledge and the level of their knowledge of affixes. Students are instructed to write as many words as they can with words that begin or end with these prefixes and suffixes, respectively. Two lists of 10 suffixes and prefixes with examples are presented. Most of the prefixes and suffixes in Part I are more frequent and/or transparent than those in Part II. Students are asked to write the meanings of the prefixes.

Directions.   The directions are printed at the top of the student copy. The time to take the assessment can vary for purpose. In whole-group settings, students can be given eight minutes to complete each part. Go on to Part II to complete the assessment if students generate at least two words for 8 of the 10 affixes.

Scoring and Interpretation.   Score 2 points for each correct word that is also spelled correctly. Score 1 point for each word that could be correct but is misspelled. In the prefixes test, award 1 point for each prefix defined correctly.

Examine the types of suffixes and prefixes that were more difficult for students to understand to determine the types of prefixes the students would benefit from examining in vocabulary study. There should be a developmental pattern in the students' errors. Students usually produce more words for the words with common prefixes and suffixes. Instruction can begin by making the meaning connections among known affixes and explaining the explicit grammatical functions of suffixes.

In Part I of the prefix test, students who score between 30 and 40 points are likely to be in the middle of the intermediate stage of reading and in the syllables and affixes stage of spelling. Students who score between 30 and 40 points in Part II of the prefixes tests are likely to be in the middle of the advanced stage of reading and in the derivational relations stage of spelling. For the suffixes test, students are not asked for the meanings of the suffixes. Students who score between 25 and 35 on Part I of the suffix test are likely to be in the middle of the intermediate stage of reading and in the syllables and affixes stage of spelling. Students who score between 25 and 35 on Part II of the suffix test are likely to be in the middle of the advanced stage of reading and in the derivational relations stage of spelling.

Students who score below 30 on Part I of the prefix test and below 25 on Part I of the suffix test are ready to focus on some of the easier and more common prefixes and suffixes. They need to look more deeply at the familiar affixes and focus on several of the affixes they do not know well.

Student Form for Producing Words with the Same Suffix

Part I. Here are 10 suffixes with examples. Think of words that have the same suffix. Write up to four related words on the line. Do not include words with *plurals*, words that end with *s* (*basketfuls* would not count). Do not spend too much time on any one suffix. Spell the words the best you can. Your teacher will tell you how much time you have.

Student's Name _____ Teacher _____ Period/Grade ___ Date _____

suffix (example)

1. *-ful* (basketful) _____
2. *-ing* (contracting) _____
3. *-y* (lucky) _____
4. *-ish* (childish) _____
5. *-ly* (seriously) _____
6. *-er* (reporter) _____
7. *-al* (magical) _____
8. *-ness* (goodness) _____
9. *-less* (painless) _____
10. *-ion* (eruption) _____

Part II. Here are 10 suffixes with examples. Think of words that have the same suffix. Write up to four related words on the line. Do not include words with *plurals*, words that end with *s* (*punishment*s would not count). Do not spend too much time on any one suffix. Spell the words the best you can. Your teacher will tell you how much time you have.

Student's Name _____ Teacher _____ Period/Grade ___ Date _____

suffix (example)

1. *-ment* (punishment) _____
2. *-ist* (specialist) _____
3. *-ial* (presidential) _____
4. *-ism* (symbolism) _____
5. *-ous* (dangerous) _____
6. *-ence* (competence) _____
7. *-ure* (indenture) _____
8. *-ive* (retrospective) _____
9. *-ous* (poisonous) _____
10. *-able* (affordable) _____
    or
    -ible (contemptible) _____

Student Form for Producing Words with the Same Prefix

Part I.   Here are 10 prefixes with examples. Think of words that have the same prefix. Write up to four related words on the line. Do not include words with *plurals,* words that end with *s* (*returns* would not count). Write down the meaning of the prefixes. Do not spend too much time on any one prefix. Spell the words the best you can. Your teacher will tell you how much time you have.

Student's Name _____   Teacher _____   Period/Grade ___   Date _____

prefix (example)

1. re-   (return) _____

         re- means: _____

2. *un-*   (unreliable) _____

         un- means: _____

3. *mis-*   (misleading) _____

         mis- means: _____

4. *non-*   (nonfiction) _____

         non- means: _____

5. *mono-* (monochrome) _____

         mono- means: _____

6. *auto-* (autograph) _____

         auto- means: _____

7. *pre-*   (prejudge) _____

         pre- means: _____

8. *semi-* (hemisphere) _____

         semi- means: _____

9. *dis-*   (discontinue) _____

         dis- means: _____

10. *in-*   (incorrect) _____

         in- means: _____

Part II.   Here are 10 prefixes with examples. Think of words that have the same prefix. Write up to four related words on the line. Do not include words with *plurals,* words that end with *s* (*supersonics* would not count). Write down the meaning of the prefixes. Do not spend too much time on any one prefix. Spell the words the best you can. Your teacher will tell you how much time you have.

Student's Name _____   Teacher _____   Period/Grade ____   Date _____

prefix   (example)

1. *super-* (supersonic) _____

   super- means: _____

2. *anti-*   (antibiotic) _____

   anti- means: _____

3. *micro-* (microbiologist) _____

   micro- means: _____

4. *tri-*   (triangle) _____

   tri- means: _____

5. *mal-*   (malformation) _____

   mal- means: _____

6. *sub-*   (subsection) _____

   sub- means: _____

7. *inter-* (interact) _____

   inter- means: _____

8. *con-/* (connect, company) _____
   com-

   con-/com- means: _____

9. *de-*   (debug, dejected) _____

   de- means: _____

10. *trans-* (transport) _____

   trans- means: _____

Part I Answers

1.	*re-*	back, again	report, realign, retract, revise, regain, reflect, rename, restate, recombine, recalculate, redo
2.	*un-*	not	uncooked, unharmed, unintended, unhappy
3.	*mis-*	bad, badly	misinform, misinterpret, mispronounce, misnomer, mistake, misogynist
4.	*non-*	not	nonferrous, nonabrasive, nondescript, nonfat, nonfiction, nonprofit, nonsense, nonentity
5.	*mono-*	single, one	monopoly, monotype, monologue, mononucleosis, monorail, monotheist
6.	*auto-*	self	automobile, automatic, autograph, autonomous, autoimmune, autopilot, autobiography
7.	*pre-*	before	predetermine, premeditated
8.	*semi-*	half	semifinal, semiconscious, semiannual, semimonthly, semicircle
9.	*dis-/dys-*	away, not, negative	dismiss, differ, disallow, disperse, dissuade, disconnect, dysfunction, disproportion, disrespect, distemper, distaste, disarray, dyslexia
10.	*in-*	not	incomplete, indirect, indecent, inaccurate, inactive, independent

Part II Answers

1.	*super-/ supra-*	above	superior, suprarenal, superscript, supernatural, supercede, superficial, superhero, superimpose
2.	*anti-*	against	antisocial, antiseptic, antithesis, antibody, antichrist, antinomies, antifreeze, antipathy, antigen, antibiotic, antidote, antifungal, antidepressant
3.	*micro-*	small	microscope, microprocessor, microfiche, micrometer, micrograph
4.	*tri-*	three	triangle, trinity, trilateral, triumvirate, tribune, trilogy, tricycle, trillion
5.	*mal-*	bad, badly	maladjusted, malady, malcontent, malfeasance, maleficent, malevolent, malice, malaria, malfunction, malignant
6.	*sub-*	under, below	submerge, submarine, substandard, subnormal, subvert, subdivision, submersible, submit
7.	*inter-*	between	international, intercept, intermission, interoffice, internal, intermittent
8.	*con-/ com-*	with, together	convene, compress, contemporary, converge, compact, confluence, concatenate, conjoin, combine, convert, compatible, consequence
9.	*de-*	remove, opposite	decode, deceive, definite, deduct, defend, detach
10.	*trans-*	across	transaction, transform, transmit, transcribe, translate, transplant, transcontinental

G.2 TEST OF MORPHOLOGICAL STRUCTURE

There are two ways to administer this assessment. The oral form is conducted individually and the written form can be conducted in small group or whole class.

Directions

For the oral administration, follow the directions. Write down what the student says.

In the written format, make copies of the written form. Use the oral form, and read the word and then the sentence. Students use the written form to write the word form that fits the sentence.

Scoring and Interpretation

Oral Scoring and Interpretation.   Carlisle has written extensively to interpret the results for several populations (2000).

Adding together the scores for derivation and decomposition for the oral form, there is a possible score of 40. Students who score below 50% (20/40) are probably late transitional to early intermediate readers. For them, the study of morphology may begin by focusing on bases with more transparent meanings, and few if any changes to the bases in spelling or pronunciation when suffixes are added; for example, *reach/reachable; act/action; grace/graceful.* Students who score 70% (28/40) may study more systematically the types of meaning, spelling, and pronunciation changes that occur when suffixes are added; for example, *fragile/fragility; oppose/opposition; acclaim/acclamation.*

Written Scoring and Interpretation.   There are 40 items. Score 1 point for each correct item that is spelled correctly, and ½ point for entries that contain the correct number of syllables and can be read.

Students who score below 40% (16/40) are probably late transitional to early intermediate readers. For them, the study of morphology may begin by focusing on bases with more transparent meanings, and few if any changes to the bases in spelling or pronunciation when suffixes are added; for example, *reach/reachable; act/action; grace/graceful.* Students who score 60% (24/40) may study more systematically the types of meaning, spelling, and pronunciation changes that occur when suffixes are added; for example, *fragile/fragility; oppose/opposition; acclaim/acclamation.*

Important Note.   While recommending that students who score less than 50% on the oral form or 40% on the written form begin with more transparent morphological relationships, this is not meant to suggest that such students not be exposed to, think about, and discuss more opaque relationships. This does suggest, however, that their systematic study of morphological relationships begin with and focus primarily on more straightforward and obvious relationships. A secure foundation at this level will ensure a more productive and secure systematic study of less transparent relationships later on.

Written Form

Students listen and complete the sentence in writing.

Part I: Derivation

Student's Name _____ Teacher _____ Period/Grade ____ Date _____

Directions: "I am going to say a word, and then I am going to read you a sentence that contains a form of the word I say. However, the word in the sentence will be left out, and I'd like you to write what you think that word is. For example: 'farm'; 'My uncle is a _____.' [farmer]. Let's try another one: 'help'; 'My sister is always _____.' [helpful]. Spell the words the best you can."

1. *warm.* He chose the jacket for its _____. [warmth]

2. *permit.* Father refused to give _____. [permission]

3. *profit.* Selling lemonade in summer is _____. [profitable]

4. *appear.* He cared about his _____. [appearance]

5. *protect.* She wore glasses for _____. [protection]

6. *perform.* Tonight is the last _____. [performance]

7. *expand.* The company planned an _____. [expansion]

8. *revise.* This paper is his second _____. [revision]

9. *reason.* Her argument was quite _____. [reasonable]

10. *major.* He won the vote by a _____. [majority]

11. *deep.* The lake was well known for its _____. [depth]

12. *equal.* Boys and girls are treated with _____. [equality]

13. *adventure.* The trip sounded _____. [adventurous]

14. *absorb.* She chose the sponge for its _____. [absorption]

15. *active.* He tired after so much _____. [activity]

16. *human.* The kind man was known for his _____. [humanity]

17. *humor.* The story was quite _____. [humorous]

18. *assist.* The teacher will give you _____. [assistance]

19. *mystery.* The dark glasses made the man look _____. [mysterious]

20. *glory.* The view from the hilltop was _____. [glorious]

Part II: Decomposition

Student's Name _____ Teacher _____ Period/Grade ___ Date _____

Directions: "I am going to say a word, and then I am going to read you a sentence that contains a form of the word I say. However, the word in the sentence will be left out, and I'd like you to write what you think that word is. For example: 'driver'; 'Children are too young to _____.' [drive]. Let's try another one: 'improvement'; 'My teacher wants my spelling to _____.' [improve]. Spell the words the best you can."

1. *growth.* She wanted her plant to _____. [grow]

2. *dryer.* Put the wash out to _____. [dry]

3. *variable.* The time of his arrival did not _____. [vary]

4. *width.* The mouth of the river is very _____. [wide]

5. *density.* The smoke in the room was very _____. [dense]

6. *famous.* The actor would achieve much _____. [fame]

7. *description.* The picture is hard to _____. [describe]

8. *strength.* The girl was very _____. [strong]

9. *decision.* The boy found it hard to _____. [decide]

10. *popularity.* The girl wants to be _____. [popular]

11. *publicity.* His views were made _____. [public]

12. *difference.* Do their opinions _____? [differ]

13. *originality.* That painting is very _____. [original]

14. *courageous.* The man showed great _____. [courage]

15. *admission.* How many people will they _____? [admit]

16. *dangerous.* Are the children in any _____? [danger]

17. *reduction.* The overweight man was trying to _____. [reduce]

18. *continuous.* How long will the storm _____? [continue]

19. *reliable.* On his friend he could always _____. [rely]

20. *acceptance.* Is that an offer you can _____? [accept]

Oral Form

Student responds individually to teacher.

Part I: Derivation

Directions: "I am going to say a word, and then I am going to read you a sentence that contains a form of the word I say. However, the word in the sentence will be left out, and I'd like you to tell me (or write down) what you think that word is. For example: 'farm'; 'My uncle is a _____.' [farmer]. Let's try another one: 'help'; 'My sister is always _____.' [helpful].

1. *warm.* He chose the jacket for its _____. [warmth]

2. *permit.* Father refused to give _____. [permission]

3. *profit.* Selling lemonade in summer is _____. [profitable]

4. *appear.* He cared about his _____. [appearance]

5. *protect.* She wore glasses for _____. [protection]

6. *perform.* Tonight is the last _____. [performance]

7. *expand.* The company planned an _____. [expansion]

8. *revise.* This paper is his second _____. [revision]

9. *reason.* Her argument was quite _____. [reasonable]

10. *major.* He won the vote by a _____. [majority]

11. *deep.* The lake was well known for its _____. [depth]

12. *equal.* Boys and girls are treated with _____. [equality]

13. *adventure.* The trip sounded _____. [adventurous]

14. *absorb.* She chose the sponge for its _____. [absorption]

15. *active.* He tired after so much _____. [activity]

16. *human.* The kind man was known for his _____. [humanity]

17. *humor.* The story was quite _____. [humorous]

18. *assist.* The teacher will give you _____. [assistance]

19. *mystery.* The dark glasses made the man look _____. [mysterious]

20. *glory.* The view from the hilltop was _____. [glorious]

Part II: Decomposition

Directions: "I am going to say a word, and then I am going to read you a sentence that contains a form of the word I say. However, the word in the sentence will be left out, and I'd like you to tell me (or write down) what you think that word is. For example: 'driver'; 'Children are too young to _____.' [drive]. Let's try another one: 'improvement'; ' My teacher wants my spelling to _____.'" [improve]

1. *growth.*   She wanted her plant to _____. [grow]

2. *dryer.*   Put the wash out to _____. [dry]

3. *variable.*   The time of his arrival did not _____. [vary]

4. *width.*   The mouth of the river is very _____. [wide]

5. *density.*   The smoke in the room was very _____. [dense]

6. *famous.*   The actor would achieve much _____. [fame]

7. *description.*   The picture is hard to _____. [describe]

8. *strength.*   The girl was very _____. [strong]

9. *decision.*   The boy found it hard to _____. [decide]

10. *popularity.*   The girl wants to be _____. [popular]

11. *publicity.*   His views were made _____. [public]

12. *difference.*   Do their opinions _____? [differ]

13. *originality.*   That painting is very _____. [original]

14. *courageous.*   The man showed great _____. [courage]

15. *admission.*   How many people will they _____? [admit]

16. *dangerous.*   Are the children in any _____? [danger]

17. *reduction.*   The overweight man was trying to _____. [reduce]

18. *continuous.*   How long will the storm _____? [continue]

19. *reliable.*   On his friend he could always _____. [rely]

20. *acceptance.*   Is that an offer you can _____? [accept]

Source: From Carlisle, J. F. (2000). Awareness of the structure and meaning of morphologically complex words: Impact on reading. *Reading and Writing: An Interdisciplinary Journal, 12,* 169–190. Adaptation has been made in length and for a written format. Used by permission.

Test of Morphological Structure

APPENDIX G

G.3 UPPER-LEVEL SPELLING INVENTORY

General Instructions for Administering the Inventories

Students should not study the words in advance of testing. Assure the students that this is not for a grade but to help you plan for their needs. Tell students, "I am going to ask you to spell some words. Spell them the best you can. Some of the words will be easy to spell; some may be difficult. When you do not know how to spell a word, spell it the best you can."

Ask students to number their paper. Call each word aloud (from p. 256) and repeat it. Say each word naturally, without emphasizing phonemes or syllables. Use it in a sentence, if necessary, to be sure students know the exact word. Sample sentences are provided along with the words. After administering the inventory use a Feature Guide, Class Composite Form, and, if desired, a Spelling-by-Stage Classroom Organization Chart to complete your assessment.

Scoring the Inventory Using the Feature Guides

1. Make a copy of the Feature Guide (p. 257) for each student. Draw a line under the last word called if you called less than the total amount and adjust the possible total points at the bottom of each feature column.
2. Score the words by checking off the features spelled correctly that are listed in the cells to the right of each word. For example, if a student spells *switch* as SWICH they get a check in the Digraphs and Blends cell and the Vowel cell, but not for the Complex Consonants. Write in the misspelling (*ch* in this case) but do not give a point for it. If a student spells *illiterate* as ILITERATE they get a check in the Unaccented Final Syllable cell, but not for the Assimilated Prefix. Put a check in the "correct" column if the word is spelled correctly. Do not count reversed letters as errors but note them in the cells. If unnecessary letters are added, give the speller credit for what is correct but do not check correct spelling.
3. Add the number of checks under each feature and across each word, allowing you to double-check the total score recorded in the last cell. Modify the ratios in the last row, depending on the number of words called aloud.

Interpreting the Results of the Spelling Inventory

1. Look down each feature column to determine instructional needs. A student who misses only one (or two if the features sample eight to ten words) can go on to other features. A student who misses two or three needs some review work, but students who miss more than three need careful instruction on this feature. If a student did not get any points for a feature, then earlier features need to be studied first.
2. To determine a stage of development, note where students first make more than one error under the stages listed at the top of the Feature Guide.

Using the Class Composite, Spelling By Stage Form, and Upper-Level Spelling Inventory Class Composite

1. Staple each feature guide to the student's spelling paper and arrange the papers in rank order from highest total points to lowest total points.
2. List students' names in this rank order in the left column of the appropriate Classroom Composite form (p. 258) and transfer each student's feature scores from the bottom row of the individual Feature Guides to the Classroom Composite Form. If you call out less than the total list, adjust the totals on the bottom row of the Classroom Composite.
3. Highlight cells where students make two or more errors on a particular feature to get a sense of your groups' needs and, if possible, to form groups for instruction.

Note: See Chapter 2 and Appendix A in *Words Their Way* for more detailed directions for choosing, administering, scoring, interpreting, and using the inventories to form instructional groups.

Word List and Sentences

The Upper-Level Spelling Inventory can be used in intermediate, middle, high school, and postsecondary classrooms. The 31 words are ordered by difficulty to sample features of the within-word pattern to derivational relations spelling stages. With normally achieving students, you can administer the entire list, but you may stop when students misspell more than eight words and are experiencing noticeable frustration.

1. *switch*. We can switch television channels with a remote control. *switch*

2. *smudge*.   There was a smudge on the mirror from her fingertips.   *smudge*

3. *trapped*. He was trapped in the elevator when the electricity went off. *trapped*

4. *scrape*. The fall caused her to scrape her knee. *scrape*

5. *knotted*. The knotted rope would not come undone. *knotted*

6. *shaving*. He didn't start shaving with a razor until 11th grade. *shaving*

7. *squirt*. Don't let the ketchup squirt out of the bottle too fast. *squirt*

8. *pounce*. My cat likes to pounce on her toy mouse. *pounce*

9. *scratches*. We had to paint over the scratches on the car. *scratches*

10. *crater*. The crater of the volcano was filled with bubbling lava. *crater*

11. *sailor*. When he was young, he wanted to go to sea as a sailor. *sailor*

12. *village*. My Granddad lived in a small seaside village. *village*

13. *disloyal*. Traitors are disloyal to their country. *disloyal*

14. *tunnel*. The rockslide closed the tunnel through the mountain. *tunnel*

15. *humor*. You need a sense of humor to understand his jokes. *humor*

16. *confidence*. With each winning game, the team's confidence grew. *confidence*

17. *fortunate*. The driver was fortunate to have snow tires on that winter day. *fortunate*

18. *visible*. The singer on the stage was visible to everyone. *visible*

19. *circumference*. The length of the equator is equal to the circumference of the earth. *circumference*

20. *civilization*. We studied the ancient Mayan civilization last year. *civilization*

21. *monarchy*. A monarchy is headed by a king or a queen. *monarchy*

22. *dominance*. The dominance of the Yankees baseball team lasted for several years. *dominance*

23. *correspond*. Many students correspond through email. *correspond*

24. *illiterate*. It is hard to get a job if you are illiterate. *illiterate*

25. *emphasize*. I want to emphasize the importance of trying your best. *emphasize*

26. *opposition*. The coach said the opposition would give us a tough game. *opposition*

27. *chlorine*. My eyes were burning from the chlorine in the swimming pool. *chlorine*

28. *commotion*. The audience heard the commotion backstage. *commotion*

29. *medicinal*. Cough drops are to be taken for medicinal purposes only. *medicinal*

30. *irresponsible*. It is irresponsible not to wear a seat belt. *irresponsible*

31. *succession*. The firecrackers went off in rapid succession. *succession*

Upper-Level Spelling Inventory Feature Guide

Student's Name _____ Teacher _____ Period _____ Grade _____ Date _____

Words Spelled Correctly: _____ / 31   Feature Points: _____ / 68   Total _____ / 99   Spelling Stage _____

| Stages and gradations | Within-Word Pattern | | | Syllables and Affixes | | | Derivational Relations | | | Word Spelled Correctly | Feature Points |
| | Early | Middle | Late | Early | Middle | Late | Early | Middle | Late | | |
Words	Digraphs and Blends	Vowels	Complex Consonants	Inflected Endings and Syllable Juncture	Unaccented Final Syllables	Affixes	Reduced Vowels in Unaccented Syllables	Greek and Latin Elements	Assimilated Prefixes		
1. switch	sw	i	tch								
2. smudge	sm	u	dge								
3. trapped	tr			pped							
4. scrape		a-e	scr								
5. knotted		o	kn	tted							
6. shaving	sh			ving							
7. squirt		ir	squ								
8. pounce		ou	ce								
9. scratches		a	tch	es							
10. crater	cr	ai		t	er						
11. sailor					or						
12. village				ll	age						
13. disloyal		oy			al	dis					
14. tunnel				nn	el						
15. humor				m	or						
16. confidence						con	fid				
17. fortunate					ate			fortun			
18. visible						ible		vis			
19. circumference						ence		circum			
20. civilization							liz	civil			
21. monarchy								arch			
22. dominance						ance	min				
23. correspond							res		rr		
24. illiterate					ate				ll		
25. emphasize						size	pha				
26. opposition							pos		pp		
27. chlorine						ine		chlor			
28. commotion						tion			mm		
29. medicinal					al			medic			
30. irresponsible						ible	res		rr		
31. succession						sion			cc		
Totals	/5	/9	/7	/8	/9	/10	/7	/7	/6	/31	/68

Upper-Level Spelling Inventory

APPENDIX G

Upper-Level Spelling Inventory Class Composite

Student's Name _____ Teacher _____ Period _____ Grade _____ Date _____

Words Spelled Correctly: ____ / 31   Feature Points: ____ / 68   Total ____ / 99   Spelling Stage _____

Stages and Gradations for Features (possible points in parentheses)

| Students | Within-Word Pattern | | | Syllables and Affixes | | | Derivational Relations | | | |
| | Early | Middle | Late | Early | Middle | Late | Early | Middle | Late | Total Points (99) Rank Order |
	Digraphs and Blends (5)	Vowels (9)	Complex Consonants (7)	Inflected Endings and Syllable Juncture (8)	Unaccented Final Syllables (9)	Affixes (10)	Reduced Vowels in Unaccented Syllables (7)	Greek and Latin Elements (7)	Assimilated Prefixes (6)	
1.										
2.										
3.										
4.										
5.										
6.										
7.										
8.										
9.										
10.										
11.										
12.										
13.										
14.										
15.										
16.										
17.										
18.										
19.										
20.										
21.										
22.										
23.										
24.										
25.										
26.										
27.										
Number who miss more than 1 on feature										

G.4 HOMOPHONE VOCABULARY AND SPELLING ASSESSMENT FOR PACING VOCABULARY INSTRUCTION

Teacher Instructions

The assessment on pages 261–262 provides a quick way to assess students' knowledge of the meanings and spellings of increasingly less familiar and less frequent homophone pairs. In a general way, performance on this productive spelling task illustrates students' vocabulary and orthographic knowledge, the knowledge of words that underlies students' reading and spelling.

Pause after the first two pairs to see if students understand the directions. You may want to pause or stop after 10 pairs to see how students performed. All students may not pronounce the words as homophones. In these instances, explain to students that they are close and that they are to think of the two words that are similar in pronunciation.

Directions to Students.   "A homophone is a word that sounds like another word, but which has a different spelling and meaning. For example, if I read this sentence: *I went to the sale to buy fresh fruit*, which spelling of *sale/sail* would you write? *Sale.* This homophone assessment will help us to understand your vocabulary development and spelling knowledge of how these homophones are spelled. This assessment will help us think about instruction. There are two parts to the assessment."

Part I.   "I am going to say a word and read a sentence, and then I will say the word again. Please write the word on your paper. Each word is part of a homophone pair."

Part II.   "On your own, think of the second spelling of the word and write that word underneath. For example, in the *sale/sail* homophone pair, write *sail* underneath *sale*. A second spelling of *sale* is *s-a-i-l*, as in *to sail on a sailboat* or *the sail of a sailboat*. Write s-a-i-l below *sale*. Make a guess if you are not sure of the answer."

sale

sail

Other examples of homophone pairs to share with students are *heard/herd* and *way/weigh*.

"After I call out the first homophone to the pair, you will have 10 seconds to write the first word and then the second homophone."

Scoring and Interpretation.   The pairs are arranged roughly in order of difficulty and frequency. These words are also arranged by their spelling complexity. A total of 40 points is possible. The interpretation of the score in the table below is a pacing guide that gives direction on what types of words students are ready to study.

Students' knowledge of the meanings of the words will vary with their literacy. There will be a close relationship between students' knowledge of these homophones and their reading and spelling development. See the pacing table that accompanies the directions.

As can be seen in the table on the following page, students who score less than 20 words spelled correctly will need a slower pace to learn polysyllabic vocabulary words. They may be able to read the words in the first half of the assessment, but vocabulary like the words in pairs 11–20 may well be too difficult for the students to read and spell. Consider the scores in the context of the developmental sequence outlined at the end of Chapters 1 and 8. These students are probably transitional readers who are within-word pattern spellers.

Students who score between 50 and 80 percent may be intermediate readers in the syllables and affixes stage of spelling. Over the course of this stage they grow more comfortable reading polysyllabic words greater than five syllables. At the beginning of this stage they need more time to learn to read and spell specialized vocabulary (e.g.,

Guide for Interpretation of the Homophone Assessment for Pacing Vocabulary Instruction		
Number and Percent of Words Spelled Correctly	**Pacing Guide for Pacing Vocabulary Instruction**	**Probable Reading/ Spelling Stages**
Number Correct: ≤20 Percent Correct: <50%	• Read 1 to 3-syllable words with ease in context. • Spell most single-syllable words correctly. • Study homophones, inflectional morphology, and easy prefixes and roots. • Benefit from support in reading text that is filled with polysyllabic words.	Transitional/Within-Word Pattern
Number Correct: 28–32 Percent Correct: 50%–80%	• Read words having 6 or fewer syllables with ease in context. • Spell 3- to 5-syllable words correctly with practice. • Learn affixes and easy roots. Vocabulary instruction can include polysyllabic words. Study the way two-syllable words combine.	Intermediate/ Syllables and Affixes
Correct: >32 Percent Correct: >80%	• Read nearly all words in texts with ease. • Spell new vocabulary words with a little practice. • Explore the history of specialized vocabulary, learn roots and harder affixes.	Advanced/ Derivational Relations

metamorphoses). Their vocabulary study can deal conceptually with more challenging words, provided time is given to learning more challenging word patterns (for example, Greek and Latin roots) in less transparent combinations such as *circumspect* and *transpire*. Students who score between 70 and 80 percent will find words like those in pairs 13–20 somewhat easy, and students will be able to concentrate on the meanings of the words. Words that are much more complicated in structure will be too difficult to read and spell. Students who spell more than 80 percent of the homophones correctly are probably advanced readers who are derivational relations spellers. They need further challenges and will benefit from explaining and sharing what they know with others.

Variations in Administration. The directions above are the most difficult assessment option. Here are variations that are less difficult.

1. *Students match the words with the definitions.* Create a sort or letter the homophones for students to write beside the matching definition. Recognition is easier than the writing task above. Keep in mind that those students in the transitional reading stage will be able to read the words through the first 12 pairs. The last eight words may be difficult to read if they are unfamiliar to students. Intermediate and advanced readers will be able to read all the words.

2. *Students write the correct homophone beside the sentence.* Students are given the sentences, and the teacher calls out the homophone pair. The students write the correct form beside the sentence. If the assessment calls for students to write and spell the words correctly, students in the transitional reading and within-word pattern spelling stage will usually not be able to spell more than four word pairs correctly. Students in the syllables and affixes and derivational relations stages will spell most of these words correctly.

Word Pairs

Word[1]	Definitions[2]	Sentences[3]
1. *rose*	flower	The rose had a prickly stem.
	moderate purplish red	That rose-colored rug matches the color of my chair.
	to rise or stand up	The audience rose to their feet and cheered.
rows	propels boat with oars	The fisherman rows his boat away from the shore.
	continuous lines or stripes	He planted the carrot seeds in three rows.
2. *meat*	animal tissue used for food	Many sharp-toothed dinosaurs were meat eaters.
meet	come into contact with	You meet many people at school.
3. *steal*	to take property of another illegally, pilfer	It is illegal to steal money from a bank.
steel	commercial iron containing carbon	Strong steel beams support the weight of the skyscraper.
4. *marry*	to unite in wedlock	The princess hoped to marry a prince.
merry	cheerful, joyous	The merry guests greeted each other happily.
5. *threw*	propelled through air by the hand	The boy threw the ball to his friend.
through	denoting penetration or passage	I poked a needle through the buttonhole.
6. *soared*	flew aloft, rose	The eagle soared high above its nest.
sword	long-bladed weapon for cutting, slashing, and thrusting	The king drew his sword fiercely.
7. *weather*	atmospheric state at specific time and place	Our weather today is cloudy and cool.
whether	conjunction indicating a choice between alternatives	She could not decide whether to walk or ride her bike to school.
8. *bolder*	more fearless in meeting danger or difficulty	He grew bolder over time to make his voice heard.
boulder	detached mass of rock	A large boulder blocked the entrance to the cave.
9. *trader*	person who barters, buys, and sells	She works as a stock trader on Wall Street.
traitor	person who commits treason against his or her country, betrays another's trust, or is false to an obligation	He argued with the king and was declared a traitor.
10. *altar*	place of worship or sacrifice	The church's altar was decorated with beautiful flowers.
alter	to become different or cause to become different	The seamstress will alter my pants to make them fit better.
11. *bridal*	nuptial festival or ceremony	The bridal party arrived at the church two hours before the wedding.
bridle	headgear by which a horse is controlled	The jockey held the horse's bridle with a firm grip.
12. *accept*	to take without protest	Please accept our invitation to the party.
except	to omit something	She remembered to pack everything except for her toothbrush.

13.	profit	excess of returns over expenditures, net income (revenues and gains less expenses and losses)	The company increased their profit this year.
	prophet	person gifted with extraordinary spiritual and moral insight; spiritual seer	The prophet shared his vision with his followers.
14.	reflects	turns, throws, or bends back at angle	The water reflects the image of the trees above.
		thinks about, considers	At the end of the game, the team reflects on its play.
	reflex	reaction to stimulus, often unconscious	Your gag reflex prevents choking.
15.	sensor	a device that detects	The sensor detected smoke and set off an alarm and the sprinkler system.
	censor	person who decides if communication material is to be deleted	The censor decided that the video was not suitable for television broadcasting.
16.	patience	ability to not be upset	Birdwatchers show great patience while waiting to see rare birds.
	patients	people under a doctor's care	The doctor treated several patients.
17.	ascent	rising	We watched the hot air balloon's ascent into the morning sky.
	assent	concurrence	Nodding his head in agreement, the judge indicated assent.
18.	penance	sorrow or contrition	He performed a penance for the sin he committed.
	pennants	nautical flags usually tapering to a point	The boat's pennants fluttered gently in the ocean breeze.
19.	depose	to remove from high position	The organization voted to depose their leader.
	depots	railroad or bus stations	The passengers changed trains at several depots.
20.	parity	close equivalence, likeness	After choosing players to play baseball, they felt there was parity between the two sides.
	parody	literary style characterized by reproduction of stylistic peculiarities of a work for comic effect or ridicule	The hilarious parody made fun of popular musicians.

[1]Word frequency (Zeno et al., 1995), and orthographic pattern were considered to select words.
[2]Definitions are from J. B. Hobbs (Compiler). (1986). *Homophones and homographs: An American dictionary*. Jefferson, NC: McFarland & Company.
[3]Assisted by Mandy Grotting.

G.5 FUNCTIONAL READING LEVELS AND READING RATE RANGES BY DEVELOPMENTAL LEVELS

Functional Reading Levels (Comfort Level)	Criteria for Functional Level	Reading Activities
Independent Level (Easy)	• Excellent reading comprehension (at least 90% accuracy) • Fluent reading rate and good oral reading expression • Few oral reading errors (3 or fewer errors per hundred words)	• Pleasure reading • Sustained silent reading • All independent work
Instructional Level (Comfortable)	• Good comprehension (at least 70% accuracy) • Fairly fluent reading rate and some oral reading expression • Good accuracy in oral reading (5 errors or less per 100 words; 12 errors or less for beginning readers)	• Teacher support • Small-group activities • Partner reading
Frustration Level (Too Difficult)	• Poor comprehension (less than 50% accuracy) • Disfluent, slow reading rate, hesitant and unexpressive • Numerous reading errors (7 errors or more per 100 words)	• For overviews and figures • Skimming and scanning • When interest is strong

Reading Rates By Developmental Stages (words per minute)

Reading Stages	Independent		Instructional		Frustration	
	Oral	*Silent*	*Oral*	*Silent*	*Oral*	*Silent*
Emergent	In a story reading voice or register, mimicking a reader.					
Beginning	60–80	—	40–70	—	< 35	—
Transitional	80–130	90–140	70–120	70–120	40–60	40–60
Intermediate	110–120	140–250	80–100	100–200	≤ 80	≤ 100
Advanced	120–150	250–500	100–120	180–200	≤ 100	≤ 120

Rates vary by the difficulty of the text and the student's development within a stage. For example, an advanced (teenage) reader may hit 160 wpm orally in easy text. An early beginning reader may read relatively difficult material at 40 wpm.

G.6 A CONCEPT SCIENCE SORT

Elements, Compounds, and Mixtures/Solutions

Elements	Compounds	Mixtures/Solutions
gold	different atoms	one kind of atom
can be separated	seawater	isotopes
soil	parts retain identities	metallic
molecules H_2O	pure	air
molecules H_2	covalent bonds	water bonds
made of elements and compounds	ionic bonds	oxygen
spices in a sauce or cake	hydrogen	salt

Additional Sorting Cards Added to the Sort during and after Studying Elements, Compounds, and Mixtures/Solutions

Additional Vocabulary to Add during and after Sorts			
unique properties	elements chemically joined	no reaction when joined	**Oddball**
molecules	atoms lose individual properties	homogeneous	particles
exist independently	composition	heterogeneous	chemistry
metals	chemical formulas	not chemically joined	gases
nonmetals	sugar	H_2	liquids
2 is a subscript for oxygen	solids	gases	

G.7 CHECKLIST OF VOCABULARY IN WRITING

Student's Name _____   Teacher _____

Period _____   Grade _____   Date _____

Check the items based on writing samples.

Teacher's question: When you look at students' writing what do you usually see?

Student's question: What do I see when I look at my vocabulary? How often?

	Always	Often	Occasionally	Never
Accuracy: Vocabulary is used correctly in writing				
T: Is the vocabulary's meaning accurate in writing?	_____	_____	_____	_____
S: Did the vocabulary make sense? Did I choose the right words?	_____	_____	_____	_____
Word frequency and variety: Variety of single-syllable and polysyllabic words				
T: Were there 4+-syllable words in the writing?	_____	_____	_____	_____
S: How complex was the vocabulary that I used? Did I use polysyllabic words?	_____	_____	_____	_____
Word choice: Combination of common and less frequent words				
T: Were there interesting words used in the writing?	_____	_____	_____	_____
S: Did I use unusual and interesting vocabulary in my writing?	_____	_____	_____	_____
Richness: Colorful and descriptive vocabulary				
T: Was the vocabulary colorful and descriptive?	_____	_____	_____	_____
S: Did the vocabulary paint a picture and show what I was trying to say?	_____	_____	_____	_____
New vocabulary: Recently acquired vocabulary				
T: Did the writing include recently acquired vocabulary?	_____	_____	_____	_____
S: Did I use new vocabulary?	_____	_____	_____	_____
Metaphor, simile, analogy, and idioms: Figurative language				
T: Did the student use figurative language?	_____	_____	_____	_____
S: Did I use figurative language? Did I compare my ideas to others' ideas?	_____	_____	_____	_____

Other observations and examples of note:

_____

_____

_____

_____

G.8 QUALITATIVE SPELLING CHECKLIST

Use this checklist to analyze students' uncorrected writing and to locate their appropriate stages of spelling development. Examples are in parentheses. The spaces for dates at the top of the checklist are used to follow students' progress. Check when certain features are observed in students' spelling. When a feature is always present, check "Yes." The last place where you check "Often" corresponds to the student's stage of spelling development.

Student _____   Observer _____

Dates _____   _____   _____

	Yes	Often	No
Letter Name–Alphabetic			
Late			
• Are short vowels spelled correctly? (b<u>e</u>d, sh<u>i</u>p, wh<u>e</u>n, l<u>u</u>mp)	___	___	___
• Is the *m* or *n* included in front of other consonants (lu<u>m</u>p, sta<u>n</u>d)	___	___	___
Within-Word Pattern			
Early			
• Are long vowels in single-syllable words used but confused? (FLOTE for *float*, TRANE for *train*)	___	___	___
Middle			
• Are most long vowel words spelled correctly, while some long vowel spelling and other vowel patterns are used but confused? (DRIEV for *drive*)	___	___	___
• Are the most common consonant digraphs and blends spelled correctly? (<u>sl</u>ed, <u>dr</u>eam, fri<u>ght</u>)	___	___	___
Late			
• Are the harder consonant digraphs and blends spelled correctly? (<u>sp</u>eck, <u>sw</u>it<u>ch</u>, <u>sm</u>u<u>dge</u>)	___	___	___
• Are most other vowel patterns spelled correctly? (sp<u>oi</u>l, ch<u>ewe</u>d, s<u>er</u>ving)	___	___	___
Syllables and Affixes			
Early			
• Are inflectional endings added correctly to base vowel patterns with short-vowel patterns? (shopp<u>ing</u>, march<u>ed</u>)	___	___	___
• Are junctures between syllables spelled correctly? (ca<u>tt</u>le, ce<u>ll</u>ar, ca<u>rri</u>es, bo<u>tt</u>le)	___	___	___
Middle			
• Are inflectional endings added correctly to base words? (chew<u>ed</u>, march<u>ed</u>, show<u>er</u>)	___	___	___
Late			
• Are unaccented final syllables spelled correctly? (bott<u>le</u>, fortun<u>ate</u>, civil<u>ize</u>)	___	___	___
• Are less frequent prefixes and suffixes spelled correctly? (<u>con</u>fident, fav<u>or</u>, rip<u>en</u>, cell<u>ar</u>, pleas<u>ure</u>)	___	___	___
Derivational Relations			
Early			
• Are most polysyllabic words spelled correctly? (*fortunate, confident*)	___	___	___
Middle			
• Are unaccented vowels in derived words spelled correctly? (conf<u>i</u>dent, civ<u>i</u>lize, cat<u>e</u>gory)	___	___	___
Late			
• Are words from derived forms spelled correctly? (*pleasure, opposition, criticize*)	___	___	___

G.9 KNOWLEDGE OF GREEK AND LATIN ROOTS

Matching Assessment of Some Greek and Latin Roots

Greek			*Latin*		
______	1. *ver*	a. bad	______	1. *duc*	a. flow
______	2. *mal*	b. breathe	______	2. *sect*	b. small
______	3. *ante*	c. all	______	3. *flu*	c. death
______	4. *spir*	d. turn	______	4. *gen*	d. judge
______	5. *omni*	e. foot	______	5. *sequ*	e. lead
______	6. *poly*	f. before	______	6. *hydr*	f. land
______	7. *cap*	g. good	______	7. *min*	g. water
______	8. *ped*	h. life	______	8. *dent*	h. cut
______	9. *bene*	i. head	______	9. *mort*	i. follow
______	10. *corp*	j. many	______	10. *terra*	j. tooth
______	11. *astr*	k. body	______	11. *jud*	k. hand
______	12. *bio*	l. star	______	12. *man*	l. birth

Answer Key for Matching

Greek

1. d **2.** a **3.** f **4.** b **5.** c **6.** j **7.** i **8.** e **9.** g **10.** k **11.** l **12.** h

Latin

1. e **2.** h **3.** a **4.** l **5.** i **6.** g **7.** b **8.** j **9.** c **10.** f **11.** d **12.** k

Words for Students to Spell and Define

Ask students to spell and define the following words.

1. consecutive
2. affluence
3. beneficial
4. malevolent
5. omnivore
6. corporal
7. aerosol
8. hydraulic
9. conspiracy
10. sectarian
11. judiciary
12. privilege
13. vertigo
14. anterior
15. equation
16. terrarium
17. asteroid
18. antibiotic
19. progeny
20. allegiance

G.10 RUBRIC FOR VOCABULARY LEARNING

Name _____   Period/Grade _____

Teacher _____

Dates _____ _____ _____

Student: How would you rate your understanding of the vocabulary?

5   I have a complete understanding.

4   I have a good understanding.

3   I have some knowledge.

2   I am learning the vocabulary.

1   The vocabulary is very new to me.

Teacher: How would you rate the student's understanding of the vocabulary?

5   Uses the vocabulary accurately in writing and speech; understands the words in various reading contexts; can explain to others; completes assignments using vocabulary; can brainstorm several closely related words; spells vocabulary accurately and easily

4   Uses the vocabulary accurately in writing and speech; understands the words in various reading contexts; learning to explain the words to others; completes assignments using the vocabulary in writing; can brainstorm two closely related words; spells most vocabulary accurately and easily

3   Learning how the vocabulary is used in speech and writing; broadening knowledge of the context in which the vocabulary is learned; takes notes on the key vocabulary, may not spell the word correctly; can recognize which words may not be spelled accurately

2   Knows the word fits in broad categories; can associate a few related words; does not spell the words accurately

1   Is hearing and seeing the vocabulary for the first time; learning to associate meanings with the words; learning to pronounce and spell all of the syllables in the words and meaning units; has an adjusted vocabulary list; receives extra instruction

G.11 GENERATING WORDS FROM BASES AND ROOTS

Teacher Information

Directions. Decide on a time limit; eight minutes is adequate for most students. Let students know when half the time is over, and when 30 seconds is left. If you see that students have stopped writing, you can stop the test. Read the directions aloud to students.

Scoring. Score 1 point for each correct response that is spelled correctly. Score ½ point when the word is misspelled, but is recognizable, with each syllable represented.

Here is a list of words for scoring. Consult a dictionary when in doubt.

1. *turn:* downturn, lecturn, overturn, nocturnal, return, returnable, returning, taciturn, turning, turnkeys, turnouts, turnover, turnpikes, turnstile, turntable, upturn, woodturning
2. *fuse:* confuse, confused, effuse, defuse, diffuse, diffuser, infuse, perfuse, profuse, refuse, reinfuse, suffuse, transfuse, unconfuse
3. *bio:* autobiography, biocontrol, biodiversity, biodynamic, bioelectronics, biofeedback, biographical, biography, biohazard, biological, biologist, biology, biomass, biomechanical, biometrics, bionic, biotechnology, biochemistry, biologic, biomedical, microbiology
4. *graph:* autograph, autobiography, biograph, biography, cardiograph, grapheme, graphics, graphically, lithograph, monograph, orthography, photograph, photography, pornographic, radiograph, spectrograph, telegraph, tomography, topographic
5. *spec, spect:* aspect, inspect, introspect, irrespective, prospect, respect, spectacles, spectrograph, specs, speculate, speculative, species
6. *tract:* attract, attraction, attracting, attractive, abstract, contract, contraction, contractual, detract, distraction, extract, extraction, retract, tractor
7. *tain:* retain, retaining, unattainable, contain, container, pertain, sustain, certain, certainly, certainty, distain, uncertain, tainting, tainted, taint, curtain, obtain, maintain, mountain

Interpretation. Score one point for each entry that is a real word and that is spelled correctly. These base words and roots are for advanced readers to consider. Students who score between 12 and 20 should study common prefixes and suffixes. Students who produce three words for most items and have a score between 16 and 21 are ready to study roots and less frequent affixes more systematically. Students who score 22 and above are probably advanced readers who can study principles of sound change, including assimilated prefixes and vowel reduction.

Generating words related to these roots requires a flexible, quick, and deep vocabulary knowledge. Because students are thinking of the words and not hunting for them on a page, these are probably words students know.

Student Form for Generating Words

Student's Name _____   Teacher _____

Period _____   Grade _____   Date _____

Directions. Make as many words as you can by adding prefixes, suffixes, and by making compound words with these base words and roots. Do not include any words with plurals, words that end with *s* (turns would not count). The blank spaces are for you to write your words. Spell the words the best you can. Your teacher will tell you how much time you have.

    Here is an example: In 1. below, four new words were made. Can you think of other words to make? There are four more blank spaces, and this is where you begin. Skip around as you brainstorm, and take the full time. Turn your paper over when time is called.

1. *turn*   return   returnable

                  turned   downturn

_____   _____

2. *fuse*   confuse   confusing

_____   _____

_____   _____

3. *bio*   _____   _____

_____   _____

_____   _____

4. *spec, spect*   _____   _____

_____   _____

_____   _____

5. *tract*   _____   _____

_____   _____

_____   _____

6. *tain*   _____   _____

_____   _____

_____   _____

G.12 VOCABULARY SELF-ASSESSMENT TEMPLATE

Vocabulary Self-Assessment

Student _____   Dates _____ (X)

_____ (O)

_____ (✓)

Vocabulary	Knowledge Rating			
	Never Heard of It	Heard It	Have Some Ideas	Know It Well

G.13 MY STRATEGIES FOR LEARNING VOCABULARY

Strongly agree ◄──────► Strongly disagree

Do I know the meaning of the vocabulary?

I learn the vocabulary by reading the textbook.
_____ _____ _____ _____ _____ _____

I learn the vocabulary in the class lectures.
_____ _____ _____ _____ _____ _____

I learn the vocabulary through classroom activities.
_____ _____ _____ _____ _____ _____

I learn the vocabulary from reading.
_____ _____ _____ _____ _____ _____

Do I know how to learn new vocabulary?

I see inside words to find meaningful parts.
_____ _____ _____ _____ _____ _____

I can think of related words to make meaning connections.
_____ _____ _____ _____ _____ _____

I can find references and other resources to study vocabulary.
_____ _____ _____ _____ _____ _____

When I read a chapter in the textbook, how many words are new to me? How many vocabulary words do I need to study?

0–1	2–4	5–9	10–19	≥ 20
_____	_____	_____	_____	_____

Can I read the vocabulary?

When I read, I know the meanings of most of the words.
_____ _____ _____ _____ _____ _____

I can pronounce the words.
_____ _____ _____ _____ _____ _____

I can read the words easily, without having to pronounce the words.
_____ _____ _____ _____ _____ _____

There are a few words I do not know when I read. (≤ 5 per 100)
_____ _____ _____ _____ _____ _____

There are many words I cannot read. (≥ 10 per 100)
_____ _____ _____ _____ _____ _____

When I read a chapter in my textbook(s), there are words I cannot pronounce. Check how many words on a page were difficult to read:

0–1	2–4	5–9	≥ 10
_____	_____	_____	_____

What are my next steps learning the vocabulary?

How many vocabulary words will I study each week?

0–1	2–4	5–9	≥ 10
_____	_____	_____	_____

How many days a week will I review the vocabulary to learn the vocabulary words?

0–1	2–4	5–7
_____	_____	_____

I would benefit from working with others to study the vocabulary.
_____ _____ _____ _____ _____ _____

I can learn the assigned vocabulary with ease.
_____ _____ _____ _____ _____ _____

I benefit from having note cards.
_____ _____ _____ _____ _____ _____

I need more resources to learn about the words.
_____ _____ _____ _____ _____ _____

I can assist others.
_____ _____ _____ _____ _____ _____

APPENDIX H

Templates

COMPARISON AND CONTRAST

TOPIC _____

Item of Contrast:		Feature Being Contrasted	Item of Contrast:	
Differences			Differences	
	Features in Common			

WORD SORT TEMPLATE

CONCEPT OF DEFINITION

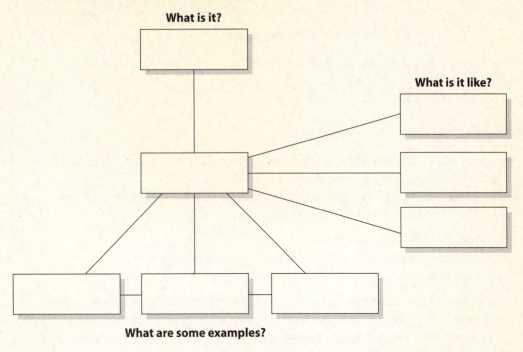

What is it?

What is it like?

What are some examples?

4-SQUARE CONCEPT MAP

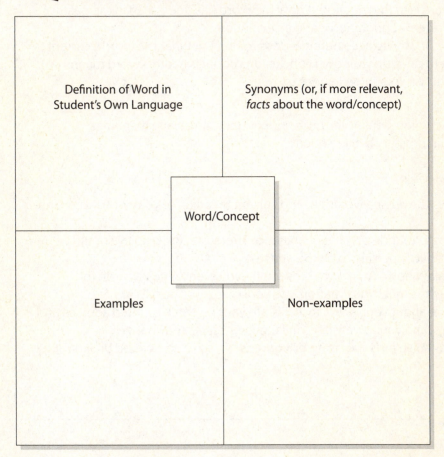

Definition of Word in Student's Own Language

Synonyms (or, if more relevant, *facts* about the word/concept)

Word/Concept

Examples

Non-examples

WORD MUSEUM HANDOUT

Word Museum Assignment

A "Word Museum" is a celebration of words, word histories, and the diversity of the English language. On November 21st, we will construct a Word Museum in class. You are **each** responsible for creating **your own** display for our museum.

The Word Museum—Research

I will assign you a word from the word wall. If you love a particular word and want to work on it, please let me know BEFORE I hand out the words to the class.

Read about the history and origins of your word in *The Oxford English Dictionary*. **Copy** your word's entry in the dictionary. **Answer** these questions:

1. From which language did your word derive?
2. What is the first recorded instance of its use in the English language?
3. Write down some of the most interesting or surprising citations recorded over the years.

Find and copy an encyclopedia article that helps to explain what your word means or meant in the past. **Write** 1–3 sentences that explains why this information is important.

Find and copy a poem that helps to explain what your word means. **Write** 1–3 sentences that explain what your poem has to do with your word.

In Google, type your word into the search bar. **Write a paragraph** that tells how many sites use your word and explains how at least three of the sites use your word differently.

Collect evidence of your word in print, on TV, or another public source like a billboard. Simply write down how your word was used; then cite your source. **Do this** WITHOUT USING A COMPUTER. Your goal here is to find out about how the word has been used in the past, how it is used today, its different connotations, and its evolution.

Interview three people of varying ages **outside class** to find out what the word's current meaning is. Use these data to develop your own conclusions about what this word means in current and common usage. Ask your interviewees to

1. Define the word
2. Describe the word's connotations, overtones, innuendoes, and slang meanings
3. Use it as they would in ordinary conversation

The Word Museum—The Display

Create a display that shows the origin, evolution, and current meaning of your word. There are only a few requirements:

Your word is multifaceted. Your display should be, too. Therefore, the display should be **multidimensional.** Think about appealing to **all the senses.**

Make sure that the display shows ALL of your research—you won't receive credit for research that I can't see. Pack as much information into your display as possible.

Write a **1-page narrative** about your word. Incorporate your research (printed sources and interviews), course readings, and your own views on language usage and change.

An important part of your display is the **citing of sources.** Attach a completed bibliography to your display.

Have fun!

References

Allen, J. (2007). *Inside words*. Portsmouth, NH: Stenhouse.

The American Heritage® Dictionary of the English Language: Fourth Edition. (2000). Retrieved December 12, 2008, from www.bartleby.com/61/roots/IE76.html

Anderson, L. (1999). *Speak*. New York: Farrar, Strauss, & Giroux.

Anderson, R., Wilson, P., & Fielding, L. (1988). Growth in reading and how children spend their time outside of school. *Reading Research Quarterly, 23,* 285–303.

Angelou, M. (1999). *I know why the caged bird sings*. New York: Bantam.

Anglin, J. M. (1993). *Vocabulary development: A morphological analysis*. Monographs of the Society for Research in Child Development (Serial No. 238), *58*(10).

August, D., & Shanahan, T. (2006). *Developing literacy in second-language learners: Report of the National Literacy Panel on Language-Minority Children and Youth*. New York: Taylor and Francis.

Ayers, D. M. (1986). *English words from Latin and Greek elements* (2nd ed.; revised by Thomas Worthen). Tucson: The University of Arizona Press.

Badders, W., Carnine, D., Feliciani, J., Jeanpierre, B., Sumners, C., & Valentino, C. (2007). *Houghton Mifflin California science*. Boston: Houghton Mifflin.

Bailey, A. (Ed.). (2006). *The language demands of school: Putting academic English to the test*. New Haven, CT: Yale University Press.

Bartel, R. (1983). *Metaphors and symbols: Forays into language*. Urbana, IL: National Council of Teachers of English.

Bauer, M. D. (1986). *On my honor*. New York: Clarion.

Baumann, J. F., Edwards, E. C., Font, G., Tereshinski, C. A., Kame'enui, E. J., & Olejnik, S. (2003). Teaching morphemic and contextual analysis to fifth-grade students. *Reading Research Quarterly, 37*(2), 150–176.

Baumann, J. F., Kame'enui, E. J., & Ash, G. E. (2003). Research on vocabulary instruction: Voltaire redux. In J. Flood, D. Lapp, J. R. Squire, & J. M. Jensen (Eds.), *Handbook of research on teaching the English language arts* (2nd ed., pp. 752–785). Mahwah, NJ: Lawrence Erlbaum Associates.

Bear, D. R. (1992). The prosody of oral reading and stages of word knowledge. In S. Templeton & D. R. Bear (Eds.), *Development of orthographic knowledge and the foundations of literacy: A memorial festschrift for Edmund H. Henderson* (pp. 137–189). Hillsdale, NJ: Lawrence Erlbaum Associates.

Bear, D. R. (2005). *Language and literacy survey*. Reno: Center for Learning & Literacy, University of Nevada, Reno.

Bear, D., Helman, L., Templeton, S., Invernizzi, M., & Johnston, F. (2007). *Words their way with English learners*. Upper Saddle River, NJ: Merrill/Prentice Hall.

Bear, D., & Templeton, S. (2000). Matching development and instruction. In N. Padak & T. Rasinski (Eds.), *Distinguished educators on reading: Contributions that have shaped effective literacy instruction* (pp. 363–376). Newark, DE: International Reading Association.

Bear, D. R., Templeton, S., & Warner, M. (1991). The development of a qualitative inventory of higher levels of orthographic knowledge. In J. Zutell & S. McCormick (Eds.), *Learner factors/teacher factors: Issues in literacy research and instruction* (Fortieth yearbook of the National Reading Conference, pp. 105–110). Chicago: National Reading Conference.

Bear, D. R., Truex, P., & Barone, D. (1989). In search of meaningful diagnosis: Spelling-by-stage assessment of literacy proficiency. *Adult Literacy and Basic Education, 13,* 167–185.

Beck, I., & McKeown, M. (2008). *Improving comprehension with questioning the author*. New York: Scholastic.

Beck, I. L., McKeown, M. G., & Kucan, L. (2002). *Bringing words to life: Robust vocabulary instruction*. New York: Guilford.

Beck, I., McKeown, M., & Kucan, L. (2008). *Creating robust vocabulary*. New York: Guilford.

Blachowicz, C. L. Z. (1986). Making connections: Alternatives to the vocabulary notebook. *Journal of Reading, 29,* 643–649.

Blachowicz, C., & Fisher, P. J. (2009). *Teaching vocabulary in all classrooms* (4th ed.). Boston: Allyn & Bacon.

Blachowicz, C., & Ogle, D. (2008). *Reading comprehension: Strategies for independent learners*. New York: Guilford.

Black, R. W. (2005). Access and affiliation: The literacy and composition practices of English-language learners in an online fanfiction community. *Journal of Adolescent and Adult Literacy, 49*(2), 118–128.

Booth, W. (2007, September 30). Angelenos' new refrain: "I love (downtown) L.A." City's once-wasteland is hipster heaven. *The Washington Post,* p. A1.

Bravo, M. A., Hiebert, E. H., & Pearson, P. D. (2005). Tapping the linguistic resources of Spanish/English bilinguals: The role of cognates in science. In R. K. Wagner, A. E. Muse, & K. R. Tannenbaum (Eds.), *Vocabulary acquisition: Implications for reading comprehension* (pp. 140–156). New York: Guilford.

Brown, J. I., Fishco, V. V., & Hanna, G. S. (1993). *Nelson-Denny reading test*. Itasca, IL: Riverside Publishing.

California Department of Education. (2008). *Standards and frameworks*. Retrieved July 5, 2008, from www.cde.ca.gov/be/st

Carlisle, J. F. (2000). Awareness of the structure and meaning of morphologically complex words: Impact on reading. *Reading and Writing, 12,* 169–190.

Carlisle, J. F., & Stone, C. A. (2005). Exploring the role of morphemes in reading. *Reading Research Quarterly, 40*(4), 428–449.

Claiborne, R. (1989). *The roots of English: A reader's handbook of word origins*. New York: Times Books.

Cooper, S. (1986). *Silver on the tree*. New York: Collier Books.

Corson, D. (1995). *Using English words*. Dordrecht, Netherlands: Kluwer Academic Publishers.

Coxhead, A. (2000). A new academic word list. *TESOL Quarterly, 34,* 213–239.

Cummings, D. W. (1988). *American English spelling: An informal description*. Baltimore: Johns Hopkins University Press.

Cunningham, A. E., & Stanovich, K. (1998). What reading does for the mind. *American Educator, 22*(1–2), 8–15.

Dale, E. (1965). Vocabulary measurement: Techniques and major findings. *Elementary English, 42,* 895–901.

Davies, M. (2006). *A frequency dictionary of Spanish: Core vocabulary for learners*. New York: Routledge.

Diamond, L., & Gutlohn, L. (2007). *Vocabulary handbook*. Baltimore: Paul H. Brookes.

Dickinson, D. K., McCabe, A., & Sprague, K. (2003). Teacher Rating of Oral Language and Literacy (TROLL): Individualizing early literacy instruction with a standards-based rating tool. *The Reading Teacher, 56*(6), 554–564.

Echevarria, J., Vogt, M., & Short, D. (2004). *Making content comprehensible for English learners: The SIOP model*. Boston: Allyn & Bacon.

Ehri, L. C. (1997). Learning to read and learning to spell are one and the same, almost. In C. A. Perfetti, L. Rieben, & M. Fayol (Eds.), *Learning to spell: Research, theory, and practice across languages* (pp. 237–269). Mahwah, NJ: Lawrence Erlbaum Associates.

Fadiman, A. (2006). The melting pot. In D. M. Newman & J. A. O'Brien (Eds.), *Sociology: Exploring the architecture of everyday life* (pp. 84–100). Thousand Oaks, CA: Pine Forge Press.

Fisher, D., & Frey, N. (2007). *Improving adolescent literacy: Content area strategies at work* (2nd ed.). Upper Saddle River, NJ: Prentice Hall.

Flanigan, K., & Greenwood, S. (2007). Effective content vocabulary instruction in the middle: Matching students, purposes, words, and strategies. *Journal of Adolescent and Adult Literacy, 51*(3), 226–238.

Flanigan, K., Hayes, L., Templeton, S., Bear, D., Invernizzi, M., & Johnston, F. (in press). *Words their way with struggling readers*. Boston: Allyn & Bacon.

Frayer, D., Frederick, W., & Klausmeier, H. (1969). *A schema for testing the level of cognitive mastery* (Working Paper No. 16). Madison: Wisconsin Research and Development Center.

Freedman, R. (1989). *Lincoln: A photobiography*. Boston: Houghton Mifflin.

Freeman, D., & Freeman, Y. (2002). *Between worlds: Access to second language acquisition*. Portsmouth, NH: Heinemann.

Friedman, T. (2007). *The world is flat 3.0: A brief history of the 21st century*. New York: Picador Press.

Gee, J. P. (2005). *An introduction to discourse analysis: Theory and method*. New York: Routledge.

Gelb, I. J. (1963). *A study of writing*. Chicago: University of Chicago Press.

Goerss, B., Beck, I., & McKeown, M. (1999). Increasing remedial students' ability to derive word meaning from context. *Reading Psychology, 20*, 151–175.

Graves, M. F. (2006). *The vocabulary book: Learning and instruction*. New York: Teachers College Press.

Graves, M. F., & Watts-Taffe, S. M. (2002). The place of word consiousness in a research-based vocabulary program. In A. E. Farstrup & S. J. Samuels (Eds.), *What research has to say about reading instruction* (3rd ed., pp. 140–165). Newark, DE: International Reading Association.

Hacker, D. (2008). *A pocket style manual* (5th ed.). Boston: Bedford/St. Martin's.

Havelock, E. (1982). *The literate revolution in Greece and its cultural consequences*. Princeton, NJ: Princeton University Press.

Hawthorne, N. (1955). *The scarlet letter*. New York: Washington Square Press.

Henderson, E. (1981). *Learning to read and spell: The child's knowledge of words*. DeKalb: Northern Illinois University Press.

Houston, J. W., & Houston, J. D. (1973). *Farewell to Manzanar*. New York: Bantam.

Invernizzi, M. (2007, April). Word study before, during, and after reading and writing in the content areas: Using word study to facilitate comprehension, deepen knowledge, and increase vocabulary. Presentation to the Annual George Graham Lecture, University of Virginia, Charlottesville.

Invernizzi, M., & Hayes, L. (2004). Developmental-spelling research: A systematic imperative. *Reading Research Quarterly, 39*, 216–228.

Jesperson, O. (1938). *Growth and structure of the English language*. Garden City, NY: Doubleday.

Johnson, D. D., & Pearson, P. D. (1984). *Teaching reading vocabulary*. New York: Holt.

Johnston, F. (2000/2001). Spelling exceptions: Problems or possibilities? *The Reading Teacher, 54*, 372–378.

Johnston, F. (2001). The utility of phonic generalizations: Let's take another look at Clymer's generalizations. *The Reading Teacher, 55*, 132–143.

Kieffer, M., & Lesaux, N. (2007). Breaking down words to build meaning: Morphology, vocabulary, and reading comprehension in the urban classroom. *The Reading Teacher, 61*(2), 134–144.

Krashen, S. (1985). *The input hypothesis: Issues and implications*. New York: Longman.

Lanham, R. A. (1993). *The electronic word: Democracy, technology, and the arts*. Chicago: University of Chicago Press.

Lederer, R. (1991). *The miracle of language*. New York: Atria.

Lehr, S. (2007). *Inventing English: A portable history of the language*. New York: Columbia University Press.

Lemke, J. (1988). Genres, semantics, and classroom education. *Linguistics and Education, 1*, 81–99.

Lowry, L. (1993). *The giver*. Boston: Houghton Mifflin.

Lubliner, S., & Scott, J. A. (2008). *Nourishing vocabulary: Balancing words and learning*. Thousand Oaks, CA: Corwin Press.

Lunsford, A. A. (2006). *Easy writer: A pocket reference* (3rd ed.). Boston: Bedford/St. Martin's.

MacGinitie, W. H., MacGinitie, R. K., Maria, K., & Dreyer, L. (2000). *Gates-MacGinitie reading tests* (4th ed.). Itasca, IL: Riverside Publishing.

Marzano, R. J. (2004). *Building background knowledge for academic achievement*. Alexandria, VA: Association for Supervision and Curriculum Development.

McBride-Chang, C., She, H., Ng, J. Y.-W., Meng, X., & Penney, T. (2007). Morphological structure awareness, vocabulary, and reading. In R. K. Wagner, A. E. Muse, & K. R. Tannenbaum (Eds.), *Vocabulary acquisition: Implications for reading comprehension* (pp. 104–122). New York: Guilford.

McKeown, M. G., & Curtis, M. E. (Eds.). (1987). *The nature of vocabulary acquisition*. Hillsdale, NJ: Lawrence Erlbaum Associates.

Moloney, K. (2008). *"I'm not a big word fan": An exploratory study of ninth-graders' language use in the context of word consciousness-oriented vocabulary instruction*. Unpublished doctoral dissertation, University of Nevada, Reno.

Moore, A. (1980). *Watchmen #1*. DC Comics.

Myers, W. D. (1992). *Somewhere in the darkness*. New York: Scholastic.

Nagy, W. (2007). Metalinguistic awareness and the vocabulary-comprehension connection. In R. K. Wagner, A. E. Muse, & K. R. Tannenbaum (Eds.), *Vocabulary acquisition: Implications for reading comprehension* (pp. 52–77). New York: Guilford.

Nagy, W., & Anderson, R. C. (1984). How many words are there in printed school English? *Reading Research Quarterly, 19*, 304–330.

Nagy, W., & Scott, J. (2000). Vocabulary acquisition. In R. Barr, M. L. Kamil, P. B. Mosenthal, & P. D. Pearson (Eds.), *Handbook of reading research* (Vol. 3). New York: Longman.

Nation, I. S. P. (2001). *Learning vocabulary in another language*. Cambridge, U.K.: Cambridge University Press.

Nilsen, A. P., & Nilsen, D. L. F. (2004). *Vocabulary plus: High school and up*. Boston: Allyn & Bacon.

O'Dell, S. (1989). *Black star, bright dawn.* Boston: Houghton Mifflin.

Olson, D. (1994). *The world on paper: The conceptual and cognitive implications of writing and reading.* Cambridge, U.K.: Cambridge University Press.

Orwell, G. (1946). *Animal farm.* New York: Harcourt, Brace, & World.

Patterson, J., Patterson, J., & Collins, L. (2002). *Bouncing back: How your school can succeed in the face of adversity.* Larchmont, NY: Eye on Education.

Pearson, P. D., Hiebert, E. H., & Kamil, M. L. (2007). Vocabulary assessment: What we know and what we need to know. *Reading Research Quarterly, 42,* 282–296.

Pinker, S. (1999). *Words and rules: The ingredients of language.* New York: Basic Books.

Pullman, P. (1997). *The golden compass.* New York: Del Rey.

Raphael, T. E., & Au, K. H. (2005). QAR: Enhancing comprehension and test taking across grades and content areas. *The Reading Teacher, 59*(3), 206–221.

Read, J. (2004). *Assessing vocabulary.* Cambridge, U.K.: Cambridge University Press.

Reinking, D. (1998). Introduction: Synthesizing technological transformations of literacy in a post-typographic world. In D. Reinking, M. C. McKenna, L. D. Labbo, & R. D. Kieffer (Eds.), *Handbook of literacy and technology: Transformations in a post-typographic world* (pp. xi–xxx). Mahwah, NJ: Lawrence Erlbaum Associates.

Robinson, S. (1989). *Origins.* New York: Teacher Writers Collaborative.

Rylant, C. (1990). *A couple of kooks and other stories about love.* New York: Dell.

Sagan, C. (1977). *The dragons of Eden: Speculations on the evolution of human intelligence.* New York: Random House.

Santa, C. M., Havens, L. T., & Valdes, B. J. (2004). *Project CRISS: Creating independence through student-owned strategies* (3rd ed.). Dubuque, IA: Kendall/Hunt.

Schleppegrell, M. J. (2004). *The language of schooling: A functional linguistics perspective.* Mahwah, NJ: Lawrence Erlbaum Associates.

Schwartz, R. M., & Raphael, T. E. (1985). Concept of definition: A key to improving students' vocabulary. *The Reading Teacher, 39,* 198–205.

Scragg, D. G. (1974). *A history of English spelling.* New York: Barnes & Noble.

Smith, D., Ives, B., & Templeton, S. (2007, December). The construction and analysis of the Degrees of Relatedness Interview: A measure of students' explicit morphological knowledge. Paper presented at the 57th Annual Meeting of the National Reading Conference, Austin, TX.

Snow, C., & Kim, Y. (2007). Large problem spaces: The challenge of vocabulary for English language learners. In R. K. Wagner, A. E. Muse, & K. R. Tannenbaum (Eds.), *Vocabulary acquisition: Implications for reading comprehension* (pp. 123–139). New York: Guilford.

Stahl, S. A., & Nagy, W. (2006). *Teaching word meanings.* Mahwah, NJ: Lawrence Erlbaum Associates.

Steinbeck, J. (1939). *The grapes of wrath.* Sherborne, U.K.: Sun Dial Press.

Sterbinsky, A. (2007). *Words their way spelling inventories: Reliability and validity analyses.* Memphis, TN: Center for Research in Educational Policy, University of Memphis. Available at www.allynbaconmerrill.com/content/images/9780132239684/support/WTWReport.doc

Strunk, W., & White, E. B. (2005). *The elements of style.* Mayville, NY: Paramount Press.

Taylor, T. (1993). *Timothy of the cay.* New York: Harcourt.

Templeton, S. (1979). Spelling first, sound later: The relationship between orthography and higher order phonological knowledge in older students. *Research in the Teaching of English, 13,* 255–264.

Templeton, S. (1980). Logic and mnemonics for demons and curiosities: Spelling awareness for middle- and secondary-level students. *Reading World, 20,* 123–130.

Templeton, S. (1983). Using the spelling/meaning connection to develop word knowledge in older students. *Journal of Reading, 27*(1), 8–14.

Templeton, S. (1991). *Teaching the integrated language arts.* Boston: Houghton Mifflin.

Templeton, S. (1997). *Teaching the integrated language arts* (2nd ed.). Boston: Houghton Mifflin.

Templeton, S. (2003a). Comprehending homophones, homographs, and homonyms. *Voices from the Middle, 11*(1), 62–63.

Templeton, S. (2003b). Spelling. In J. Flood, D. Lapp, J. R. Squire, & J. M. Jensen (Eds.), *Handbook of research on teaching the English language arts* (2nd ed., pp. 738–751). Mahwah, NJ: Lawrence Erlbaum Associates.

Templeton, S. (2004a). Spelling and the middle school English language learner. *Voices from the Middle, 11*(4), 48–49.

Templeton, S. (2004b). The vocabulary-spelling connection: Orthographic development and morphological knowledge at the intermediate grades and beyond. In J. F. Baumann & E. J. Kame'enui (Eds.), *Vocabulary instruction: Research to practice* (pp. 118–138). New York: Guilford.

Templeton, S. (2006). Dispelling spelling assumptions: Technology and spelling, present and future. In M. McKenna, L. Labbo, R. Kieffer, & D. Reinking (Eds.), *Handbook of literacy and technology* (2nd ed., pp. 335–339). Mahwah, NJ: Lawrence Erlbaum Associates.

Templeton, S. (2009). Spelling-meaning relationships among languages: Exploring cognates and their possibilities. In L. Helman (Ed.), *Literacy development with English learners: Research-based instruction in grades K–6* (pp. 196–212). New York: Guilford.

Templeton, S., & Bear, D. R. (Eds.). (1992). *Development of orthographic knowledge and the foundations of literacy: A memorial festschrift for Edmund H. Henderson.* Hillsdale, NJ: Lawrence Erlbaum Associates.

Templeton, S., Johnston, F., Bear, D. R., & Invernizzi, M. (2009). *Words their way: Word sorts for derivational relations spellers* (2nd ed.). Boston: Allyn & Bacon.

Texas Education Agency. (2008). *Texas essential knowledge and skills.* Retrieved July 5, 2008, from www.tea.state.tx.us/teks/index.html

Thomas, L., & Tchudi, S. (1998). *The English language: An owner's manual.* Upper Saddle River, NJ: Longman.

Tolkien, J. W. (1937). *The hobbit.* London: George Allen & Unwin, Ltd.

Townsend, D., Bear, D. R., & Templeton, S. (2008). *Intermediate academic vocabulary spelling inventory.* Reno: Center for Learning and Literacy, University of Nevada, Reno.

Vacca, R. T., & Vacca, J. L. (2007). *Content area reading: Literacy and learning across the curriculum* (9th ed.). Boston: Allyn & Bacon.

Venezky, R. (1999). *The American way of spelling: The structure and origins of American English orthography.* New York: Guilford.

Viise, N. M., & Austin, O. F. (2005). Can adult low-skilled literacy learners assess and discuss their own spelling knowledge? *Journal of Adolescent and Adult Literacy, 48*(5), 402–414.

Weber, D. J. (2006). Many truths constitute the past: The legacy of the U.S.-Mexican war. Retrieved July 7, 2008, from www.pbs.org/kera/usmexicanwar/aftermath/many_truths.html

West, M. (1953). *A general services list of English words*. Retrieved July 9, 2008, from http://jbauman.com/aboutgsl.html

Whitaker, S. (2008). *Word play: Building vocabulary across texts and disciplines grades 6–12*. Portsmouth, NH: Heinemann.

White, T. G., Sowell, J., & Yanagihara, A. (1989). Teaching elementary students to use word-part clues. *The Reading Teacher, 42*, 302–308.

Yolen, J. (1984). *Heart's blood: The pit dragon chronicles, volume two*. New York: Doubleday.

Yolen, J. (1988). *Favorite folktales from around the world*. New York: Pantheon.

Zeno, S. M., Ivens, S. H., Millard, R. T., & Duvvuri, R. (1995). *The educator's word frequency guide*. Brewster, NY: Touchstone Applied Science Associates.